African Americans and the Pacific War, 1941–1945

In the patriotic aftermath of Pearl Harbor, African Americans demanded the right to play their part in the war against Japan. As they soon learned, however, the freedom for which the United States and its allies was fighting did not extend to African Americans. Focusing on African Americans' experiences across the Asia-Pacific Theater during World War Two, this book examines the interplay between national identity, the racially segregated US military culture, and the possibilities of transnational racial advancement as African Americans contemplated not just their own oppression, but that of the colonized peoples of the Pacific region. In illuminating neglected aspects of African American history and of World War Two, this book deepens our understanding of the connections between the US role as an international power and the racial ideologies and practices that characterized American life during the mid-twentieth century.

Chris Dixon is Professor of History at Macquarie University, Australia. His publications include *African America and Haiti: Emigration and Black Nationalism in the Nineteenth Century* (2000), *Perfecting the Family: Antislavery Marriages in Nineteenth-Century America* (1997), and *Hollywood's South Seas and the Pacific War: Searching for Dorothy Lamour* (with Sean Brawley, 2012).

D1711073

African Americans and the Pacific War, 1941–1945

Race, Nationality, and the Fight for Freedom

CHRIS DIXON

Macquarie University, Sydney

CAMBRIDGE
UNIVERSITY PRESS

CAMBRIDGE
UNIVERSITY PRESS

University Printing House, Cambridge CB2 8BS, United Kingdom

One Liberty Plaza, 20th Floor, New York, NY 10006, USA

477 Williamstown Road, Port Melbourne, VIC 3207, Australia

314–321, 3rd Floor, Plot 3, Splendor Forum, Jasola District Centre,
New Delhi – 110025, India

79 Anson Road, #06-04/06, Singapore 079906

Cambridge University Press is part of the University of Cambridge.

It furthers the University's mission by disseminating knowledge in the pursuit of
education, learning, and research at the highest international levels of excellence.

www.cambridge.org
Information on this title: www.cambridge.org/9781107112698
DOI: 10.1017/9781316285619

First published 2018

Printed in the United States of America by Sheridan Books, Inc.

A catalogue record for this publication is available from the British Library.

Library of Congress Cataloging-in-Publication Data

NAMES: Dixon, Chris, 1960– author.
TITLE: African Americans and the Pacific war, 1941–1945 : race, nationality,
    and the fight for freedom / Chris Dixon.
DESCRIPTION: New York : Cambridge University Press, 2018. | Includes
    bibliographical references and index.
IDENTIFIERS: LCCN 2018012842| ISBN 9781107112698 (hardback : alk. paper) |
    ISBN 9781107532939 (pbk. : alk. paper)
SUBJECTS: LCSH: World War, 1939–1945—African Americans. | African Americans—Race
    identity. | Racism—United States—History—20th century. | United States—Armed
    Forces—African Americans.
CLASSIFICATION: LCC D810.N4 D59 2018 | DDC 940.5403—dc23
    LC record available at https://lccn.loc.gov/2018012842

ISBN 978-1-107-11269-8 Hardback

ISBN 978-1-107-53293-9 Paperback

For Nik

In a thousand subtle ways, in a thousand brutal ways, we were taught that we were not part of American culture and history. Here, we were *making* history. We were part of the vanguard of a new revolution – part of the struggle of the colored nine-tenths of humanity to gain democracy and dignity.

Nelson Peery, *Black Fire: The Making of a Revolutionary* (247)

Contents

Figures

Acknowledgments

Completing this book has only been possible due to the generous support of numerous people and institutions, both in Australia and the United States. I wish to acknowledge at the outset the vital support provided by the Australian Research Council (ARC). An ARC Discovery Project grant enabled me to travel to the United States to conduct the archival research that remains at the heart of historical endeavor, relieved me of some of my teaching responsibilities, and allowed me to employ Samantha Bedggood and Dominic Hennessy – two members of the coterie of bright and enthusiastic graduate students I have had the privilege of supervising in recent years – as research assistants. I'm grateful for their contributions to this project. Macquarie University generously provided me with time to complete the manuscript, and I especially thank Martina Möllering, Dean of the Faculty of Arts, and my colleagues in the Department of Modern History, Politics and International Relations. I also acknowledge support from the University of Queensland's Institute for Advanced Studies in Humanities. Thanks go also to John Maynard and Vicky Haskins, from the University of Newcastle (Australia), for their interest in, and support of, this project.

I acknowledge, too, the Australian-American Fulbright Commission, whose Professional Scholarship in Australian-United States Alliance Studies enabled me to consider in detail the implications of the African American presence in wartime Australia; that work forms the basis of Chapter 4 of this book. The Fulbright Scholarship allowed me to spend four months as a Visiting Research Fellow in the Institute of Historical Research (IHR) at the University of Texas at Austin (UT Austin). I'd like to thank Seth Garfield, Director of the IHR, and Juliet Walker – who offered a constructive and supportive reading of my work – for helping ensure that my time in Austin was productive. I wish also to acknowledge Courtney Meador, of the UT History Department, who went above and beyond the call of duty in organizing the logistics of my visit to the IHR. Special thanks go to Rhonda Evans and John Higley, present and past directors of UT's Edward A. Clark Center for Australian and New Zealand Studies, for their help and hospitality both before and during my visit to Austin.

In this age of digitization, librarians and archivists remain the often-unsung heroes of historical research. At the Library of Congress, Megan Harris provided invaluable assistance as I navigated my way through the Veterans History Project. I'm sincerely thankful for her help. I am also grateful to Eric Van Slander, in the National Archives and Records Administration, at College Park, Maryland. As anyone who has researched in the National Archives can attest, the mass of material can seem overwhelming, and the systems to access that material occasionally obtuse – negotiating both was made easier with Eric's expertise and friendly help. I also thank Carol Leadenham for her assistance during my brief visit to the Hoover Institution Library and Archives at Stanford University. Thomas J. Wood, at the Norris L. Brookens Library, University of Illinois at Springfield, helped provide access to Edwin Lee's memoir of his Pacific War service. At the Lyndon B. Johnson Presidential Library (Austin, Texas), Liza Talbot procured materials relating to the African American presence in wartime Australia. Staff at the United States Army Military History Institute (Carlisle, Pennsylvania), and at the Schomburg Center for Research in Black Culture (New York Public Library) also helped locate sometimes-obscure sources. Yorick Smaal very generously shared with me documents he had located in the National Archives.

I'm especially grateful to Deborah Gershenowitz at Cambridge University Press, both for her initial interest in this project and for her patience and encouragement as I have brought it to completion. My thanks go also to Kristina Deusch, Julie Hrischeva, and the rest of the team at Cambridge, for their assistance in turning the manuscript into a book. I am deeply grateful, too, to the readers who offered astute and helpful comments, initially on the proposal and subsequently on the completed draft of the manuscript.

For nearly three decades I have been fortunate to benefit from the friendly support provided by colleagues in the Australian and New Zealand American Studies Association: Shane White, Trevor Burnard, David Goodman, Clare Corbould, Mike McDonnell, Douglas Craig,

Frances Clark, and Timothy Minchin have helped furnish the collegial network that remains fundamental to academic life. In particular, I'd like to acknowledge Ian Tyrrell's contribution. It is more than a few years since Ian supervised my PhD thesis, but he has given steadfast support ever since. Similarly, Tony Barker has been a friend and mentor for longer than we'd perhaps care to remember; while my visits back to the University of Western Australia are infrequent, my lunches with Tony inevitably stretch into the late afternoon, as we traverse important academic matters and even more important matters of cricket.

As ever, family and friends have provided steadfast support. I wish to thank Selina Ward, Malcolm Quekett, Andrew Robertson, Sarah Pinto, Ian Hood, Angus Gorman, and Alan "Hamstrung" Peacock. Wish and Anita welcomed me to Austin and kept me nourished with regular Friday night Tex-Mex. Sean Brawley is a coauthor, colleague, and friend: his steadfast support over three decades is much appreciated. Thanks, also, to Lorna Davin for her encouragement during the early stages of this project. When I started this book, my son, Sam, was halfway through high school; he's now more than halfway through his undergraduate degree. Along the way he's tackled illness and other challenges – keep on motoring, matey. For her care and love, I dedicate this book to Nikki Percival.

Introduction

In the opening chapter of his fictional account of the Pacific War, the black writer and Pacific War veteran John Oliver Killens depicts an exchange between the novel's principal character, Solomon "Solly" Saunders, and his new bride, Millie. As Solly bewails the relentless injustices he confronts as a black man in mid-twentieth America, Millie counsels him to put the racial struggle on hold during his impending military service. "[F]orget about the race problem," she pleads, "at least for the duration of the war." Suggesting that the advantages Saunders enjoys over the majority of black recruits – "he was personable, and he was educated," and, perhaps most significantly, he was more fair-skinned than many African Americans – will enable him to advance his career and set the newlyweds on the path to postwar prosperity and advancement, Millie worries that Solly will squander those advantages. Exasperated, she implores him to be "an American instead of a Negro."[1]

Published in 1963, Killens's *And Then We Heard the Thunder* served as a bridge, a literary connection between the African American experience during the Pacific War – a "racial war" as Solly Saunders put it – and the increasingly assertive civil rights movement of the 1960s.[2] While

---

[1] John Oliver Killens, *And Then We Heard the Thunder* (New York, NY: Knopf, 1963), 6.

[2] Killens, *And Then We Heard the Thunder*, 459. Jonathan Yardley has noted that "as a work of literature," Killens's novel had "large flaws." See Jonathan Yardley, "The Thunder of Protest Without the Lightning of Art," *Washington Post*, July 24, 2003. See also Jennifer C. James, *A Freedom Bought with Blood: African American War Literature from the Civil War to World War II* (Chapel Hill, NC: University of North Carolina Press, 2007), 276. On Killens, see Keith Gilyard, *John Oliver Killens: A Life of Literary Black Activism* (Athens, GA: University of Georgia Press, 2010).

Killens's account of the war was fictional, it was informed by his own wartime experiences, and the tension he described between race and nationality – between an African American identity and an American identity – was played out time and again during the Pacific War. By bringing to the fore this enduring tension in African American history and culture, Killens linked African Americans' wartime experiences to the wider political, economic, and social transformations that occurred across the wartime Asia-Pacific.[3] "Race" was at the center of those transformations, as Japan depicted its quest for regional hegemony as a crusade of liberation against the tyranny of Western colonialism.[4] The racial implications of the Pacific War, however, transcended the contest between Asia and the West, as the white supremacist values upon which both the colonial enterprise and American racism were predicated were tested in myriad ways between 1941 and 1945. The wartime Asia-Pacific was a world turned upside down as prevailing hierarchies within, as well as between, nations were tested by the tumult of total war, and as oppressed groups fought for freedom and demanded democracy.

African Americans were active participants in that complicated and convoluted quest for liberation. In part, black military service in the Pacific Theater was an adventure, a chance to see the world. Calvin C. Miller, a young recruit from North Carolina, spoke for hundreds of thousands of his African American peers. Relishing opportunities to travel "around the world" and "see things" that his teachers had not – could

---

[3] A word on nomenclature is necessary at the outset. In using the phrases "Pacific War," "Pacific Theater," and "Asia-Pacific Theatre" throughout this study, I am conscious that Allied commanders separated the Pacific region into distinct "Pacific" and "Southwest Pacific" Theaters, and – more significantly – that the conflict also stretched over much of Asia. (I note, too, that American veterans of the conflict were eligible to receive the "Asiatic-Pacific" Campaign Medal.) Similarly, in referring to the "Asia-Pacific region," I recognize the diversity of the societies and cultures across that vast area. No less importantly, I acknowledge that while Americans' Pacific War began on December 7, 1941, Japan's 1931 invasion of Manchuria anticipated the full-scale Sino-Japanese conflict beginning in 1937, and that the Japanese occupation of Indochina, beginning in September 1940, foreshadowed further Japanese conquests across Asia.

[4] Historians have long emphasized the racial dimensions of the Pacific War. See Christopher Thorne, *Allies of a Kind: The United States, Britain, and the War against Japan, 1941–1945* (New York, NY: Oxford University Press, 1978), 7. Writing during the mid-1980s John Dower noted that "[a]part from the genocide of the Jews, racism remains one of the great neglected subjects of World War Two." In part, this present study should be seen as another step in addressing that neglect. See John Dower, *War Without Mercy: Race and Power in the Pacific War* (New York, NY: Pantheon Books, 1986), 4. See also Gerald Horne, *Race War!: White Supremacy and the Japanese Attack on the British Empire* (New York, NY: New York University Press, 2004).

not – teach him, Miller recalled that notwithstanding the dangers of battle and the disappointments of racism, his military service had been largely positive: "I learned a lot. It was a great experience."[5] But Miller's wartime contribution, along with those of the tens of thousands of other African Americans who served across the Asia-Pacific, had a wider significance. While almost certainly apocryphal, the story of a young African American draftee who asked that his epitaph read "Here lies a black man, killed fighting a yellow man for the protection of a white man" captured succinctly the complex racial dynamics of the conflict that raged across Asia and the Pacific.[6] The power of that anecdote rests not only on the explicit, oft-stated tension between American rhetoric and the realities of American racism, but also on the ways in which that tension was shaped by the war against the "yellow" adversary.

For African Americans, the Pacific War connected these racial issues to their nation's foreign policy. Indeed, as well as a subject of analysis, race is a lens through which the complicated, multiracial history of the Pacific War can be uncovered. As a September 1945 editorial in the black *New York Amsterdam News* explained, American racism was linked ineludibly to both the outbreak and the conclusion of the Pacific War. Just as the "extent of the disaster at Pearl Harbor was caused by American racial thinking" – white Americans' complacency and sense of superiority led them to assume that the Japanese were incapable of executing an intricate military strike against Western forces – so too the "Japanese surrender was drenched with U.S. racial arrogance."[7] White American commanders' condescension toward their vanquished foes, the *News* suggested, was symptomatic of a racial haughtiness that threatened the prospects for interracial harmony and the future peace. At war's end, America's unresolved racial issues assumed even more urgency, as the United States became the preeminent power across the Asia-Pacific.

Questions of race were fundamental to African Americans' musings on the Pacific War, and the transformations it wrought within the United States and across Asia and the Pacific. Although the black press reported proudly at war's end that 200,000 "tan yanks" had played a "vital role" in defeating Japan, and while African Americans served across the breadth

[5] Calvin C. Miller, AFC/2001/001/74496, Veterans History Project Collection, American Folklife Center, Library of Congress, Washington, DC (VHP-LoC).
[6] The story of the African American draftee can be found in Neil A. Wynn, "The Impact of the Second World War on the American Negro," *Journal of Contemporary History* 6, no. 2 (1971): 49.
[7] "Has America Learned?" *New York Amsterdam News*, September 15, 1945.

of the vast Asia-Pacific Theater, they regarded the Pacific War as much more than an opportunity to defend the United States.[8] As exemplified by the "Double V" campaign – the dual struggle against racism at home and fascism abroad – African Americans' participation in their nation's war effort was also a fight to secure their own rights. The war, therefore, was an opportunity to transform, as well as defend the United States. Conscious that service for the nation was a potent means of establishing their rights of citizenship, between 1941 and 1945 African Americans reiterated the significance of military duty. In this respect they were continuing a long tradition: recognizing that race, war, and citizenship have always been linked in American life, since the War of Independence African Americans had offered their service to their nation, hoping that their wartime efforts and sacrifices would be repaid with the full measure of rights to which they were entitled. By connecting black military service across the Pacific Theater to wider questions of transnational racial liberation, this book casts new light on a conflict that was substantially about race. Shifting the geographic center of the African American wartime experience to the Asia-Pacific region provides a fresh, international perspective on blacks' wartime struggle against white supremacy at home and abroad.

Racial issues were of course also central to the war in Europe. Yet a 1943 remark from the prominent black correspondent Vincent Tubbs – that the conflict in the Pacific had "more ramifications of race and color than Hitler's war" – reflected the concerns of millions of African Americans and other nonwhite peoples.[9] Writing in late 1943, the black journalist and educator Lewis K. McMillan explained that in order to "understand the true character of World War II," one need only "cast" their "eyes over the vast expanse of the great old Pacific Ocean." It was there, he asserted, that "all that is bad, all that is diseased in a western white man's dominated world, a world that breeds and nurtures war," was "laid bare" for all to see.[10] African Americans were situating themselves at the center of what the black sociologist and writer Horace R. Cayton

[8] "Tan Yanks, Now 200,000 Strong, Played Vital Role in Pacific since Pearl Harbor," *Afro-American*, September 1, 1945. See also "Tally of Pacific War Cost Shows Negroes Paid Dearly for Victory," *Norfolk Journal and Guide*, September 1, 1945.

[9] Vincent Tubbs, "Too Far Out to Swim Back," *Afro-American*, May 8, 1943. See also Will V. Neely, "Color Lines Vague as Net Tightens on Japanese in Pacific," *Philadelphia Tribune*, August 12, 1944; "Fighting a Racial War," *Afro-American*, July 28, 1945.

[10] Lewis K. McMillan, "Is World War II Another Scramble for Plunder: How Will the Colored People Fare?" *Cleveland Call and Post*, October 23, 1943.

described as the "global battle of words and ideas." While "the American Negro" was "relatively unimportant except as a symbol of America's racial injustices," he argued, the "stake for which the battle" was "being fought" was "world domination." "Propaganda about the American Negro," wrote Cayton, was "effective in the Philippines, Burma, India, Palestine and South America." African Americans' struggle for equality thereby assumed a global significance. And even while the United States was continuing to renege on its promise of democracy, Cayton invoked principles of American exceptionalism to press his case. The United States, he explained, was "the microcosm" being scrutinized "by the non-white world to see what role they will play if democracy triumphs."[11]

Exceptionalist ideas also underpinned African Americans' perception of their own role as agents of liberation across the Asia-Pacific. Although Japan had figured significantly in what Etsuko Taketani has labeled the "Black Pacific," the Pacific War tested the racial imperatives that had underpinned such ideas during the interwar years.[12] Contending that Japan's anticolonialism was tainted by militarism and self-interest, African Americans assumed they were better-placed to carry freedom to the oppressed peoples of the Asia-Pacific. That confidence was underpinned by a faith that in the global contest of ideas American "civilization" – despite its obvious flaws – was preferable to the alternatives proffered by the nation's enemies. Across the Pacific Theater, that contrast was evidenced not only by Japanese brutality, but also by African Americans' belief that they were destined to play a key role in elevating the uncivilized "others" over whose territories the war was being fought. Anticipating that they would fulfill an important part in America's international mission, and articulating a racially nuanced version of American exceptionalism, black leaders presumed African Americans were uniquely qualified to carry the virtues of civilization to other, less-advanced, non-white peoples. Consequently, while African Americans – as the black journalist Roi Ottley put it in 1943 – felt "a great resurgence of racial kinship to other colored peoples of the world," that sense of kinship did not connote equality.[13] Rather, African Americans' imagined racial community of

[11] Horace R. Cayton, "Japanese Propaganda: Follows Axis Lines of Racial Superiority," *Pittsburgh Courier*, October 9, 1943. See also "Japs Tell Asia U.S. Won't Bring Equality," *Afro-American*, March 7, 1942.
[12] See Etsuko Taketani, *The Black Pacific Narrative: Geographic Imaginings of Race and Empire between the World Wars* (Hanover, NH: Dartmouth College Press, 2014).
[13] Roi Ottley, *"New World A-Coming": Inside Black America* (Boston, MA: Houghton Mifflin, 1943), v.

nonwhite peoples was marked by hierarchies – a form of black, or African American orientalism – that reflected many of the racial assumptions and values that underpinned Western colonial endeavors.[14] African Americans were thus casting their own, neocolonial shadow over the Pacific.

Black servicemen stationed in Asia and the Pacific were alert to the racial dimensions of the conflict raging around them. African American demands for equality, subdued during the desperate days of the Depression, were voiced more loudly as the United States embarked on a great international crusade on behalf of freedom and democracy. For African Americans, the contradiction between their nation's stated wartime goals, and the ongoing realities of racial subjugation and segregation, was all too stark. Hundreds of thousands of African Americans joined the National Association for the Advancement of Colored People (NAACP); the Congress of Racial Equality was established in 1942; and in communities, factories, and fields, and in the still steadfastly segregated barracks of the armed forces, African Americans discussed, lobbied, and organized on behalf of their race. As the Swedish sociologist Gunnar Myrdal remarked in 1944, there was "bound to be a redefinition of the Negro's status in America as a result of this war."[15]

Besides recognizing the immediate, parochial dimensions of the war – rather than fighting "to preserve our way of life," African Americans "were fighting to change it!" – blacks knew that military service in the wartime Asia-Pacific was raising important questions concerning their role in extending US power.[16] During the middle decades of the twentieth century that ascendant American power was expressed economically, politically, and culturally. Above all, however, American hegemony rested on military power, and in the aftermath of Pearl Harbor the United States projected itself as a liberating force, whose soldiers carried with them not just their rifles but also the virtues of liberal democracy. Even during the desperate months of late 1941 and early 1942, American military power was infused with a higher, transformational responsibility

---

[14] Other scholars have also referred to the notion of "Black Orientalism," although their analyses have generally been confined to discussions of African Americans' perceptions of Asians. See, for example, Helen H. Jun, "Black Orientalism: Nineteenth-Century Narratives of Race and U.S. Citizenship," *American Quarterly* 58, no. 4 (2006): 1047–66. See also Bill V. Mullen, *Afro-Orientalism* (Minneapolis, MN: University of Minnesota Press, 2004).

[15] Gunnar Myrdal, *An American Dilemma: The Negro Problem and Modern Democracy* (New York, NY: Harper and Row, 1944), 997.

[16] Nelson Peery, *The Making of an American Revolutionary* (New York, NY: The New Press, 1994), 233.

to liberate and democratize the world. That mission, however, was compromised by the realities of American racism, which African Americans connected explicitly to the meaning of freedom in the postwar world.

Those questions – still unresolved many decades later – transcended the borders of the United States, as the Pacific War cast African Americans as both liberators and occupiers throughout Asia and the Pacific. Grasping the transnational implications of their wartime role, African Americans knew that at the same time as they were victims of American racial prejudice they were also instruments of American power. Black participation in the Pacific War, then, was tied to the rise of American power. As the United States extended its global authority, African Americans were active agents for their race as well as their nation. By raising questions regarding the ways in which African Americans understood, negotiated, and fought for their place in the United States, the Pacific War threw African American' longstanding struggle to reconcile their black identity with their American identity into sharp relief. Indeed, for African American servicemen in the Pacific War – fighting across a region long scarred by racism and colonialism, and where the United States would soon be claiming the mantle of international democratic leadership – the "double consciousness" identified by W. E. B. Du Bois at the beginning of the twentieth century was all the more challenging.[17]

The Pacific War cast that tension between racial and national identity in an explicitly transnational context. Although prevailing Western constructions of Pacific Islanders as a mythologized "Other" rested on binary distinctions between "white" and "black," the Orientalist assumptions underpinning such a dichotomy were tested by the Pacific War. Paul Lyons's claim that black Americans constructed the Pacific as essentially "African" raises questions regarding African Americans' perceptions of both Africa and the Pacific.[18] Inevitably, at a time when scholars such as Melville J. Herskovits were tracing the links between black Americans and their African past, African Americans were keenly interested in the ways in which World War Two disrupted the European colonial presence in Africa.[19] More significantly for this study, however, black Americans'

---

[17] On the notion of "double consciousness," see W. E. B. Du Bois, *The Souls of Black Folk*, eds. Henry Louis Gates, Jr and Terri Hume Oliver (New York, NY: W. W. Norton, 1999), 11.

[18] Paul Lyons, *American Pacificism: Oceania in the U.S. Imagination* (New York, NY: Routledge, 2006), 37–8.

[19] In reviewing Melville J. Herskovits's 1941 *Myth of the Negro Past*, J. A. Rogers commended Herskovits for refuting notions of African savagery and backwardness. See J. A. Rogers, "The Truth about Negroes," *Pittsburgh Courier*, February 21, 1942.

calls for an "African Charter," predicated on a belief that African nations were ready for self-government, were paralleled by African American demands for a "Pacific Charter."[20] These demands were encouraged by the turmoil of the Pacific War, and while previous scholars have recognized that that conflict disturbed the racial hierarchies that had prevailed across the prewar Asia-Pacific, they have not explored the part that African Americans – military personnel, journalists and editors, activists, and others – played in that process. Likewise, although Pacific historians have demonstrated that Pacific Islanders were impressed by the part played by black Americans in the massive wartime American military presence, little has been said about African Americans' perceptions of those interactions.[21]

These omissions can be traced to the wartime marginalization – cultural, as well as political – of the African American contribution to Allied victory. Noting that forms of black popular culture are products of both "engagement across different cultural boundaries," and negotiations between "dominant and subordinate" positions, the ways in which African Americans were depicted – or not depicted – in wartime cultural productions was both revealing and contentious.[22] While "the idea of black film is always a question, never an answer," black commentators recognized the particular power of film to shape popular attitudes.[23] Bemoaning the absence of African Americans from popular narratives about the Pacific War, the black press railed, in particular, against the persistent neglect of African Americans in wartime news reports. "[W]hite people," complained the NAACP's *The Crisis* in February 1944, "get the impression" that "Negroes are doing little if anything to win the victory." The "scheme to keep from white America the news that the Negro

---

[20] "Wanted: An African Charter," *Pittsburgh Courier*, December 19, 1942.

[21] Echoing Margaret Mead's suggestion that African Americans had played a significant role in building a "bridge" that helped Manus Islanders develop a "sense of racial identification," Lamont Lindstrom and Geoffrey White contended that the "example" of African American troops contributed to the "transformations" in Pacific Islanders' self-image. See Margaret Mead, *New Lives for Old: Cultural Transformations–Manus, 1928–1953* (1956; New York, NY: William Morrow and Co., 1966), 173; Lindstrom and White, "War Stories" in *Island Encounters: Black and White Memories of the Pacific War* (Washington, DC: Smithsonian Institution Press, 1990), 22. See also Sean Brawley and Chris Dixon, *Hollywood's South Seas and the Pacific War: Searching for Dorothy Lamour* (New York, NY: Palgrave Macmillan, 2012), 221, n.67.

[22] Stuart Hall, "What Is This 'Black' in Black Popular Culture?" *Social Justice* 20, nos. 1–2 (1993): 110.

[23] Michael Boyce Gillespie, *Film Blackness: American Cinema and the Idea of Black Film* (Durham, NC: Duke University Press, 2016), 16.

minority is doing its part in the war," wrote the editors, "is a dastardly trick, as mean as any perpetrated against the race." Compounding that frustration, even when accounts detailing African Americans' contributions to the war in the Pacific were available, cinemas and news companies rarely made use of such reports. Although companies such as Pathé and Paramount denied having a "policy of excluding Negroes from their films," African Americans were not placated. Despairing that the "story of Negro soldiers on the battlefront" would never be known "if the telling was left" to white-owned newsreel corporations, the editors of *The Crisis* expressed exasperation that a film highlighting the contribution of black engineers in the Southwest Pacific Theater was "not handled at all by the newsreel companies." Instead, the film was "turned over" to "All American Newsreel," a company "said to be organized by owners of strictly jim crow Negro theatres throughout the Southern and border states." African American commentators argued that the cumulative effect of these practices was "to keep 122,000,000 white Americans in ignorance of what Negro troops" were "doing to win victory over the Axis."[24] Moreover, when efforts were made to present African Americans – and their wartime relations with white Americans – in a positive light, such as in certain official, government productions, the intention was often transparently propagandistic, rather than pedagogic. Therefore, while government-sponsored documentaries such as *The Negro Soldier* (1944) and *The Negro Sailor* (1945) acknowledged African Americans' contributions to America's military history, by overlooking the persistence of racial segregation in the armed forces, they implied that the black struggle for civil rights was complete.[25]

On the surface, Hollywood's wartime productions offered an alternative means of subverting white racism. Several films made during the war featured blacks in minor but nonetheless significant roles, and as one historian has noted, black "figures' best chance to bend the bars

[24] "Omissions from Newsreels" and "Along the N.A.A.C.P. Battlefront," both in the *The Crisis*, February, 1944, 39, 51–2.
[25] See Carlton Moss, *The Negro Soldier*, directed by Frank Capra, War Activities Committee of the Motion Picture Industry, 1944; Department of the Navy, *The Negro Sailor*, directed by Henry Levin, United States Navy Motion Film Productions, 1945. See also Andrew J. Huebner, *Warrior Image: Soldiers in American Culture from the Second World War to the Vietnam Era* (Chapel Hill, NC: University of North Carolina Press, 2008), 45–7; Thomas Cripps, *Slow Fade to Black: The Negro in American Film, 1900–1942* (New York, NY: Oxford University Press, 1977), 379–81; Thomas Cripps, *Making Movies Black: The Hollywood Message Movie from World War II to the Civil Rights Era* (New York, NY: Oxford University Press, 1993), 102–25.

of the cage of unity occurred in combat pictures, where Hollywood gave" African Americans "more equality than the war or navy departments were prepared to consider."[26] Yet with occasional exceptions – as a subsequent chapter explains, *Bataan*, released in 1943, presented an African American soldier in a positive light – wartime productions typically perpetuated, rather than challenged, prevailing racial stereotypes.[27] Hollywood was complicit in marginalizing the African American contribution to the Pacific War.

This marginalization persisted during the postwar period. In the well-known 1958 movie version of James A. Michener's 1947 *Tales of the South Pacific*, there was just "one lonely" African American soldier.[28] And while some World War Two novels – most notably Killens's *And Then We Heard the Thunder* – were penned by black writers or veterans, or featured African American characters, such works constitute a tiny minority of the vast outpouring of literature devoted to the Pacific War.[29] Similarly, African American veterans remain frustrated by the fact that with the notable, if belated exception of Doris "Dorie" Miller, the black hero of Pearl Harbor, they remain largely absent from popular narratives of the Pacific War. As

[26] See Clayton R. Koppes, "Hollywood and the Politics of Representation: Women, Workers, and African Americans in World War II Movies," in *The Home Front War: World War II and American Society*, eds. Kenneth Paul O'Brien and Lynn Hudson Parsons (Westport, CT: Greenwood, 1995), 36. While *In This Our Life* (1942) did not deal with the war, it did raise racial issues. Conversely, wartime black musicals such as *Cabin in the Sky* (1942) and *Stormy Weather* (1943) did little to challenge white stereotypes of African Americans. See Neil A. Wynn, *The Afro-American and the Second World War* (London: Paul Elek, 1976), 81–4; Cripps, *Making Movies Black*, 32–4; Cripps, *Slow Fade to Black*, 377–9.

[27] Cripps, *Making Movies Black*, 76. On blacks' efforts to ameliorate their marginalization in wartime popular culture, see Stephen Tuck, "'You Can Sing and Punch … But You Can't Be a Soldier or a Man': African American Struggles for a New Place in Popular Culture," in *Fog of War: The Second World War and the Civil Rights Movement*, eds. Kevin M. Kruse and Stephen Tuck (New York, NY: Oxford University Press, 2012), 5. See also Benjamin L. Alpers, "This Is the Army: Imagining a Democratic Military in World War II," *Journal of American History* 85, no. 1 (1998): 146–7.

[28] See Margaret Jolly, "From Venus Point to Bali Ha'i: Eroticism and Exoticism in Representations of the Pacific," in *Sites of Desire, Economies of Pleasure: Sexualities in Asia and the Pacific*, eds. Lenore Manderson and Margaret Jolly (Chicago, IL: University of Chicago Press, 1997), 116.

[29] For a survey of African American literature of World War Two, see Jennifer Corrine James, "'Sable Hands' and National Arms: African-American Literature of War, the Civil War-WWII" (PhD dissertation, University of Maryland, 2001). African American resistance to segregation within the military was one of the major themes of James Gould Cozzens's Pulitzer-Prize winning novel, *Guard of Honor*. See James Gould Cozzens, *Guard of Honor* (New York, NY: Harcourt, Brace, 1948).

one black Army veteran opined, "you never see" African Americans in cinematic accounts of the Pacific War. Blacks, he insisted, "were there. Why not put them in there now?"[30] Contending that there was nothing accidental about the exclusion of African Americans from popular accounts of the bloody 1945 battle on Iwo Jima, black Marine Steven Robinson concluded wryly that the omission "was purposely done."[31]

Paralleling their neglect in popular depictions of the Pacific War, African Americans have long been marginalized in historical accounts of the conflict.[32] Curiously, although historians have long recognized the significance of World War Two for African Americans, and while scholars have examined the relationship between black military service, the Cold War, and the postwar civil rights movement, even recent studies of the Pacific War continue to neglect blacks' roles in a conflict in which questions of race loomed so large.[33] Just as American military power across the wartime Pacific was racialized, so too are memories of the conflict.

---

[30] John David Jackson, AFC/2001/001/38452, VHP-LoC.

[31] See Robinson, cited in Melton A. McLaurin, *The Marines of Montford Point: America's First Black Marines* (Chapel Hill, NC: University of North Carolina Press, 2007), 101. On the controversy regarding the near-complete exclusion of African Americans from Clint Eastwood's 2006 film, *Flags of Our Fathers*, see Alex Altman, "Were African-Americans at Iwo Jima?" *Time*, June 9, 2008, http://content.time.com/time/nation/article/0,8599,1812972,00.html (accessed October 9, 2016); Earl Ofari Hutchinson, "Flags of Our Fathers Whitewashes War History," *The Huffington Post*, May 26, 2011, www.huffingtonpost.com.au/entry/flags-of-our-fathers-whit_b_32402 (accessed October 9, 2016).

[32] Ulysses Lee's study of the use of African American troops during World War Two includes considerable detail concerning the deployment of black troops to the Pacific War. While *Black Soldier Blues*, a 2005 television documentary, paid particular attention to the wartime discrimination endured by African American servicemen based in Australia, it also drew attention to the extent and depth of white American racism across the Pacific Theater. See Ulysses Lee, *The Employment of Negro Troops* (Washington, DC: Office of the Chief of Military History, United States Army, 1966); Nicole McCuaig and Veronica Fury, *Black Soldier Blues*, directed by Nicole McCuaig (Sydney: Australian Broadcasting Corporation/Big Island Pictures, 2005). See also Horne, *Race War!*; Debra J. Latourette et al., *African Americans in World War 2: Struggle against Segregation and Discrimination*, directed by Jonathan J. Nash (Miami, FL: Department of Defense 50th Anniversary of World War II Commemorative Committee, 1997).

[33] Peter Schrijvers has justified his neglect of black troops on the grounds that "in a war that was to a large extent racial in nature," the "African-American experience was inevitably quite distinct from that of white Americans." The black experience in the Pacific War, he suggested, warrants "special treatment in a separate study." See Peter Schrijvers, *Bloody Pacific: American Soldiers at War with Japan* (New York, NY: Palgrave Macmillan, 2010), xii. See also John Bodnar, *"The Good War" in American Memory* (Baltimore, MD: Johns Hopkins University Press, 2010), 167–83. On the shifting views of the significance of World War Two in the history of the struggle for civil rights, see Kevin M. Kruse and Stephen Tuck, "Introduction," *Fog of War: The Second World War and the*

The exclusion of African Americans from popular and historical accounts of the Pacific War affirms the significance of the politics of history for black America. Bearing in mind the central role accorded to military valor in constructions of American citizenship – a process rendered all the more potent by the valorization of World War Two's "Greatest Generation" – the continuing elision of African Americans from narratives of the Pacific War perpetuates longstanding ideas regarding blacks' willingness, or unwillingness, to fight for their own freedom. As Francois Furstenberg has explained, notions of black passivity have long been a powerful weapon in the armory of those contending that African Americans are both unworthy of freedom, and complicit in their own oppression.[34] Accordingly, while scholars such as John Bodnar and Andrew J. Huebner are right to argue that the mythologized notion of World War Two as the "good war" overlooks important wartime divisions within the United States, and that veterans of that conflict found reintegration into postwar society more fraught than popular memory suggests, it remains the case that veterans of World War Two occupy a special, exceptional place in American memory.[35] For African Americans, however, the "good war" paradigm remains problematic, as they seek inclusion into the dominant narrative. While the "Allied war epic" exerts a hegemonic influence over popular and scholarly memories of the Pacific

---

Civil Rights Movement, eds. Kevin M. Kruse and Stephen Tuck (New York, NY: Oxford University Press, 2012), 3–6. See also Harvard Sitkoff, "Racial Militancy and Interracial Violence in the Second World War," *Journal of American History* 58, no. 3 (1971): 661; Richard Dalfiume, "The 'Forgotten Years' of the Negro Revolution," *Journal of American History* 55, no. 1 (1968): 90–106. On the relationship between African American military service and the postwar civil rights struggle, see Christine Knauer, *Let Us Fight as Free Men: Black Soldiers and Civil Rights* (Philadelphia, PA: University of Pennsylvania Press, 2014). Studies of African Americans and the Cold War include Mary L. Dudziak, *Cold War Civil Rights: Race and the Image of American Democracy* (Princeton, NJ: Princeton University Press, 2000); Brenda Gayle Plummer, *Rising Wind: Black Americans and U.S. Foreign Affairs, 1935–1960* (Chapel Hill, NC: University of North Carolina Press, 1996); Jonathan Rosenberg, *How Far the Promised Land? World Affairs and the American Civil Rights Movement from the First World War to Vietnam* (Princeton, NJ: Princeton University Press, 2006); Michael Cullen Green, *Black Yanks in the Pacific: Race in the Making of the American Military Empire after World War II* (Ithaca, NY: Cornell University Press, 2010); Carol Anderson, *Eyes off the Prize: The United Nations and the African American Struggle for Human Rights, 1944–1955* (Cambridge: Cambridge University Press, 2003).

[34] See Francois Furstenberg, "Beyond Freedom and Slavery: Autonomy, Virtue, and Resistance in Early American Political Discourse," *Journal of American History* 89, no. 4 (2003): 1302–28. See also Tom Brokaw, *The Greatest Generation* (New York, NY: Random House, 1998).

[35] See Bodnar, *"The Good War" in American Memory*; Huebner, *Warrior Image*.

War, the "dominant stories" associated with those memories are not defined solely along national lines. The power of those stories to "simplify and transform troublesome or dissonant memories" applies equally to marginalized and silenced groups – such as African Americans – within nations.[36]

The neglect of African Americans in studies of the Pacific War reflects the fact that military historians' gaze has typically been directed at the battlefield, where relatively few blacks served. And although some studies situate African Americans' Pacific War experiences within broader surveys of the black contribution to the military history of the United States, their analysis of African Americans' roles in the war against Japan remains meager.[37] The most valuable discussion of African Americans and the Pacific War is Robert Jefferson's 2008 study of the 93rd Infantry Division – the principal black combat unit deployed to the Pacific Theater. In rich and careful detail, Jefferson traces the views and military careers of the men of the 93rd, from the prewar period through to the ways in which their postwar experiences were shaped by their military service.[38] While Jefferson's study demonstrates comprehensively the discrimination endured by the men of the 93rd, and highlights the long-term significance of their military service, only a minority of African Americans were given the opportunity to serve in combat units. Absent, too, from the historiography, too, is an examination of the deeper social and political dimensions of African Americans' Pacific War, which provided a key platform for blacks' contribution to postwar US foreign policy. This book fills this historiographical lacuna.

---

[36] See Takahashi Fujitani, Geoffrey M. White, and Lisa Yoneyama, "Introduction," in *Perilous Memories: The Asia-Pacific War(s)*, eds. Takahashi Fujitani, Geoffrey M. White, and Lisa Yoneyama (Durham, NC: Duke University Press, 2001), 4.

[37] Surveys of African American military history include Robert B. Edgerton, *Hidden Heroism: Black Soldiers in America's Wars* (Boulder, CO: Westview Press, 2001); Gerald Astor, *The Right to Fight: A History of African Americans in the Military* (Novato, CA: Presidio, 1998); Gail Buckley, *American Patriots: The Story of Blacks in the Military from the Revolution to Desert Storm* (New York, NY: Random House, 2001). Important studies of African Americans during World War One include Chad L. Williams, *Torchbearers of Democracy: African Americans Soldiers in the World War I Era* (Chapel Hill, NC: University of North Carolina Press, 2019), and Arthur Barbeau, *The Unknown Soldiers: Black American Troops in World War I* (Philadelphia, PA: Temple University Press, 1974).

[38] Robert Jefferson, *Fighting for Hope: African American Troops of the 93rd Infantry Division in World War II and Postwar America* (Baltimore, MD: Johns Hopkins University Press, 2008).

Like many exercises in African American history, this study exploits an eclectic range of primary sources. The starting point for any analysis of black participation in the Pacific War are the materials held at the National Archives and Records Administration (NARA), in College Park, Maryland. The vast military bureaucracy that developed during World War Two produced voluminous records, detailing almost every conceivable aspect of the American war effort. Military authorities, like their civilian counterparts, expended vast amounts of time and energy seeking to contain what they regarded as "race problems" – both in the United States, and internationally. Yet while racial issues loom large in many of those official military records, African Americans voices are marginalized in and frequently absent from such sources. For scholars interested in African American history, reading archival materials such as those held at NARA, or in records held by the other official repositories, such as the US Military History Institute, at Carlisle Barracks, Pennsylvania, the challenge is often one of listening out for silences.

While black voices were frequently muted in official military and government sources, they spoke loudly in the records of the NAACP and in the African American press. The records of the NAACP, housed in the Library of Congress, provide valuable insights into African Americans' wartime experiences, grievances, and aspirations. Black newspapers – which according to one survey had a combined weekly circulation of over 1.2 million in 1941, rising to more than 1.8 million by 1945 – remain an essential source for tracing African American wartime experiences.[39] As well as presenting African Americans' wartime courage and virtue as affirmations that they were entitled to equality and the rights of citizenship, black editors, correspondents, and commentators deliberated over and debated the political and racial implications of the Pacific War. Predictably, those deliberations attracted the scrutiny of white civil and military authorities, who were determined to present non-confrontational images of African Americans. Moreover, although the relationship between white authorities and the black press was not entirely antagonistic – both were seeking to emphasize that African Americans were playing their part in securing Allied victory – there were differences regarding the nature of that black contribution. The African American press, therefore, worked to overcome white America's ignorance regarding

---

[39] On circulation figures of African American newspapers, see Paul Alkebulan, *The African American Press in World War II: Toward Victory at Home and Abroad* (Lanham, MD: Lexington Books, 2014), 23.

blacks' role in the war effort. Individual African American journalists had a vital part to play in overcoming that neglect. Here again, however, there were instances when white and black interests coincided.[40] While the United States War Department employed just one black officer in its press section, it did accredit approximately twenty African Americans as war correspondents. For the black press, this process could be mutually advantageous: as Lee Finkle has observed, "widespread coverage of the black soldier's role in the war effort was the most effective means of stimulating sales."[41]

Throughout the Asia-Pacific war zone, African American journalists documented the frustrations and aspirations of black service personnel. Most would have described themselves as "reporters," or "correspondents," but those phrases understate their contribution to the black freedom struggle. The distinction between "reporter" and "activist" was ambiguous, and whatever the journalistic conventions regarding objectivity, African American reporters exploited their wartime role to become – in the words of Bernard P. Young, editor of the *Norfolk Journal and Guide* – "crusaders" and "advocates" for their race.[42] There were also occasions when black correspondents intervened directly to challenge racist practices. Writing from Manila in early 1945, well-known African American reporter Charles H. Loeb detailed his participation in

[40] John F. Dille, Jr., a white officer assigned to organize black journalists, recalled being told by the "senior public-information officer" of the Pacific Fleet that he should "say that these [black] sailors are doing well in the Navy and are performing worthwhile missions." See John F. Dille, cited in *The Golden Thirteen: Recollections of the First Black Naval Officers*, ed. Paul Stillwell (Annapolis, MD: Naval Institute Press, 1993), 112.

[41] See Lee Finkle, *Forum for Protest: The Black Press during World War II* (Cranbury, NJ: Fairleigh Dickinson University Press, 1975), 54.

[42] See P. Bernard Young, Jr., "Credo for the Negro Press," *Norfolk Journal and Guide*, July 22, 1944. Noting the historiographical neglect of African American correspondents during the Pacific War, David J. Longley has analyzed Vincent Tubbs's wartime writings about Australia and Japan. See David J. Longley, "Vincent Tubbs and the Baltimore *Afro-American*: Although completed too late to inform this study, David J. Longley's PhD thesis provides a careful and detailed analysis of African American correspondents during World War Two. See Longley, "Victory at Home and Abroad: Overseas Correspondents, the African American Press, and the Long Civil Rights Movement, 1939–1946" (PhD dissertation, Monash University, 2018). See also Jinx Coleman Broussard and John Maxwell Hamilton, "Covering a Two Front War: Three African American Correspondents during World War II," *American Journalism* 22, no. 3 (2005): 33; John D. Stevens, *From the Back of the Foxhole: Black Correspondents in World War II*, Journalism Monographs, 27, Lexington, KY: Association for Education in Journalism, February, 1973, 7.

a successful protest against the imposition of segregationist practices in that recently liberated city.[43]

Black reporters such as Loeb had little trouble recording their wartime experiences. Uncovering the stories of African American servicemen – few black women were given opportunities to serve across the Pacific Theater – is more challenging. Only a relative handful of servicemen wrote and published memoirs, private correspondence is scant, and diaries are elusive. Yet such sources, highlighting African Americans' more private emotions, as well as the racialized politics of black military service, are immensely valuable. Fortunately for the historian, tracing the experiences and memories of black veterans of the Pacific War is made easier thanks to the Veterans History Project, at the Library of Congress. This vast collection, comprising interviews with veterans of every conflict in which Americans have fought since World War One, is a rich resource for historians of the American military experience. As with all oral histories, the interviews included in the Veterans History Project must be used judiciously. Along with the fact that the project is in many respects celebratory rather than scholarly, most of the interviews with Pacific War veterans were recorded several decades after the war's end: inevitably, memories fade, details become blurred, and the interviewees' recollections regarding specific events should be treated cautiously. Blacks' recollections of their frontline experiences are complicated by the continuing marginalization of African Americans from popular memories of the Pacific War, and former servicemen's views of the war are often limited to what they experienced in their own barracks, or foxhole. Furthermore, many of those conducting the interviews with veterans were untrained in the techniques of oral history.[44] Those caveats notwithstanding, the materials included in the Veterans History Project have given voice to otherwise silenced men and women, and helped elevate them from the footnotes of history to which they were too long consigned.

African Americans and the Pacific War consists of a series of thematic chapters, bookended by an analysis of the meaning of Pearl Harbor for black America, and an examination of black reactions to the end of the war and the ascending power of the United States across the Asia-Pacific. As Chapter 1 reveals, while African Americans shared their compatriots'

[43] Charles Loeb, "A 'Daily News' Reporter Helps Lick Jim Crow," *New York Amsterdam News*, March 24, 1945.
[44] On the Veterans History Project see Christopher Michael Jannings, "Lest We Forget: The Library of Congress's Veterans History Project and 'Radical Trust'" (PhD dissertation, Western Michigan University, 2010).

outrage at Japan's surprise attack at Hawaii, the nation's response to Pearl Harbor highlighted the racism that remained so deeply embedded in American life. African American patriotism was hence shaped not just by the events of December 1941, but also by blacks' dual loyalties to race and nation. For African Americans, the post-Pearl Harbor patriotic imperative was further muddled by the fact that the nation's enemy had, during the prewar period, claimed a friendship and common fraternity with black Americans. Japan's international effort to position itself as the nemesis of white authority and colonialism was thus connected to African Americans' struggles for freedom and equality. Pearl Harbor was not just the beginning of a new and bloody phase in the long-running contest between Japan and the United States: for black Americans, it explicitly connected their challenge to American racism to the wider, international struggle to overthrow the old colonial order.

In Chapter 2, attention turns to the interlocking patterns of racism that characterized the wartime Asia-Pacific. During World War Two, African Americans were victims of a racially segregated military system, extending from training camps scattered across the United States to the most distant reaches of America's military apparatus. However, while African Americans everywhere challenged the US military's segregationist practices, the Double V campaign took a particular form in the Pacific Theater, where blacks were fighting on islands and territories previously under the thrall of Western colonial authority. Examining the racial dynamics of black military service in regions stained by colonial hierarchies of race and power raises questions concerning African Americans' attitudes toward and treatment of other nonwhite peoples. Across the Pacific Theater, as African Americans simultaneously challenged and reinforced prevailing racial practices, and navigated their loyalties to race and nation, the line between "liberator" and "occupier" was frequently indistinct. These issues of national and racial identity were framed by the harsh realities of war as blacks navigated the complex interplay between place, imagination, and experience through distinctly African American eyes.

Tensions between race and nationality also underpin Chapter 3, exploring the vexed relationship between war and gender across the Pacific Theater. In tracing the wartime intersections between gender and race – as they were understood, negotiated, and experienced by African Americans – gender, like race, is both a subject for historical scrutiny and a lens through which the complex history of the Pacific War can be considered. Amid that most masculine of spaces – the military – African Americans were waging war across a region that Western culture had long portrayed in highly sexualized terms. For black men, the friction between race and gender across the wartime Pacific was sharply felt. Although the perils of transgressing the line between race and sex were all too familiar to African American servicemen, the sensual freedoms promised by the much-mythologized "South Seas" complicated the tension between sex and race, and contributed to a kind of moral panic regarding the perils of black sexuality. These issues were of deep concern to American commanders, whose apprehensions were both moral and military. Not only was controlling African American sexuality deemed necessary to protect the virtue of women across the Asia-Pacific, but commanders also worried that inappropriate behavior on the part of black servicemen would antagonize local communities, whose support for the Allied war effort was considered essential. Regulating or prohibiting black servicemen's interactions with women of all races was a means of maintaining white masculine hegemony.

The following three chapters explore ways in which the Pacific War presented opportunities for African Americans to remake the world. Chapter 4 examines the African American presence in wartime Australia. That presence exposed the contradictions of Australian and American racism, and further empowered African Americans to press their case as agents of transnational liberation. Australia was more than just an ally of the United States. It was also an outpost of "white civilization" in the Asia-Pacific region. African Americans' prewar knowledge of Australia was generally limited to a vague awareness of the nation's notorious racial policies which restricted the immigration of nonwhite peoples and which reflected a deep-seated racism toward its own indigenous inhabitants. In practice, however, African Americans were frequently surprised by the friendly reception they received in Australia, and their wartime encounters there – with their white compatriots, as well as with Australians – constitute an important, if often neglected, aspect of the transnational African American experience during World War Two. For many white Americans, the apparent willingness of Australians to forgo principles of white supremacy constituted a provocative challenge to the racial – and in some cases, sexual – order. As one white American war correspondent reported from Australia: "I have never seen the racial problem brought home so forcibly as it is over here."[45]

[45] Robert Sherrod, undated report, with processing note, "[Public activities-Biographical Information-Navy] Australia Material," Lyndon Baines Johnson Archives Collection, Lyndon B. Johnson Presidential Library, Austin, Texas.

In Chapter 5, the focus turns to black combat service across the Pacific Theater. While *African Americans and the Pacific War* does not provide detailed discussions of specific battles in which blacks participated, front-line military service was inherently political and racialized. During the Vietnam War, blacks believed they were overly represented in combat units; during World War Two, however, recognizing that the "future of the Negro in America" was "being decided in the foxholes of the world," they articulated very different frustrations.[46] Incensed by the "widespread opinion that Negroes make poor fighting soldiers," and by the obstinate refusal of white authorities to deploy African Americans to combat, during the 1940s black leaders campaigned for the right to fight.[47] Seeking to protect their own cultural and political authority, white men recognized that refusing black men the opportunity to serve in combat was a means of denying them their manhood – and the rights of citizenship. The connections between black military service, masculinity, and citizenship had been evident in America's earlier wars.[48] But during World War Two African Americans believed that service in combat zones of the Pacific Theater would help ensure that the American power that was being projected abroad was a racially progressive contrast to both the illiberal segregationist practices still commonplace throughout much of the United States and the colonial systems that had characterized the prewar Asia-Pacific.

Having been active participants in the momentous transformations across the wartime Asia-Pacific, when the conflict concluded, black servicemen, reporters, and leaders reflected on the meaning of the war and the part that African Americans would play in the postwar world. As Chapter 6 explains, at the end of the Pacific War blacks' interactions with their wartime adversaries and allies were shaped by the racial dynamics

---

[46] "Writing the Future in Foxholes," *Chicago Defender*, February 24, 1945. On African Americans and the Vietnam War, see James Westheider, *Fighting on Two Fronts: African Americans and the Vietnam War* (New York, NY: New York University Press, 1997); Westheider, *The African American Experience in Vietnam: Brothers in Arms* (Lanham, MD: Rowman and Littlefield, 2008); Herman Graham, III, *The Brothers' Vietnam War: Black Power, Manhood, and the Military Experience* (Gainesville, FL: University Press of Florida, 2003).

[47] Ruth Danenhower Wilson, *Jim Crow Joins Up*, Revised edn. (New York, NY: William J. Clark, 1944), 41.

[48] Adriene Lentz-Smith has noted that manhood "was the idiom of black soldiers' political discourse before and during" World War One. See Lentz-Smith, *Freedom Struggles: African Americans and World War I* (Cambridge, MA: Harvard University Press, 2009), 7. See also Steve Estes, *I Am a Man! Race, Manhood, and the Civil Rights Movement* (Chapel Hill, NC: University of North Carolina Press, 2005), 13.

of the rise of American internationalism, and by the nation's attempt to establish itself as the dominant power in the postwar Asia-Pacific. Certain that racial issues were fundamental to debates regarding the international order across the postwar the Pacific and Asia, black leaders envisaged a unique role for African Americans. And as they contemplated that role, African Americans' perceptions and politics continued to be determined by the dual imperatives of race and nationality. Reconciling those often-contradictory imperatives remained a complicated, fraught process. As Chapter 1 explains, these tensions were exposed at the beginning of America's Pacific War, as African Americans responded to the Japanese attack at Pearl Harbor.

CHAPTER I

"Jim Crow on the Run"

Black America, Pearl Harbor, and the Patriotic Imperative

Pearl Harbor put Jim Crow on the run.
That Crow can't fight for Democracy
And be the same old Crow he used to be—
Although right now, Even yet today,
He still tries to act in the same old way.
But India and China, and Harlem, too,
Have made up their minds Jim Crow is through.[1]

Written just ten months after the US traumatic entry into World War Two, Langston Hughes's poetic pronouncement of the demise of American racism was aspirational rather than descriptive. Racism, as Hughes well knew, was a stubborn beast to slay. At the same time, however, in heralding "Jim Crow's Last Stand" he recognized the profound significance of the events of December 7, 1941. Japan's attack at Pearl Harbor, Hughes declared, had precipitated an upsurge in civil rights activism, and highlighted the international dimensions of the struggle against racism. Pearl Harbor was instrumental in bolstering black consciousness, as nonwhite peoples everywhere took matters into their own hands and asserted their rights with a newfound confidence. As Hughes implied, black Americans' racially distinct understandings of Pearl Harbor complicate traditional narratives regarding national unity and patriotism in wartime America.

---

[1] See Langston Hughes, "Jim Crow's Last Stand," in *The Collected Works of Langston Hughes: Volume 2, The Poems, 1941–1950*, ed. Arnold Rampersad (Columbia, MO: University of Missouri Press, 2001), 98. A slightly revised version of Hughes's poem was published in the *Afro-American*, October 24, 1942.

Few events have shaken the United States like Japan's surprise attack at Pearl Harbor. What President Franklin D. Roosevelt described as "a date which will live in infamy" was a transformational event in American history.[2] The enduring interpretation of Pearl Harbor as a unifying event in American history underpins popular representations of wartime America, and of the role of the "Greatest Generation" in saving not just the United States, but freedom loving people everywhere, from the ravages of fascist totalitarianism. At first glance "Pearl Harbor" – the phrase soon connoted not just a place, but principally the events of that fateful December morning – was invested with similar meanings for African Americans as it was for their white compatriots. Enraged by Japan's act of treachery, Eddie Will Robinson – a self-described "seventeen-year-old patriot" – recalled "burning with a desire to smite the little bastards who had dared to fire on the flag of my country."[3]

Articulating a sentiment common among African Americans, Robinson's patriotic fervor suggests that besides signaling an end to American isolationism, the surge of patriotism prompted by Pearl Harbor transcended the racial divide. African Americans reacted to the Japanese attack with a sense of vengeance that seemingly left no doubt regarding their commitment to their nation and its war against Japan. According to popular narratives, African Americans recognized that their goal of racial advancement was contingent upon the survival of the United States. As it did for white Americans, the phrase "Remember Pearl Harbor" resonated in the African American community, and was a powerful tool for encouraging service on behalf of the war effort, from civilians as well as military personnel. Indeed, far from exhibiting "a strong current of apathy" toward the war, African Americans took a keen interest in its outcome.[4] By the war's end over one million blacks had served in the military, and all but a small minority who were called to do so "accepted induction and served effectively."[5]

[2] Franklin D. Roosevelt, "Pearl Harbor Speech: Day of Infamy," at http://www.digitalhis tory.uh.edu/disp_textbook.cfm?smtID=3&psid=1082 (accessed April 4, 2016).

[3] Robinson cited in *The Invisible Soldier: The Experience of the Black Soldier*, ed. Mary Penick Motley (Detroit, MI: Wayne State University Press, 1975), 111. For other African Americans' recollections of the events of December 7, 1941, see, for example, Ivan J. Houston, *Black Warriors: The Buffalo Soldiers of World War II* (New York, NY: iUniverse, 2009), 1.

[4] The quote comes from Clayton R. Koppes and Gregory D. Black, "Blacks, Loyalty, and Motion-Picture Propaganda in World War II," *Journal of American History* 73, no. 2 (1986): 383.

[5] See George Lipsitz, "'Frantic to Join ... the Japanese Army': The Asia Pacific War in the Lives of African American Soldiers and Civilians," in *The Politics of Culture in the*

Yet, for African Americans, Pearl Harbor raised questions very different from those confronting white Americans. Despite sharing the national rage at Japanese perfidy, blacks understood the causes and consequences of Pearl Harbor in racially distinct terms, which raised anew the persistent tension in African American culture between national and racial identity. Their responses to Japan's attack, therefore, not only reflected immediate, patriotic imperatives: "Pearl Harbor" became a powerful referent point to denounce racism everywhere, as the white supremacy underpinning both American racism and the colonial enterprise was challenged in myriad ways during the Pacific War. Underpinning this analysis, moreover, are questions concerning the ways in which black service personnel bound for the Pacific regarded themselves as harbingers of a new order, including a new racial order, which would overturn established racial values and racist practices – in the US military, in the American nation, and across the Asia-Pacific. As this chapter reveals, Pearl Harbor was a key moment for African Americans, highlighting the connections between US foreign policy, the nation's mistreatment of its black citizens, and the systems of colonialism and racism in the areas over which the Pacific War was fought. Examining African Americans' responses to Pearl Harbor thus adds a new dimension to our understandings of its meaning in American history, culture, and foreign policy.

When African Americans are incorporated into the dominant narrative regarding the meaning of Pearl Harbor in United States history – and they have often occupied, at best, a marginal place in that narrative – their role is frequently explained through the actions of one man, Doris "Dorie" Miller.[6] His valor during the Japanese attack defied white stereotypes regarding African Americans, and rendered him an exemplar, both for his race and for his nation. African Americans' reactions to Pearl Harbor, however, transcended Miller's individual heroism and highlighted the relationship between American and international racism: sections of the black community had long been aware of Japan's challenge

---

Shadow of Capital, eds. Lisa Lowe and David Lloyd (Durham, NC: Duke University Press, 1997), 325. Ulysses Lee has noted that between the end of November 1941 and the end of December 1942 the "active enlisted strength" of African Americans in the United States Army increased from 97,725 to 467,883. See Ulysses Lee, *The Employment of Negro Troops* (Washington, DC: Office of the Chief of Military History, United States Army, 1966), 88.

[6] For an analysis of the ways in which Doris Miller "has been reinscribed as a marker of the US military's triumph over racism," see Robert K. Chester, "'Negroes' Number One Hero': Doris Miller, Pearl Harbor, and Retroactive Multiculturalism in World War II Remembrance," *American Quarterly* 65, no. 1 (2013): 31–61 (quote on 31).

to the prevailing racial and colonial order, and during the prewar period Japan had been integral to African American internationalism, particularly across the Asia-Pacific region.

African American internationalism must be seen within the context of the rising global tensions of the late 1930s and early 1940s. Regardless of those tensions, many Americans clung to the illusion of isolationism, imagining that the Pacific and Atlantic oceans provided impermeable barriers that would continue to shield the United States from the wars already raging through much of Europe and Asia. While many African Americans were relatively unmoved by events across the Atlantic, others anticipated that the war in Europe would inflict a "death blow" on the "idea of white supremacy."[7] Consequently, even as the African American press regarded the European war as a contest between imperial rivals, by December 1941 black newspapers recognized Nazi Germany as a pitiless enemy of nonwhites. Elements of the black leadership explicitly connected the war in Europe to African Americans' fight for their civil rights. Criticizing those who contended it would make "no difference who wins" the war in Europe, the *Chicago Defender* urged "all the forces of progress and democracy" to "get together." The conflict in Europe was of direct consequence to African Americans: "Is it not true," the *Defender* editorialized, "that behind Hitler, supporting his false racial theories, stand the American advocates of 'white supremacy'?" The war, urged the *Defender*, provided an opportunity – an obligation, really – to disprove the "believers in the inherent inferiority of black men."[8]

The racial implications of the deepening international crisis were also evident in the European powers' continuing subjugation of their colonial subjects. Italy's 1935 assault against Ethiopia provoked wide condemnation from the black press, which denounced the invasion as conspicuous evidence of the lasting power of colonialism.[9] African Americans also

---

[7] George Schuyler, "War Will Be a Boon to Darker Races," *Pittsburgh Courier*, September 2, 1939.

[8] "Our Stake in the European War," *Chicago Defender*, September 23, 1939. See also Lee Finkle, *Forum for Protest: The Black Press during World War II* (Cranbury, NJ: Fairleigh Dickinson University Press, 1975), 200, 203.

[9] Byron Richard Skinner, "The Double 'V': The Impact of World War II on Black America" (PhD dissertation, University of California, Berkeley, 1978), 8–9; Penny M. Von Eschen, *Race against Empire: Black Americans and Anticolonialism, 1937–1957* (Ithaca, NY: Cornell University Press, 1997), 11; John Hope Franklin and Alfred A. Moss, Jr., *From Slavery to Freedom: A History of African Americans*, 8th ed. (New York, NY: Alfred A. Knopf, 2000), 476; James H. Meriwether, *Proudly We Can Be Africans: Black Americans and Africa, 1935–1961* (Chapel Hill, NC: University of North Carolina Press, 2002),

condemned Hitler's racial policies, and took pride in Jesse Owens's successes at the 1936 Olympic Games in Berlin, and in boxer Joe Louis's famous 1938 victory over German Max Schmeling.[10] Internationally, elements of the African American community supported the Soviet Union, which – at least until the Nazi-Soviet accord of 1939 – stood as an alternative to fascism and Nazism. Subsequently, in June 1941, some African Americans expressed outrage when Germany invaded Russia.[11] Moreover, while many African Americans regarded the war in Europe as principally a contest between Old World powers, and a distant distraction from their more pressing problems in the United States, their endorsement of isolationism did not equate to disinterest in matters of foreign policy. Rather, black Americans were keenly interested in their nation's role in the growing international crisis.

Central to that growing black concern for international events, and a sign that even before the United States had formally entered World War Two African Americans had one eye fixed firmly on the postwar world, was their interest in the Atlantic Charter. Framed during an August 1941 meeting between President Franklin D. Roosevelt and British Prime Minister Winston Churchill, the Atlantic Charter articulated a series of principles – the "Four Freedoms" – to guide the international order following the eventual defeat of the Axis powers. Joining notions of universal human rights to the democratic principles for which the Allies were ostensibly fighting, the Charter was an ambitious declaration of idealistic intent. Victims of Western colonialism, recognizing the significance of the Atlantic Charter, quickly appropriated its rhetoric and sentiments. In particular, the Charter's third principal – "all peoples had a right to self-determination" – was of direct consequence for nonwhite people everywhere. While Churchill conceived the principal of self-determination chiefly in terms of the European war and European territorial disputes, in the wake of Pearl Harbor Roosevelt interpreted the Charter more expansively than the British Prime Minister. Issues of colonial authority and race could not be ignored. The prominent black leader W. E. B. Du Bois, who initially

---

Chapter 1. See also Waldo E. Martin, Jr., *No Coward Soldiers: Black Cultural Politics and Postwar America* (Cambridge, MA: Harvard University Press, 2005), 19.

[10] William Patterson, "Joe Louis Killed Nazi Supremacy Theory," *Pittsburgh Courier*, July 9, 1938. See also Lauren Rebecca Sklaroff, "Creating G. I. Joe Louis: Cultural Solutions to the 'Negro Problem' During World War II," *Journal of American History* 89, no. 3 (2002): 970; Robert F. Jefferson, *Fighting for Hope: African American Troops of the 93rd Infantry Division in World War II and Postwar America* (Baltimore, MD: Johns Hopkins University Press, 2008), 31–5.

[11] See, for example, Nelson Peery, *Black Fire: The Making of an American Revolutionary* (New York, NY: The New Press, 1994), 83–4.

discounted the Atlantic Charter as a ruse to preserve white supremacy, described Roosevelt's new stance as an "admission" that "a world revolution" was underway, which would transform the "relation of the white and colored peoples."[12]

By late 1941 the Atlantic Charter had "captured the attention of a wide array of African American activists."[13] But while those activists and editors shared the growing unease over the deteriorating situation in Asia, the Japanese attack at Pearl Harbor came as a complete surprise. Marking an end to American isolationism, Pearl Harbor transformed America's wartime role from that of a quasi-combatant into the decisive power on the Western Front in Europe and across the Asia-Pacific Theater. Although Germany declared war on the United States just four days after Pearl Harbor, and while American policymakers agreed that the war in Europe was a more immediate priority than the conflict in the Pacific, Pearl Harbor exercised an almost mystical influence over American wartime patriotism. "Remember Pearl Harbor" was much more than a wartime mantra, however: the phrase symbolized the contrast between American virtue and Japanese treachery, and signified Americans' collective devotion to military victory. That collective effort, and the assumptions of national unity upon which it rested, raised vexing questions for African Americans as they confronted American racism and negotiated the tensions between racial and national identity.

These tensions shaped black American attitudes toward Japan, both before and during the Pacific War. Conscious of the transnational dimensions of the twin struggle against racism and colonialism, during the interwar period African Americans had contemplated the implications of Japan's rise to power across the Asia-Pacific. Examining the relationship between African Americans and Japan, historians have emphasized the significance of Japan's rise as an anti-imperialist and antiwhite power. As Marc Gallicchio has explained, from the late nineteenth century an amorphous, but influential group of "black internationalists" in the United States were excited by the prospect of a prosperous and confident Japan, whose status and authority were potentially powerful weapons in the global fight against racism.[14]

[12] W. E. B. Du Bois, "A Chronicle of Race Relations," *Phylon* 3, no. 2 (1942): 207. See also Finkle, *Forum for Protest*, 210–11.

[13] Von Eschen, *Race against Empire*, 26.

[14] See Marc Gallicchio, *The African American Encounter with Japan and China: Black Internationalism in Asia, 1895–1945* (Chapel Hill, NC: University of North Carolina Press, 2000).

A substantial body of opinion within the African American community perceived Japan as a thorn in the side of the white powers.[15] "Japan has white imperialism on the run," noted the *Pittsburgh Courier* in August 1939, and "the white imperialists don't like it."[16] And while Japan's increasingly assertive foreign policy alarmed the American political and military leadership, sections of the black community expressed sympathy for Japanese ambitions. On the eve of Pearl Harbor, the Baltimore *Afro-American* suggested it was a "great mystery to many people" that the United States had insisted on the Monroe Doctrine while denying Japan "similar political leadership in Asia." That contradiction, noted the *Afro-American*, disqualified Americans from preaching "morality and consistency to the Japanese."[17] Although the *Afro-American's* apparently benign interpretation of the Monroe Doctrine implied that US foreign policy toward its southern neighbors was fundamentally benevolent, the paper's principal concern was to condemn American hypocrisy regarding Japanese ambitions.

Despite an ongoing admiration for Japan's defiance against Western colonialism and racism, however, and notwithstanding Japanese attempts to foment pro-Japan organizations in a number of urban black communities, African Americans betrayed an underlying ambivalence toward

---

[15] Gerald Horne has noted that during the years before the Pacific War "Japan was – without question – the nation most admired by African Americans." Subsequently, Horne tempered his argument slightly: "In the period before World War II, Japan was probably the nation most admired among African Americans." Conversely, John Dower concluded that Japan's attempts to "influence black opinion in the United States" were "desultory and ineffective." See Gerald Horne, *Race War!: White Supremacy and the Japanese Attack on the British Empire* (New York, NY: New York University Press, 2004), 43; Gerald Horne, "Tokyo Bound: African Americans and Japan Confront White Supremacy," in *Transnational Blackness: Navigating the Global Color Line*, eds. Manning Marable and Vanessa Agard-Jones (New York, NY: Palgrave MacMillan, 2008), 191; John Dower, *War Without Mercy: Race and Power in the Pacific War* (New York, NY: Pantheon Books, 1986), 174. See also Yuichiro Onishi, *Transpacific Antiracism: Afro-Asian Solidarity in 20th-Century Black America, Japan, and Okinawa* (New York, NY: New York University Press, 2013); Reginald Kearney, *African American Views of the Japanese: Solidarity or Sedition?* (Albany, NY: State University of New York Press, 1998); Ernest Allen, Jr., "When Japan Was the 'Champion of the Darker Races': Satokata Takahashi and the Flowering of Black Messianic Nationalism," *Black Scholar* 24 (Winter 1994): 32–4; Gallicchio, *African American Encounter*, 112–14; Michael Lee Lanning, *The African American Soldier: From Crispus Attucks to Colin Powell* (Secaucus, NJ: Birch Lane Press, 1997), 174; Yuichiro Onishi, "The New Negro of the Pacific: How African Americans Forged Racial Cross-Solidarity with Japan, 1917–1922," *Journal of African American History* 92, no. 2 (2007): 191–213.

[16] "The World This Week," *Pittsburgh Courier*, April 8, 1939.

[17] "In Fighting Japan Our Own Hands Are Not Clean," *Afro-American*, December 6, 1941.

Japan and its imperial and territorial aspirations. During the 1930s Japan's increasingly assertive foreign policy placed African Americans in a complicated position. Apprehensive about the rise of international fascism, many black leaders regarded Japan's attempt to subdue China as blatant territorial ambition. Dismissing Japan's claim to be a beacon for the world's nonwhite people, the *Norfolk Journal and Guide* asserted in July 1939 that Tokyo was "as heartless as London, Paris, Rome and Berlin in subjugating helpless peoples." Japan's malevolent foreign policy was reflected in the vicious treatment meted out to the victims and opponents of Japanese expansion. The Japanese occupation of "Korea, Manchukuo, and the conquered Chinese provinces," the *Journal and Guide* explained, provided "a startling example of how Negro Americans, Africans and Siamese would fare under the military heels of imperial Japan."[18] Agreeing that Japan's invasion of China offered convincing evidence of Japanese brutality, African American historian and reporter Joel Augustus Rogers pointed out that while Japanese governments had not always been militaristic and expansionist, the current regime was no friend of African Americans – nor other oppressed races. "What sort of freedom," asked Rogers, "could such cut-throats and robbers" bring? Noting that he did not "give a damn how liberal has been the reception accorded" to "one or two Negro visitors to Japan," Rogers declared he would not want "freedom from such bloody, murderous hands."[19]

Reflecting the nexus between foreign policy and domestic racial politics, African American attitudes toward Japan were also shaped by their interpersonal relations with both the Japanese and Japanese Americans. Relations between Japanese Americans and African Americans during the prewar period defy easy categorization. Although the occasional tensions between Japanese Americans and African Americans were diluted because relatively few blacks lived on the West Coast, where the majority of Japanese Americans lived, historians have argued that the Japanese rejection of "any attempt to classify them as Negroes" caused resentment among African Americans living in California.[20] Particularly after Pearl

---

[18] "Japanese Bunk," *New Journal and Guide*, July 22, 1939.
[19] J. A. Rogers, "Present Jap Rulers Exploit Darker Races Same as Dominant Whites," *Pittsburgh Courier*, December 6, 1941. Subsequently, the *Cleveland Call and Post* used its review of the 1942 film *Ravaged Earth* to link Japan's "unprovoked and brutal invasion" of China to its subsequent "treacherous stab" at Pearl Harbor. See "Action-Packed Film of Jap Atrocities," *Cleveland Call and Post*, May 15, 1943.
[20] Gallicchio, *African American Encounter*, 55. See also Allen, "Satokata Takahashi," 29.

Harbor, that resentment contributed to black suspicions toward Japanese Americans.

African Americans expressed ambivalence toward Japanese visitors to the United States. Again, interpersonal relations complicated the notion of a racial alliance between black Americans and Japanese. The often-tenuous attempts to forge political links between the two groups are best seen in the context of African American reactions to Japanese expressions of animosity toward blacks, and other nonwhite peoples. Anticipating the views of a black British interpreter who lived in Japan for three years prior to the war, and who would state in 1944 that the Japanese "feel as superior to the Negro as any bigoted white American," the *Chicago Defender* referred in August 1941 to the "deep seated antagonism that is nurtured by the Nipponese against the sons of Ham." As the *Defender* explained, Japanese antipathy toward African Americans was manifested on a local, individual level: Japanese students in the United States had "nothing to do with" their black counterparts and were "even less friendly than hard-shell southerners from Georgia or Mississippi." Conceivably, Japanese visitors' lack of interaction with African Americans reflected cultural and linguistic differences, rather than racial arrogance. But if the *Defender's* editors contemplated that possibility in private, they focused publicly on perceptions of Japanese racial condescension toward African Americans. Determined to correct the "popular fallacy" among blacks that Japan was sympathetic to African Americans, the *Defender* dismissed as "sentimental bunkum" the notion that Japan was "interested in the black races." The Japanese, the paper concluded, "look upon Negroes as inferior people."[21]

It would be going too far to claim that African American ambivalence toward Japan evaporated in the aftermath of Pearl Harbor – sections of the black leadership continued to acknowledge Japan's role as an opponent of colonialism and racism – but the Japanese attack generated widespread and predictable hostility among African Americans. Japan, concluded the *Pittsburgh Courier*, was intent on securing "world domination."[22] Japanese conquests throughout Asia, argued the *Courier* in the aftermath of Pearl Harbor, demonstrated that contrary to her claims of international friendship with other nonwhite peoples, Japan was "one of their great enemies and exploiters." While the "barbaric atrocities"

---

[21] "Says Japs Feel Superior to Negro," *New Journal and Guide*, April 8, 1944; "Japan and the Negro," *Chicago Defender*, August 16, 1941.
[22] "The World a Part of Asia," *Pittsburgh Courier*, April 25, 1942.

committed on Allied prisoners by Japanese troops had "stunned the American people," the *Courier* editorialized in February 1942 that there had been ample warnings that Japan had already resolved that "mercy shall play no part" in the war.[23] International racial politics found expression in individual behavior, including on the battlefield. Responding to a letter from one "Negro soldier," who questioned whether the "Japs" were "as bad as we are led to believe," and who wondered whether "the Negro would lose anything by America's defeat or gain anything by a Jap victory," the paper warned black servicemen that they "must have no illusions regarding the attitude of the Japanese." Recognizing "no racial ties" with African Americans, the Japanese "hate Negroes more than they do American whites, for their hatred of Negroes is intensified by contempt for their inferiority." Echoing the language used by white Americans in their wartime representations of the Japanese, the *Courier* warned black troops that they "must expect to share all the brutalities that the maniacal mind of Japan can contrive."[24]

African American criticisms of Japanese behavior and character underpinned their post-Pearl Harbor conviction that their future was as part of the United States. As the *Pittsburgh Courier* reported in August 1942, "the average American Negro is American first, with less [sic] foreign ties than any other group in the country." Although African Americans "sympathize with the plight of colored people elsewhere," and "understand the world wide character of the color problem," they did not "believe in Santa Claus."[25] No lesser of an authority than A. Philip Randolph, national director of the March on Washington Movement and president of the Brotherhood of Sleeping Car Porters, denounced the notion that Japan was sincerely interested in advancing the interests of African Americans. "Any Negro," he declared, "who thinks the Negro people have anything to gain by the victory of Japan in this war, is hopelessly dumb, ignorant and ridiculous."[26] Describing the handful of blacks arrested by the

[23] Editorial, "The Lesson of Bataan and Corregidor," *Pittsburgh Courier*, February 12, 1942.
[24] A Negro Soldier, "How Would Japs Treat Negroes," *Pittsburgh Courier*, January 24, 1942; Editorial, "The Lesson of Bataan and Corregidor." *Pittsburgh Courier*, February 12, 1942.
[25] "The Pacific Movement," *Pittsburgh Courier*, August 8, 1942. See also Neil A. Wynn, "Black Attitudes toward Participation in the American War Effort, 1941–1945," *Afro-American Studies* 3, no. 1 (June, 1972): 17–18. On the FBI's continuing suspicions regarding Japanese influence among African Americans, see Patrick S. Washburn, *A Question of Sedition: The Federal Government's Investigation of the Black Press during World War II* (New York, NY: Oxford University Press, 1986), 172–4.
[26] "Randolph Hits Pro Japanese Negro Groups," *Chicago Defender*, October 3, 1942.

Federal Bureau of Investigation (FBI) for collaborating with the Japanese as "people on the lunatic fringe," Randolph concluded it was "almost inconceivable that a Negro in his right mind would advocate the victory of the Japanese over his own country."[27] Even those sent by the Japanese to stir trouble within the African American community concurred that black loyalties lay with the United States. Mimo D. Guzman, a Filipino acting at the behest of the Japanese, conceded after his arrest by the FBI in 1942 that his efforts to build support among African Americans for a "world-wide movement" against the white race had been "futile." The "basic loyalty of Negro Americans," he suggested, was too strong.[28] African Americans' identity as Americans was prevailing over exaggerated claims – and fears – of a shared racial identity with the Japanese.

Transforming their shock and anger at Japanese treachery into a sense of wartime purpose, black leaders urged African Americans to devote their energies to winning the war. In so doing, they reflected an almost-instinctive sense of national loyalty. Any gesture of black patriotism – such as an incident in May 1942, when an African American waiter was stabbed after refusing to mail a letter on behalf of an interned Japanese diplomat – was presented as evidence of "the unquestioned loyalty of Negroes to the United States."[29] Writing from Pearl Harbor in early 1942, Associate Negro Press correspondent Mamie G. Hoffman recalled that while she had previously undertaken to comment on "analogous race problems," the gravity of the immediate wartime situation led her to conclude that "[t]his is not the time to emphasize race." "Just now we Negroes have no time to waste on race problems that cannot be immediately remedied or eradicated." Nor did African Americans have time, she contended, "to beat our breasts in despair over what has happened to our disadvantage." "Instead," she continued, "we must summon every resource and make a way to live with dignity and for a purpose." "By doing so," she concluded, "we can turn any tragedy into victory."[30]

Hoffman was not alone in expressing such views. Others, too, prioritized national defense over the racial contest. Imploring African

[27] A. Philip Randolph, "Pro-Japanese Activities among Negroes," *The Black Worker,* September, 1942, 4.
[28] "Jap Agent Admits Futile Effort to Win Negroes," *New Journal and Guide,* August 15, 1942.
[29] "Stabbed by Jap Diplomat after He Refused $500 Bribe to Mail Letter," *Chicago Defender,* May 23, 1942. See also "Jap Diplomat Stabs Waiter Who Wouldn't Mail Letter," *Afro-American,* May 9, 1942.
[30] Mamie G. Hoffman, "Second Pearl Harbor Hero?" *Atlanta Daily World,* March 8, 1942.

Americans to "present a united front to the world," Dr. Leonidas L. Berry, Secretary and Treasurer of Missions for the African Methodist Episcopal Church, declared in early 1942 that blacks "must fight for the democracy that makes all mankind act, think and feel free."[31] Premised on deeply held assumptions concerning the United States as a model of freedom – in promise if not in reality – Berry's statement reflected popular views regarding the redemptive power of American democracy. *Afro-American* columnist and World War One veteran Elliot Freeman was unequivocal in declaring his support for the US war effort: This "is our country, we know no other, [and] our country is fighting with ruthless enemies, who are determined to destroy all the good for which the country stands."[32] Asked whether African Americans would "finally attain the equal measure of democracy to which they are entitled," one black survivor of Pearl Harbor recalled in 1943 that such questions were "a bit too deep" for him. "All I know," he stated, "is that there is a war to be won first." "[W]e can talk about the rest," he concluded, "after it's over."[33]

Even as some blacks were willing to accept the promise of American democracy, and suspend the quest for civil rights while the war raged, others refused to do so, even in the immediate, patriotically charged period after Pearl Harbor. At first blush, the white author and "sincere friend and champion of" African Americans, Pearl Buck, whose views were publicized widely in the black press, appeared to endorse a deferral of the fight for civil rights. As "[f]aulty as our democracy is," she argued, "the United States must be the leader in this war for the right of people to be free."[34] But Buck, in concert with black leaders and editorialists, contended that US leadership of the global community was contingent upon the nation granting equality to African Americans. Only then, she argued, could the United States repudiate Japanese claims that the oppression of black Americans was proof that the United States was unfit to assume a position of international leadership.[35]

---

[31] "A. M. E. Leader Flays Cowardly Japan's Attack," *Pittsburgh Courier*, January 3, 1942.

[32] Freeman, "The Whirling Hub," *Afro-American*, October 30, 1943.

[33] Richard Dier, "Japs Will Be Hard to Beat, Nazis Easier, Seaman Says," *Afro-American*, October 2, 1943.

[34] "Pearl Buck's Plea," *Afro-American*, March 7, 1942; "May Guide Way to Universal Freedom: Pearl Buck's Plea to Colored Americans," *Afro-American*, March 7, 1942. See also Lucius C. Harper, "Dustin' Off the News," *Chicago Defender*, March 14, 1942.

[35] See "Japs Cite Race Prejudice in U.S. as Argument among Pacific Folk," *Philadelphia Tribune*, February 21, 1942. See also "Japanese Use Us in Their Propaganda," *Philadelphia Tribune*, August 8, 1942.

A January 1942 editorial in *The Crisis* summed up the sentiments of many African Americans. Careful to declare their fidelity to the United States – "let there be no mistake" about blacks' patriotism, they wrote – and emphasizing that African Americans should express their "loyalty to the democratic ideal as enunciated by America," the journal's editors insisted nonetheless that war had made the struggle for black civil rights all the more important. During "a death struggle between the brutalities and indecencies of dictatorships, and the dignity and decency of democracies," *The Crisis* contended, black Americans "dare not keep silent." Characteristically, *The Crisis* viewed these issues through a transnational lens. And in highlighting the racial injustices practiced by America's "British ally" – whose colonial empire included significant possessions across Asia and the Pacific – *The Crisis* hinted at the centrality of the Asia-Pacific Theater in shaping African American perceptions of the significance of World War Two.[36]

African Americans thus understood Pearl Harbor as a watershed in the history of race relations. Insisting that "remember Pearl Harbor" was far more than a rhetorical device, African Americans invested the phrase with a racially distinct meaning that merged calls for victory over Japan with demands that the United States fulfill its democratic promises – to all its citizens. In July 1942, the *Afro-American* explicated the connections between Pearl Harbor and the long history of American racism: while white Southerners "did not hear the bombs falling on Pearl Harbor because they were still listening to the echoes of Fort Sumter," and whereas "Dixie" regarded Pearl Harbor as "just a historical event, the significance of which has no effect on the consciousness of those who are psychologically still fighting the battle of Appomattox," African Americans appropriated Pearl Harbor as a means of reminding the nation of the realities of discrimination and segregation.[37] Wartime "race prejudice" declared the *Afro-American*, was analogous to the "blunder at Pearl Harbor."[38]

When white Americans urged their compatriots to "remember Pearl Harbor" they implied that victory in the war would restore the nation; African Americans, however, employed the phrase to demand not restoration, but change. Accordingly, while Japan's attack on Pearl Harbor transformed African Americans' discussions concerning the relationship between race and nationality into a common quest to win the war,

[36] "Now Is Not the Time to Be Silent," *The Crisis*, January, 1942, 7.
[37] "The Big Parade," *Afro-American*, July 21, 1942.
[38] "War Race Prejudice Like Blunder at Pearl Harbor," *Afro-American*, April 11, 1942.

the surge of black patriotism was predicated on the conviction that the American democratic experiment was incomplete, and that US leadership across the Asia-Pacific was contingent upon the fulfillment of the nation's democratic promise.[39] For African Americans this entailed two, interconnected responsibilities: besides being compelled to make clear their views regarding the contest between democracy and dictatorship, they were also obliged to transform the ideal of American democracy into a reality. It was not until February 1942 that a black Kansan, James G. Thompson, labeled the dual fight against fascism abroad and racism at home as the "Double V" campaign; however, the ideas articulated by Thompson were apparent to African Americans in the immediate aftermath of Pearl Harbor.[40] Explicating the connection between the patriotism provoked by Pearl Harbor and the African American quest for civil rights, the Double V campaign remained a rallying cry for black Americans for the duration of the war.[41] Long after Pearl Harbor, that dual struggle against fascism abroad and racism at home required a careful balancing act for African Americans, as they confronted accusations of disloyalty, and weighed the competing imperatives of race and nationality.

In the wake of Pearl Harbor, however, African American loyalty to the nation transcended their doubts regarding their place in the United States. Agreeing that the immediate priority was the survival of the United States, thousands of blacks offered their services to the military. Although some African Americans recalled that before the Japanese attack they "didn't know what Pearl Harbor was," and that they had "never heard of the place," they were not alone in their geographic naiveté, and it did not diminish the significance of what took place there on December 7, 1941.[42] George Ruth Jr., was just thirteen years old when the Japanese

---

[39] "Now Is the Time Not to Be Silent," 7.

[40] James G. Thompson, "Should I Sacrifice to Live 'Half American'?" *Pittsburgh Courier*, January 31, 1942.

[41] The *Pittsburgh Courier* was instrumental in publicizing and popularizing the Double V campaign, but the campaign enjoyed support from other newspapers, including the *Afro-American* and the *Chicago Defender*. See Patrick S. Washburn, "The *Pittsburgh Courier's* Double V Campaign in 1942," *American Journalism* 3, no. 2 (1986): 73–86; Earnest L. Perry, Jr., "A Common Purpose: The Negro Newspapers Publishers Association's Fight for Equality during World War II," *American Journalism* 19, no. 2 (2002): 31–43. Ethan Michaeli, *The Defender: How the Legendary Black Newspaper Changed America* (Boston, MA: Houghton Mifflin Harcourt, 2016), 243.

[42] Robert Quarles, AFC/2001/001/80199, Veterans History Project Collection, American Folklife Center, Library of Congress, Washington, DC (VHP-LoC); John David Jackson, AFC/2001/001/38452, VHP-LoC.

attacked at Pearl Harbor, but his determination "to help end the war" was typical among African Americans.[43]

Black men's reaction to Pearl Harbor was more than a characteristically masculine response to the Japanese affront to American national pride. African Americans went to considerable trouble – both at the time, and later – to explain their motivations for enlisting. One black Clevelander was insistent: "I know we get pushed around pretty bad in this country," but "what the h – l, we're Americans aren't we? It's America's war, so sign me up, I want to fight."[44] Like other members of the much-vaunted "Greatest Generation," African Americans were conscious that they were invested with important responsibilities – which could, for the moment at least, transcend, racial distinctions. As Navy veteran Luther James McNeal recalled, "we all had the idea, whether you were black or white that the war had to be won by the United States."[45] McNeal was far from alone in rushing to enlist. Having volunteered to join the Army in 1942, Linzey Donald Jones recalled his "patriotic duty to serve in the armed forces."[46] Many African Americans, moreover, concurred with Allen T. Hayes's optimistic assertion that they were playing a part in solving "all the problems."[47] Inevitably, not all black men were swept up by wartime jingoism: rather than volunteering, many waited to be drafted; and a minority resisted the draft on account of their religious conviction. But most black men, like Bennett J. Cooper, who recalled "literally kicking and screaming" when he was drafted, "went, like everyone else did, and made the most of it."[48]

Joining that patriotic imperative to more immediate material concerns, some African Americans recalled the effect of Pearl Harbor in starkly personal terms. Unsurprisingly, given that the nation was still emerging from the Great Depression, some African Americans perceived the outbreak of war as an opportunity to escape poverty and deprivation. Oliver R. Walker, working as a "delivery boy" in Baltimore, was blunt: "everybody wanted a

---

[43] Ruth, World War II Veterans Survey. 93rd Infantry Division. Box 1, File 4655, United States Army Military History Institute, United States Army Heritage and Education Center, Carlisle, Pennsylvania (USAHEC).

[44] "Clevelanders United in Opinion on War," *Cleveland Call and Post*, December 13, 1941.

[45] James Henry McNeal, AFC/2001/001/24011, VHP-LoC.

[46] Linzey Donald Jones, AFC/2001/001/38128, VHP-LoC.

[47] Allen T. Hayes, AFC/2001/001/30629, VHP-LoC.

[48] Bennett, J. Cooper, Jr., AFC/2001/001/68243, VHP-LoC. On blacks resisting the draft on account of their religious faith, see Jack D. Foner, *Blacks and the Military in American History: A New Perspective* (New York, NY: Praeger, 1974), 145–6.

war job."[49] One "of twelve children," Navy veteran Richard Lucas recalled that his "main reason for going into service" was "economic."[50] Yet those individual material aspirations – like the oft-stated recognition that military service was one way to "see the world" – were almost always seen in the collective context of the post-Pearl Harbor national emergency.[51] Interviewed nearly seven decades after the United States entered the war, Herman Melvin Parker was emphatic: "I remember Pearl Harbor. I remember when President Roosevelt declared war. I never forget what he said, 'I hate war. My wife Eleanor hates war. But we gotta go to war.'" Painting a picture of American national innocence, Parker remembered that prior to Pearl Harbor life "was going along so peacefully and so calm. We didn't know there were those kind of people in the world. People that would attack us. We just think a war is something that happens someplace else. It don't have nothin' to do with America." With his father's agreement, and following the example of his older brother, who had enlisted in 1939, the fourteen-year-old Parker joined the Navy.[52] Describing the "shock" of Pearl Harbor, Army veteran William Earl Lafayette recalled that while he had been "living with full knowledge of what was going on in the world" since the outbreak of war in Europe in 1939, it was only after Japan's attack that he and his friends "began to personalize it." Lafayette's response was unambiguous: "There was no way we were not going to go."[53]

Reflecting and encouraging those declarations of African American patriotism, the black press declared that "Japan's foul attack upon Pearl Harbor" had led to "national unity."[54] Although African American newspapers continued to rail against racial discrimination, and notwithstanding the continuing suspicions of government agencies and white politicians, the black press played a key role in fostering African American support for the war effort.[55] Sustaining black morale could take many

---

[49] Oliver R. Walker, AFC/2001/001/33034, VHP-LoC.
[50] Richard Lucas, interview published in Glenn A. Knoblock, *Black Submariners in the United States Navy, 1940–1975* (Jefferson, NC: McFarland & Co., 2005), 315.
[51] Willie J. Clemens, AFC/2001/001/45487, VHP-LoC.
[52] Herman Melvin Parker, AFC/2001/001/72903, VHP-LoC.
[53] William Earl Lafayette, AFC/2001/001/43118, VHP-LoC.
[54] Emmett J. Scott, "Any National Unity Must Include the Negro," *Cleveland Call and Post*, January 10, 1942. Lee Finkle has argued that the African American press edged "toward" a position of encouraging African Americans to "close ranks" with other Americans to ensure the survival of the United States. See Finkle, *Forum for Protest*, 112.
[55] On the Federal Government's suspicions regarding the loyalty of the black press, see Washburn, *A Question of Sedition*. (2014): 7–97; Jinx Coleman Broussard, *African American Foreign Correspondents: A History* (Baton Rouge, LA: Louisiana State University Press, 2013), 111–12. See also Michael S. Sweeney and Patrick S.

forms. Beyond the obvious use of their papers' columns to explain the
meaning of the war for African Americans, black editors emphasized the
importance of local, community-based expressions of patriotism. Sensing
an opportunity to repudiate those who questioned African American loyalty, black newspapers supported the morale-building stamp and bond
rallies that raised funds for the war effort. In so doing, they stressed that
the participants had "remembered Pearl Harbor."[56]

Millions of African Americans read, shared, and discussed black newspapers. They also shared in, and contributed to, the national cultural
response to Pearl Harbor. In verse and song, blacks linked their grief, love,
and patriotism to the trauma of December 1941. Harry Wilson Patterson,
a black messenger in the Navy Department, penned "Sleep On!" in tribute
to a former colleague killed at Pearl Harbor. Patterson's poem, the *Afro-
American* reported proudly, was "published in over 300 newspapers."
The US Navy, recognizing the value of publicizing black expressions
of Pearl Harbor-inspired patriotism, also published Patterson's work.[57]
Blues singers also referred to Pearl Harbor. Doctor Clayton's 1942 "The
Pearl Harbor Blues," praised by one African American reviewer as "timely
and unique," compared the "ungrateful" Japanese to "a stray dog in the
street"; Lonnie Johnson assured the subject of "Baby, Remember Me"
that he did not "mind dyin,'" and that "every Jap" he killed would be for
his lover.[58] Personal sacrifice – and killing an enemy deemed less-than-
human – were thereby linked to personal love, and to the wider patriotic
imperative to "Remember Pearl Harbor."

African Americans' patriotic endeavors, however, were not always
welcomed by white America. Although Pearl Harbor served as a rallying
cry for all Americans, the initial response of civil and military authorities to blacks' attempts to volunteer highlighted the tension between

---

Washburn, "Aint Justice Wonderful": The *Chicago Tribune's* Battle of Midway Story
and the Government's Attempt at an Espionage Act Indictment in 1942," *Journalism &
Communication Monographs* 16, no. 1 (2014): 7–97.

[56] "They Remembered Pearl Harbor," *Afro-American*, January 2, 1943. See also
"Remembering Pearl Harbor with Bonds," *Atlanta Daily World*, January 12, 1943.

[57] Ric Roberts, "Messenger Tells Afro How He Got Inspiration for Pearl Harbor Poem,"
Afro-American, March 14, 1942; Associated Press, *Pearl Harbor: Day of Infamy* (np: AP
Publishers, 2015), unpaginated. See also "Tribute to the Dead of Pearl Harbor," *Afro-
American*, December 12, 1942.

[58] Guido van Rijn, *Roosevelt's Blues: African-American Blues and Gospel Songs on
President FDR* (Jackson, MS: University Press of Mississippi, 1997), 152–4; and F. M.
Davis, "'Pearl Harbor Blues': Given Okay for Originality and Timeliness," *New Journal
and Guide*, June 27, 1942.

black patriotism and American racism. That tension was apparent even in the immediate, hyper-patriotic aftermath of Pearl Harbor. While it might have been anticipated that blacks who volunteered their services would be viewed with suspicion, and even hostility, by white Southerners, those suspicions extended north of the Mason Dixon Line. The day after "Japan's treacherous and underhanded attack," reported the *New York Amsterdam Star-News*, "[s]everal hundred young patriotic Harlem boys of the required age and physical qualifications" hurried "to the Whitehall Street Naval Recruiting Depot." These young men, the paper noted, "were as angered at the action of the Japanese as any of the thousands of whites who rushed to volunteer." The Navy's recruiting policies, however, reflected the long-standing institutional racism that affirmed African Americans' second-class status. "Without exception," protested the *Star-News*, the black volunteers "were told they were not wanted except as cooks, mess hall attendants and flunkies."[59]

New York military authorities' response to African Americans' attempts to serve their nation was characteristic of a wider white ambivalence – and in some instances contempt – toward the surge of black patriotism. Across the nation, thousands of blacks responded to Pearl Harbor by volunteering for military service. All but a handful were turned down. During December 1941, as President Roosevelt called the nation to war and urged Americans to make whatever sacrifices were necessary to defeat the Axis, 30,000 African Americans were "passed over" in that month's draft call.[60]

So deeply entrenched was that racial prejudice that even African American volunteers with prized skills – such as Caesar S. Bassette, Jr., a qualified radio operator whose services were initially rejected by military recruiters in St. Louis, but who later served as an instructor to the famed Tuskegee Airmen – were frequently denied the chance to "remember Pearl Harbor."[61] Frustrated by white authorities' refusal to accept black volunteers, civil rights advocates linked such segregationist policies to the

[59] Dan Burley, "Louis Starts Drilling for Buddy Baer; Navy Very Busy Refusing Volunteers," *New York Amsterdam Star-News*, December 27, 1941.

[60] Finkle, *Forum for Protest*, 93. See also Richard M. Dalfiume, *Desegregation in the US Armed Forces: Fighting on Two Fronts, 1939–1953* (Columbia, MO: University of Missouri Press, 1969), 51. The wartime military draft system continued to discriminate against African Americans. See George Q. Flynn, "Selective Service and American Blacks during World War II," *Journal of Negro History* 69, no. 1 (1984): 14–25.

[61] "Radio Expert would 'Remember Pearl Harbor' but Army-Navy won't let him Serve Country," *Pittsburgh Courier*, January 3, 1942. See also "Dr. Caesar Stephens Bassette, Jr.," www.bassettbranches.org/tng//getperson.php?personID=I40&tree=276B (Accessed

nation's military fortunes. Writing in early 1942, civil rights leader Roy Wilkins pointed to the contradiction between the Navy's "frantic appeals for radio technicians," and its unwillingness to accept the services of "skilled Negroes." The Navy, Wilkins suggested, "would rather not have a vital radio message get through than to have it sent by black hands or over equipment set up by black technicians."[62] The treatment of African American volunteers from Army and Navy recruiters, declared the black journalist and activist Emmett J. Scott, was "chilling, callous, [and] discouraging, to state it mildly."[63] Relegated to the status of what *Time* magazine described in early 1942 as "semi-citizens," black Americans remained on the periphery of civic and military life in the United States.[64] Nothing better symbolized that marginalization than the fact that during World War Two, as in the nation's earlier conflicts, African Americans continued to be relegated to segregated units.

African Americans understood these issues in explicitly transnational terms. While the racial complexities of a potential conflict across the Asia-Pacific had been the subject of considerable discussion among the black leadership since the late 1930s, Pearl Harbor transformed the abstract into the tangible, and engaged the attention of the African American community. As the *Pittsburgh Courier* reported in May 1942, Walter White, Executive Secretary of the National Association for the Advancement of Colored People (NAACP), had asserted that Pearl Harbor, and the defeat of British power at Singapore, "marked the end of an epoch." Not only would the "black, brown and yellow peoples who constitute four-fifths of the world's population" no longer acquiesce to white supremacy, but the "disproportionate power wielded" in the "national affairs" of the United States by "Southern Congressman and Senators with a Ku Klux Klan philosophy" would "mean only tragedy" for the world's nonwhite peoples.[65]

The Crisis also contemplated the connections between domestic and international racism. Although the editors conceded that institutionalized racism within the US military could not be overturned immediately – "the Army" had to "weigh everything in relation to winning

---

May 26, 2015.) On the Tuskegee Airmen, see J. Todd Moye, *Freedom Flyers: The Tuskegee Airmen of World War II* (New York, NY: Oxford University Press, 2010).

[62] Roy Wilkins, "The Watchtower," *New York Amsterdam Star-News*, January 10, 1942.

[63] Emmett J. Scott, "The Right to Fight for One's Country Is God-Given," *Cleveland Call and Post*, February 21, 1942.

[64] "White Man's War," *Time*, February 3, 1942.

[65] "'White Invincibility' Doomed," *Pittsburgh Courier*, May 23, 1942.

the war" – the editors' patience was not inexhaustible, and they emphasized the global military consequences of American segregation. Both the
United States and Britain were "depending upon 'colored' nations and
nationals as allies in the Far East," and with ten percent of the American
population "not white," the "handling of racial matters in our own
nation, and particularly in our armed services, becomes of the greatest
importance."[66] Besides linking America's segregative practices to the battlefield fortunes of the United States, *The Crisis* was explicating the racial
dimension to the wartime alliance with Britain and other Western nations.

Black commentators stressed that the military fortunes of that alliance
rested on the renunciation of racism and colonialism. Tracing a range of
wartime insults and slights directed at nonwhite peoples by Allied leaders,
in March 1942 the *Afro-American* asserted that "race and color" were now
a "chief issue" in the war. African Americans were skeptical of attempts to
distinguish US international power from European colonialism. Referring
to "Japanese whisperings" regarding the colonial powers' ongoing mistreatment of their colonized subjects, the *Afro-American* did not excuse the United
States from the mistreatment of subject people across the Asia-Pacific: "every
anti-racial step" taken by the United States and other colonial powers, the
Afro-American noted, had been "dramatized by the skillful Jap propaganda
machine." Colonialism and racism were no mere abstractions. In the wake
of Pearl Harbor, as the Japanese juggernaut brushed aside Allied resistance,
African Americans insisted that racism and colonialism had made it easier
for "the Japanese military machine to crush all Allied opposition in Asia."[67]

Averring that the United States, and the nascent United Nations,
should not repeat the errors of the colonial powers who had ruled the
Asia-Pacific region, black leaders joined the failures of colonial rule to
the crises confronting Allied forces on the battlefield. "Blinded by greed"
and "mentally warped by stupidity," European colonists had not realized that if the "natives" of the region had been "trained for defense
and treated as human beings" they "could have delayed the Japanese
sufficiently long to upset their treacherous strategy." Britain's failing in
this regard was particularly abject, opined the *New Journal and Guide*.
The "United Nations may well profit," the paper suggested, "from the
experience of the British in the Pacific and Asia."[68] The unseemly haste

---

[66] See "The Negro in the United States Army," *The Crisis*, February, 1942, 47.
[67] Editorial, "Race and Color Are Now a Chief Issue in the War," *Afro-American*, March
21, 1942.
[68] "Antidote for Fear," *New Journal and Guide*, May 23, 1942.

with which the British had abandoned their colonial subjects in Malaya and Singapore to an unknown fate at the hands of the Japanese, suggested the *Chicago Defender*, had provided a significant "advantage for Japan." Britain's failure to win the loyalty of its colonial subjects was exposed by the inability – or refusal – of those peoples to defend British colonial authority in the face of Japanese aggression.[69] Self-government, even within the context of a continuing imperial connection, would have encouraged resistance to Japan's military onslaught.[70] And while they distinguished themselves from the colonized subjects of the Asia-Pacific, African Americans explained the oppression of nonwhite people in transnational terms: the ill-treatment they suffered within the United States, as victims of a form of internal colonization, was analogous to the exploitation of Asians and other victims of Western colonialism. In the same way as Indians were victims of British imperialism, noted the *Chicago Defender* in August 1943, African Americans were victims of "American imperialism, greed, terror and rapacity."[71]

When African Americans articulated these transnational connections, or criticized American racism, they exacerbated white doubts regarding blacks' allegiance to the United States. Any hint of black dissatisfaction with the United States was easily misunderstood or misconstrued as evidence of disloyalty. Notwithstanding the overwhelming expressions of African American patriotism prompted by Pearl Harbor, and despite black leaders' renunciations of their earlier endorsement of Japan's anticolonial stance, those prewar expressions of black support for Japan's anticolonial stance remained a matter of deep disquiet among white authorities. Amid the national paranoia in the period following Pearl Harbor, white Americans' suspicions regarding the prospect of African American collusion with militant nonwhites abroad fueled concerns that the Japanese "had succeeded in gaining many converts among" groups of "dissatisfied Negroes."[72] These wartime concerns were fueled by Japan's attempts to

[69] "Under the Lash: Criticism of Men and Conditions Which Make or Mar the Future of a Race," *Chicago Defender*, February 21, 1942. See also George Padmore, "Crisis in the British Empire," *The Crisis*, July, 1942, 216.

[70] Frank E. Bolden, "'White Racial Superiority Myth Being Shattered in War' – Bolden," *Pittsburgh Courier*, May 9, 1942; Von Eschen, *Race against Empire*, 23–4.

[71] *Chicago Defender*, August 22, 1943, cited in Von Eschen, *Race against Empire*, 35. For an early and important contribution to the notion of "internal colonialism," refer to Robert Blauner, "Internal Colonialism and Ghetto Revolt," *Social Problems* 16, no. 4 (1969): 393–408.

[72] "Memorandum to the Assistant Chief of Staff, G-3. Subject: The Negro," June 17, 1942, Box 472, NM84, Entry 418, RG 165, Records of the War Department General and

sow racial discord in the United States. Having earlier denounced the
United States as no different from other colonizing powers, after Pearl
Harbor Japan continued to criticize America's treatment of nonwhite peoples, and continued to woo African Americans. As the African American
correspondent and author Roi Ottley declared in 1943, racial conflicts
in the United States were "propaganda meat to the Japanese, who would
persuade the darker millions of the world that Japan is fighting a war to
liberate oppressed colored peoples."[73]

Japanese propagandists, alleged a widely publicized 1942 counter-
intelligence report, were seeking to create "dissatisfaction among
American Negroes," with the twin goals of fostering "race riots and
organized revolts against the United States government and authority"
and engendering "sympathy with Japanese aggressions." Tracing the history of Japanese attempts to win the hearts and minds of black Americans,
the wartime report suggested that in 1940 "between eighty and ninety
percent of the American colored population who had any views on the
subject" had been "pro-Japanese." While it was subsequently conceded
that estimate was "alarmist" – assessing the level of support for Japan
among African Americans was an unavoidably imprecise exercise – the
1942 report concluded that Japan's "intensive propaganda amongst"
African Americans had yielded "considerable effect." Of particular concern were Japanese attempts to "promote" the "subversion of Negro
troops in the United States Army." Lending weight to these claims, the
authors of the 1942 report claimed that a meeting of the "allegedly representative National Negro Associations" had "refused, by a vote of 36
to 5, to state that the Negro" was "100% in support of our war effort."
In an effort to undermine African American loyalty to the United States,
a long list of "Japanese-Negro front organizations," including "several
religious and semi-religious organizations," had reportedly disseminated
"seditious propaganda" within the black community. While stories of
"Japanese propagandizing" and "fifth columnists" resonated north of the
Mason Dixon line, reports of "agitation" among African Americans in
the Southern states, where the tradition of attributing racial unrest to foreign influences had a long and powerful history – and where many of the
nation's military bases, with their thousands of potentially troublesome

---

Special Staffs, National Archives and Records Administration, College Park, Maryland
(NARA).

[73] Roi Ottley, *"New World A-Coming": Inside Black America* (Boston, MA: Houghton
Mifflin, 1943), 327. See also Editorial, "Opinion," *Afro-American*, March 7, 1942;
Horne, *Race War!*, 227–8.

African American recruits, were located – prompted particular concerns for white authorities.[74]

Analyses of Japanese attempts to enlist the support of African Americans reputedly confirmed US government and military fears concerning the corruption of African American loyalty by foreign ideas. Conflating deeply held apprehensions regarding political subversion with concerns regarding African Americans' religious identity, government officials noted that "Negro organs of suspected Communist party affiliations" were susceptible to "exploitation by the Japanese." Not for the last time, moreover, Islamic beliefs were deemed a particular threat, as the "Nation of Islam" was considered to be essentially "a military organization." Any expression of African American internationalism – including the Universal Negro Improvement Association (UNIA), which had sought to foster an international alliance among nonwhites, but whose heyday had long since passed – was the subject of considerable concern. African American churches, and the black press, were allegedly complicit in Japan's attempts to win support within the African American community. While it was conceded that some depictions of African American sympathy for, or even collaboration with, Japan were unduly alarmist, in the aftermath of Pearl Harbor, when fear frequently triumphed over reason, Japan's propaganda efforts among African Americans continued to provoke angst among white officialdom.[75]

Fears of black disloyalty were fueled by African Americans' wartime efforts to secure equality. In the heated atmosphere of the post-Pearl Harbor period, the Double V campaign caused considerable anxiety among US military leaders, who agonized about the possible effects of black "militancy" within the armed forces, and who feared that African Americans' interest in Japan's anti-colonialist stance was tantamount to black support for Japan's war effort. Therefore, while a majority of African Americans agreed with black Cincinnatian Harvey Kerns that there was "no danger of an alliance of Negroes with Japanese," and

---

[74] *Japanese Racial Agitation among American Negroes* (Prepared by the Evaluation Unit, C.I.C), 7–10, 291.2, 4/15/42, Box 472, NM84, Entry 418, RG 165, NARA.

[75] *Japanese Racial Agitation*, 11–16, 291.2, 4/15/42, Box 472, NM84, Entry 418, RG 165, NARA. See also Takashi Fujitani, *Race for Empire: Koreans as Japanese and Japanese as Americans* (Berkeley, CA: University of California Press, 2011), 91; Walter Atkins, "Is Negro Press 'Agitating?': Soldiers Reply to Critics," *Chicago Defender*, January 23, 1943; Masaharu Sato and Barak Kushner, "'Negro Propaganda Operations': Japan's Short-Wave Radio Broadcasts for World War II Black Americans," *Historical Journal of Film, Radio and Television* 10, no. 1 (1999): 5–26. On the UNIA, see Judith Stein, *The World of Marcus Garvey: Race and Class in Modern Society* (Baton Rouge, LA: Louisiana State University Press, 1986).

although "sympathy for Japan" was "self-generated," with "little connection to Tokyo," fears of such an alliance remained powerful, especially among American military commanders.[76] These anxieties were compounded by black resentment regarding racial discrimination in the armed forces, and by Japanese criticism of what the civil rights advocate Roy Wilkins described in January 1942 as "the special American crime of lynching."[77] Detecting an opportunity to win the favor of African Americans, the Japanese wasted no time after Pearl Harbor in depicting the lynching of blacks in the Southern states and Americans' conduct on the battlefield as manifestations of the same racist traits. American soldiers' "cruelty," reported Japanese radio in December 1941, "was not surprising," given the prevalence of "lynchings in the Southern states."[78]

White Americans' doubts regarding African American loyalty were encouraged by black expressions of support for Japanese Americans – both groups, their critics imagined, were beholden to the Japanese government. Significantly, too, like African Americans, but unlike Hispanic Americans, who were classified as "white," those Japanese Americans who were allowed to serve in the US military did so in segregated units. While the immediate post-Pearl Harbor response among African Americans was to endorse the national paranoia about Japanese Americans – the black press reported, for example, that "Japanese farmers" across Southern California had "secretly plotted to poison their produce and carry death into the homes of thousands of Americans, and that the Japanese had "quietly" secured "control of a large number" of the "farms upon which Los Angeles" depended for much of its fruit and vegetables – African Americans soon began expressing more nuanced views of Japanese Americans.[79] In the frenzy of post-Pearl Harbor patriotism, drawing parallels between the wartime internment of Japanese Americans and the segregation of African Americans was politically perilous. Some black commentators, however, drew such comparisons. Correspondents for the *Chicago Defender*, in particular, not only looked on with some

---

[76] "300 Hear Kerns at Interracial Forum," *Cleveland Call and Post*, January 16, 1943; Gallicchio, *African American Encounter*, 116, 132. Neil A. Wynn has noted that the Federal Bureau of Investigation blamed the "widespread mood of rebelliousness" among African Americans on "foreign-inspired agitators." See Wynn, *The African American Experience during World War II* (Lanham, MD: Rowman and Littlefield, 2010), 78.

[77] Wilkins, "The Watchtower." Japanese authorities had earlier translated a novel by Walter White, in which the theme of lynching had figured prominently. See Horne, *Race War!*, 51.

[78] "Americans are Brutal; 'They Lynch', Say Japs," *Pittsburgh Courier*, January 3, 1942.

[79] "Japs Control Coast Food," *Afro-American*, January 17, 1942.

sympathy at the denial of civil liberties to Japanese Americans, but also contemplated the racial assumptions that contrasted presumptions of white American patriotism against a skepticism concerning black loyalty to the United States. Similar racial assumptions, it was contended, underpinned the relocation and internment of Japanese Americans.[80]

The *Defender's* correspondents were not alone in critiquing the treatment of Japanese Americans. In October 1942, shortly after Harry Paxton Howard had used the columns of *The Crisis* to warn African Americans that the mistreatment and internment of Japanese Americans – "these Americans" – was a "result of the color line," and "of direct consequence for the American Negro," *Afro-American* correspondent Ralph Matthews suggested that Japanese American internees were "better Americans than those intolerant contemptible bigots who call themselves Americans while denying the rights of citizenship to their fellowmen of dark skin."[81] Referring to the contentious tension between race and nation, Matthews suggested that national loyalties were not determined inevitably by race. African Americans recognized that the wartime racialization of patriotism and the rights of citizenship was privileging white Americans and disempowering nonwhites such as African Americans and Japanese Americans. This insight was not new, but African Americans understood it had been rendered more urgent by the paranoia unleashed by Pearl Harbor.

Matthews's *Afro-American* colleague, Vincent Tubbs, also reflected on the plight of Japanese American internees, and connected the racialization of patriotism to the racial composition of the US military. In May 1943 Tubbs detailed the process by which Japanese Americans were taken from their homes and relocated in what the *Afro-American* and *The Crisis* labeled "Concentration Camps." Describing the efforts of Hearst newspaper columnists and editors to provoke anti-Japanese American sentiment, Tubbs denounced the privations inflicted upon the internees. Japanese Americans, he argued, were victims of a deep-seated American racism, which treated all nonwhites with similar disdain. Exacerbating matters, the "majority of the military policemen assigned

[80] See C. K. Doreski, "'Kin in Some Way': The *Chicago Defender* Reads the Japanese Internment, 1942–1945," in *The Black Press: New Literary and Historical Essays*, ed. Todd Vogel (New Brunswick, NJ: Rutgers University Press, 2001), 161–87. On the wartime internment of Japanese Americans, see Roger Daniels, *Prisoners without Trial: Japanese Americans and World War II* (New York, NY: Hill and Wang, 1993).
[81] Harry Paxton Howard, "Americans in Concentration Camps," *The Crisis*, September, 1942, 284; Ralph Matthews, "The Big Parade: Little People of War Coast Jap Victims: How Guilty Are They? Good Americans," *Afro-American*, October 10, 1942.

to guard duty at the camps" were "illiterate Southerners" harboring "inbred racial prejudice."[82] As the next chapter explains, the behavior of those military policemen was symptomatic of an entrenched racism, which African Americans encountered time and again during their wartime military service across the Asia-Pacific Theater. Furthermore, while those military policemen were acting with the imprimatur of the US government, African Americans remained certain that such abuses of power contradicted the democratic ideals upon which the American war effort was purportedly predicated. And, most significantly, given the continuing doubts regarding African American patriotism, black sympathy for Japanese American internees did not equate to support for Japan.

African Americans' refusal to countenance an alliance with Japan, regardless of the latter's status as an enemy of white imperialism, reflected blacks' Christian faith, and their conviction that notwithstanding its faults, the United States – in contrast to Japan – was a nation founded on Christian principles. These Christian principles, it was argued, were both peaceful and universal, and a contrast to Japanese religious values, which were depicted as fiercely nationalistic and subject to the devious whim of the Emperor and the Japanese elite. "Emperor Hirohito and the high priests of Shintoism," warned S. A. Haynes in May 1942, "have decreed that all religions in East Asia," including Christianity, "must be merged in the interests of [Japanese] self preservation." If such a merger could not be achieved by "persuasion," warned Haynes, it would be achieved "by fire and sword."[83] Such methods, contended African American leaders, were inimical to American democratic principles. Insisting that African Americans' "destiny was in the United States," and linking religious faith to political values, Benjamin E. Mays, the black President of Morehouse College, declared in May 1942 that African Americans' "salvation must be worked out" in the United States, where "the religion is Christian" and "the ideals are democratic."[84] As Langston Hughes argued in 1944, black Americans had no reason to sympathize with the Japanese on account of some imagined racial bond: Japan's fascist ideology was contrary to American democratic values.[85]

[82] "How Japs Were Forced Out of Their West Coast Homes," *Afro-American*, May 1, 1943; Howard, "Americans in Concentration Camps," 281–5, 301–2.

[83] S. A. Haynes, "The World Horizon: Japan Plans Religious Regimentation," *New Journal and Guide*, May 30, 1942.

[84] Benjamin E. Mays. "The Negro and the Present War," *The Crisis*, May, 1942, 160, 164.

[85] "Don't Sympathize with the Jap on Color, Says Hughes," *Afro-American*, December 30, 1944.

During the Pacific War, as word spread of Japan's "uncivilized meth-ods of war," and of Japanese maltreatment of those whom it was claiming to liberate, the disjunction between Japanese and African American polit-ical and religious philosophies became more apparent. Japan's attempts to present itself as a friend of the colonized peoples of the Asia-Pacific appeared ever more implausible to African Americans.[86] In the words of Benjamin E. Mays, "Japan has no particular love or interest in the darker peoples of the earth." Mays, who had traveled widely, and who admitted to being "greatly impressed" by what he saw in Tokyo, was nevertheless adamant in his May 1942 declaration that "Japan is for Japan": argu-ing that Japan was suppressing "her darker brothers in the same way as imperialist whiter nations," May derided as "utter nonsense" the notion "that Japan would be the nation around which the darker races" could "rally and look to for guidance." African Americans, Mays asserted, "need have no sympathy for Japan."[87]

Following Pearl Harbor, as African Americans distanced themselves from Japan, they betrayed many of the same racial stereotypes that char-acterized white Americans' depictions of the Japanese. Leon W. Taylor's December 1942 analysis of Japan's efforts to win support among the black community casts light on African Americans' post-Pearl Harbor perceptions of Japanese attempts to encourage a transnational alliance of nonwhite peoples. On one level Taylor's intention was clear: detailing the various attempts of the Japanese "foreign office" to establish an "under-standing with the darker races within the United States" – with the ulti-mate goal of establishing "control over all Negroid groups throughout the world" – served as a warning to all Americans about Japanese inten-tions.[88] Counseling caution about Japanese methods, Taylor's depiction of deceitful Japanese was congruent with popular wartime American views of a sneaky adversary who launched surprise attacks and flouted the rules of civilized warfare.

Referring to "three kinds of propaganda" used by the Japanese, Taylor described Japan's attempts to, firstly, win over "the cultured Negro." Having convinced themselves that "certain Negro leaders possessed a greater hold upon the masses than really existed," the Japanese had attempted to forge an alliance with African American leaders, who would

---

[86] "The War," *New Journal and Guide*, January 3, 1942.
[87] Mays, "The Negro and the Present War," 160, 165.
[88] Leon W. Taylor, "Find Japanese Tried Three Kinds of Propaganda on Us," *Atlanta Daily World*, December 27, 1942. See also Leon Taylor, "Japs Use 3 Propaganda Approaches among Us," *Afro-American*, December 26, 1942.

serve as "fifth-columnists." Arguing that Japan had underestimated the "intelligence, loyalty and patriotism of American Negroes," Taylor contended that Japan's attempt to recruit the African American leadership had "evaporated entirely in the late '20s with the tour of Japan by the scholarly Dr. Du Bois." The Japanese "foreign office," Taylor argued, then attempted to woo "the teeming lower ranks of American Negroes." Alleging that "Nipponese agents" sought to lay "the sympathetic foundation" for African American protest, Taylor suggested that the second phase of propaganda was a prelude to a "third and most dangerous phase," conducted by "Japan's black allies" in major cities and industrial centers. Japanese agents, Taylor claimed, had used volatile propaganda, along with an appeal to superstition, to try and sow seeds of discontent within the black populace. Realizing that a large-scale uprising among African Americans was unlikely, Japanese agents remained hopeful that black restlessness would divert resources from the US war effort. In Taylor's view, African American loyalty to the United States, coupled with "the high educational standards" among segments of the black "community," had thwarted Japan's appeals to African Americans.[89]

The black skepticism toward Japan described by Taylor underpinned African American reactions to Pearl Harbor – and was further strengthened by growing evidence of Japanese contempt for other nonwhite peoples. The Japanese, it seemed, shared many whites' negative perceptions of black people. Discounting the "loose talk" regarding Japan's "friendship for the darker races," *Chicago Defender* editor Lucius C. Harper declared in May 1942 that the "Japanese have little respect for black folk." Evoking racial stereotypes used commonly by white Southerners, and reiterating the African American critique of Japanese disdain for black peoples, Harper warned that the Japanese considered African Americans "too docile and subservient" to become anything more than "a servant or a hireling." The implication was clear: Japan was no better than the Southern slaveocracy, and its attempt to present itself as a friend of African Americans, and the leader of an international alliance of nonwhite peoples, was disingenuous and self-serving. Reprising a theme common in black discourse, Harper also advised that African Americans who imagined they would attain "manhood rights" through an association with Japan's wartime conquests were mistaken.[90] Finally,

[89] Taylor, "Find Japanese Tried Three Kinds of Propaganda on Us." On Du Bois's visit to Japan, see Kearney, *African American Views of the Japanese*, 72.
[90] Lucius C. Harper, "Dustin' Off the News: How Do We Get That Way about Japan?" *Chicago Defender*, May 9, 1942.

in distinguishing between the Japanese and Japanese Americans – both the motives and methods of the former were suspect, while those of the latter were fundamentally honorable – African Americans implied the latter group had essentially been "Americanized." That assumption shaped African American attitudes and behavior as they made their way across the wartime Asia-Pacific.

In the aftermath of Pearl Harbor, then, African Americans were largely unconvinced by Japan's claims of racial fraternity and friendship. While many whites continued to imagine that African Americans were susceptible to Japanese propaganda, those blacks who most forcefully demonstrated the boundaries of black loyalty to the United States, such as Malcolm X and John Hope Franklin, did so principally because of homegrown American racism.

Malcolm Little – it was not until 1950 that he began calling himself "Malcolm X" – went to some lengths to avoid military service. In doing so, he revealed an astute awareness of transnational racial politics, and provided an early example of his sometimes-mischievous ability to merge his individual life experience with wider racial and political currents. Knowing that military intelligence agents – "black spies in civilian clothes," in Malcolm's words – were on the lookout for evidence of subversion within the African American community, in 1943 Malcolm made it known that he was "frantic to join ... the Japanese Army." If this evidence of his disloyalty was not sufficient to persuade the authorities that he was unsuited for military service, Malcolm told a psychiatrist at his physical examination that he was keen to join the US Army, so he could be sent South, where he could "steal" weapons, organize "nigger soldiers," and "kill crackers." Predictably, Malcolm was judged unfit for military service.[91]

The experience of John Hope Franklin, who subsequently became a preeminent historian of the African American experience, was very different from Malcolm's. Caught up in the post-Pearl Harbor wave of patriotism, Franklin answered a Navy advertisement for skilled office workers. Amply qualified – overqualified, in fact – for such a position,

---

[91] Malcolm X and Alex Haley, *The Autobiography of Malcolm X. With the Assistance of Alex Hailey.* (1965; reprinted, New York, NY: Grove Press, 1966), 104–5; Lipsitz, "Frantic to Join ... the Japanese Army," 323–4; Nat Brandt, *Harlem at War: The Black Experience in World War II* (Syracuse, NY University Press, 1996), 110–11. See also Kimberley L. Phillips, *War! What Is It Good For? Black Freedom Struggles and the US Military, from World War II to Iraq* (Chapel Hill, NC: University of North Carolina Press, 2012), 34.

and learning there was "a shortage of personnel to handle the crush of office work," Franklin "rushed" to the "recruitment office" to volunteer his "services to relieve the navy of its distress." Franklin was told that the Navy would not recruit him because African Americans were "not wanted." With a doctorate in history from Harvard University, Franklin then sought to secure a position with the Department of War, "which was assembling a staff of historians to do the definitive history of the great conflagration." Aware that "several white historians who had not obtained their advanced degrees" had recently been employed, Franklin was disappointed when the Department did not even reply to his application. Franklin's disappointments were not yet over, however. Invited to deliver the commencement address at the Tulsa high school from which he had graduated, Franklin was required to seek permission from his local draft board to leave North Carolina where he was then living. Told that such permission would only be granted if he agreed to "get a blood test," Franklin suffered further humiliation and indignation from the draft board's physician. His patience now exhausted, Franklin was forced "reluctantly to one irrevocable conclusion": "however much" the United States "was devoted to protecting the freedoms and rights" of others, it "had no respect" for Franklin, "no interest" in his "well-being," and no desire to "utilize" his "services." For the "remainder of the war years" Franklin devoted his energies to "outwitting" his "draft board and the entire Selective Services establishment."[92] In different ways, Malcolm's and Franklin's attempts to avoid military service highlighted the deep wartime disappointments felt within black America, and revealed that the surge of patriotism that swept through the African American community following Pearl Harbor could be tempered by individual experiences and circumstances.

In 1942 Malcolm and Franklin were relatively obscure figures. Examining the response of two well-known blacks further complicates understandings of African American patriotism. Just weeks after Pearl Harbor, world heavyweight boxing champion, and newly inducted soldier, Joe Louis, was reputedly "anxious to get a crack at 'those Japanese.'" The black press fêted Louis's patriotism and enthusiasm for the war effort, and with the support of civil and military authorities, he became an important

---

[92] John Hope Franklin, "Their War and Mine," *Journal of American History* 77, no. 2 (1990): 576–7; Lipsitz, "Frantic to Join … the Japanese Army," 324–5. See also John Hope Franklin, *Mirror to America: The Autobiography of John Hope Franklin* (New York, NY: Farrar, Straus, and Giroux, 2005), 105.

wartime symbol of American defiance and martial determination.[93] During early 1944, the *Pittsburgh Courier* ran advertisements for "eleven-by fourteen-inch color drawings" of "Joe Louis the Fighter," wherein he was depicted as the embodiment of armed, masculine patriotism. Proudly wearing his uniform as the US flag flew in the background, Louis was portrayed as an archetype of African American manhood, defiant in the face of danger, and "with no fears for the future."[94] Adolph Newton, a black sailor who served in the Pacific between 1943 and 1945, attested to Louis's significance. Describing a wartime argument with a white sailor, Newton later declared he "wasn't afraid of this guy," or of "any white man." A "certain boxing champion," he wrote, "had led me and all Negroes I knew to believe that no white man could beat a Negro."[95]

Joe Louis was more than a symbol of African American patriotism and manhood, however. Following Pearl Harbor, invoking his name and formidable reputation was also a means of highlighting American racism. Urging the Navy to allow blacks to move beyond the menial roles to which they had long been consigned, Walter White wondered "What will Joe be thinking?" "At this time in our national peril," White asked, "what will be in Joe Louis's mind as he climbs through the ropes at Madison Square Garden." For White, the contradiction between Louis fighting for the "Naval Relief Fund" while the Navy denied "his thirteen million colored American fellow citizens" the right to serve as equals was a damning indictment of the institutionalized racism that scarred the American military.[96]

While there is no reason to doubt the sincerity of Louis's patriotism, examining the ways in which he was constructed as an exemplar of African American patriotism suggests a more nuanced reading of black Americans' response to the outbreak of the Pacific War. Amid criticisms of Louis's determination to proceed with a planned bout in the aftermath of Pearl Harbor, it was argued that he "could render no better service to his country in this time of extreme emergency." As evidence of Louis's honorable and patriotic motives, and connecting his fight directly to the

---

[93] "Louis Anxious to Get Crack at Japanese: Lesson No. 1: How to Smash the Japanese," *Atlanta Daily World*, January 13, 1942. See also Sklaroff, "Creating G.I. Joe Louis," 958–83.

[94] See advertisement, *Pittsburgh Courier*, January 31, 1942.

[95] Adolph Newton, *Better than Good: A Black Sailor's War, 1943–1945* (Annapolis, MD: Naval Institute Press, 1999), 68.

[96] "Well, Even the South Can't Blame Negroes for Pearl Harbor Incident," *Chicago Defender*, December 27, 1941; "Navy Bias Leaves Pearl Harbor Stain on Whites," *Afro-American*, December 27, 1941. See also Juliete Parker, *A Man Named Doris* (Longwood, FL: Xulon Press, 2003), 60.

war effort, it was noted that he had promised to "donate the full share of his purse" from the fight to the Navy Relief Society. Most significant, however, was his manager's admission that if Louis had refused to fight, "he would have been promptly stigmatized as 'un-American.'"[97] The obligations of African American patriotism were far from straightforward.

Even more contentious than Joe Louis was Dorie Miller. Relegated, like other African Americans in the Navy, to the role of messman, Miller had received no formal training to operate weapons: the Navy command assumed African Americans were incapable of fulfilling a combat role.[98] During Japan's "infamous sneak attack" on the morning of December 7, however, Miller not only tried gallantly to save the life of the mortally wounded captain of the *West Virginia*, but also manned a machine gun, firing at the attacking aircraft. In the process he "won lasting fame" – and several months later, following a sustained campaign from sections of the black press, a Navy Cross – for his courage.[99] Amid the jingoistic aftermath of Pearl Harbor, Miller became a symbol of African American defiance, determination, and patriotism (Figure 1.1).

Extolled as "the first hero of World War II," and lauded as "the outstanding hero of Pearl Harbor," Miller quickly became a source of intense pride for African Americans.[100] While other African Americans were commended for their sacrifices at Pearl Harbor, Miller was elevated to the status of a celebrity, and called upon to motivate other African Americans to avenge Japan's attack. Along with the attentions lavished on Miller in the press, his deeds were celebrated on stage, in song, and in verse. "They

---

[97] Art Carter, "Joe's Charity Fight for Navy Will Help Us All – Roxborough," *Afro-American*, December 27, 1941. See also "Attention, U.S. Navy!" *Pittsburgh Courier*, January 17, 1942.

[98] Morris J. MacGregor, Jr., has noted that the Navy's treatment of African Americans during the interwar period marked the "nadir of the Navy's relations with black America." See MacGregor, Jr., *Integration of the Armed Forces, 1940–1965* (Washington, DC: Center of Military History, United States Army, 1981), 58.

[99] "Dorie Miller, Pearl Harbor Hero, First to Get Award," *Afro-American*, May 12, 1945. See also "Navy Cross Awarded to Dorie Miller," *Afro-American*, May 16, 1942; Washburn, *A Question of Sedition*, 53–4; Stephen Tuck, "'You Can Sing and Punch ... But You Can't Be a Soldier or a Man': African American Struggles for a New Place in Popular Culture," in *Fog of War: The Second World War and the Civil Rights Movement*, eds. Kevin M. Kruse and Stephen Tuck (New York, NY: Oxford University Press, 2012), 104.

[100] "Dorie Miller, Pearl Harbor Hero, First to Get Award," *Afro-American*, May 12, 1945; Nancy MacDonald and Dwight MacDonald, *The War's Greatest Scandal!: The Story of Jim Crow in Uniform* (New York, NY: The March on Washington Movement, 1943), 3. See also "Dorie Miller, Pearl Harbor Hero, Commended by Knox," *Afro-American*, April 11, 1942; "Dorie Miller Awarded Navy Cross by F.D.R." *Atlanta Daily World*, May 31, 1942.

FIGURE 1.1. Admiral C. W. Nimitz pins the Navy Cross on Doris "Dorie"
Miller, May 27, 1942
Courtesy: National Archives 208-NP-8PP-2.

found Dorie Miller, behind that great big Navy gun," sang Josh White,
and he "made them wish they'd stayed in the land of the risin' sun." [101]

[101] See "Dorie Miller Ballad Staged at Great Lakes," *New Journal and Guide*, August 21,
1943; Elijah Wald, *Josh White: Society Blues* (Amherst, MA: University of Massachusetts
Press, 2000), 106; A. Russell Buchanan, *Black Americans in World War II* (Santa

Miller's deeds at Pearl Harbor were likened by the African American civil rights advocate Earl B. Dickerson to those of the Revolutionary-era black hero, Crispus Attucks.[102] Comparing Miller with Attucks was significant not just because of the two men's valor, but also because Attucks's presence at the creation of the American republic – he was often praised as the first martyr, black or white, of the Revolution – tied him very directly to the *idea* of the American nation.[103] Drawing a parallel between Attucks and Miller was an unequivocal assertion of African American determination to use memories of Pearl Harbor – and of World War Two more generally – to remake American democracy, and fulfil the promises of the Revolutionary era.

Even before Miller was identified as the valorous messman aboard the *West Virginia*, his heroism exposed the contradiction between American wartime rhetoric and the treatment of its black citizens. The black press seized upon this contradiction. "Nothing could be more tragic," noted the *Afro-American* in January 1942, than in the "emergency" situation "when the air was filled with Japanese planes, when the chief was dying and the country needed trained men most," the only "available machine gun was operated by a man who never before had fired one."[104] As the *Pittsburgh Courier* put it: "Negro mess attendants, although they are only taught to flunky in the United States Navy, seized weapons which were strange to them and put up a gallant fight."[105] Agreeing that Miller's actions were

---

Barbara, CA: Clio Books, 1977), 117. Subsequently, a "Dorie Miller Chorus" performed in Norfolk, Virginia. See "Churches," *New Journal and Guide*, December 16, 1944. See also J. Farley Ragland's poetic tribute to Miller, "Dorie Miller," *Afro-American*, August 8, 1942. For an example of the praise given to other black servicemen at Pearl Harbor, see "Brothers Killed at Pearl Harbor: Mess Attendants Lose Their Lives," *Atlanta Daily World*, January 7, 1942. In an effort to build African American morale, Miller addressed other black sailors. See "Dorie Miller Talks to Camp Smalls Grads," *Afro-American*, January 16, 1943.

[102] "'I Too, Am an American' Program Attracts 2000," *Cleveland Call and Post*, January 17, 1942.

[103] While Attucks is widely remembered as the first American casualty of the Revolutionary War, eleven-year-old Christopher Seider had been shot a few weeks earlier by the British. Attucks, moreover, was of African and Native American descent. On Attucks, see Benjamin Quarles, *The Negro in the American Revolution* (1961; reprinted, Chapel Hill, NC: University of North Carolina Press, 1996), 5–8; Mitch A. Kachun. *First Martyr of Liberty: Crispus Attucks in American Memory* (New York, NY: Oxford University Press, 2017).

[104] Editorial, "We Have Not Begun to Fight," *Afro-American*, January 3, 1942. See also "Unidentified Messman Is Hero of Pearl Harbor," *Afro-American*, January 3, 1942.

[105] "Navy Messman Proves Hero in Pearl Harbor Disaster," *Pittsburgh Courier*, January 3, 1942. See also Robert B. Edgerton, *Hidden Heroism: Black Soldiers in America's Wars* (Boulder, CO: Westview Press, 2001), 130.

FIGURE 1.2. US military recruiters made extensive use of Dorie Miller's heroism
at Pearl Harbor
Courtesy: National Archives 208-COM-43 535613.

"an inspiring example of patriotism," that could "open up the eyes of those in authority" who had been "discounting the Negro's ability to discharge the obligations of higher naval ranks," the *Chicago Defender* further insisted that the "incident" provided "the best argument against" the "limitations and restrictions that loyal and courageous black citizens are made to endure in the Navy." "If a humble, segregated mess attendant can perform such a deed of valor," asked the *Defender*, "what would a proud black naval lieutenant" do during a similar "emergency"?[106]

The celebration of Miller's deeds at Pearl Harbor also raised questions for the Baltimore *Afro-American* editorialist Ralph Matthews.

[106] "Negro Heroism at Pearl Harbor," *Chicago Defender*, January 10, 1942.

Responding to reports that a company was profiting from Miller's deeds by selling "Dorie Miller buttons," Matthews was irked that "a percentage of the profit" from the sale of the buttons was reportedly going to Miller's parents and that "the rest" was "to be divided in devious ways." For Matthews, this seemed "like a cheap way" to "cash in on" both "the accidental valor of an American boy who was only doing his duty," and exploit "the hunger of our race for a hero to worship." Denouncing the sale of the buttons as "pure shysterism," analogous "to the numerous schemes, trinkets and mementoes" that had been "put on the market when Joe Louis had first become famous," Matthews's contempt was clear. The commercialization of Louis's and Miller's deeds, he wrote, "was designed to take advantage of the gullibility of a hero-poor race." By manufacturing "synthetic heroes," or by drawing inappropriate comparisons between Dorie Miller and Douglas MacArthur, Matthews argued, African Americans risked losing their "sense of perspective," their "sense of proportion," and their "sense of fundamental values."[107]

The *Afro-American's* critique of the commodification of Miller's heroism rested in part on a belief that his bravery had already been acknowledged – most significantly, the President had "bestowed upon this young man an honor in keeping with the deed." But the paper also repudiated attempts to profit from Miller's courage. If Miller's parents were "a party" to the plan to sell buttons, argued Matthews, "they should immediately and irrevocably renounce any share of the profits," since they had "no more right to profit by the deeds of their son than the thousands of other mothers and fathers who have given their lads to their country at just as great a sacrifice."[108] In spite of those concerns, the *Afro-American* and other black newspapers continued to refer to Miller's heroism – and, after his death when the USS *Liscome Bay* was torpedoed by a Japanese submarine in November 1943, his legacy – to condemn the racism to which African Americans continued to be subjected.[109]

Eighteen months after American entry in the war, Ralph Matthews reflected on the significance of Pearl Harbor. Suggesting ironically that "the late Admiral Isoroku Yamamoto of Japan" would be a worthy recipient of the "Spingarn Medal for Contribution to Racial Advancement,"

---

[107] Editorial, "Heroes Made, Not Born!" *Afro-American*, May 30, 1942.
[108] Editorial, "Heroes Made, Not Born!"
[109] See "This Is What Dorie Miller Died to Protect," *Afro-American*, December 22, 1945. See also "Navy Reports Hero Dorie Miller Missing in Action," *New Journal and Guide*, December 25, 1943.

Matthews contended that in "scheming up the Pearl Harbor raid" Yamamoto had "indirectly been a shot in the arm for American democracy." Prior to Pearl Harbor, Americans had been complacent, taking their "democracy pretty much for granted" and "enjoying the questionable luxury of disunity and business as usual." Since Pearl Harbor, however, African Americans had seized the day, proving their valor on the battlefield, and taking every opportunity to prove "their right to full citizenship."[110]

Matthews summarized succinctly the important questions Pearl Harbor raised for black Americans. While African American-Japanese relations during the prewar period had reflected a common repudiation of white racism and colonialism, following Pearl Harbor a majority of African Americans shared their white counterparts' almost visceral response to what they considered Japanese treachery. Indeed, while blacks' ambivalent prewar attitudes toward Japan complicated their analysis of the US wartime mission of liberation across the Asia-Pacific, after Pearl Harbor there was near-unanimous support among African America for the nation's war effort. Moreover, although government and military officialdom within the United States continued to fret about Japanese subversion among the African American community, those fears were largely misplaced: while many black Americans understood questions of race in transnational terms, and condemned Western colonialism across the Asia-Pacific, they saw their future as Americans. Loyalty to nation proved a more powerful imperative than tenuous racial connections between Japanese and African Americans. Yet the relationship between race, nation, and patriotism remained contentious. Even as African Americans saw their future as bound inseparably with the United States, in the period following Pearl Harbor they were soon reminded of the limits of the American commitment to democracy and equality. The nation's response to Pearl Harbor revealed that the outbreak of war did not signal the demise of the prevailing racist culture and practices. The war that for Americans began at Pearl Harbor thus became – as earlier wars had done – a means of demonstrating that African Americans were both loyal citizens of the United States and harsh critics of its endemic racism. By attacking the United States at Pearl Harbor, Japan had played an important, if inadvertent, part in putting Jim Crow "on the run."

---

[110] Ralph Matthews, "Watching the Big Parade: Yamamoto Is Worthy of Spingarn Medal for Contribution to Racial Advancement," *Afro-American*, May 29, 1943.

CHAPTER 2

The Segregated South Seas

Hierarchies of Race in the Pacific War

During World War Two, as in earlier conflicts, the inherently conservative US military establishment followed, rather than led, the nation toward more enlightened racial practices. Although white military commanders conceded that "separate facilities are rarely equal," only a few criticized racial segregation. Denying that the "separate organization" of white and black troops was "an endorsement of beliefs in racial distinction," commanders defended the practice as "a matter of practical military expediency."[1] Black servicemen, however, were unpersuaded by such claims. Segregation, they asserted, was militarily inexpedient and unjust, and an embarrassing contradiction of US claims to be fighting for international freedom and democracy. From Baton Rouge to Berlin, and from Tampa to Tokyo, black service personnel denounced segregation and the white supremacist values upon which it rested.

Yet while racism was endemic within the US armed forces, blacks' wartime military experiences were not universal. Rather, they were conditioned by specific historical and geographical circumstances. Across the Asia-Pacific, the long history of colonialism complicated African Americans' wartime struggle against discrimination. Consequently, as blacks serving in the Pacific Theater fought for their own rights, they fought also to ensure that the US military power extending across the region fulfilled, rather than contradicted, America's democratic rhetoric and mission. But there was another dimension to the African American wartime mission. Certain that the Asian and Pacific regions had only

---

[1] United States War Department, *Command of Negro Troops* (Washington, DC: U.S. Government Printing Office, 1944), 12.

"a semblance" of "democracy" and "civilization" – ideas widely regarded by African Americans as inseparable – black soldiers, sailors, and correspondents believed their wartime mission entailed carrying both to the unenlightened peoples of the Asia-Pacific.[2] Across the Pacific Theater, African Americans' challenge to segregation within the military was therefore part of a wider transnational mission of liberation and elevation – and a projection of the principles upon which American exceptionalism was predicated. Confronting intricate, interlocking racial hierarchies, and facing profound tensions between racial and national identity, African Americans were variously victims, agents, and symbols of the racial upheavals arising from the Pacific War. Above all, they were tangible symbols of American racism as well as American opportunity.

African Americans' military experiences began at enlistment, when they became part of the massive US military machine that by war's end had dispatched nearly twelve million Americans overseas. But before black recruits, volunteers and draftees alike, could take part in the campaign against Japan, they had to endure the travails of basic training. As any veteran will affirm, the early stages of military life entail a degree of trauma, as recruits are assimilated – sometimes violently – into military service and culture. For African Americans, that shock was exacerbated by the sometimes-fierce experiences of racism. Clarence Johnson was just eighteen years old when he joined the Navy in 1944, and his admission that he "was not emotionally prepared" for military life was true for many of his peers. For Johnson, the shock of military service was compounded by the disjunction between his desire to serve his country and the ruthless realities of racism: although slavery "was supposed to be over," he remembered, segregation had "created a chasm between the races" that fostered "isolation and mistrust."[3]

While some black veterans recalled boot camp as "tough but impartial," many endured intimidation and brutalization far beyond that encountered by other recruits.[4] Recalling his basic training, in Alabama John David Jackson's assessment was blunt, but typical: "my first days in service were hell."[5] Confronted by what one black Pacific War veteran

---

[2] Vincent Tubbs, "Papuans Chop Up Tax Collector, Bake Him Slowly; Eat Him," *Afro-American*, September 25, 1943.

[3] Clarence Johnson, AFC/2001/001/82459, Veterans History Project Collection, American Folklife Center, Library of Congress, Washington, DC (VHP-LoC).

[4] Henry Howard, AFC/2001/001/16244, VHP-LoC. See also Mortimer Augustus Cox, AFC/2001/001/43735, VHP-LoC.

[5] John David Jackson, AFC/2001/001/38452, VHP-LoC.

described as "pretty nasty" drill instructors, African American recruits routinely endured what *The Crisis* somewhat benignly described as "mistreatment" in "many of the army camps of the country, particularly those situated in the South."[6] Despite repeated black protestations, the War Department continued to locate many training facilities in the Southern states. During a time of "national emergency," it was argued, "matters of efficiency and timesaving" took precedence over the "costs in interracial terms."[7] For many African American recruits the shock of military life was compounded by their first direct experiences with southern segregation.[8]

The wartime influx of thousands of African American recruits into training camps exacerbated white Southerners' racial antipathies. In 1942, with memories of Pearl Harbor still fresh in Americans' minds, the Southern Governors Conference went so far as to object unanimously to the presence of black servicemen in their states.[9] Two years later, military authorities' belated and reluctant steps to curtail segregative practices on military bases prompted renewed complaints from Southern whites, who sought to defend "state laws" as well as "traditional customs and racial relationships."[10] It was a "grievous error," lamented Georgian Senator Richard Russell in unreconstructed language no different from that of his antebellum predecessors, "to require officially a promiscuous comingling of the races."[11] Many white Southerners, moreover, like whites in other states, regarded the sight of "niggers with guns" as confronting, even when – or, most likely, because – the "niggers" were in US military uniform. Although the Acting Mayor of DeRidder, Louisiana, praised the "orderly and well disciplined" behavior of the black troops of the

---

[6] Theodore R. Orr, AFC/2001/001/15260, VHP-LoC; Editorial, "Give Our Soldiers Protection," *The Crisis*, July, 1941, 215. See also Harry Benjamin Washington, Jr., AFC/2001/001/86605, VHP-LoC; Morris D. Pasqual, AFC/2001/001/48929, VHP-LoC; A. Russell Buchanan, *Black Americans in World War II* (Santa Barbara, CA: Clio Books, 1977), 79–82.

[7] United States War Department, *Command of Negro Troops*, 15.

[8] See Thomas A. Pincham, AFC/2001/001/10503, VHP-LoC; Marcus Alphonso Cranford, Sr., AFC/2001/001/43075, VHP-LoC. See also Russell Taylor McCabe, AFC/2001/001/7757, VHP-LoC.

[9] See Gerald Astor, *The Right to Fight: A History of African Americans in the Military* (Novato, CA: Presidio, 1998), 161. See also Richard M. Dalfiume, *Desegregation in the U.S. Armed Forces: Fighting on Two Fronts, 1939–1953* (Columbia, MO: University of Missouri Press, 1969), 49; Buchanan, *Black Americans in World War II*, 79–80.

[10] John Newsome, 9th District of Alabama, to Henry L. Stimson, Secretary of War, August 31, 1944, RG 407, Box 1064, 291.2 Race, Records of the Adjutant General's Office, National Archives and Records Administration, College Park, Maryland (NARA).

[11] Richard Russell, August 8, 1944, RG 407, Box 1064, 291.2 Race, NARA.

93rd Infantry Division, and reported that they had caused "no trouble or apprehension," members of the Division recalled the "less than cordial" reception from the locals in "Cajun country."[12] With admirable understatement, Samuel Nelson Burroughs concluded simply that his wartime experiences in Louisiana "weren't very good."[13] The reception given to black servicemen in Louisiana was characteristic of the treatment they received across the South, but many blacks also encountered animosity north of the Mason-Dixon Line.[14] "The Negro recruit," recalled one veteran of the 93rd Division, "was never allowed to forget he was a Negro," and that "the Negro had a place to stay," both "in and out of camp."[15]

The hostility directed toward black recruits rested on violence – and on the ever-present threat of violence. As well as being a source of deep frustration within the African American community, there were national and international ramifications of the violence directed at black troops. In mid-1943 the Assistant Secretary of War, John J. McCloy, admitted that "[d]isaffection among Negro soldiers" had become so widespread that it constituted "an immediately serious problem."[16] Japanese propagandists, alert to that disaffection, sought to turn it to their advantage. Japan's "exposé of American race prejudice," contended the *Chicago Defender* in 1943, was undermining American claims of moral superiority in the global war of ideas.[17] The "bloody story" of racial violence in Detroit in 1943, wrote Baltimore *Afro-American* correspondent Elmer Carter, was undeniable

[12] See W. A. Simmons, Acting Mayor, City Council, DeRidder, Louisiana, to Henry L. Stimson, Secretary of War, June 29, 1943, RG 407, Box 1067, 291.2 Race, NARA; Walter B. Sanderson, Jr., AFC/2001/001/76450, VHP-LoC. See also Maggi M. Morehouse, *Fighting in the Jim Crow Army: Black Men and Women Remember World War II* (Lanham, MD: Rowman and Littlefield, 2000), 95–9.

[13] Samuel Nelson Burroughs, AFC/2001/001/71767, VHP-LoC. See also Rueben Bertram Wheatley, AFC/2001/001/73030, VHP-LoC; George Edward Knapp, *Buffalo Soldiers at Fort Leavenworth in the 1930s and Early 1940s* (Fort Leavenworth, KS: Combat Studies Institute, U.S. Army Command and General Staff College, 1991), 40–1.

[14] See Phillip McGuire, ed., *Taps for a Jim Crow Army: Letters from Black Soldiers in World War II* (Lexington: University Press of Kentucky, 1983), Chapter 8; Studs Terkel, *"The Good War": An Oral History of World War II* (1984; reprinted, New York, NY: Ballantyne Books, 1985), 149.

[15] Willie Laughton, cited in *The Invisible Soldier: The Experience of the Black Soldier, 1941–1945*, ed. Mary Penick Motley (Detroit, MI: Wayne State University Press, 1975), 100.

[16] "Memorandum, John J. McCloy, Assistant Secretary of War, for Chief of Staff, July 3, 1943: Subject: Negro Troops," in *Blacks in the Military: Essential Documents*, eds. Bernard C. Nalty and Morris J. MacGregor (Wilmington, DE: Scholarly Resources, 1981), 121.

[17] Lucius C. Harper, "Dustin' Off the News: American Race Prejudice Is Winning for Japan?" *Chicago Defender*, September 4, 1943.

evidence of Americans' racial hypocrisy: "How can America condemn Japan?" asked Carter, when America "sprinkles the pavements of her cities with the blood of citizens whose only offense is the color of their skin?"[18]

While black recruits were disturbed by the wartime violence to which they, and other African Americans were subjected, military service was widely considered a transformative, even liberating experience. "I was 19," recalled Thomas A. Pincham, "and everything was an adventure."[19] Sergeant Joe McHaney spoke for many black veterans, whose wartime journey – political, as well as physical and psychological – to the Pacific Theater began when they left home for the uncertainty of basic training. Born in Montgomery, Alabama, and raised in Gulfport, Mississippi, McHaney explained that joining the military, and being stationed briefly in Chicago, "marked the beginning" of his "independence."[20] Thousands of black Pacific War veterans expressed similar sentiments. For Fred Linwood Simmons, Sr., joining the Navy in 1943 was a means of fulfilling his dream to "see the world."[21] Samuel Nelson Burroughs was even more emphatic: his induction into the military was the point where he "really got to understand the real world."[22]

Reflecting the long American tradition of the citizen soldier, the military occupied a vital part in national life, and the values it sought to inculcate, along with the opportunities it provided for self-improvement, were widely respected in wartime America. While those values transcended race, military service assumed particular significance for African Americans as they linked their burgeoning sense of personal independence and their quest for racial justice to America's great crusade to liberate the Asia-Pacific region from Japanese tyranny. Nelson Peery's explicitly left-wing politics did not preclude him from recognizing the merits of military service. In his "final week" of school in rural Minnesota, Peery noticed a "poster on the bulletin board," advertising the Army's "Civilian Military Training Camp." "It was what" Peery was "looking for – a chance to learn to fight. I believed in the military. It was the highest level of organization and force. That was the route to

[18] Elmer Carter, "Detroit Promotes Japanese Victory," *Afro-American*, July 10, 1943.
[19] Thomas A. Pincham, AFC/2001/001/10503, VHP-LoC.
[20] Enoch P. Waters, Jr., "Chicagoans Proud of Co. 'A' in South Pacific Area," *Chicago Defender*, November 6, 1943.
[21] Fred Linwood Simmons, Sr., AFC/2001/001/74559, VHP-LoC. See also Christopher C. Hough, AFC/2001/001/71829, VHP-LoC; David Jeff Keys, AFC/2001/001/79317, VHP-LoC; James Randolph, AFC/2001/001/77320, VHP-LoC.
[22] Samuel Nelson Burroughs, AFC/2001/001/71767, VHP-LoC.

freedom."[23] A politically conscious – and indeed precocious, judging by his autobiography – young man, Peery identified a symbiotic relationship between his own, individual advancement as a black man in a deeply racist society and the democratic, racially liberal principles for which the United States claimed to be fighting.

The African American leadership seized every opportunity to press home the principles and aspirations identified by Peery. Following Pearl Harbor, while the black leadership and press incorporated African Americans into the unfolding American narrative of gallantry, and emphasized that white and black Americans were fighting together on the frontlines, most African Americans serving in the Pacific Theater were confined to noncombatant duties.[24] As Chapter 5 explains, the systematic underuse of highly trained African American combat troops throughout the Pacific Theater, and their common deployment to laboring roles that both reflected and perpetuated their second-class status, prompted a bitter political debate. However, with the connivance of large sections of the nation's political leadership, the exploitation of black servicemen as laborers was pervasive through-out the Pacific Theater. As Howard Leslie Gregg put it, he and his fellow "Seabees" in the 22nd Special Naval Construction Battalion, stationed on the Admiralty Islands, were "more or less" the "labor gang."[25] While the role of a Seabee inevitably entailed hard physical toil, regardless of the unit's racial composition, the abuse of black servicemen as laborers remained commonplace across the Pacific Theater.

African Americans recognized the political and racial implications of their common relegation to laboring duties. Referring to one of the tasks considered most demeaning by African Americans, Linzey Donald Jones recalled that many black troops "considered it very insulting" that they were required to work as stevedores, "rather than fight."[26] Marcus Alphonso Cranford, Sr., was even more forthright: invoking the most troubling aspect of the nation's troubled racial past, he condemned ste-vedoring as "slavery in a military manner."[27] One 1943 report, describ-ing the military's segregationist policies as "the war's greatest scandal," argued that in "return for their patriotism," African Americans were being

---

[23] Nelson Peery, *Black Fire: The Making of an American Revolutionary* (New York, NY: The New Press, 1994), 80.
[24] "Army Mum on Race Soldiers with MacArthur: Admires Courage Shown by Fighters," *Pittsburgh Courier*, February 14, 1942.
[25] Howard Leslie Gregg, AFC/2001/001/76549, VHP-LoC.
[26] Linzey Donald Jones, AFC 2001/001/38128, VHP-LoC.
[27] Marcus Alphonso Cranford, AFC/2001/001/43075, VHP-LoC.

"jim crowed into segregated regiments and used largely as servants and laborers."[28] Compounding black frustration was the military's practice of redesignating "Negro soldiers with special training for some skilled branch of the Army" into labor units.[29] The consequences of these discriminatory practices were clear: the "Negro soldier sees himself [as] a miserable pawn in the inexorable hands of a fate which has already stacked the cards against him."[30] Accordingly, while some black servicemen were not disappointed to avoid the perils of combat, and although some suggested that service in noncombat units was likely to equip them with more useful work experience and employable skills than service in the infantry, many others were dismissive of claims that "white and colored troops" were serving together in "soldierly understanding."[31] Condemned as a waste of military resources that would prolong the war, the misuse of black troops was also an affront to African American masculinity. Repudiating white depictions of African Americans as happy to perform laboring tasks – which reprised slaveholder's self-serving depictions of contented slaves – black servicemen concluded, in the words of Navy veteran Ray Carter, that by "trying to make menials out of us at every opportunity," white military commanders' racial policies "struck at our manhood."[32]

In the face of this disquiet, the Federal Government provided little comfort to African Americans, and scant hope that the war would lead to positive change. Long-held racial stereotypes remained pervasive among white Americans. And even when racial traits attributed to African Americans were presented positively, such as in a magazine report suggesting that using the cadence of jazz music was the most effective way to instruct black troops to march and drill, they reflected and reinforced whites' unreconstructed views. Asserting that the military could not "change civilian ideas of the Negro," Colonel E. R. Householder of the Adjutant General's Office declared that the "Army's job" was simply

[28] Nancy MacDonald and Dwight MacDonald, *The War's Greatest Scandal!: The Story of Jim Crow in Uniform* (New York, NY: The March on Washington Movement, 1943), 3.
[29] Ruth Danenhower Wilson, *Jim Crow Joins Up*, Revised edn. (New York, NY: William J. Clark, 1944), 97.
[30] Grant Reynolds, "What the Negro Soldier Thinks about This War," *The Crisis*, September 1944, 291.
[31] Enoch P. Waters, *American Diary: A Personal History of the Black Press* (Chicago, IL: Path Press, 1987), 390; "Tan Yanks," *Time*, May 29, 1944.
[32] Ray Carter, cited in Motley, ed., *Invisible Soldier*, 110. For a wartime representation of African Americans as content to be relegated to laboring roles, see Sgt. Barrett McGurn, "Guadalcanal Goes Garrison," in *The Best from Yank, The Army Weekly: Selected by the Editors of Yank* (New York, NY: E. P. Dutton, 1945), 232.

to "train soldiers." Speaking the day after Pearl Harbor, Householder asserted that the Army was "not a sociological laboratory." Addressing "racial problems," he claimed, would "endanger efficiency and morale." In a characteristic evasion of responsibility, and misrepresenting the racism endemic to the military, he contended that "responsibility" was "upon the complainant in racial friction or clashes."[33] The persistence of what one white Pacific War veteran labeled a "K[u] K[lux] K[lan] attitude" within the military was a factor behind the ongoing restriction of black servicemen to menial laboring roles and a cause of the often-strained relations between African American and white servicemen across the Asia-Pacific Theater.[34]

That relegation of black troops to noncombat tasks placed the black leadership and press in an awkward position. They insisted that African Americans must be allowed to serve equally in all branches of the military. Yet they also understood that the work being performed by African Americans – however tedious, and however much that work appeared to confirm blacks' second-class status within American military and civil life – should be valued as essential to the nation's war effort, and regarded as evidence of their capacities and fidelity to the United States. As the *New York Amsterdam News* reported in January 1944, "although the Negro soldiers are winning no battle glory," they "are an important connecting line in the vital link which handles supplies for the men at the front."[35] The following month, correspondent Fletcher P. Martin described African Americans' logistical contributions to the Pacific War in dramatic, masculinist, terms:

When two-thousand pounds of hurtling missiles of steel and powder smash enemy installations on Bougainville it is a safe wager that these flying fragmentations of death were handled by a Negro ordnance unit. It is safe to add that when Mitchells and Liberators, pregnant with blockbusters, hover

[33] Colonel E. R. Householder, cited in *The Crisis*, May 1945, 131; Corporal George Norford, "Negro GIs in the Fijis Prefer the Manual of Arms in Jazz Time," in *Best from Yank*, 135.
[34] Questionnaire, 27th Infantry Division, Daniel J. Brown Papers, United States Army Military History Institute, United States Army Heritage and Education Center, Carlisle, Pennsylvania.
[35] Fletcher P. Martin, "Marines on Guadalcanal Reinforced," *New York Amsterdam News*, January 22, 1944. See also Will V. Neely, "Ordnance Men Do Fine Work in S. Pacific," *Atlanta Daily World*, December 23, 1943; Scoop Jones, "Troops Continue Heroic Work in New Guinea," *New Journal and Guide*, August 21, 1943. For an example of whites' praise for "Negro soldiers" in service roles, see Sgt. Ed Cunningham, "The Road to Tokyo," in *Best from Yank*, 177–9.

above Rabaul, strong brown hands are they which shoved the bombs up through the bomb bays before the ships took flight.[36]

African American military service was also inscribed with a higher, transformational, and transnational purpose. Acclaiming the efforts of a "battalion of colored Seabees" who had landed in the Solomons, the *Afro-American* cataloged the battalion's efforts to transform the "jungle-covered island." Logging and milling "their own lumber," and constructing roads and other communications facilities, the black Seabees also "installed lights and telephones" and "provided a supply of water."[37] Those blacks serving in noncombat roles also described the significance of their contribution to the Allied war effort. Insisting that his unit had "served our country well," Marcus Cranford stressed they had "done a fine job."[38] In spite of spending much of his time in the Pacific swabbing ships' decks and cleaning laundry, Calvin Collins enjoyed his time in the service, took pride in his work, and emphasized that he had provided an invaluable service for the nation's military machine.[39]

Collins's memories were an understandable attempt on the part of a noncombatant to write himself into the narrative of war. But military commanders' efforts to restrict black servicemen to physical and often menial labor was a potent expression of the deeply embedded racism within the armed forces – as well as a powerful imperative driving the struggle to overcome that racism.[40] Cowie Taylor, one of the first African American Marines, highlighted these connections. Having helped secure the island of Saipan from the Japanese, Taylor and his fellow black Marines suffered the ignominy of being consigned to segregated camps – an experience, he recalled, that was "[j]ust like being in Mississippi."[41] Further complicating matters, reports that white servicemen treated "every dark-skinned person better than the American Negro" reflected the frustrations of African American servicemen, and underscored the complex hierarchies

---

[36] Fletcher P. Martin, "Colored Unit Is Backbone of Attack on Japs at Bougainville," *Afro-American*, February 19, 1944. See also Fletcher P. Martin, "Ordnance Unit Guarding Vital So. Pacific Area," *New York Amsterdam News*, February 26, 1944.

[37] "Seabee Units Build Solomon's Defenses," *Afro-American*, July 3, 1943. See also "Sea-Bees in S. Pacific Perform Miracles in Construction Work," *Cleveland Call and Post*, December 25, 1943.

[38] Marcus Alphonso Cranford, AFC/2001/001/43075, VHP-LoC.

[39] Calvin Collins, AFC/2001/001/32840, VHP-LoC.

[40] On the struggle for integration within the United States armed forces, see Morris J. MacGregor, Jr., *Integration of the Armed Forces, 1940–1965* (Washington, DC: Center of Military History, United States Army, 1981).

[41] Cowie Taylor, AFC/2001/001/50909, VHP-LoC.

of race and nationality prevailing across the Pacific Theater. One white Mississippian, seen playing with a group of Guamanian children, was asked by National Association for the Advancement of Colored People Executive Secretary White whether he would "be as nice to kids of that color back home?" "These kids are not niggers," the indignant white soldier replied.[42]

Even when African American service personnel encountered racially enlightened whites, apprehensions remained. Describing the "relationship" between "the Negro and white soldier in the South Pacific" as "farcical," Sergeant Willie Lawton of the 93rd Infantry Division, recalled that "the very guy who would make your life miserable in the states was your best buddy" in the war zone. Although Lawton recalled that social interactions between African American and white troops could be cordial, black servicemen commonly remembered their time in the Pacific War zone very differently. Consequently, while Lawton "accepted the friendship" of white servicemen, the men in his unit "never forgot" that "one day" they would be "going home" and that the "buddy-buddy bit" would not survive in peacetime.[43] In September 1942, Private Louis G. Alexander, stationed in the New Hebrides, wrote to his unit chaplain, describing relations between white and black servicemen. Emphasizing his own background – Alexander was a successful businessperson who enjoyed the advantages of a good education – his letter revealed both the diversity among black service personnel as well as his frustration. "Men in this regiment," he explained, "are talked to and treated more like animals of a lower class than like human beings."[44]

The institutionalized racism of the various branches of the armed forces was manifested in many ways. Following a sustained campaign in the black press, the Navy's policy of restricting African Americans to the role of messmen – or "seagoing bellhops," as the black newspapers described them – was reversed in April, 1942.[45] Yet while the policy was

---

[42] "Negro Soldiers Treated Worse Than Other Dark-Skinned Peoples," *Atlanta Daily World*, March 9, 1945.

[43] Sergeant Willie Lawton, cited in Motley, ed., *The Invisible Soldier*, 102. See also David Scott, Sr., AFC/2001/001/78823, VHP-LoC.

[44] Private Louis G. Alexander to Luther M. Fuller, September 12, 1942, RG 165, Records of the War Department General and Special Staffs, NM84, Entry 418, Office of the Director of Plans and Operations, General Records – Correspondence – Security – Classified General Correspondence, 1942–1945, 291.2, Operations Division, War Department General Staff, Records Section, Box 472, NARA.

[45] See George Hemingway Isom, *What Is That Boy Going to Do Next?: A Memoir* (Lincoln, NE: iUniverse, 2005), 29.

FIGURE 2.1. Seamen Dodson B. Samples, Raymond Wynn, Edward L. Clavo, and Jesse Davis load shells in the Naval Ammunition Depot, Espiritu Santo, New Hebrides N.d.
Courtesy: National Archives 80-G-123941.

modified, reforming the culture of racism proved immeasurably more difficult. Derided by *The Crisis* as a "gesture," the new policy signified only a minor change to the racist culture permeating the Navy.[46]

Black frustrations were compounded by the promotion policies of the armed forces. Asking bluntly why there was just one black general amongst the "700,000 Negro troops in the army," the *New York Amsterdam News* suggested in late 1944 that the US Army was "about as Nazi-like as Hitler's."[47] Although they acknowledged that "the failure to promote Negro officers" or "give them positions of command" was a chief source of "racial friction," military authorities were reluctant to

---

[46] See "The Navy Makes a Gesture," *The Crisis*, May, 1942, 151. See also MacGregor, *Integration of the Armed Forces, 1940–1965*, 58; Dennis D. Nelson, *The Integration of the Negro into the U.S. Navy* (New York, NY: Farrar, Strauss and Young, 1951), 14; Michael Lee Lanning, *The African-American Soldier: From Crispus Attucks to Colin Powell* (Secaucus, NJ: Birch Lane Press, 1997), 200.

[47] "Is Our Army Nazi-Like?" *New York Amsterdam News*, October 28, 1944.

adopt more racially enlightened and equitable promotion policies.[48] By the end of the Pacific War, when there were 165,000 African American enlisted men serving in the Army, there were just fifty-two commissioned officers. Not only did some Army commanders insist that black troops "prefer service under white officers," but the perception that a majority of African American officers "exhibit a total lack of responsibility" remained pervasive in many quarters. "Negro officers," it was alleged, were "generally not as effective as white officers of comparable grade due to [a] lack of leadership ability."[49] Within the Marine Corps, only four African Americans received commissions during the war.[50] The Navy's record was no better: in the words of Walter White, the Navy's promotion policies for African Americans were "woefully behind" those of the US Army – whose record in that regard was hardly progressive.[51] Despite repeated protests from the black leadership and press, it was not until January 1944 that a select group of sixteen African Americans began training as Naval officer cadets.[52]

Across the Pacific Theater, black servicemen voiced their frustrations with the military's promotion policies. Writing in January 1945, a black officer from the 1315th Engineer Construction Battalion complained that "only one colored officer has been promoted" since the unit had been activated in July 1943.[53] Regardless of "how good you are," concluded another black officer, "the army will still not promote you if that will put

[48] Memo from Captain George W. W. Little (Division Psychiatrist) to Division Surgeon, 93rd Infantry Division, May 8, 1944, RG 337, Records of Headquarters Army Ground Forces, General Correspondence, 337/55/184, NARA. See also Wilson, *Jim Crow Joins Up*, 98–9. On African American officers during the interwar period, see Gerald W. Patton, *War and Race: The Black Officer in the American Military, 1915–1941* (Westport, CT: Greenwood Press, 1981), Chapters 7 and 8. See also William H. Hastie, "The Negro in the Army Today," *The Annals of the American Academy of Political and Social Science* 223, no. 1 (September 1942): 58–9.

[49] See "Letter from Commanding General, 93rd Division," April 8, 1953; Colonel Edward S. Greenbaum, "Report of the 93rd Division," n.d.; "COMGENSOPAC" TO "AGWAR," October 2, 1943, all in RG 165, 165/390, Box 61, NM84, NARA.

[50] Nelson, *The Integration of the Negro*, 12. See also "Mr. President, What of the Marines?" *Afro-American*, August 19, 1944.

[51] Walter White, *A Man Called White: The Autobiography of William White* (London: Gollancz, 1949), 273.

[52] Lanning, *African-American Soldier*, 205–6.

[53] See "United States Army Forces in the Far East," *Censorship Survey of Morale-Propaganda Rumors*, 23, Issued by the A.C. of S., G-2, February, 1945, RG 496, Records of the General Headquarters, Southwest Pacific Area and United States Armed Forces, Pacific (World War II), 290/47/28/2, NARA.

you over an inferior white officer."[54] African Americans' frustrations with the military's promotion policies were well summed up by Willie Lawton. "Promotions," he wrote, "were given on the basis of whether you were a 'good nigger.'" During his time in the service, recalled Lawton, "the Negro of some intelligence and freedom of thought" was "not wanted and wasn't going very far."[55] For African Americans to gain promotion, it was assumed, they had to conform to whites' self-serving preconceptions regarding blacks' capacities. Inevitably, too, there were instances when African Americans put their quest for individual advancement ahead of the collective racial well-being. In their quest "to get a stripe," noted "Marcus" Cranford, these "Uncle Toms" were willing to betray other African Americans.[56]

Promotion to the officer corps did not end the racial discrimination – social as well as professional – endured by African Americans. Rarely promoted to senior officer ranks, and precluded from commanding white troops, black officers faced segregative practices paralleling those endured by black enlisted personnel. Walter B. Sanderson recalled there were "always two different officers' clubs" during his time with the 93rd Division: one reserved for whites, and the other for blacks. "And of course," he recalled, "the differences in furnishings was obvious and expected."[57] African American officers, like black enlisted men, were also subjected to public humiliation. An officer from the 369th Infantry Regiment described how he and other black officers had attended a United Services Organization (USO) show, only to be told they could not use seats clearly reserved for visiting officers. Understandably, the "embarrassment of having to leave in front of a vast crowd" rankled.[58]

The Army's monthly censorship reports provide an invaluable window into racial tensions across the Pacific Theater. Confirming that the question of race relations was a persistent issue for military authorities, these summaries reveal both the worst and the best of race relations across the Pacific Theater. Following the lead of the black press, whose

---

[54] See "United States Army Forces in the Far East," *Censorship Survey of Morale-Propaganda Rumors*, 22, Issued by the A.C. of S., G-2, September, 1944, RG 496, 290/47/28/2, NARA.

[55] Lawton, cited in Motley, ed., *Invisible Soldier*, 101.

[56] Cranford, AFC/2001/001/43075, VHP-LoC.

[57] Sanderson, AFC/2001/001/76450, VHP-LoC.

[58] See "United States Army Forces in the Far East," *Censorship Survey of Morale-Propaganda Rumors*, 23, Issued by the A.C. of S., G-2, September, 1944, RG 496, 290/47/28/2, NARA.

condemnation of racism within the armed forces was occasionally countered by optimistic declarations that "the cause of interracial relations" was being boosted by blacks and whites sharing certain military experiences, censorship reports provide evidence of mutual amity and respect, from white and African American servicemen.[59] In mid-1944, the white commander of one black unit concluded that his men were "good boys," who "really soak up knowledge like a sponge."[60] Another white officer, writing in early 1945, admitted that working alongside African Americans had led him to revise his previously skeptical views of their capacities. While he had initially been "disgusted," by the "bunch of colored boys now" he was "handling" – even as he embraced a more tolerant attitude toward blacks his language betrayed the condescension that so infuriated African Americans – he was "often surprised at the ability of some of them." "The longer I serve with these [black] men," confessed another officer, "the better I like them and the smarter I discover them to be." Having previously assumed that African Americans were incapable of progress or advancement, he concluded that "the colored race is just as intelligent and as good" as "the white" race. Americans of all races, he contended, should "enjoy the same privileges and act as equals."[61]

Regardless of such expressions of racial goodwill, relations between black and white service personnel across the Asia-Pacific Theater were frequently less amicable. As the Censorship Survey of February 1945 concluded, only a "small minority of letters," indicated that "relations between the races" were "cordial."[62] In their private correspondence, many white officers recorded their contempt for African American troops. "I'm going nuts working with these damned niggers," wrote one officer, while another described the "[l]azy, good for nothing niggers" in his command as "[r]ascals" and "[p]oor human specimens." Frustrated that "[t]his black scum," with "intelligence below the age of ten" had "gotten

---

[59] "Colored, White Soldiers Travel to Battle Zone in 'Swing Time,'" *Pittsburgh Courier*, July 4, 1942.

[60] See Headquarters, United States Army Forces in the Far East, Office of the Theater Censor, A.P.O. 501, *Censorship Survey of Morale-Propaganda Rumors*, Issued by the A.C. of S., G-2, July, 1944, 60, RG 496, Records of the General Headquarters, Southwest Pacific Area and United States Armed Forces, Pacific (World War II), 290/47/28/2, NARA.

[61] See United States Army Forces in the Far East, Office of the Theater Censor, A.P.O. 501, *Censorship Survey of Morale-Propaganda Rumors*, 41–2, Issued by the A.C. of S., G-2, March, 1945, RG 496, 290/47/28/2, NARA.

[62] See United States Army Forces in the Far East, *Censorship Survey of Morale-Propaganda Rumors*, 24, Issued by the A.C. of S., G-2, February, 1945, RG 496, 290/47/28/2, NARA.

me down," another white officer concluded that African Americans were "simply sullen animals."[63]

In the face of such antipathy, it was unsurprising that many African Americans were sharply critical of their white officers. Arguably, what is most notable is the restraint that African Americans exercised in dealing with the racism they encountered on a daily basis. While some black servicemen noted that not all white servicemen and officers were racist, for every African American who spoke positively about their white compatriots, many more spoke critically.[64] Echoing the views of one white officer, who conceded that the "Southern boys" were "not overburdened with intelligence," and were incapable of recognizing that their treatment of African American service personnel was no different from the behavior of the Japanese fascists they so vehemently denounced, black troops often distinguished between Northern and Southern whites. Writing from New Guinea, a black officer in the 1311th Engineer Regiment noted that his commanding officer "is a southerner and he is giving everybody hell."[65] And although John David Jackson recalled that "some" of the white officers in his unit were "pretty good," he emphasized that others were not. Alluding to a much-despised character from Harriet Beecher Stowe's *Uncle Tom's Cabin*, Jackson likened some white officers to "Simon Legree, if you know what I mean."[66]

Pandering to those white prejudices, and reflecting their doubts concerning the capacity of black troops, white military authorities continued to stifle African Americans' ambitions for advancement within the military. Yet although promotion opportunities for African Americans were few and far between during the Pacific War, the concept of "leadership" transcended the formal structures of the armed forces. Black servicemen who had received more than a rudimentary education felt an obligation to other, less fortunate blacks. Mortimer Augustus Cox, one of the first African Americans permitted to enlist in the Marine Corps, recalled

[63] See Headquarters, United States Army Forces in the Far East, Office of the Theater Censor, A.P.O. 501, *Censorship Survey of Morale-Propaganda Rumors*, 60, Issued by the A.C. of S., G-2, July, 1944, 6G 496, 290/47/28/2, NARA.

[64] Charles Strother, Jr., stationed on the island of Tinian, in the Marianas, was one African American who spoke positively about white officers. Recalling that he "never" heard "one bad word about his [white] lieutenant or any of the officers," Strother claimed that the "whole company got along great together." See Strother, Jr., AFC/2001/001/63802, VHP-LoC.

[65] See United States Army Forces in the Far East, Office of the Theater Censor, A.P.O. 501, *Censorship Survey of Morale-Propaganda Rumors*, 61, 43, Issued by the A.C. of S., G-2, July and August, 1944, RG 496, 290/47/28/2, NARA.

[66] See John David Jackson, AFC/2001/001/38452, VHP-LoC.

that "educated blacks" realized they could not "let the race down." Confronting hostility from white Marines on a daily basis, Cox and others believed they "were responsible for the group." As he put it, he "felt close" to black leaders such as A. Phillip Randolph.[67]

All African Americans, from national leaders such as Randolph to the lowest-ranked enlisted serviceman, realized that racism was predicated on negative racial stereotypes of nonwhite peoples. Black servicemen bemoaned these stereotypes and the language associated with them. The language used by white Americans to describe black servicemen was at once a symptom of white racism and a powerful symbol of their continuing degradation of African American men whose military service was an important expression of their masculine self-identity. While black naval veteran Adolph Newton explained that the "word *nigger* is a funny word," and that the response it elicited was determined by tone, intent, and context, the use of that phrase by white officers and servicemen – and their depiction of African American men as "boys" – caused deep offence and frustration.[68] Although military authorities recognized that African Americans resented "derogatory" phrases such as "colored boys" or "niggers," their efforts to educate white troops about the politics of language were both half-hearted and ineffectual as white servicemen and officers continued to degrade black troops with offensive language. Nelson Peery was just one black soldier incensed to be called "boy" by white officers.[69] And highlighting African Americans' unwillingness to be characterized alongside other nonwhite peoples, their resentment at whites' use of the term "nigger" was likely exacerbated by the fact that the phrase was sometimes also used by white Americans and their Australian allies to describe Pacific Islanders.[70]

---

[67] See Mortimer Augustus Cox, AFC/2001/001/43735, VHP-LoC.

[68] Adolph Newton, *Better than Good: A Black Sailor's War, 1943–1945* (Annapolis, MD: Naval Institute Press, 1999), 94.

[69] United States War Department, *Command of Negro Troops*, 23; Peery, *Black Fire*, 141–4; See also Louis A. Perkins, AFC/2001/001/32840, VHP-LoC; Alfred S. Campbell, *Guadalcanal Round-Trip: The Story of an American Red Cross Field Director in the Present War* (Lambertville, NJ: Printed privately, 1945), 90; Ruben Hines, cited in Melton Alonza McLaurin, *The Marines of Montford Point: America's First Black Marines* (Chapel Hill, NC: University of North Carolina Press, 2007), 98; McGuire, *Taps for a Jim Crow Army*, 99, 113. The novelist Sloan Wilson – who had commanded an Army supply ship during the Pacific War – also referred to black anger at whites' use of the term "nigger." See Ruth Danenhower Wilson, *Voyage to Somewhere* (New York, NY: A. A. Wyn, 1946), 185.

[70] See, for example, Charles Walmsby Diary, July 21, 1942, Papers of Sergeant Charles Walmsby, PR00742, Australian War Memorial, Canberra.

Determined to resist such expressions of white racism, black service-men demonstrated a newfound confidence, and nascent sense of political consciousness, in a variety of ways. As one black Pacific War veteran noted, while some African Americans "were broken" by the racism they encountered in the armed forces, "the majority" who served "fought back in innumerable ways."[71] That resistance could take many forms. A minority of African Americans embraced overt resistance to white racism. Such a course of action was fraught, as the institutionalized power of white military authority could be brought to bear violently and quickly on African Americans deemed "troublesome." The inequalities of military justice were among the most obvious and debilitating expressions of the racism inherent in American military culture. Statistically more likely than white servicemen to be charged and prosecuted for a range of offences, African Americans were also more likely to be found guilty and punished more severely than their white peers.[72] During, and in the immediate aftermath of the war, of the twenty-one American soldiers executed by US authorities across the Pacific Theater, eighteen were black.[73]

Black servicemen referred frequently to these institutionalized injustices. Claude Norfleet, a Navy steward, and the informal leader of a group of African Americans who found themselves in dispute with their white officers, suggested a hunger strike as one way to seek redress for their grievances. A hunger strike was a relatively peaceful way to challenge white racism, but Norfleet was evidently considered a troublemaker, and was singled out for punishment by his white commanders. Following a fracas involving black and white servicemen, Norfleet was arrested. If his recollection of the details of the incident was imprecise – understandable given the passage of time – Norfleet was clear about its consequences. Found guilty "of destroying property or something," he was sent back to the United States, sentenced to a year in prison, and dishonorably discharged. After considerable effort, which included sending letters to politicians in Washington, DC, Norfleet's discharge was altered to "honorable." Many years later, recalling his wartime experiences, Norfleet was self-effacing about his role in confronting the institutionalized racism that was commonplace in the services. He was, however, certain

---

[71] Ray Carter, cited in Motley, ed., *Invisible Soldier*, 110.
[72] Wilson, *Jim Crow Joins Up*, 99. See also Grant Reynolds, "What the Negro Soldier Thinks about the War Department," *The Crisis*, October, 1944, 318, 328.
[73] Lanning, *The African-American Soldier*, 177. See also Walter A. Luszki, *A Rape of Justice: MacArthur and the New Guinea Hangings* (Lanham, MD: Madison Books, 1991), 107.

about the reason for his arrest and imprisonment: he had been fighting segregation.[74]

Given the white determination to maintain the subjugation of African Americans, it was understandable that only a handful of blacks confronted white racism head-on. Yet African Americans serving in the Pacific War challenged the social etiquette of American racism in myriad ways. Drafted into the Army in late 1942, Franklin Harold Tinsley, Sr., found himself performing clerical duties in the Pacific Theater. Temporarily delegated to other duties, he missed reveille one morning. Tinsley's commander punished him by denying him his rations. In response, Tinsley "made a mistake" and twice forgot to process that particular officer's pay sheet. When the officer realized what was going on, Tinsley began receiving his proper rations.[75] Tinsley's resistance was not without risk, and was contingent upon specific circumstances as well as the personality of the officer involved. But it was also congruent with the type of "mistake" that occurred routinely in the heavily bureaucratized military machine with which the United States waged war during the 1940s, and was one means of negotiating a resolution to the racism encountered routinely by African American servicemen. Tinsley's actions – and similar forms of defiance from black servicemen across the Pacific Theater – were twentieth-century analogs of the resistance offered daily by African Americans during the era of slavery.

The legacies of these wartime acts of resistance were profound. Tracing the subsequent advances achieved by the civil rights movement to African Americans' wartime experiences, black veterans described the Pacific War as personally and racially transformational. During "World War Two," noted Herman Parker, a black Navy veteran of the conflict against Japan, "we learned about race relations." While the war was being fought, he remembered, black servicemen were "kinda half-way scared of white people." Notwithstanding the formalities of military life, however, wartime contact with white Americans demystified and undermined white authority, and set the scene for the postwar challenge to prevailing racial hierarchies: "I guess from being around them and seeing they were nothing but men just like you, you kinda just lost that fear ... we learned that he was nothing but a man just like we were." No longer willing to

---

[74] See Claude Norfleet, AFC/2001/001/27843, VHP-LoC. Norfleet's black compatriots were not the only ones to stage a hunger strike to draw attention to racial injustices. See "Seabees Herded with Bayonets," *Afro-American*, May 5, 1945.

[75] See Franklin Harold Tinsley, Sr., AFC/2001/001/21551, VHP-LoC.

acquiesce to white bullying, Parker and his peers "came back with a different attitude and a different feeling." Whereas prior to the war African Americans were "scared, scared, scared," having "got in there and saw what they were all about, it weren't nothin'."[76] The Pacific War destabilized racial hierarchies within the US armed forces and – by extension – within all corners of American life.

The Pacific War also disturbed colonial hierarchies based on race. This raises questions regarding African Americans' wartime encounters with the peoples of the Asia-Pacific. The region's physical and human geography, which so sharply highlighted the contrast between modern Western society and the premodern world inhabited by Asians and – in particular – Pacific Islanders, was significant in shaping the lived experiences of black servicemen. These experiences, in turn, influenced blacks' perception of the war against Japan as a contest over "civilization." Although many African Americans considered Pacific Islanders and Asians as far more than anthropological curios, their wartime interactions highlighted the distinctions rather than the similarities between Islanders, Asians, and African Americans. The racially specific political questions arising from black military service in the Pacific Theater – notably the prospects for an imagined community of nonwhite peoples – were informed by deep-seated cultural assumptions. African Americans had long been part of the American project across the Pacific and Asia, and tracing their preconceptions of those regions informs this analysis of their wartime experiences. It was one of the paradoxes of the Pacific War that while African Americans criticized the negative stereotypes imposed upon them by white Americans, their own views of Pacific Islanders and Asians reflected longstanding racial stereotypes.

The Asian and the Pacific regions had long fascinated Americans of all races. While the United States had eschewed the formal trappings of empire, African Americans' perceptions of the Pacific – and here they had much in common with their white compatriots – reflected popular misconceptions of the region, of which the most potent were a series of myths about an illusory "South Seas." For the generation of African Americans venturing to the South Seas during World War Two, their misperceptions of the region had been reinforced and reinvigorated during the interwar period by Hollywood's enthusiastic embrace of the "South Seas" genre. As the entertainment pages of the black press during the 1930s reveal, African Americans were exposed to Hollywood's

---

[76] Herman Parker, AFC 2001/001/80199, VHP-LoC.

fictionalized depictions of the Pacific region.[77] Informed by these misrepresentations, African Americans' knowledge of the Pacific region was
predicated on preconceptions regarding the virtues of Western – and
particularly American – "civilization." These assumptions were widely
shared by all Americans, but the endemic racism within the US military
complicated African Americans' wartime perceptions of, and interactions
with, Pacific Islanders and Asians.

The disillusioning realities of war transformed the Pacific region from
a site of fantasy to a site of conflict: from a place of pleasure to a place
of devastation and death.[78] In spite of the attempts of military authorities
to avert disillusionment with the Pacific by educating service personnel
about the region, illusions of the South Seas remained popular among
black servicemen.[79] For servicemen bound for the Pacific Theater, a gen-
eralized and often romanticized vision of the South Seas could provide
a welcome distraction from the looming realities of war. While servicemen's wartime experiences were not directly analogous to those of the
peacetime traveler or tourist, many black service personnel appreciated
their military service as an opportunity to travel and experience locales
that would otherwise have remained distant dreams.[80] Although some
middle-class Americans had opportunities to travel to the Pacific during
the interwar period, for a much larger number of Americans – particularly
African Americans – the Pacific was a fantasy, glimpsed via Hollywood's
lens or through the pages of *National Geographic*. Although Europe's
attractions were well documented, glamorized images of the "South
Seas" were especially alluring. Black veteran Harry W. Leavell summed
up the sentiments of many servicemen bound for the Pacific Theater:
"I always wanted to go to the South Pacific as a youngster. I thought, God,

---

[77] See Chris Dixon and Sean Brawley, "'Tan Yanks' Amid a 'Semblance of Civilization':
African American Encounters with the South Pacific, 1941–1945," in *Through
Depression and War: Australia and the United States*, eds. Peter Bastian and Roger Bell
(Sydney: Australian-American Fulbright Commission, 2002), 93.

[78] For an analysis of the enduring power of the mythology through various forms of Western
culture, see Sean Brawley and Chris Dixon, *The South Seas: A Reception History from
Daniel Defoe to Dorothy Lamour* (Lanham, MD: Lexington Books, 2015).

[79] See Sean Brawley and Chris Dixon, *Hollywood's South Seas and the Pacific War:
Searching for Dorothy Lamour* (New York, NY: Palgrave Macmillan, 2012), Chapters
2 and 3.

[80] For a case study of the "soldier as tourist," see Sean Brawley and Chris Dixon, "Colonel
Zimmer's Sea Shell Collection: Souvenirs, Experience Validation, and American Service
Personnel in the Wartime South Pacific," in *Coast to Coast and the Islands in Between:
Case Studies in Modern Pacific Crossings*, eds. Prue Ahrens and Chris Dixon (Newcastle-
upon-Tyne: Cambridge Scholars Publishing, 2010), 77–87.

this is going to be great."[81] Notwithstanding the common discomfort of sea-sickness, traversing the Pacific was, as one veteran remarked, "something that's unimaginable unless you've done it."[82]

For many African Americans, Hawaii provided their first taste of the fabled "South Seas." Hoping to forestall racial tensions in Hawaii, during the early months of the Pacific War some US military commanders had regarded the deployment of black troops there as "most undesirable."[83] However, military expediency took precedence over racial anxieties, and African Americans found themselves dispatched to Hawaii. As Beth Bailey and David Farber have noted, of all those who visited Hawaii during World War Two, none found it "stranger than the 30,000" African Americans "who came through the islands." Blacks' wartime experiences on the Hawaiian Islands were far from uniformly positive, but as Bailey and Farber have contended, "Hawaii's wartime racial fluidity" provided "a more welcoming environment than the one they had left behind."[84] Certainly, African Americans found much to admire in Hawaii, beginning with the physical environment. John David Jackson's description of Hawaii as "the prettiest place" he had "ever seen" was typical.[85] Later in the war, too, for African Americans who had served elsewhere in the Pacific, Hawaii's allure was undiminished. After enduring the horrors of Iwo Jima, Mortimer Augustus Cox regarded Hawaii as a peaceful counterpoint to the ferocity of the frontlines. "It was just like being in Paradise," he recalled.[86]

---

[81] See Harry Leavell, AFC/2001/001/2658, VHP-LoC.

[82] See *Dr. Edwin A. Lee Memoir*, 55, held in Archives/Special Collections, Norris L. Brookens Library, University of Illinois at Springfield. See also Linzey Donald Jones, AFC/2001/001/38128, VHP-LoC. See also, for example, Earl V. Root, AFC/2001/001/71839, VHP-LoC. On the "King Neptune Ceremony" held as units of the 93rd Division crossed the Equator, see "Quarterly History," January – March 1944, HQ and Hq Battery, 93rd Infantry Division Artillery, RG 407, Box 11333, 291.2 Race, NARA.

[83] "H.L.S.," Memorandum for the Chief of Staff. Subject: The Colored Troop Problem, March 25, 1942, RG 165, Box 472, NM 84 – Entry 418, Classified General Correspondence, 1942–45, NARA.

[84] See Beth Bailey and David Farber, *The First Strange Place: The Alchemy of Race and Sex in World War II Hawaii* (New York, NY: The Free Press, 1992), 133. See also Perry E. Fischer and Brooks E. Gray, *Blacks and Whites Together through Hell: U.S. Marines in World War II* (Turlock, CA: Millsmont Publishing, 1994), 38–40.

[85] John David Jackson, AFC/2001/001/38452, VHP-LoC. See also Claude Norfleet, AFC/2001/001/27843, VHP-LoC; Hayden Bernard Williams, AFC/2001/001/55426, VHP-LoC.

[86] Cox, AFC/2001/001/43735, VHP-LoC. Hayden Bernard Williams remembered the "wonderful time" he spent in Honolulu, and former Marine Lawrence Reginald Lucas,

Yet Hawaii could also be a let-down. "When I landed in Pearl Harbor," recalled James Luther McNeal, "it was a big disappointment." Having read "so much about Hawaii," he had "anticipated a great big beautiful place." Instead, he "found a place like all other places, only more military."[87] Although Hawaii's physical geography was an anticlimax for some black servicemen, the racism they encountered on the island group was a more pressing problem. Despite its physical attractions, remembered John David Jackson, Hawaii was "quite prejudiced."[88] While Hawaii reputedly "had no 'Negro Problem'" prior to World War Two, race relations changed dramatically after December 1941.[89] The segregationist practices of the US military, coupled with the wartime policies of Hawaiian authorities and businesses, meant that although race relations there were generally less hostile than in the segregated South, significant difficulties arose for African Americans stationed in, or passing through, wartime Hawaii. Further, blacks stationed in Hawaii were forced to overcome a series of racial preconceptions ranging from the familiar – that their presence posed a threat to the local women, for instance – to the absurd, including the rumor – which persisted across a number of sites to which African Americans were deployed during the Pacific War – that they "had tails."[90] And while their own views of Pacific Islanders were influenced by Hollywood's representations of the South Seas, African Americans lamented that Hawaiians' stereotypical views of blacks could be traced to the "parts given" to blacks "in movies and on the radio."[91]

Hollywood's influence ran deep and served to exacerbate black servicemen's disappointments. Because the islands evoked images of a relaxed, carefree lifestyle, it is perhaps unsurprising that African Americans expressed frustration when they were denied the same social or recreational activities as their white compatriots. Robert Quarles's experiences were typical. When the ship on which he was traveling stopped at Hawaii the black troops on board hoped to "go on shore" in Hawaii, and "have drinks" and "meet girls." But Quarles and the men in his unit were "terribly disappointed" when they were prohibited from doing so by commanding

who was stationed briefly in Hawaii soon after the war ended, recalled that the people of Hilo were "very friendly." See Williams, AFC/2001/55436, VHP-LoC; Lucas, AFC/2001/001/67012, VHP-LoC.
[87] James Luther McNeal, AFC/2001/001/24022, VHP-LoC.
[88] John David Jackson, AFC/2001/001/38452, VHP-LoC.
[89] Bailey and Farber, *First Strange Place*, 139.
[90] See Willie Bruce, AFC/2001/001/49801, VHP-LoC. See also Bailey and Farber, *First Strange Place*, 150–1; White, *A Man Called White*, 273–4.
[91] "War Workers Take Wives to Hawaii," *Afro-American*, March 27, 1943.

officers apprehensive about potential "trouble between the white and black troops." Rather than risking an altercation with white authorities, some black servicemen decided to stay on base.[92] Others, however, such as Charles Berry, who felt like he was "back in Chattanooga or Mississippi," challenged the racism they encountered in Hawaii. Prohibited from entering the Royal Hawaiian Hotel, Berry and the men in his unit "formed a line beside the building and slept there on the concrete." That "was probably the first sleep in," recalled Berry, alluding to one of the tactics of the postwar civil rights movement.[93] As Bailey and Farber suggest, at the same time as wartime "Hawaii was a place of eye-opening possibilities," it "was also a place in which racial struggle became a necessity."[94]

Many black service personnel regarded Hawaii as a brief, and largely "Westernized" interlude on their long journey to the "South Seas" – an often-indeterminate region, that variously included Polynesia, Melanesia, and Micronesia, and which sometimes stretched as far west as the Philippines. Harry Leavell spoke for many of his contemporaries, servicemen and correspondents alike. Recalling that as "a youngster" he had always wanted to travel to the "South Pacific," Leavell was not disappointed by his initial encounters with the region. Guam, he remembered, was "beautiful."[95] Mirroring a wider pattern among the United States and Allied service personnel throughout the Pacific Theater, however, for many African Americans their arrival in the South Pacific shattered their preconceived, romanticized views of the region. New Guinea proved particularly disappointing: while the island's Markham Valley was a "beauteous spot from the air," wrote Fletcher P. Martin, once "on the ground" it became a "conglomeration of troops, mud, malaria and jungles."[96] Fellow correspondent Vincent Tubbs remarked that while the New Guinean "vista" was like "paradise," the jungle was "hell."[97] African Americans'

[92] Robert Quarles, AFC/2001/001/80199, VHP-LoC. See also Charles Edward Orgain, AFC/2001/001/48764, VHP-LoC; Marcus Alphonso Cranford, AFC/2001/001/43075, VHP-LoC.

[93] Charles Berry, AFC/2001/001/5950, VHP-LoC. See also Bailey and Farber, *First Strange Place*, 151–2.

[94] Bailey and Farber, *First Strange Place*, 135.

[95] Harry W. Leavell, AFC/2001/001/2658, VHP-LoC. See also Newton, *Better than Good*, 48; Company History, 793rd Ordnance (Light Maintenance) Company, March, 1944, RG 407, Box 11343, 291.2 Race, NARA.

[96] Fletcher P. Martin, "No Women, No Movies – Lonely Soldier Talks to Dodo Birds," *Pittsburgh Courier*, January 1, 1944.

[97] Vincent Tubbs, "Tubbs Flies to New Guinea Battle Area in Papuan Jungle," *Afro-American*, July 17, 1943.

representations of the "savage" but "wonderful" islands of New Guinea were congruent with well-established representations of the island as both mysterious and menacing.[98] But those images extended well beyond New Guinea. Tubbs's description of Java as "a strange medieval world" captured many men's views of the wider Pacific Theater.[99] The fact that many black servicemen were stationed in Melanesia or Micronesia added to their disillusionment, since those regions differed most starkly from the mythologized images of the "South Seas," which had been based principally on an imagined Polynesia.[100]

This disillusionment was compounded by the horrors, and even the detritus, of battle. By early 1944, when units of the 93rd Division arrived on Guadalcanal, the remaining Japanese forces there no longer posed a serious threat to American units. Yet, like their white compatriots, the men of the 93rd had not heeded the lessons that military authorities had sought to inculcate. "Our arrival at Guadalcanal," reported the Division's artillery battery, "was somewhat disappointing to put it mildly." Suggesting the enduring appeal of the South Seas fantasy, it was reported that some men's belief that the island was "a Utopia" was "quickly dispelled."[101]

Compounding that sense of alienation, the "hot and wet" climate and the unfamiliar fauna of the Asia-Pacific Theater exposed servicemen to debilitating and sometimes life-threatening diseases.[102] Typhus and dysentery affected service personnel in all theaters of war. But the relentless tropical climate and unforgiving jungle environment in which much of the Pacific War was waged carried particular risks. Although African American servicemen's fears were often overstated – rumors abounded of virulent, drug-resistant diseases – enough soldiers and sailors were affected by various tropical ailments to render the risk more than theoretical. African American units lost many men – some temporarily; others

---

[98] See Brawley and Dixon, *The South Seas: A Reception History*, 59–73.

[99] Vincent Tubbs, "Javanese a Quaint People," *Afro-American*, September 11, 1943.

[100] See Brawley and Dixon, *Hollywood's South Seas*, 58, 71–4, 85.

[101] See "Quarterly History," January – March 1944, HQ and HQ Battery, 93rd Infantry Division Artillery, RG 407, Box 11333, 291.2 Race, NARA.

[102] See Howard Hickerson, cited in Morehouse, *Fighting in the Jim Crow Army*, 139. On African American servicemen's descriptions of South Pacific wildlife, see Company History, 793rd Ordnance (Light Maintenance) Company, March, 1944, RG 407, Box 11343, 291.2, NARA; Newton, *Better than Good*, 48; Theodore R. Orr, AFC/2001/001/15260, VHP-LoC; Carl Tuggle, AFC/2001/001/49547, VHP-LoC; Samuel Gibson, AFC/2001/001/8445, VHP-LoC.

permanently – to the various diseases that ravaged the military forces of every nation fighting across the Pacific Theater.

Malaria was a major concern. In the 24th Infantry Regiment, the first African American combat unit deployed to the Pacific Theater, the "medical problem" was "mainly one of a struggle against malaria."[103] The common means of avoiding malarial infection – a daily dose of Atabrine – provided a measure of protection. Its efficacy, however, was dependent on servicemen taking it regularly. Alarmed by stories regarding the drug's side-effects – rumors persisted that it "might affect" what one black veteran euphemistically described as the men's "masculinity" – some black troops took their chances, rather than their Atabrine.[104] Black servicemen were not the only ones concerned by the potential side-effects of anti-malarial medication. Lieutenant Prudence Burrell, an African American nurse serving with the 268th Station Hospital in New Guinea, refused to take Atabrine, partly because she believed that her childhood exposure to malaria provided immunity as an adult, and also "because it made us black ones look gray."[105] US military authorities sought to control the mosquito infestations that spread malaria, but those efforts were incomplete, and never reached all the way to the frontlines. Inevitably, some servicemen contracted malaria. Dengue fever, another mosquito-borne infection, also affected many men.[106]

Alongside the unremitting struggle to maintain physical well-being, military service in the Pacific Theater entailed particular challenges to servicemen's psychological welfare. With "not much entertainment," remembered Elum Richson, who had been stationed in Elum Richson, a veteran of the New Guinea campaign, recalled that with little "entertainment" on offer, black servicemen did what troops everywhere did to entertain themselves. They played cards, watched movies, complained about "unbearable food," reminisced about home and family, and longed for an end to war.[107] Yet, if those were

[103] "Historical Record and History of the 24th United States Infantry, from July 1, 1943 to September 30, 1943," RG 407 Records of the Adjutant General's Office, 1917. World War II Operations Reports, 1941–49. Infantry. INRG 24-01, Entry 427, Box 16958, NARA. See also L. Albert Scipio, *Last of the Black Regulars: A History of the 24th Infantry Regiment (1869–1951)* (Silver Springs, MD: Roman Publications, 1983), 75.

[104] See Walter B. Sanderson, AFC/2001/001/76450, VHP-LoC.

[105] See Prudence Burrell, AFC/2001/001/4747, VHP-LoC.

[106] See Roy B. Sutton, AFC/2001/001/63967, VHP-LoC; Earl V. Root, AFC/2001/001/71839, VHP-LoC.

[107] David Parker Barnes, AFC/2001/001/27781, VHP-LoC. See also Elum Richson, AFC/2001/001/23258, VHP-LoC; John W. Dominick, AFC/2001/001/38356, VHP-LoC; Carl Tuggle, AFC/2001/001/49547, VHP-LoC; Morehouse, *Fighting in the Jim Crow Army*, 151–6.

familiar habits and sentiments among servicemen, they were rendered distinctive by the physical and human geography of the Pacific Theater. Concomitant with the harsh climate and physical environment, the cultural gulf between African American troops and the local populations – about which more will be said later – limited the opportunities for relaxation and recreation during servicemen's time off-duty. Whereas service personnel in the European Theater often had opportunities to venture into large towns and cities, their counterparts in the Pacific Theater had few such prospects. African American servicemen were not the only ones to suffer such disappointments, but racial segregation and discrimination further curtailed their opportunities for recreation and interaction with local populations – indigenous or European. Furthermore, like other forms of field entertainment, the "quite infrequent" visits from USO shows were often segregated, with black entertainers performing for African American audiences.[108] Even in Honolulu – the most "American" point in the Pacific Theater to which black servicemen were deployed – African Americans "didn't feel welcomed" at the local USO facilities.[109]

Segregationist principles also characterized US military authorities' determination to regulate African Americans' interactions with the indigenous peoples of the Asia-Pacific. Although African Americans were depicted as an integral part of an army of liberation which was repelling Japanese brutality and extending civilization across the Asia-Pacific, US commanders feared both the immediate military consequences as well as the potential long-term political and racial consequences of liaisons between African Americans and native populations. Those concerns – like white authorities' fears of collaboration between African Americans and Japanese – were exaggerated, but they were powerful. Fearing that black Americans would foment discord among Islanders, American commanders referred to earlier examples of racial collusion. A 1942 Navy report on the "Psychology of Solomon Islanders," for instance, claimed that in 1931 African Americans arriving at Rabaul on a merchant ship had incited a race riot, which allegedly lead to the death of several whites and a large number of natives.[110] Anxious to avoid such incidents, US

[108] Walter B. Sanderson, AFC/2001/001/76450, VHP-LoC. On the segregation of USO shows, see Thomas A. Pincham, AFC/2001/001/10503, VHP-LoC.
[109] Leon Allison Fraser, AFC/2001/001/5184, VHP-LoC. See also Earl V. Root, AFC/2001/001/71839, VHP-LoC.
[110] Robert L. Ghormley, "Psychology of Solomon Islanders," October 7, 1942, RG 313, Records of the Naval Operating Forces, Box 6786, 370/35-36/35-01, NARA. The "idea

commanders feared that liaisons between African Americans and local populations would jeopardize the supply of native labor which was a vital part of the Allied war effort.

Military commanders' attempts to regulate interactions between African American servicemen and indigenous populations functioned alongside the continuing dehumanization of African Americans by white American officers and enlisted men. Louis R. Perkins recalled that when he arrived on Guam, blacks initially enjoyed considerable freedom. Soon, however, the Navy introduced regulations prohibiting African Americans from visiting the populated centers of the island. Perkins also learned that like the Hawaiians before them the Guamians had been told that African Americans had tails.[111] That rumor – purportedly evidence that African Americans were "monkeys" – remained powerful during the Pacific War.[112]

African Americans repudiated such rumors, but their interactions with native peoples betrayed their own hierarchical perceptions of race. And although cultural and commercial exchanges with native populations were contingent upon local circumstances, interactions were inevitable given that the US military was systematically exploiting native labor. African American military personnel were complicit in that process. Many black servicemen used Islanders to do their laundry, for example, and while some African Americans – such as Averitte Wallace Corley, who recalled cordial relations with "the natives" – described their interactions with Islanders in positive terms, the relationship was far from equal.[113] African Americans' treatment of Islanders resembled relations between white and black Americans, and by exploiting native labor, black servicemen perpetuated patterns of labor relations that had characterized the prewar colonial regimes across the Asia-Pacific. All of this suggests that African Americans accepted their white compatriots' assumptions regarding the superiority of Western culture. Reporting on the "Use of

---

of a 'strike' among indentured workers in Rabaul," reported anthropologist Margaret Mead, had come from "American Negro seamen." See Margaret Mead, *New Lives for Old: Cultural Transformations–Manus, 1928–1953* (1956; reprinted, New York, NY: William Morrow and Co., 1966), 80. Charles J. Weeks, Jr., has noted concerns that wartime breaches of discipline among African American troops stationed in Tonga were especially troubling because they "involved the civilian population." See Charles J. Weeks, Jr., "The American Occupation of Tonga, 1942–1945: The Social and Economic Impact," *Pacific Historical Review* 56, no. 3 (1987): 411.

[111] Louis A. Perkins, AFC/2001/001/22540, VHP-LoC.
[112] See Norman R. Payne, AFC/2001/001/ 49177, VHP-LoC; Benjamin Patterson, cited in McLaurin, *Marines of Montford Point*, 103.
[113] Averitte Wallace Corley, AFC/2001/001/43821, VHP-LoC.

FIGURE 2.2. African Americans serving with the 34th Naval Construction
Battalion trade with Solomon Islanders, September 23, 1943
Courtesy: National Archives 80-G-8916.

Natives," the Intelligence Section of the 369th Infantry Regiment referred
specifically, if unwittingly, to these issues. "Carefully selected" and "well
handled" natives, wrote the Regiment's intelligence officer, had been "a
boon" to the allied "cause."[114] While that officer was white, his report
affirmed that the black troops of the 369th Regiment had taken advantage
of native labor.

Pacific Islanders were of course more than just a source of labor for
African Americans. On a personal level, however, blacks' interactions with
the indigenous peoples of the Pacific Theater reflected long-established
racial and cultural stereotypes. African Americans, in common with other
servicemen, were both curious and apprehensive about indigenous peoples. Above all, notwithstanding their expressions of sympathy for the
colonized subjects of the Asia-Pacific region, African Americans emphasized their differences from native peoples. Marine veteran Norman Payne
described his sense of difference from the Pacific Islanders he encountered.

[114] S2, 369th Infantry Regiment, "Use of Natives," in G2 Weekly Summary, No. 29, May
26, 1945, RG 407, Box 11331, 291.2 Race, NARA.

Although the two peoples were "the same color," he explained, they "talked," "reacted," and "thought differently."[115] For a majority of black servicemen, that sense of cultural difference transcended the bonds of race.

Islanders, and subsequently Asians, were often exoticized and – as Chapter 3 explains, eroticized – by African American servicemen and correspondents. Reflecting long-held views in Western culture, images of benign or childlike indigenes coexisted alongside assumptions regarding "primitive" or even "savage" natives. During the 1930s and 1940s much of what African Americans "knew" about the peoples of Pacific region was derived from the popular press. Claims of scientific authenticity were commonplace, but such claims served principally to highlight both Hollywood's pedagogic power as well as the limits of anthropological research. An August 1942 article by the black journalist Louis Lautier was typical. Describing the inhabitants of the Solomon Islands – where American forces were then locked in bloody battles with the Japanese – Lautier declared authoritatively that "[i]nvestigation" had revealed that the island group was "inhabited by warriors" who had "consistently resisted 'civilization.'" Lautier might well have been correct in noting that the Solomon Islanders continued to practice "cannibalism," and engage in "head-hunting expeditions against rival tribes." More significant, however, was his statement – his tone was certainly not that of an admission – that his "investigation" had relied upon information provided by the National Geographic Society.[116] Lautier's depiction of the Solomon Islanders, moreover, reflected popular views among African Americans regarding their deep sense of difference from natives whom they commonly regarded as uncivilized.

Wartime experiences frequently confirmed, rather than challenged, prevailing racial stereotypes. There were several elements of these stereotypes. Black reporters affirmed many of the long-standing images regarding life in the tropics and the indigenous inhabitants of the Pacific region. Jimmy Hick's reference to natives as "angels," Vincent Tubbs's description of "quaint" Javanese, and Fletcher P. Martin's depiction of the inhabitants of Samar Island in the Philippines as "childlike in their simplicity," were representative of many African Americans' views of native peoples.[117] African American condescension toward native peoples rested

---

[115] Norman R. Payne, AFC/2001/001/49177, VHP-LoC.
[116] Louis Lautier, "Solomon Islands Populated by Dark Skinned Natives," *Pittsburgh Courier*, August 29, 1942.
[117] Jimmy Hicks, "This Is My Island," *Cleveland Call and Post*, November 27, 1943; Tubbs, "Javanese a Quaint People,"; Fletcher P. Martin, "Guerrilla War Waged by the People," *New Journal and Guide*, December 23, 1944.

on assumptions regarding the merits of Christianity and civilization.[118] Although the "Kanakas" of New Caledonia had "accepted Christianity," and while "nearly every baby" was "baptized in the Christian faith," Martin suggested that the natives there were maintaining "some of their early beliefs." "[M]odern civilization," he explained, was "creeping in" only "slowly." Describing the Kanakas as, "[b]are footed, graceful, and picturesque in costumes of brilliant color," Martin perpetuated deeply Ingrained stereotypes of native peoples as somehow unaffected by the demands of modernity. When they were "not working in the fields or in Army service," the Kanakas would "stand and smile in a lazy sort of way at the hustling, bustling troops."[119] Noting that "life is lazy," and that it "seemingly floats without rhyme or reason," Martin's reference to "[h]alf clad natives" on one undisclosed location in the former Dutch East Indies, who would "walk by" Americans "and grin," echoed depictions of the region offered by Europeans since the beginning of their colonial endeavor. Yet Martin also suggested that the same natives were more than just indolent bystanders to the conflict raging around them, as some demonstrated considerable commercial and entrepreneurial zeal by charging inflated prices for goods and services.[120]

Both of these stereotypes – the passive native and the wily native – had long coexisted in Western discourses about Islanders in particular and colonized subjects more generally. We should perhaps not be surprised that African Americans reflected and perpetuated those stereotypes, were it not for the fact that rhetorically some claimed to be advancing a transnational union of nonwhite peoples that would transcend and challenge prevailing racial hierarchies and structures. Even in these cases, however, the wartime writings of African American journalists suggest that their perceptions of such a transnational racial union were also characterized by hierarchies – just as had been the case for earlier proponents of what has sometimes been described as "Black Nationalism."

These cultural and racial hierarchies were widely accepted by African American troops. While they agreed "there was little difference" between the "facial appearance of the native of Fiji and New Caledonia and that of the American Negro," black servicemen were astounded by the "abject

---

[118] Hicks, "This Is My Island."

[119] Fletcher P. Martin, "Describes Life of Our Boys in Pacific's New Caledonia," *Atlanta Daily World*, December 31, 1943.

[120] Fletcher P. Martin, "G.I.'s Poised to Blast Philippines, Just Ahead," *New York Amsterdam News*, September 9, 1944. See also "Race-Baiting Governor to Leave New Caledonia as Terror Charges Refuted," *New Journal and Guide*, January 1, 1944.

poverty" of native peoples.[121] Poverty was interpreted as one sign of the lack of development, or modernity, among Pacific island societies. And even when they acknowledged the natives' intelligence, African American servicemen referred frequently to the primitive nature of native societies and cultures: while "[s]ome" of the New Guinea natives, wrote Sergeant J. L. Hawkins, were "very intelligent," they were nonetheless "very primitive in their dress and customs."[122] Of all the pejorative stereotypes rendering the South Pacific "primitive," the association of the region with cannibalism was one of the most persistent. Noting that visiting the "very primitive" native communities of the Solomons "was like going back 10,000 years," Walter B. Sanderson explained that the inhabitants of the island group had only "recently converted from cannibalism."[123] Sharing Sanderson's views, black service personnel were frequently wary of Pacific Islanders. Explaining why she declined an opportunity to visit one New Guinea Island, Army nurse Prudence Burrell explained that the island in question was reputedly inhabited by "headhunters."[124]

Informed by such preconceptions, African American service personnel kept their distance from the indigenous populations of many Pacific islands. When black servicemen encountered the natives of New Guinea, recalled Adolph Newton, they "stared at each other." Conceding that he probably "looked as strange to them as they looked" to him, Newton noted that the best course of action was to leave the area quickly.[125] William Earl Lafayette's description of his unit's encounter with the natives of the Bismarck Archipelago, off the coast of New Guinea, hinted at the extent to which African Americans perceived themselves as intruders in an essentially alien environment: the natives, he noted, "would walk right through our area but there was no communication at all."[126] This was no meeting of equals in a transnational struggle against racism and colonialism.

The difficulties of communication described by Lafayette, most apparent in Melanesia and Micronesia but evident across the Asia-Pacific

[121] "Says Soldiers Restricted in Melbourne," *Journal and Guide*, October 17, 1942.
[122] Hawkins, cited in Christopher Paul Moore, *Fighting for America: Black Soldiers – The Unsung Heroes of World War II* (New York, NY: One World/Ballantine, 2005), 69.
[123] Sanderson, AFC/2001/001/76450, VHP-LoC. See also Calvin C. Miller, AFC/2001/001/74496, VHP-LoC; Edwards, AFC/2001/001/68079, VHP-LoC; Douglas Hall, "Wounded Sgt. Tells of Fight with Japs," *Afro-American*, July 7, 1943.
[124] Prudence Burrell, AFC/2001/001/4747, VHP-LoC.
[125] Newton, *Better than Good*, 51.
[126] William Earl Lafayette, AFC/2001/001/43118, VHP-LoC.

Theater, remained a problem for the duration of the war. Military authorities made some efforts to surmount those linguistic barriers – James A. David was just one black veteran who recalled being given phase books for "every place" where his unit spent time – but only a tiny handful of African Americans learned the local languages and dialects.[127] Referring to these linguistic shortcomings, Army Chaplain David S. Harkness noted that while the Philippine tribesmen among whom he was based learned "very quickly" how to "speak the English language," those tribesmen told him "humorously, 'You are very slow to speak our language.'"[128]

Notwithstanding those linguistic differences, when black service personnel felt it safe to do so they often defied warning against mingling with native peoples. Harry W. Leavell's experiences were typical of many African American servicemen. Having secured a pass to visit a local village on the island of Guam, Leavell recalled being offered octopus to eat. The novelty of such a delicacy was not lost on Leavell, but along with his sense of difference from the native population, he praised them for their honesty and courage – particularly the sacrifices they made on behalf of George Tweed, a US Navy radioman who, with the assistance of the Guamanians, eluded capture by the Japanese from December 1941, until his rescue in July 1944. Yet Leavell remained wary of the locals, particularly after two men in his unit who had gone "AWOL" had been killed after trying "to break into some native's village." If the runaway soldiers had anticipated that the natives would provide refuge from the military police, their gruesome demise – one soldier was allegedly decapitated, and the other "shot in the middle of the head with a .45" – was a stark lesson for other black servicemen. If those men's fate was not sufficient to encourage a cautious relationship with Islanders, the discovery of "a whole bunch" of Japanese bodies buried near the village evidenced the local population's hostility toward wartime interlopers – Allied and Japanese alike.[129]

Despite such stories, African Americans' curiosity frequently led them to seek out local populations. This was even the case for African American women, who presumably had most to fear from so-called "primitive"

[127] James A. David, AFC/2001/001/56158, VHP-LoC. See also "ARC Worker Tells of Pacific Life," *Pittsburgh Courier*, March 31, 1945.
[128] "Chaplain Harkness Writes 'Briefs of the Philippines,'" *Atlanta Daily World*, June 30, 1945.
[129] Leavell, AFC/2001/001/2658, VHP-LoC. See also George R. Tweed, *Robinson Crusoe, USN: The Adventures of George R. Tweed, RM1C, on Jap-held Guam*, as told to Blake Clark (New York, NY: Whittlesey House, 1945).

tribesmen. Ignoring orders to avoid "any contact whatsoever" with the natives living near the base of the 268th Station Hospital, Prudence Burrell remembered the nurses sneaking out to the local village, to satisfy their curiosity regarding "what was going on."[130] Additionally, in spite of reports of collusion between native peoples and the Japanese, there were occasions when African Americans sought to help – materially, and sometimes spiritually – people they regarded as less advanced than themselves.[131] African Americans were sometimes represented as intermediaries between the West and those deemed uncivilized. "Somewhere in India," it was reported in September 1943, a "Negro Engineers' Orchestra" had "brought boogie woogie to the Naga headhunters." While the Nagas' "only music" had previously been "the rhythm of war drums," they had reportedly taken "to jive like natural-born hepcats."[132]

Cultural interactions such as these were a means of smoothing the path for African Americans' attempts to help Pacific Islanders. William B. Rice, Jr., a black medic, sought to alleviate the wartime sufferings endured by Solomon Islanders. Emphasizing his personal responsibility to provide help – that was "what a medic is supposed to do" – Rice also stressed the underlying humanity of both groups. "God made all nations, and races of all people," he recalled.[133] Humanity might have had common origins, but in Rice's telling, African Americans embraced the wider American self-perception of the United States as a benefactor for other nations, and of American military power as an irresistible force carrying civilization, and by implication, Christianity, to otherwise benighted peoples. Amid reports that Pacific Islanders regarded African Americans as the most "civilized" or "advanced" of the nonwhite "races" – "the people of our islands," recalled Chief Vissuk of Vanuatu, worshipped "black American soldiers" as "gods" or "deities" who "had come to deliver us from the European devils who had ruled us" – it was unsurprising that some black servicemen were happy to believe that the peoples of the Pacific region considered African Americans as "the Prince of the Black Races."[134]

---

[130] Prudence Burrell, AFC/2001/001/4747, VHP-LoC. Howard Leslie Gregg, stationed on the Admiralty Islands, summed up the official policy regarding interactions with the local population: "we wasn't (sic) allowed to fraternize with them." See Gregg, AFC/2001/001/76549, VHP-LoC.

[131] For an example of a report of natives assisting the Japanese, see "Native Spies Betray Allies," *Pittsburgh Courier*, May 22, 1943.

[132] *Yank Down Under*, September 24, 1943.

[133] William B. Rice, AFC/2001/001/05205, VHP-LoC.

[134] Vissuk, cited in Moore, *Fighting for America*, 77; L. J. Taggart, "What the People Say: Natives of S. W. Pacific Area Appreciate American Negro," *Chicago Defender*, June 30, 1945.

African Americans' sense of difference from local populations extended beyond the South Pacific. By war's end tens of thousands of blacks had spent time in the Philippines, which had been part of the American empire since the end of the nineteenth century. Shaped by that unequal political relationship, African Americans' views of Filipinos also reflected the racial values evident in blacks' relations with other peoples across the Asia-Pacific Theater. Lauding the Filipinos' courage in the face of Japanese aggression and occupation, African Americans considered Filipinos less primitive – and more "Americanized" – than other foreign peoples encountered during the course of the Pacific War. Robert Quarles's description of the "wonderful" Filipinos was revealing. Impressed by the linguistic skills and social acumen of the young Filipinos, Quarles "really enjoyed" his time in the Philippines. Part of the credit, he implied, for what he labeled the Philippines' "civilization," could be attributed to the presence of Americans – including African Americans – in the colony.[135]

Quarles's statement suggested that even as the black press and leadership denounced US colonial authority over the Philippines, African Americans accepted many of the racial assumptions that underpinned that colonial endeavor. These assumptions were evidenced by African Americans' descriptions of Filipino stewards serving on board US Navy vessels. Like African Americans, Filipinos were relegated to the role of steward, or messman. Harold E. Ward, an African American whose "attitude" led to him being thrown "out of the ward room" of the USS *San Francisco*, believed the Filipino stewards "had a different philosophy." Coming from the poverty of the Philippines, he wrote, the Filipinos were grateful for the opportunity to establish "a career in the United States Navy" – however humble it might seem to Americans, of any race. "Being a servant," noted Ward, "didn't bother" the Filipinos. But what Filipinos regarded as satisfactory, Ward averred, was not good enough for "us black kids," many of whom "were angry." "[W]e were Americans for God's sake," and [s]upposed to be citizens," he insisted.[136] As Ward described it, the differences – political and cultural – between Filipinos and African Americans, who positioned themselves first and foremost as Americans, were clear.

African Americans stationed in Asia, like those serving in the Pacific, were struck by their differences from those they encountered. They

---

[135] Robert Quarles, AFC/2001/001/80199, VHP-LoC.
[136] Harold E. Ward, AFC/2001/001/76010, VHP-LoC.

also discerned differences between "natives" of the "South Pacific" and "Asiatics."[137] As ever, the categories of "race" and "nationality" proved problematic, as "Asiatic" included allies as well as enemies. The Japanese were examples of "bad" Asiatics, but, building on sympathies articulated during the prewar period, African Americans commended the positive characteristics of the Chinese. Those sympathies rested in part on images of toiling, if often ignorant peasants, with little or no understanding of political matters, who were stoically resisting the Japanese invaders. Yet African Americans also recognized that Asians – including the Chinese – were in some respects more enlightened, particularly on questions of race, than white Americans who purported to be "civilized." In December 1943, the *Afro-American* reported that Chinese blood banks, unlike their American counterparts, did not "segregate colored blood." The "whole idea of keeping separate blood banks for peoples of different races," stated Dr. Chien Lung Yi, was "ridiculous."[138]

African Americans' relations with Indians also defy straightforward characterization. While African Americans were reportedly "highly popular" with Indians, such descriptions served principally to highlight the differences between black Americans and Asians.[139] Conscious of those differences, African Americans' disdain for the material conditions under which Asians and Pacific Islanders lived shaped their perceptions of both groups. While black leaders and correspondents reflected on the political inequalities that underpinned the destitution of colonized subjects, African American servicemen were struck principally by the poverty and squalor they confronted. Louis Douglas, stationed in India during 1944, recalled that the people were "poor," and "living and sleeping on the ground."[140] Misunderstanding could be mutual. Charles Pitman, serving with the 518th Trucking Battalion, was stationed in Bombay during the latter stages of the war. During his time in India, Pitman encountered "East Indian" troops, serving under British command, who "would have nothing to do" with African American servicemen. The Indians' "cool" response, he explained, could be attributed to two factors: perceiving African Americans through the lens of the "caste system," with its contempt for "untouchables," the Indians regarded black Americans as "outcasts"; that contemptuous attitude, moreover, was fueled by demeaning stories about African Americans.

---

[137] "They Prefer to Fight for Uncle Sam," *Pittsburgh Courier*, August 7, 1943.
[138] Richard R. Dier, "Chinese Blood Bank Has No Jim Crow," *Afro-American*, December 4, 1943.
[139] "Race Troops Win Friends in India," *Pittsburgh Courier*, November 21, 1942.
[140] Louis Douglas, AFC/2001/001/50356, VHP-LoC.

However, when the Indians encountered African Americans and learned they "were not like the lies" that had been used to belittle them, they "became friendly" toward the visiting black troops. "[I]t ended well," Pitman concluded.[141] Besides highlighting African Americans' endeavors to correct racist misconceptions, Pitman's experiences affirmed that the racial hierarchies exposed and tested by the Pacific War were more nuanced than a simple demarcation between "black" and "white." While African Americans and the nonwhite peoples of the Asia-Pacific understood the wartime challenges to racism and colonialism in distinct ways, each recognized that the Pacific War marked a watershed between the old, colonial order, and a postwar world based on very different political systems and racial assumptions.

African Americans in the Pacific Theater were both victims of American racism, and agents of America's expanding international power. Contending that American racism was undermining US claims to be a force for international freedom, African Americans believed that as well as defeating Japan, the Allies' wartime mission should extend freedom and democracy. African Americans were thus embarking on a transnational war of liberation. Not only was the United States a tardy, or even reluctant liberator – the nation had stayed out of the war, at least formally, as Japan had invaded China, and occupied other parts of Asia – but African Americans knew that the notion of American "freedom" was itself a matter of ongoing dispute. African Americans were part of a military force and alliance whose interactions with Pacific Islanders and Asians reflected racial values and racist practices that were at odds with the principles for which the United States claimed to be fighting. That contradiction was evident on many levels. Even as the United States declared it was fighting the war to guarantee principles of freedom and democracy, African Americans across the Pacific Theater found themselves confronting the entrenched racism of the American military machine. The individual and institutionalized racism of the US military could seem overwhelming: the tasks assigned to African Americans, and the military regulations and justice to which they were subjected, laid bare the contrast between American rhetoric and the realities of American racism. This had profound implications, as the illusion of American unity was exposed vividly by African Americans' military service. Notwithstanding the upsurge of patriotism prompted by Japan's attack at Pearl Harbor, many African Americans regarded the rhetoric of American unity – so important to

[141] Pitman, cited in Motley, ed., *Invisible Soldier*, 120.

wartime propaganda, both on the home front and internationally, and an intrinsic element of the mythology of the "Greatest Generation" – as a chimera.

Yet, in spite of the racism and tedium associated with military service across the Pacific Theater, African Americans found opportunities, learned skills, forged friendships, and encountered peoples and places that could be both exotic and exciting. In the process, they laid the groundwork for a renewed push for civil rights, and played a part in shaping the post-war challenge to transnational racism. Grasping opportunities to demand and secure their own rights, African Americans' wartime encounters with native peoples across the Pacific Theater also highlighted the challenges standing in the way of an imagined community of nonwhite peoples. As the next chapter reveals, the tensions between race and nationality were further reflected in, and shaped by, the wartime interactions between African American men and the women they encountered – or did not encounter – during the Pacific War.

CHAPTER 3

A Sexualized South Seas?

Intersections of Race and Gender in the Pacific Theater

War has traditionally been regarded as a quintessentially masculine endeavor. Yet while the battlefield remains largely a masculine space, and although some historians continue to argue that men on the frontlines thought little about women or sex, a bifurcated division between a "masculine" battlefield and a "feminine" home front misrepresents the complex relationship between war and gender. Across the Asia-Pacific Theater during World War Two, that vexed relationship was further complicated by the politics of race, as African Americans confronted a military system that labeled and treated black sexuality as inherently deviant. Reflecting long-standing fears in American culture, amid a war fought across a region long associated with notions of sensual freedom, it was widely assumed that black servicemen would be incapable of controlling their physical urges. As well as imperiling the moral and physical welfare of white women, black sexuality was considered a threat to white masculine hegemony. At the back of many white Americans' minds was an ever-present fear that an inability to control African American sexuality anywhere constituted a threat to the authority of white men everywhere. Accordingly, military authorities' fears of unrestrained black sexuality – a racially determined moral panic of sorts – meant African American servicemen were subject to greater restriction and censure than their white compatriots.

Across the Pacific Theater these anxieties and policies affected the everyday lives of black military personnel, sometimes in seemingly minor ways, and sometimes dramatically – such as when military justice was applied to black servicemen accused of transgressing conventions concerning the line between race and sex. These military-judicial inequalities were evident in all theaters of war, but the powerful alchemy of race and sex that characterized Western images of the "South Seas" meant these issues were played out with a particular potency across the Pacific Theater.

White fears of African American sexuality extended beyond concerns regarding interracial sex. Worried that romantic or carnal relations between black servicemen and indigenous women would antagonize the local communities providing invaluable labor to Allied forces, military authorities sought to forefend such liaisons. There was, therefore, a significant distinction between authorities' attempts to prevent African Americans from interfering with white women, and their efforts to restrict black servicemen's interactions with indigenous women: the former was born principally of concern for the sexual welfare of white women, and a determination to not offend white Americans' sensibilities regarding interracial sex; the latter reflected a pragmatic attempt to ensure a ready supply of native labor. The first imperative was principally moral; the latter principally military. Caught between these concerns, and long-standing images of the South Seas as a site of sexual freedom, African Americans negotiated the complex wartime relationship between gender and race. In treating gender as a subject, as well as a means of analysis, this chapter also suggests that the paucity of African American women across the Pacific Theater was not just a source of frustration for black servicemen – it also complicated matters for the handful of black women deployed to the region.

Central to African Americans' preconceptions of the Pacific Theater were images of a sexualized "South Seas," untainted by the constraints of "Western civilization." Perceptions of indigenous women were framed by the glamorized images presented by Hollywood's movies. While these representations said more about Westerners' views of what they wanted the South Seas to be than they did about the realities of the cultures and geography of the region, they exercised a powerful pedagogic influence over Allied service personnel.[1]

African Americans were complicit in Western misrepresentations of the Pacific region. Prior to Pearl Harbor, black newspapers frequently published advertisements for South Seas movies which, during the 1930s constituted a distinct and popular cinematic genre. Exploiting the same

---

[1] For an analysis of this issue, refer to Sean Brawley and Chris Dixon, *Hollywood's South Seas and the Pacific War: Searching for Dorothy Lamour* (New York, NY: Palgrave Macmillan, 2012). See also Christina Sharon Jarvis, "The Male Body at War: American Masculinity and Embodiment during World War II" (PhD dissertation, Pennsylvania State University, 2000), 181–9.

tropes as those used in the white press, these advertisements relied on the well-tried combination of sensuality and adventure to appeal to black moviegoers. The 1941 film *South of Tahiti* (originally titled *Captive Wild Woman*) was typical of the South Seas genre. As an advertisement in the *Chicago Defender* described it, *South of Tahiti* was "the screen's new blaze of excitement," replete with "pagan love and pagan hates."[2] Two years later, another South Seas spectacular, *White Savage*, was commended for its "romance, action and thrilling highlights." Noting that the movie's "highlights" included "native festivals and rituals," an anonymous reviewer in the Baltimore *Afro-American* declared that *White Savage* "easily heads the procession of movie hits."[3]

South of Tahiti and *White Savage* featured the sensual allure of Maria Montez. But it was another actress, Dorothy Lamour, who became synonymous with the South Seas cinematic genre. Lamour's depictions of pulchritudinous Islander women – pure, and unrestrained by Western notions of modesty or morality – were fundamental to the popularity of South Seas films. While these generic representations overlooked the significant physical and cultural distinctions between women of different Pacific regions, by the time the United States entered World War Two Lamour had become an icon, conjuring images of South Seas romance and sensuality.

Lamour's appeal transcended racial distinctions within the United States. Her films were publicized widely in black newspapers, and she remained a significant figure of attention among African Americans during World War Two. The *Chicago Defender*'s review of the 1942 film, *Beyond the Blue Horizon*, referred directly to Lamour's physical beauty. Emphasizing that a "pair of twin pleasers" was "coming to the screen," the reviewer's rapturous endorsement of the "flaming saga of love and adventure" reflected his enthusiasm for the "exotic Dorothy Lamour, waif of the wild."[4] Lamour's career, however, had a deeper significance, as her "glamourous" feminine appeal, resting principally on her depictions of a sexualized South Seas, was appropriated by civilian and military authorities to become part of the wartime patriotic project, for black as well as white Americans. Lamour's support for the US war effort attracted considerable publicity in the African American press, and

---

[2] See advertisement *Chicago Defender*, February 14, 1941.
[3] See also "'White Savage,' Lavish Thriller," *Afro-American*, June 12, 1943.
[4] See "Dorothy Lamour is Star of Regal's Friday Feature," *Chicago Defender*, October 10, 1942. For an earlier reference to Lamour, see the advertisement for *Moon over Burma*, published in the *Atlanta Daily World*, April 6, 1941.

morale-boosting films in which she starred, such as the 1942 musical *Star Spangled Rhythm*, were advertised widely in black newspapers.[5]

Although South Seas films typically presented dark-skinned characters in one-dimensional, stereotypical terms, there is no evidence that film-makers, or those charged with advertising the genre, sought to amend those images for black audiences. Presumably, filmmakers and advertisers assumed African Americans would not be insulted by simplistic or demeaning misrepresentations of dark-skinned Islanders. Presumably, too, they imagined black audiences viewing those films would do so as Americans, rather than as people joined by race with the nonwhite characters depicted in South Seas movies. In this way, national allegiances were presumed to be more powerful than an imagined racial connection between African Americans and the indigenous inhabitants of the Pacific Theater. Furthermore, while many of the characters presented as "Islanders" were depicted as racially indistinct – they were not "white," but they were often not "black" like African Americans – they were typically portrayed as "primitives," untouched by Western civilization.[6]

Hollywood's images of the South Seas were instrumental in shaping black servicemen's expectations of the Pacific Theater. For thousands of African American servicemen, their first direct encounter with Pacific womanhood occurred in Hawaii. Although the African American press reported that black servicemen were "pleasantly surprised" by the "large numbers of dark-skinned girls they saw on the sidewalks of polyglot Honolulu," Hawaii was far from a sensual or sexual nirvana.[7] Rather, responding to fears that black servicemen "would undoubtedly mix with the Hawaiians," and worried that such intermingling would damage relations between the local population and US forces, Hawaiian and military authorities sought to physically segregate African American troops and sailors from the local women.[8] The exigencies of war meant these efforts

[5] See the untitled article and photograph in the *Cleveland Call and Post*, May 16, 1942; advertisement for *Star Spangled Rhythm*, *Atlanta Daily World*, February 13, 1943. See also "Louise Beavers Presents Big Screen Stars," *Pittsburgh Courier*, February 7, 1942.

[6] See Susan Courtney, *Hollywood Fantasies of Miscegenation: Spectacular Narratives of Gender and Race, 1903–1967* (Princeton, NJ: Princeton University Press, 2005), 127; Brawley and Dixon, *Hollywood's South Seas and the Pacific War*, 22–3.

[7] "Negro Soldiers May Prove Key to South Seas Policing Following War," *Atlanta Daily World*, June 9, 1943.

[8] Major General George V. Strong, Memorandum for the Assistant Chief of Staff, O.P.D. Subject: Utilization of Negro Troops in Friendly Foreign Territory, June 17, 1942, Office of the Director of Plan and Operations, General Records – Correspondence, 1942–1945, 291.2, Box 472, NM84, Entry 418, RG 165, Records of the War Department General and

were never completely successful, but for the duration of the conflict military authorities continued to strive to separate black servicemen from local women. While African American men were generally blamed when such policies failed, women were also held responsible for preserving the lines of sexual-racial segregation. As late as October 1945 the *Chicago Defender* reported that a female civilian working for the US Navy in Honolulu had lost her job "because she had been seen associating with a Negro sailor."[9]

Adding to their frustrations, when black servicemen did encounter Hawaiian women, they were frequently disappointed. The reality could not live up to the fantasy. Articulating these disappointments, African Americans referred specifically to the iconography of the South Seas popularized by Hollywood. "Needless to say," recalled Leon Allison Fraser, "we were not greeted with the usual ceremony of pretty girls putting a Lei around your neck." "There were no grass skirts and hula dancers to be seen," he noted, "unless you paid an admission to see an Island performance." Confirming Fraser's lament that there "was very limited fraternization" with the locals, many Hawaiian women were indifferent to the black servicemen in their midst.[10] Others expressed apprehension about mingling with African Americans. Often-exaggerated stories of rapes committed by black servicemen made many Hawaiian women – of all races – nervous about socializing with black servicemen.[11] Marine Norman R. Payne recalled that when his unit visited a dance hall in Honolulu, where men paid ten cents for each dance, the women "wouldn't dance with a nigger."[12] Black servicemen learned early that the Pacific Theater was not the sexual idyll of South Seas lore.

Like other servicemen, many African Americans were willing to pay for sexual services they could not procure freely. Noting that until "the Army padlocked the bawdy houses, Honolulu was a prostitute's paradise," one

---

Special Staffs, National Archives and Records Administration, College Park, Maryland (NARA). See also Marcus Alphonso Cranford, AFC2001/001/43075, Veterans History Project Collection, American Folklife Center, Library of Congress, Washington, DC (VHP-LoC).

[9] "Navy Fires Hawaiian Girl Seen with Negro Sailor," *Chicago Defender*, October 20, 1945.

[10] Leon Allison Fraser, AFC/2001/001/5184, VHP-LoC. See also Perry E. Fischer and Brooks E. Gray, *Blacks and Whites Together through Hell: U.S. Marines in World War II* (Turlock, CA: Millsmont Publishing, 1994), 43.

[11] Beth Bailey and David Farber, "The 'Double-V' Campaign in World War II Hawaii: African Americans, Racial Ideology, and Federal Power," *Journal of Social History* 26, no. 4 (1993): 827.

[12] Norman R. Payne, AFC/2001/001/49177, VHP-LoC.

black correspondent remarked at war's end that the women working in the wartime brothels of Hawaii had provided many American servicemen's first sexual encounters.[13] "What I saw there was hard to believe," recalled one black Navy veteran. Servicemen "were standing in long lines, waiting their turns to enter houses of prostitution. I had never seen anything like that in my young life."[14] If the ready availability of prostitutes was a new experience for black servicemen, the racism they encountered in Honolulu's brothels was depressingly familiar. Although some brothels catered for black as well as white servicemen, others enforced a color bar replicating those in place in brothels in the United States.[15] Amid the conflicting cultural and commercial imperatives associated with the wartime sex trade, black servicemen were thereby reminded that the color of their skin was more important than the color of their money.

The romantic and sexual disappointments experienced by African American servicemen in Hawaii portended a deeper disillusionment with the Pacific. That disillusionment reflected the disjunction between Hollywood's images of the sexualized South Seas, and the realities of gender relations across the Pacific region. As one observer noted bluntly at the conclusion of the Pacific War, the "island women" willing to "associate" with servicemen were "far too few, and not very attractive."[16] Dorothy Lamour remained a referent point for many servicemen, whose disenchantment with the Pacific region was sometimes attributed to "Dorothy Lamour Syndrome."[17] Although servicemen's references to Lamour were not based solely on her sensual allure – black Marine Bill Downey expressed disappointment that the physical geography of the Polynesian island of Funafuti was nothing like what he had "seen in the Dorothy Lamour movies" – the Hollywood actress continued to be associated with sexualized images of the Pacific.[18]

African Americans' descriptions of indigenous women highlighted the ambiguities of racial and national identity arising from the sexualized

[13] Waller B. Fleming, "American Jim-Crow Policy Sprouting Roots in Hawaii," *Pittsburgh Courier*, December 22, 1945.

[14] William Allison, interview published in Glenn A. Knoblock, *Black Submariners in the United States Navy, 1940–1975* (Jefferson, NC: McFarland & Co., 2005), 262.

[15] "In Hawaii," *Afro-American*, August 14, 1943. Black steward's mate Eddie Will Robinson recalled that "the madam at a house of iniquity" in Honolulu "said they did not service blacks." See Robinson, cited in *The Invisible Soldier: The Experience of the Black Soldier*, ed. Mary Penick Motley (Detroit, MI: Wayne State University Press, 1975), 112.

[16] Charley Cherokee, "National Grapevine," *Chicago Defender*, November 10, 1945.

[17] See Brawley and Dixon, *Hollywood's South Seas and the Pacific War*, Chapter 3.

[18] Bill Downey, *Uncle Sam Must Be Losing the War: Black Marines of the 51st* (San Francisco, CA: Strawberry Hill Press, 1982), 167.

images that were so essential to Westerners' perceptions of the region. Black servicemen occasionally encountered native women who were more Westernized than anticipated. Arthur Busby, Sr., was surprised to discover that some Guamanian women "had high-heeled shoes, stockings, dresses, and umbrellas."[19] In other instances, indigenous women were depicted in terms reminiscent of scriptwriters' characterizations of Lamour and others who had played the part of South Seas womanhood. Writing from New Guinea in 1943, black reporter Joseph "Scoop" Jones referred to a "half-caste feminine beauty, who somehow reminded one of Dorothy Lamour in one of her tropical pictures." Describing his subject as "really something to look at," and detailing her physical appearance in close, almost voyeuristic detail, Jones left no doubt that native women were worldlier, and more enterprising, than many Americans had assumed:

> A lengthy wave of straight brunette hair falling down her back, skin with a sun-tan texture, blue eyes, a coca-cola waistline, about five feet in height and maybe 114 pounds. Unusual for a native, she wore a dress, blue and white checkered, a flower in her hair, a flowered wreath around her ankle and barefoot ... She had learned how to look demure, seductive and alluring.[20]

If Jones's description was accurate, the woman he encountered in New Guinea was self-consciously playing a "part," by conforming to the images she imagined servicemen expected of indigenous women. It is entirely possible that the woman Jones described was not complicit in that process, and that his depiction is most revealing as an affirmation of the pedagogic influence of Hollywood, and the enduring power of the South Seas fantasies it encouraged – even during wartime. For Jones, the image of New Guinean womanhood with which he was most comfortable, and which he presented as an idealized "type," was thoroughly Americanized and far removed from most servicemen's impressions of native women. Nothing better symbolized the commodification and commercialization of Islander womanhood than Jones's association of his subject's figure with Coca Cola: in this way a ubiquitous emblem of the wartime expansion of American capitalism and culture was appropriated as a symbol of the sexual fantasies of African Americans' imagined South Seas.[21]

[19] Arthur Howard Busby, Sr., AFC/2001/001/48744, VHP-LoC.
[20] Scoop Jones, "New Guinea Girls, Hep to Jive, Don Blouses to Foil Cameraman," *Afro-American*, October 2, 1943.
[21] Across the various theaters during World War Two Coca Cola constructed forty-four bottling plants. See Max Hastings, *All Hell Let Loose: The World at War 1939–1945* London: Harper Press, 2011), 349.

Jones's description also raised the question of difference among indigenous women of the Pacific. The homogenized images of the region's societies and racial groups presented by Western culture masked the significant
differences between the peoples of the Pacific. These distinctions – the
most notable of which was between Polynesians and Melanesians – were
fundamental to African Americans' disappointment with the indigenous
women they encountered across the Pacific Theater. Whereas Hollywood's
generic South Seas Islander woman was based, physically at least, on a
Polynesian "type," many black servicemen found themselves stationed in
Melanesia, where the inhabitants did not conform to the images that had
been sustained and popularized by Hollywood.

Despite the disjunction between servicemen's preconceived perceptions
of Pacific Islander womanhood, and the realities they encountered, the
African American press persisted in presenting images of Islander women
that were congruent with the South Seas tradition and fantasy. Although
these images were often flippant, and not intended to be read as literal
representations of Islander womanhood, they nevertheless relied upon
and reinforced longstanding misperceptions of a mythical South Seas. In
January 1942, as the first detachments of African American troops were
deployed to the Pacific, a *Chicago Defender* cartoon explicitly linked military service to the sexualized stereotypes of the South Seas. Highlighting
icons widely, if in some cases erroneously associated with the South Seas,
an American sailor gazes at a grass skirt-wearing Islander woman, who
is depicted leaning against a palm tree. Absent-mindedly peeling away
blades of grass from the woman's skirt, the sailor muses: "She loves
me ... She loves me not."[22] The following month the *Defender*'s cartoonist referred again to prevailing fantasies about the South Seas and took
an ironic swipe at servicemen's motives for joining the military. This cartoon depicted a soldier sitting on a beach. In spite of the presence of five
Islander women, two of whom are embracing the soldier, he asks grimly:
"I join the army to see the world and look where they send me."[23]

---

[22] Jay Jackson, "So What," *Chicago Defender*, January 17, 1942.

[23] Jay Jackson, "So What," *Chicago Defender*, February 14, 1942. In March 1943, the
Chicago *Defender* published a cartoon showing a soldier hiding in a tree, as two Island
women converse. "I think I heard that tree whistle" says one woman to the other. Another
cartoon, published in September 1943, depicted two black sailors admiring an Island
woman clad in a bikini top and the ubiquitous grass skirt. "Keep off the grass," says a
sign placed in front of the two sailors. See Jay Jackson, "So What," *Chicago Defender*,
March 3, 1943, and September 4, 1943.

Islander women frequently remained imagined objects of physical beauty and sexual allure for African American correspondents and cartoonists. In praising the physical characteristics of native women, the black press continued to rely on stereotypical images familiar to African Americans. In late 1944, black reporter Fletcher P. Martin stopped briefly in the Marshall Islands, in Micronesia. Stating that the women there were "more or less beautiful, depending on one's idea of beauty," Martin explained that the island group's inhabitants "have much in common with the Polynesians rather than the Melanesians." In case that was not sufficient to explain to his audience the physical characteristics of the local women, Martin invoked a figure with whom his readers were most certainly familiar. Although the African American performer Lena Horne "did not come from the Marshalls," wrote Martin, "her beauty is like that of a Marshallese."[24] Moreover, regardless of their cultural distance from Pacific Islanders, African Americans were not averse to appropriating the iconography of the mythical South Seas sensuality. In August 1944, under the banner "Native Maiden?," the *Cleveland Call and Post* published a photograph of the "lovely" Jannett Thompson, "garbed in a grass skirt sent to her from the South Pacific."[25]

Although this notion of mythical South Seas womanhood continued to exert a powerful appeal during the Pacific War, the absence of female company was a far more powerful imperative for African American servicemen. Indeed, although the black guitarist and United Services Organization (USO) performer Chauncey Lee claimed that military audiences were "not overly partial to women performers," the evidence from African American troops and sailors serving in the South Pacific – including from Lee himself, who conceded that servicemen "naturally like to see women performers" – suggests otherwise.[26] In addition, while Adolph Newton's observation that "the lack of available women" was having "an effect on the men" applied to servicemen of all races, and although relatively few Allied women were stationed in the Pacific Theater, the problem was most acute for African Americans. Besides confronting entrenched white apprehensions regarding black sexuality, for African American troops the common servicemen's complaint concerning the

---

[24] Fletcher P. Martin, "Martin Describes Hawaii to New Guinea Plane Trip," *Afro-American*, November 11, 1944.

[25] "Native Maiden," *Cleveland Call and Post*, August 26, 1944. On white service personnel appropriating the grass skirt, see Brawley and Dixon, *Hollywood's South Seas*, 90–1.

[26] Chauncey Lee, "USO Camp Shows and the Soldier," *The Crisis*, February, 1944, 50.

absence of Allied women was compounded by the fact that only a handful of African American women were deployed to the Pacific Theater.[27]

This lack of female company for black servicemen drew the attention of African American leaders. Presenting a predictably upbeat assessment of the black contribution to the Allied war effort, Bishop John A.
Gregg of the African Methodist Episcopal Church identified one issue
that had repeatedly been brought to his attention during his 1943 tour of
the Pacific Theater: although black servicemen were "maintaining a high
morale," he noted, they sorely missed the company of American women.
Unsurprisingly, Gregg's report spoke in wholesome terms that avoided
direct reference to sexual desires. Hoping that the Red Cross could
arrange for "just one girl" to work in their club, one group of black servicemen assured Gregg that they did not "want to 'date' her." Just "having
her to see" was all they asked.[28] In reporting Gregg's summary of black
servicemen's views, *Chicago Defender* correspondent Harry McAlpin did
not explain whether references to "American women" pertained specifically to African American women. Yet the underlying point was clear:
reflecting a continuing objectification of womanhood, black servicemen's
disappointment that Island women were few in number, and did not conform to their Hollywood-fueled expectations, was compounded by the
absence of American women across the Pacific Theater.

Although there were few opportunities for black servicemen to express
their sexuality, military authorities remained anxious about the prospect
of such interactions. Central to these anxieties were concerns regarding
venereal disease. Any loss of manpower would adversely affect the war
effort, but military and civil leaders feared that reports of venereal disease among service personnel contradicted the idealized images of the US
military as a positive force, both in the role it was playing in protecting and
projecting American values, and in ensuring that servicemen were exemplars of virtuous American manhood. Questions of military efficiency were
in this way linked to moral concerns. Further complicating matters, the
"problem" of venereal disease across the Pacific Theater was racialized.
Although military commanders' concerns regarding sexually transmitted
diseases transcended racial distinctions – they also cautioned white

---

[27] Adolph Newton, *Better than Good: A Black Sailor's War, 1943–1945* (Annapolis, MD:
Naval Institute Press, 1999), 51. See also Fletcher P. Martin, "No Women, No Movies –
Lonely Soldier Talks to Dodo Birds," *Pittsburgh Courier*, January 1, 1944.

[28] Harry McAlpin, "'Just One Girl' Is All Boys in New Guinea Ask of Gregg," *Chicago
Defender*, September 11, 1943; E. F. Joseph, "Bishop Gregg Back from Tour of the
Pacific," *Afro-American*, August 28, 1943.

troops against sexual relations with native women, and worried that venereal disease would undermine the military effectiveness of all servicemen, regardless of color – it was commonly assumed that African American men found it more difficult to exercise restraint. Here was further evidence, in the eyes of military authorities, of the necessity of containing a rampant and contaminating black sexuality. Already skeptical of the ability of African American units to perform their military duties, white commanders considered the purported prevalence of venereal disease among African American service personnel as evidence of blacks' alleged moral laxity and inability to control their sexual urges. Consequently, while military authorities attempted to regulate, or even thwart sexual relations between Allied servicemen of any race and indigenous women, much of their attention was directed toward black servicemen.

Military authorities did not have to look far for evidence of the dangers of black sexuality. Within the US military rates of infection from venereal disease were higher among African American troops than their white counterparts.[29] In September 1942, prior to its deployment to the Pacific, the 93rd Infantry Division reported 107 cases of venereal disease, leading to a loss of 2,226 "man days from duty, two and a half times as many days as any other division then under Ground Forces control."[30] More generally, it was widely assumed that rates of infection among black units deployed to the Pacific Theater remained higher than among white troops.[31]

Military authorities' concerns regarding venereal disease among black service personnel across the Asia-Pacific Theater were informed by longstanding cultural constructs. Because the region had long been portrayed and perceived as a sensual paradise, unfettered by Western inhibitions and

---

[29] Among African Americans in the Army, fifty-four percent conceded that they had suffered from a venereal disease at some point in their lives. The comparable figure for white servicemen was fifteen percent. While 21 percent of black soldiers admitted to having contracted venereal disease during their service overseas, the figure for white troops was 8 percent. See Kenneth D. Rose, *Myth and the Greatest Generation: A Social History of Americans in World War II* (New York, NY: Routledge, 2008), 41. See also Samuel Stouffer, et al, *The American Soldier. Vol. 1: Adjustment during Army Life* (Princeton, NJ: Princeton University Press, 1949), 546.

[30] Ulysses Lee, *The Employment of Negro Troops* (Washington, DC: Office of the Chief of Military History, United States Army, 1966), 278.

[31] See Captain Arthur I. Thompson, *Venereal Disease – South Pacific Area* (1946), 5, in the Maurice C. Pincoffs Papers, United States Army Military History Institute, United States Army Heritage and Education Center, Carlisle, Pennsylvania (USAHEC); "Syphilis Incidence High among Draftees," *Pittsburgh Courier*, June 26, 1943; "Let the Army Help," *Chicago Defender*, February 5, 1944.

scruples, it was feared that servicemen deployed there would succumb to sexual temptations. Paradoxically, however, these fears were compounded by the contrary, negative depictions of the South Seas, which highlighted the dangers of a region widely regarded by Westerners as uncivilized or even "savage." Not for the first time, the concurrent appeal and savagery of the Pacific region was expressed as an amalgam of temptation and fear: black servicemen who were intimate with indigenous women risked contracting venereal diseases that imperiled their own health and jeopardized their military and moral mission as models of African American manhood.

Military commanders' concerns that venereal disease was a major problem extended beyond the geographic region generally associated with the "South Seas." Even the Philippines, which until early 1942 had been occupied by the United States, was regarded as contaminated. Adolph Newton recalled that prior to the arrival of large numbers of American servicemen in liberated Manila in 1945, "the Shore Patrol and the Military Police" were "sent in" in an attempt to prevent the infection of American servicemen. While Newton's claims that military authorities "locked up all the women and young girls and treated them all for venereal disease," and that 25,000 "females were treated that first day," should be treated skeptically, they underscore the common perception that venereal disease was a major problem among native peoples. For his part, Newton's belief that it "seemed like every Filipino woman had a venereal disease of some type" dissuaded him from engaging in sexual relations with the "laundry girl" he employed.[32]

American commanders feared that black servicemen would be incapable of the same restraint that Newton claimed he exercised in his dealings with local women. Military priorities were at odds with well-established cultural constructs. Disputing the images of sensual freedom depicted in various forms of popular culture, military officials contended that the native societies of the Pacific region were instead characterized by strict codes of morality. "Moral looseness," it was argued, was "practically unheard of." Tribal leaders, finding that their own concerns coincided with those of American military commanders, frequently decreed that native women should be "confined to the village." On some islands native authorities prohibited Allied servicemen from photographing, or even talking to a native "belle" unless her father had granted permission.[33]

[32] Newton, *Better than Good*, 76, 83.
[33] Jay Greulich, "GIs and Natives Get Along Happily But the Islanders Stick to Old Traditions," *Midpacifican*, March 15, 1944.

Lest such measures prove inadequate, US military authorities issued their own, very forthright warnings against fraternization with native women. The blunt caution issued to the black troops of the 93rd Infantry Division was typical: "Don't touch the women."[34]

Reaffirming the complexities and contradictions associated with notions of "race," military authorities' strictures against sexual liaisons between black servicemen and indigenous women of the Pacific region reflected longstanding anxieties regarding racial mixing. Distinguishing between various racial "types," Marine Major General Charles F. B. Price explained the risks of allowing black servicemen to engage in sexual relations with Pacific Islanders. Although "the mix of Polynesians with white race produces a very desirable type," he wrote, "the mixture with the Negro" – as "evidenced by the few types of cross breeds with individuals of the Melanesian types in the islands" – produced "a very undesirable citizen." Black troops, Price contended, should be confined to Micronesia, where "they can do no racial harm." While his statement that basing African Americans in Micronesia might "raise the physical and intellectual standards" of the native people there was a tacit concession that African Americans possessed some of the qualities of civilization which he believed were absent from Micronesia, more significant were the racial – and racist – assumptions underpinning his attempt at social engineering.[35] The Marine Corps was the most racially recalcitrant branch of the armed services, but Price's views provided telling insights into the racial values of many senior officers in the armed forces, and highlighted the complex racial politics of the Pacific War and the postwar world it was shaping.

Inevitably, efforts to discourage liaisons with native women had an effect on black servicemen. While Captain Hyman Samuelson noted that the African American soldiers under his command believed white officers were deliberately exaggerating fears of venereal disease in order to keep the native women to themselves, even the most dubious black servicemen acknowledged the impact of the military's medical-sexual scare campaign.[36] For Thomas A. Pincham, of the 865th Port Company, the "very

---

[34] See "Solomon Islands," in "Selected Documents of the Papers of Gen. Leonard Russell Boyd," Box 1, Hoover Institution Archives, Stanford University, Stanford, California.

[35] Price, letter to General Keller E. Rockey, Director of Plans and Policies, cited in Gerald Astor, *The Right to Fight: A History of African Americans in the Military* (Novato, CA: Presidio, 1998), 259.

[36] Samuelson, Diary entry, July 13, 1943, in *Love, War, and the 96th Engineers (Colored): The World War Two New Guinea Diaries of Captain Hyman Samuelson*, ed. Gwendolyn Hall (Urbana, IL: University of Illinois Press, 1995), 213.

graphic" films used by the military were effective: "As far as sex goes, you were discouraged from that because they would show you movies and once you saw those movies, you didn't want sex. I'll tell you that."[37] Recalling his time on Green Island, New Guinea, Linzey Donald Jones described the Army's attempts to keep soldiers "out of mischief." The troops, Jones remembered, "were frightened by films" showing "soldiers having sex with the natives" and "ending up with all kinds of diseases." While "all of this was a bunch of bullshit," Jones recalled, "no soldier was willing to take a chance that they might be true."[38]

Highlighting the perils of venereal disease was not the only means of discouraging African American troops from liaising with indigenous women. Rollins Edwards, stationed at Hollandia, New Guinea, was ordered by his company commander to neither look at nor touch the "bare-breasted" women living nearby. If he did so, he was warned, the native men would "hurt" him.[39] Playing on underlying assumptions regarding the line between "civilization" and "savagery," these cautionary tales highlighted American military and political authorities' confidence that while the United States represented the former, the indigenous people of the Pacific remained closer to the latter. Military commanders' use of such rhetorical devices to caution black troops against mingling with native women suggests that they assumed African Americans accepted such a hierarchy.

Irrespective of all the warnings to African Americans against fraternizing with indigenous women, such fraternizations did occur. Identifying and describing these relations is a challenging task for the historian. Although the subject of sexual relations was much written about during the Pacific War, much of that writing was didactic, and prescriptive, and should be treated with skepticism: public discussions of the most private aspect of human behavior frequently revealed little about the realities of sexual relations, or the private values and discourses that underpinned those relations. The records left by black servicemen are characteristically incomplete. These absences from the historical record perhaps explain some historians' insistence that servicemen, particularly those in combat roles, were not distracted by sexual matters.[40] Two points are relevant

[37] Thomas A. Pincham, AFC/2001/001/10503, VHP-LoC.
[38] Linzey Donald Jones, AFC/2001/001/38128, VHP-LoC.
[39] Rollins Edwards, AFC/2001/002/68079, VHP-LoC.
[40] See Gerald Linderman, *The World within War: America's Combat Experience in World War II* (New York, NY: Free Press, 1997), 191; Eric Bergerud, *Touched with Fire: The Land War in the South Pacific* (New York, NY: Penguin Books, 1997), 475.

here. First, across the Asia-Pacific Theater a majority of black servicemen were not in combat roles, and hence had more time and opportunities to form relations with local peoples. Second, the absence from the historical record of servicemen's reflections on sexual matters reflects the fact that while servicemen undoubtedly thought about sex, the moral conventions of the 1940s meant that outside the barracks or mess room, their references to their own sexual behavior and experiences were frequently sparse, and cloaked in euphemism. Black servicemen, already labeled as a sexual threat, and all too aware that the consequences of sexual indiscretions were far graver than they were for white troops, were even less likely to candidly discuss sexual matters.

Analysis of the sexual attitudes and behavior of black servicemen is further complicated by the perils of generalization: nearly 200,000 African Americans served in the Pacific Theater. Further, the disjunction between Hollywood's images of South Seas womanhood and the women encountered by servicemen was exacerbated because those women's sexual mores rarely lived up to the uninhibited images that had been presented and popularized by anthropologists, particularly Margaret Mead, during the 1930s.[41] As many servicemen soon realized, Hollywood and science had conspired to mislead.

It is unsurprising, then, that African American veterans' recollections of liaisons with indigenous women vary widely. Some men were adamant that such interactions did not take place. Sergeant Donald McNeil, of the 93rd Infantry Division, was unequivocal: during the war, he declared, there had been no fraternization with local women.[42] While McNeil's testimony apparently affirms that combat troops, preoccupied with matters of life and death, had neither the time nor inclination to contemplate the prospect of sexual relations with native women, frontline troops were not alone in denying that black servicemen avoided intimate relations with indigenous women. Carl Hendrick Sharperson noted that the men in his unit "didn't get excited" when they encountered native women, even when those women were nearly naked.[43] Adolph Newton's depiction of

---

[41] See Jeffrey Geiger, *Facing the Pacific: Polynesia and the American Imperial Imagination* (Honolulu: University of Hawaii Press, 2007), 38–9; Brawley and Dixon, *Hollywood's South Seas and the Pacific War*, 14, 17, 89; Brawley and Dixon, *The South Seas: A Reception History from Daniel Defoe to Dorothy Lamour*. Lanham, MD: Lexington Books, 2015, 148–51.

[42] Donald McNeil, World War II Veterans Survey. 93rd Infantry Division, Box 1, File 6684, 28, USAHEC.

[43] Carl Hendrick Sharperson, AFC/2001/001/67173, VHP-LoC.

New Guinean women highlighted the contrast between the images of South Seas womanhood popularized by Hollywood, and the realities encountered by African American troops. The native women, he recalled, looked like the native men, "except their hair was longer, and the older women's breasts hung down to their navels." And while the indigenous women's dress bore a resemblance to an item widely, if often erroneously associated with the South Seas – they were wearing "skirts made of some type of grass" – Newton felt no sexual attraction toward them. It "was a tossup," he wrote, "who was more fierce, the native men or the native women." Believing that the native men "were afraid" of the women, Newton did not "want to have anything to do with either one of them."[44]

Significantly, too, many indigenous communities across the Pacific Theater sought to protect the sexual virtue of their women by physically separating them from Allied troops. This self-imposed sexual segregation rested on assumptions that black as well as white American servicemen were potential sexual aggressors. Writing from New Guinea, Archie Dawson was disappointed that the local women had "all gone up into the hills."[45] Six decades after the end of the Pacific War, Anderson Ralph Copeland was asked whether there were "hula girls" on Guadalcanal. While that question revealed more about the ongoing power of South Seas mythology than it did about the indigenous societies of the Pacific, Copeland's reply was forthright: "There weren't none."[46]

Notwithstanding the absence of native women, however, and despite some black veterans' insistence that there was no interaction with indigenous women, there is evidence of such liaisons. In some cases, although native women were initially removed from areas where Allied troops were stationed, within a few weeks or months they had returned to their homes. There were also accounts of black troops actively seeking out native women. Reports from New Guinea suggested that African Americans "roamed about the villages" of the Hanuabada area, west of Port Moresby, "looking for women."[47] Conjuring images of groups of sexually predatory servicemen, such reports were almost certainly exaggerated; without discounting the possibility that some black servicemen actively sought out native women, African Americans' roamings might

[44] Newton, *Better than Good*, 51.
[45] "South Seas Islanders Aid the United States War Effort," *Afro-American*, August 28, 1943.
[46] Anderson Ralph Copeland, AFC/2001/001/62680, VHP-LoC.
[47] See Neville K. Robinson, *Villagers at War: Some Papua New Guinea Experiences in World War II* (Canberra: Australian National University, 1979), 103.

have been born of curiosity regarding the exotic women supposedly in their midst.

Contact between African Americans and native women could develop in a range of ways. Black servicemen, for instance, utilized the labor of native women. Although such practices contravened their attempts to separate servicemen from indigenous women, military commanders were often complicit in such labor practices. Depicting various ways in which "South Seas Islanders" were aiding the Allied war effort, in August 1943 the *Afro-American* reported that "aborigenese [sic] women" had been "recruited by the navy to help" American sailors. In drawing attention to indigenous women's contribution – and the accompanying photograph of the native women included two infants as well as a young child – the editors of the *Afro-American* evidently concluded that such practices were so commonplace across the Pacific Theater that they would not draw the ire of military commanders.[48] Rather, the publication of such images suggested that both the black press and US authorities hoped to highlight the amicable relations between black servicemen and local peoples.

Predictably, such contacts could – in some instances – lead to more intimate relationships. A study by Judith A. Bennett and Angela Wanhalla, tracing the life stories of children born to indigenous women and American servicemen stationed in the wartime Pacific Theater, affirms that sexual relationships between African American servicemen and Islander women occurred.[49] Black servicemen, and their officers, have also left evidence of such interactions. Captain Percy S. Roberts, of the 25th Infantry Regiment, affirmed that black troops under his command fraternized with the local women.[50] Significantly, Roberts's unit was deployed to Guadalcanal and New Guinea – places far removed from the Polynesian idyll that most closely approximated the mythical South Seas.

Roberts's testimony was vague – he did not detail the nature of the fraternization between the men in his unit and the local women – and such evidence of liaisons between black servicemen and indigenous women must be treated cautiously: while servicemen frequently presented themselves as morally virtuous, or avoided the subject altogether when recounting their wartime experiences, others exaggerated their

---

[48] "Chicago Boys Fight Japs in Guinea Jungle," *Afro-American*, August 22, 1942.
[49] See Judith A. Bennett and Angela Wanhalla, eds., *Mothers' Darlings of the South Pacific: The Children of Indigenous Women and U.S. Servicemen, World War II* (Dunedin: Otago University Press, 2016). See also Hazel M. McFerson, "'Part-Black Americans' in the South Pacific," *Phylon* 43, no. 2 (1982): 180.
[50] See Percy S. Roberts, World War II Veterans Survey, Box 1, File 5495, 25, 28, USAHEC.

sexual experiences. Some men's reflections on this issue varied according to their audience. Returning to Chicago after a year serving in the Pacific, Sergeant Lamont Estelle "admitted" – "claimed" might have been more apposite – to having "had some rather pleasant associations with a 'couple of Caledonian chippies.'" Once again, a familiar icon of the mythical South Seas featured: one of the women, whose picture Estelle "carried in his service cap," was "clad in the grass skirt of a hula dancer." Claiming that the woman in question had written to him, Estelle maintained that although "he wasn't in the least bit familiar with French, the language spoken on the island," he had "'mastered' the tongue when the Caledonian beauties came upon the scene."[51]

Other African American servicemen, even those who established relationships with native women, were stymied by the linguistic barriers to which Estelle referred. Reporting on a performance by the "first colored USO" troupe to tour the Pacific Theater, *Afro-American* correspondent Vincent Tubbs described an exchange between one black serviceman and his "native girl friend." The African American performers, the serviceman told his girlfriend, were "home folk." "[C]ompletely baffled," the young woman replied "No compre, no compre." The soldier, according to Tubbs, looked "in dismay" at his girlfriend.[52] Although Tubbs did not dwell on the nature of the relationship between the black soldier and his girlfriend, the implication was clear: theirs was a relationship with little prospect of long-term success. Even when there was a shared determination to oust the Japanese, the cultural and linguistic chasm between African Americans and Pacific Islanders remained significant.

Reports suggesting that African American troops hoped to establish permanent relationships with indigenous women must also be treated cautiously. Without discounting the intimacy underpinning at least some of the relationships that led to the children who are the subjects of Bennett's and Wanhalla's study, it is important to remember that such relations were rare. It is also likely that some children were a result of nonconsensual sexual relations. Other evidence is no more conclusive. While Sergeant Clarence Carter, a black veteran of the New Guinea campaign, reported in mid-1943 that "[q]uite a number of the boys" had "applied for the privilege of marrying" native women, he conceded that

---

[51] Sam Lacy, "Back after Year of Jap War Service," *Chicago Defender*, May 1, 1943.
[52] Vincent Tubbs, "Flesh Show in the Pacific," in *This Is Our War: Selected Stories of Six War Correspondents Who Were Sent Overseas by the Afro-American Newspapers* (Baltimore, MD: Afro-American Company, 1945), 54–5.

no marriages had taken place by the time he left New Guinea.[53] Similarly, while the *Afro-American* noted in June 1943 that "several" black troops had "married native women," and that the newly wed African Americans had "the sincere intention of staying on," the report was vague. The islands on which such marriages had taken place were not identified, and celebrating relationships between black Americans and native women was an important element of the report's wider claim of a powerful kinship between Pacific Islanders and African Americans. Romantic attachments were thus connected to a broader racial union envisaged by the *Afro-American*.[54]

Later in the war, when US forces returned to the Philippines, some – precise numbers are predictably elusive, but it was only a few – African American troops married local Filipino women. While Filipinos remained very much an "other" to black servicemen, the cultural gap between the two groups was less significant than in other areas where black troops encountered local women. African Americans, moreover, had been included among the US forces stationed in the Philippines from the late nineteenth century.[55] In practice, not only were marriages between African American servicemen and Filipinos rare, but when such unions did occur the bride typically represented the economically privileged class of Philippine society. Reporting in April 1945 on Warrant Officer Ellis D. Williams's wedding to Filipino Eugenia Diloy, Enoch P. Waters emphasized that Diloy was "from an upper middle class land-owning family."[56] Waters's analysis contrasted sharply with Vincent Tubbs's description of the social and cultural differences that had been evident when an African American soldier had taken his native girlfriend to the USO performance. In discussing black troops' interest in Filipino women, black commentators referred to social and sexual values familiar to, and valued by, African Americans. Black servicemen, noted Charles H. Loeb, were impressed by Filipino women's sense of morality. Explaining that some African American servicemen were contemplating marriage with Filipino women, Loeb used characteristically paternalistic language to

---

[53] See Douglas Hall, "Wounded Sgt. Tells of Fight with Japs," *Afro-American*, July 7, 1943.

[54] See "Our Soldiers Seen as Asset in Island Posts," *Afro-American*, June 6, 1943.

[55] On African American military service during the Philippine-American War, see Robert B. Edgerton, *Hidden Heroism: Black Soldiers in America's Wars* (Boulder, CO: Westview Press, 2001), 56–7; Gail Buckley, *American Patriots: The Story of Blacks in the Military from the Revolution to Desert Storm* (New York, NY: Random House, 2001), 153–9.

[56] Enoch P. Waters, "L.A. Soldier Marries Tiny Leyte Girl in Philippines," *Chicago Defender*, May 19, 1945.

suggest that "the Filipino carefully guards the morals of his women."[57] In common with indigenous peoples across the Pacific, Filipinos sought to protect their sexual and moral order. And while African Americans, like their white compatriots, imagined themselves as benevolent liberators, there were occasions when others perceived them less benignly.

Alert to those concerns, US commanders' moral and sexual anxieties were compounded by their fears of homosexuality. Although they worried about homosexual behavior among white servicemen, military authorities' underlying assumption that black sexuality was both deviant and dangerous made them particularly wary of homosexual behavior among African American servicemen.

Homosexuality remains an elusive subject for historians. As scholars have demonstrated, however, homosexual practices were more common than either wartime commanders, or popular memory, would suggest. While military authorities went to some lengths to exclude homosexuals from the armed forces, the "psychiatric" screening used to identify homosexual tendencies was ineffectual.[58] Furthermore, as in other circumstances where few women were present, some servicemen who did not identify – certainly not publicly, and perhaps not privately – as homosexual, engaged in practices widely considered "homosexual."[59] As Yorick Smaal has demonstrated, although "homosex" was for some men "revelatory," arousing "feelings and desires they had been unable or unwilling to explore at home," for others it "was simply a consequence" of the segregated wartime masculine environment in which they found themselves.[60] Regardless of the circumstances, military authorities considered any expression of homosexuality deeply troubling. Paradoxically, however, in seeking to separate African American men from women, military authorities allegedly – and inadvertently – encouraged homosexual behavior. Reporting from the island of Biak, off the northern coast of New Guinea, doctors stated that black servicemen, prohibited from

---

[57] Charles H. Loeb, "Filipinos Welcome Tan-Hued Yanks; Glad Freed of Japs," *Cleveland Call and Post*, February 24, 1945.

[58] See John D'Emilio, *Sexual Politics, Sexual Communities: The Making of a Homosexual Minority in the United States, 1940–1970* (Chicago, IL: University of Chicago Press, 1983), 24–5.

[59] See Kay Saunders, "In a Cloud of Lust: Black GIs and Sex in World War II," in *Gender and War: Australians at War in the Twentieth Century*, eds. Joy Damousi and Marilyn Lake (Cambridge: Cambridge University Press, 1995), 186.

[60] See Yorick Smaal, *Sex, Soldiers and the South Pacific, 1939–45: Queer Identities in Australia in the Second World War* (Basingstoke, Hampshire: Palgrave Macmillan, 2015), 11.

socializing with the handful of white women on the island, had arranged parties where many men dressed as women, and where "homosexual practices" were commonplace.[61]

Such reports were typically anecdotal, and served principally to affirm prevailing stereotypes. Yet the public and private records of African American military service across the Pacific Theater provides further evidence of homosexual activities. One form of evidence was the violence directed at those servicemen suspected of homosexual behavior. Writing from New Guinea, Private J. F. McDonald described an incident where two soldiers had beaten up a "pansy," who had allegedly been "having an affair."[62] In December 1942 Captain Hyman Samuelson noted that "many cases of sodomy" were "becoming prevalent" among the men of the 96th (Colored) Engineers stationed in New Guinea. This "sexual perversion," he recorded in the privacy of his diary, was a "serious thing." Although this behavior was "subject to trial by General Courts Martial," and notwithstanding "the trials and convictions," Samuelson believed "the practice seems to be spreading."[63] He provided no data to substantiate his comment, but he was deeply troubled by what he considered a serious moral lapse among his troops.

As well as punishing black servicemen whom they believed had engaged in acts of homosexuality, military authorities sought to remove such men from the service. If insufficient evidence could be brought to bear to bring charges, commanders could issue a "blue discharge." These discharges did not carry the same opprobrium as a dishonorable discharge, but servicemen issued with a "blue ticket" were denied many of the benefits provided to other veterans. Blue tickets were issued in disproportionate numbers to African American troops, prompting the *Pittsburgh Courier* to campaign against a sexual-racial "witch-hunt" that highlighted the deep "wells of prejudice in the Army's pattern of segregation."[64]

---

[61] See Allan Bérubé, *Coming Out under Fire: The History of Gay Men and Women in World War Two* (New York, NY: Free Press, 1990), 193.

[62] PFC J. F. McDonald to Miss Helen McDonald, March 22, March 22, 194[?], RG 496 Records of the General Headquarters, Southwest Pacific Area and United States Armed Forces, Pacific (World War II), 290/468/06, Box 456, NARA.

[63] Samuelson, Diary entry, December 19, 1942, in Hall, *Love, War, and the 96th Engineers*, 135.

[64] John H. Young, III, "Blue Discharges under Fire: GIs Denied Benefits," *Pittsburgh Courier*, October 20, 1945; Bérubé, *Coming Out under Fire*, 232–5; Phillip McGuire, *He, Too, Spoke for Democracy: Judge Hastie, World War II, and the Black Soldier* (New York, NY: Greenwood, 1988), 72.

While homosexuality offended many Americans' sensibilities during the 1940s, and although military authorities worried about black servicemen fraternizing with indigenous women, they fretted most about the prospect of liaisons between African American servicemen and white women. These anxieties underpinned their attempts to place boundaries – including, on occasions, physical barriers – between women and African Americans. Couched in the language of protection, and reflecting white concerns that all black men were potential sexual aggressors, the wartime sexual-racial segregation across the Pacific Theater served ultimately to preserve white masculine hegemony. The confinement of American servicewomen in New Guinea, for example, implemented "to prevent" these women being raped "by Negro troops," reflected widespread white anxieties regarding the moral welfare of white women.[65] Worried about the imminent arrival of a Women's Army Corps (WAC) unit, Lieutenant Jean E. Boyle anticipated "a mess" because there were significant numbers of African American troops already stationed in the region. "I fear it will mean trouble," she stated bluntly.[66] There were also instances when women were blamed for compromising the sexual order. Highlighting the widespread "anxieties about assertive female sexuality," the alleged willingness of white WACs, nurses, and other women to date black troops was regarded as evidence of their moral laxity.[67] As one officer noted, the paucity of African American women in the Pacific War zone was problematic, particularly since some white servicewomen – preferring the company of black servicemen – refused to "go out with the white soldiers." These anxieties also portended serious complications

---

[65] Mattie E. Treadwell, *United States Army in World War II: Special Studies. The Women's Army Corps* (Washington, DC: Office of the Chief of Military History, Department of the Army, 1954), 450. See also Herbert S. Ripley and Stewart Wolf, "Mental Illness among Negro Troops Overseas," *American Journal of Psychiatry* 103 (1947): 499; Judith A. Bennett, *Natives and Exotics: World War II and Environment in the Southern Pacific* (Honolulu: University of Hawai'i Press, 2009), 37–8.

[66] Boyle to Lieutenant Barbara Berens Hall, n.d., United States Forces Far East, G2 Theater Censors' Summaries of Censorship Violations, 1942–44, 290/45/12/2–3, Box T-1422, RG338, NARA.

[67] On these anxieties, see Leisa D. Meyer, "Creating G.I. Jane: The Regulation of Sexuality and Sexual Behavior in the Women's Army Corps during World War II," *Feminist Studies* 18, no. 3 (1992), 590. For a wartime expression of anxiety regarding female sexuality, see Lieutenant J. Baranowski to Miss Ann Baranowski, n.d., and Lieutenant J. Baranowski to Second Lieutenant Donald C. Bradley, n.d., both in RG338, US Forces Far East. G2 Theater Censors' Summaries of Censorship Violations, 1942–44, 290/45/12/2–3, Box T-1422, NARA.

after the war, if "black boys" expected white women to continue going "out with them."[68]

Although there were interactions between black servicemen and white Allied women in the Pacific Theater – William Anderson, Jr., for instance, remembered securing an autograph from actress and entertainer Marilyn Maxwell – African American servicemen's memories of their time in the Pacific affirm the near-complete absence of interactions with white servicewomen.[69] In part, the absence of such interactions reflected the widespread gender imbalance among Allied forces stationed in the Pacific Theater: white servicemen also lamented the paucity of Allied women across the region.[70] But, reinforced by strict rules against liaisons between black men and white women, and underpinned by a military culture that reflected rather than challenged prevailing views, the lines of racial-sexual segregation generally held fast across the Pacific Theater.

Those lines did not go unchallenged. On occasions, black servicemen mocked prevailing racial and gender conventions. Describing how the men in his unit played basketball each evening – "mostly to tire ourselves out so we could sleep" – Adolph Newton recalled that one of the men "started appearing on the basketball court in a pair of women's under-wear." This "attracted the attention of the few white nurses who drove past." Bemused, the nurses "would stop and look and laugh." "Soon we were all playing in women's underwear," wrote Newton. "Sometimes," he noted:

> there would be four or five jeeps with nurses and officers parked along the road watching us play. They got a kick out of seeing men in women's under-wear, and we got a kick out of looking at them, especially the nurses. Now we didn't have to go find women to look at; they were coming to see us.[71]

Newton's account can be read in a number of ways. It attests, of course, to black servicemen's desire for female company – albeit company that remained at a distance and which remained strictly off-limits. His narra-tive also suggests a voyeuristic intent on the part of the white nurses and officers who stopped to observe the performance by the men in Newton's unit. Even bearing in mind the long tradition of servicemen transgressing gender lines by donning women's clothing, Newton's account suggests

[68] "Morale Report," January 1944, file Theater Censor APO, SO1/501, Theater Censor, GHQ, SWPA, 290/45/12/4–5, Box T-1433, RG 338, NARA.
[69] Anderson, AFC/2001/001/73387,
[70] See Brawley and Dixon, *Hollywood's South Seas and the Pacific War*, 102–4.
[71] Newton, *Better than Good*, 52.

that the white audience interpreted the performance as evidence of African Americans' childishness, or of their willingness to demean themselves for scant gain. Such an interpretation complicates Newton's narrative, and affirms that the white officers and nurses he described were clinging to thoroughly unreconstructed racial views. The racial authority of the white audience was thereby reinforced. Yet Newton's account did not imply disempowerment: the black troops knew they were playing a role; they believed they were obtaining something in return for their performance; and presumably they enjoyed a laugh about it all.

While Newton presented interactions between black servicemen and white women in the Pacific Theater as a novelty, these interactions typically reflected the abiding white concerns regarding black sexuality. Indeed, describing "a helluva situation" when he found himself in the company of a white WAC who had breached curfew, Newton subsequently alluded to the underlying suspicions regarding African American men's designs upon white women.[72] Concerns that white women would be raped by black men remained powerful, and reports of sexual assault by African American servicemen were commonplace in American newspapers throughout the war.[73]

An accusation of rape from a white woman could lead quickly to suspicion falling on all African American men in a particular area. Carl Hendrick Sharperson described the aftermath of an alleged rape of a nurse by a black serviceman on Banika Island, in the Russell Islands. Attempting to identify the culprit, who had been scratched as he accosted the nurse, local military commanders required all African Americans stationed on Banika Island to strip naked and walk through a mess hall. "Every black on that island was inspected," recalled Sharperson.[74] Not all black servicemen experienced such humiliation, but racially based suspicions and indignities were deeply embedded in American military culture.

The most notorious allegations of sexual assault involving African American servicemen warrant analysis. While the victims of these alleged assaults were from different racial and national groups, each case highlighted common white assumptions regarding African American sexuality, and exposed the judicial inequalities stemming from those assumptions. Wartime allegations of rape by two black servicemen stationed in the

[72] Newton, *Better than Good*, 71.
[73] Robert F. Jefferson, *Fighting for Hope: African American Troops of the 93rd Infantry Division in World War II and Postwar America* (Baltimore, MD: Johns Hopkins University Press, 2008), 201.
[74] Carl Hendrick Sharperson, AFC/2001/001/67173, VHP-LoC.

French colony of New Caledonia attracted widespread publicity in the United States. Although there had been calls to prevent blacks from being deployed to New Caledonia – a 1942 report referred to "important political and psychological reasons for not utilizing Negro troops" there – the fears of racial collusion between black troops and local indigenes underpinning that report were outweighed by the exigencies of military deployment.[75] But the American, and particularly African American, presence in wartime New Caledonia also aroused anxiety among the expatriate French community. Concerned for the welfare of European women residents of the colony, and no doubt anxious about their authority over their colonial subjects, the French expressed particular concern regarding the sexual behavior of African American troops.[76] In 1943 two black soldiers serving with the 211th Port Battalion, Privates Frank Fisher and Edward R. Loury, were accused of raping Louise Mounien, a white New Caledonian woman. Alongside the potent intersection of race and sexuality, the Fisher and Loury case highlighted the cultural and linguistic complexities of wartime relations between the United States and its allies.

Fisher's and Loury's troubles began on May 2, 1943, as they traveled to a carnival in the New Caledonian capital of Noumea. En route, nineteen-year-old Fisher and twenty-year-old Loury met a white American officer in the company of Mounien. The officer allegedly asked Fisher and Loury whether they were interested in procuring sexual services from Mounien, for a fee. Confused after the officer and the woman had conversed in French, Fisher and Loury nonetheless proceeded to have sexual relations with Mounien – although it was unclear whether they paid to do so. Later, when Fisher and Loury returned to their camp, they were arrested and charged with raping Mounien. A court martial promptly convicted the two men, and sentenced them to life imprisonment. Following the confirmation of Fisher's and Loury's sentences by the Theater commander in Melbourne, the two young men were transported to the United States to begin their incarceration.[77]

[75] Major General George V. Strong, Memorandum for the Assistant Chief of Staff, O.P.D. Subject: Utilization of Negro Troops in Friendly Foreign Territory, June 17, 1942, Box 472, NM84, Entry 418, RG 165, NARA.
[76] See Kim Munholland, *Rock of Contention: Free French and Americans at War in New Caledonia, 1940–1945* (New York, NY: Berghahn, 2005), 151–2; Stephen Henningham, "The French Administration, the Local Population, and the American Presence in New Caledonia 1943–1944," *Journal de la Société des Océanistes* 98, no. 1 (1994): 25.
[77] Jefferson, *Fighting for Hope*, 201; Harry McAlpin, "Army 'Scottsboro' Case in Australia Revealed," *Chicago Defender*, November 6, 1943; Lee Finkle, *Forum for Protest: The Black Press during World War II* (Cranbury, NJ: Fairleigh Dickinson University Press,

The response of the black press to the Fisher and Loury case revealed much about the interlocking patterns of sexism and racism prevailing in the Pacific Theater. As well as suggesting that African Americans accepted the dominant sexual values of American military culture – for some black commentators, the fact that Mounien was a "prostitute, infected with a social disease contracted long before her association with the Negro soldiers," apparently mitigated the possibility that she was raped – Fisher's and Loury's experiences highlighted the double standards of American military justice.[78] African Americans accused of raping a white woman continued to be presumed guilty until proved innocent, and the penalties to which they were subjected were almost inevitably more severe than those imposed upon their white compatriots.

As Fisher and Loury continued to protest their innocence, and as their case became a cause célèbre in the black press, tensions remained high in New Caledonia. The island's Governor, Christian L'Aigret, criticized the behavior of all American servicemen. But he was especially critical of "colored troops," whom he reportedly described as "the terror of the white women of New Caledonia."[79] Even white New Caledonian women "in the company of their husbands and brothers," he claimed, had been attacked by African American troops. Asserting that local women were "afraid to go out of the house after nightfall," L'Aigret hoped Noumea would be declared "out of bounds" for black servicemen.[80]

Perhaps because L'Aigret's critique was not confined to the alleged actions of African American troops, or perhaps because his Francophile views of the future of New Caledonia were an affront to America's stated wartime goals, US authorities were disinclined to accept his charges against black servicemen. During late 1943 and early 1944, many American observers concluded that L'Aigret's accusations had been instrumental in compounding anti-African American hostility in the French colony. L'Aigret's "particularly bitter" allegations against African Americans, according to one American report, had been instrumental in encouraging "young

---

1975), 170; Gilbert Ware, *William Hastie: Grace under Pressure* (New York, NY: Oxford University Press, 1984), 135–6.

[78] "Congressman Charges 'Frame-Up' Angle in Army 'Scottsboro Case,'" *Pittsburgh Courier*, November 6, 1943.

[79] Clipping from *Newsweek*, January 3, 1944, in RG 313, Records of the Naval Operating Forces, Secret General Administration Files, Box 6782, File A14 "Foreign Relations," NARA.

[80] Fletcher Martin, "Ranking Officers Resent Allegations: Army Authorities Refute French Governor's Charges," *Pittsburgh Courier*, January 15, 1944. See also Munholland, *Rock of Contention*, 152.

civilians" to form "organized bands" that had "threatened negroes" who had allegedly molested women. In response, the United States Army provided evidence demonstrating that African Americans were no more likely to commit offenses, of any kind, than "white troops."[81]

With L'Aigret recalled to Algeria by Free French authorities, and with no evidence to support his charges against African American servicemen, US Army authorities refused his request to declare Noumea "off limits" to black troops, and offered a measured defense of African American behavior.[82] If this was a rare occasion when US commanders defended the sexual virtue of black servicemen, it is important to acknowledge the particular context in which they did so. Against the backdrop of tense relations between American and Free French leaders in New Caledonia, American commanders' defense of black troops was a response to a perception that L'Aigret, and other Free French in New Caledonia, were challenging American authority. In this instance, American diplomatic imperatives apparently encouraged enlightened racial policies. Yet there were clear limits to these ostensibly racial liberal views. In effect, American commanders were implying that while they were entitled to discriminate against African Americans – as evidenced by the harsh sentences imposed on Fisher and Loury, and on other black servicemen accused of sexual crimes – others had no right to usurp white Americans' authority over African Americans. US commanders had in fact already imposed a form of racial segregation in New Caledonia. As Fletcher Martin noted, with "the majority of Negro camps in the area" of Noumea "out of city limits," and with "the "acute transportation problem" on the island, only a "few" African Americans visited the town.[83]

White Americans' apprehensions regarding African American sexuality were further evidenced by military authorities' attitudes toward the sex trade in New Caledonia. The "Pink House" was a well-known – and legally established – brothel in Noumea. Although business at the Pink House was brisk following the arrival of American forces in New Caledonia in late 1942, the lines of segregation were clear: African Americans were prohibited from visiting the establishment. US authorities, however, were pragmatic. By late 1943 they were proposing

[81] Unsigned telex, December 23, 1943, RG 313, Secret General Administration Files, Box 6782, File A14 "Foreign Relations," NARA.
[82] "Charge against Troops False," *Pittsburgh Courier*, January 1, 1944.
[83] Fletcher P. Martin, "Army Refutes Caledonia Misconduct Charges," *Atlanta Daily World*, January 5, 1944. See also "Race-Baiting Governor to Leave New Caledonia as Terror Charges Refuted," *The Journal and Guide*, January 1, 1944.

that the house across the road from the Pink House should become a racially segregated brothel for the exclusive use of African Americans. Local indigenous ("Kanak") women, American commanders suggested, should be recruited to work in the new facility. While sympathetic to the notion of segregating African Americans, local French authorities rejected the American proposal. Unwilling to expel the French family residing in the house where US commanders hoped to establish a brothel, local authorities were also apprehensive that missionaries, and the Kanak residents of the colony, would be outraged at the suggestion that Kanak women should be employed as prostitutes for African Americans. They suggested, instead, that American authorities should bring black women from the United States, who could be employed as prostitutes in a segregated camp outside Noumea, to be constructed using American supplies. At this point, US military commanders' moral scruples coincided with their concerns regarding American public opinion. Although they acknowledged the sexual desires of servicemen of all races, they feared a public outcry in the United States should the use of government supplies to facilitate the sex trade become common knowledge. The proposed facility was never constructed, and African Americans continued to be prohibited from the Pink House.[84]

The racial and sexual tensions in New Caledonia attracted considerable attention within the United States. Reporting in January 1944 from "filthy and squalid" Noumea, *Newsweek* correspondent William S. Boddie denounced the French administration in New Caledonia in general, and L'Aigret in particular. The Governor's disparaging remarks about Americans, Boddie asserted, "can only draw a sarcastic snigger from anyone" who had been to the French colony. Criticizing L'Aigret's "absurd" assertions concerning the behavior of African American troops, Boddie declared that if "relations" were strained it was "owing in good measure to the French themselves."[85]

African American correspondents and editors took a particular interest in the wartime tensions in New Caledonia. While romanticized images of New Caledonia as a South Seas idyll persisted – in January 1944 Fletcher P. Martin hoped that the "island paradise" of New Caledonia would not be permanently corrupted by the turmoil of war – the black press

[84] Munholland, *Rock of Contention*, 152–3.
[85] Boddie, in *Newsweek*, January 3, 1944, in RG 313, Records of the Naval Operating Forces, Secret General Administration Files, Box 6782, File A14 "Foreign Relations," NARA.

endorsed the wider American critique of L'Aigret and the behavior of the island's European inhabitants.[86] Pointing out that L'Aigret's accusations were a deliberate effort to deflect Americans' attentions from blatant war "profiteering" on the part of local New Caledonians, the *Norfolk Journal and Guide* condemned the Governor's "disquieting charges." Yet while the *Journal and Guide* insisted that US authorities "must act without delay" to refute L'Aigret's "smear" against American troops – white as well as black – African American correspondents and editors expressed specific concern regarding the treatment of black troops in New Caledonia.[87] Major-General Rush Lincoln, commander of US forces in New Caledonia, earned praise for rebutting the Governor's charges. But black editors and correspondents demanded that senior US authorities counter L'Aigret's allegations against African American servicemen. Insisting that the War Department should have provided a more categorical defense of black troops, the *Afro-American* condemned the department's silence on the matter. The possibility that L'Aigret's behavior might have been attributable to the fact that he was a "sorehead," disgruntled at being replaced by a Free French governor, did not absolve the War Department from its responsibility to defend black troops. "The fact remains," editorialized the *Afro-American*, that L'Aigret had "made charges against our soldiers, and that his statement, which escaped censorship," had "been printed in all U.S. newspapers."[88]

American criticism of L'Aigret and the French colonial administration of New Caledonia notwithstanding, Fisher and Loury were transported back to the United States, where they began their life sentences at the McNeil Island Penitentiary, in Washington state. But their case continued to attract attention, and with the support of the National Association for the Advancement of Colored People (NAACP) and the International Labor Defense (ILD), Fisher and Loury appealed their sentence. Congressman Vito Marcantonio, President of the ILD, described the conviction of Fisher and Loury as "a gross miscarriage of justice influenced by the race of the accused."[89] Despite the support of Marcantonio

---

[86] Fletcher P. Martin, "Soldiers Adopt Caledonian Customs: 'Lazy' Life Makes Impression on Men," *Philadelphia Tribune*, January 8, 1944.

[87] Editorial, "Government Must Be Firm," *The Journal and Guide*, January 1, 1944.

[88] See "Charges against Negro Troops Termed 'Absurd,'" *Chicago Defender*, January 8, 1944; Editorial, "Why Hasn't the War Department a Statement on New Caledonia?" *Afro-American*, January 8, 1944.

[89] "Seeks to Revoke Verdict of Rape Reached by Army," *Spartanburg Herald*, November 1, 1943. See also "Along the N.A.A.C.P. Battlefront," *The Crisis*, January, 1944, 21.

and William Hastie, prominent black activist, lawyer, and Chair of the NAACP's National Legal Committee, Fisher's and Loury's appeal was unsuccessful. Undeterred, Hastie and Marcantonio persisted in their efforts, and with the case continuing to attract considerable attention in the national as well as African American press, in March 1944 Robert P. Patterson, Under Secretary of War, reviewed the trial and conviction of Fisher and Loury. Emphasizing that it was "fundamental that all men, regardless of race, creed, or color" should be "treated fairly," Patterson claimed the "Army has not and will not tolerate any deviation from the elementary proposition that every soldier must be treated as an individual and every case on its merits." For African Americans, such claims rang hollow. With the black press and the NAACP demanding justice for Fisher and Loury, military authorities had little choice but to moderate the two men's sentences. Insisting that the crime of rape was a "revolting offense," made even worse when the "offense occurs in a foreign region," Patterson was also conscious of Fisher's and Loury's personal circumstances. Both were "young and of limited education," and had been "orphaned at an early age." Conceding that neither man "had a criminal record in civilian life," Patterson reduced Fisher's and Loury's sentences from life imprisonment to ten and eight years respectively.[90]

The reduction of Fisher's and Loury's sentences did not deflect attention from their case, however. To their defenders, the two soldiers were innocent of the charges for which they continued to be imprisoned. In June 1945, another appeal was launched on their behalf. As well as raising significant procedural issues pertaining to the conduct of the original trial, the fresh appeal reiterated that immediately after the alleged rape, Louise Mounien had accepted payment from Fisher. *The Crisis* reported that Hastie and Marcantonio, who were again serving as counsel for Fisher and Loury, had raised "grave doubt" regarding "a case in

---

[90] Robert P. Patterson, "Clemency Application of General Prisoners Frank Fisher, Jr and Edward Lowry (Loury)," 31 March, 1944, "Court Martials, A-J, Fisher and Loury Court Martial in New Caledonia for Rape, Veterans Affairs," Group II, Box G3, Records of the National Association for the Advancement of Colored People, Manuscript Division, Library of Congress, Washington, DC (NAACP-LoC); "Along the N.A.A.C.P. Battlefront," *The Crisis*, June, 1945, 174. See also "Four Men and a Girl," *Time*, April 10, 1944; International Labor Defense, *For Equality of Military Justice: 1,100 Leaders and Organizations Join in Endorsing Appeal for Clemency for Privates Frank Fisher, Jr. and Edward R. Loury, Victims of "the Army Scottsboro Case"* (New York, NY: International Labor Defense, 1944); Finkle, *Forum for Protest*, 172; McGuire, *He, Too, Spoke for Democracy*, 87–8; Jean Byers, *A Study of the Negro in Military Service* (Washington, DC: Department of Defense, 1950), 57–8.

Anglo-American jurisprudence where a conviction for rape" had "been permitted" when the woman had "been offered and accepted payment on the spot." Mounien's acceptance of the money, argued Hastie and Marcantonio, was "but one of many affirmative indications that she consented."[91] In speaking out on behalf of Fisher and Loury, their defenders were effectively contending that the transactional nature of the alleged relationship with Mounien precluded the possibility of rape.

In spite of the clear doubts regarding Fisher's and Loury's guilt, their convictions were not reversed. But the widespread and adverse publicity surrounding their case might go some way toward explaining why a subsequent incident in New Guinea, in which African American troops were again accused of sexual crimes against a white woman, remained largely hidden from history for nearly five decades. As with Fisher and Loury, in this later case there were significant doubts regarding the men's guilt.

At Milne Bay, New Guinea, in March 1944, six African American troops were accused of accosting two Army nurses, Ruth Irvine and Marie Weaver.[92] As in so many cases where black men were accused of sexually assaulting white women, details of the alleged incident were murky. Accompanied by two white servicemen, James Flanagan and Thomas Havers, Irvine and Weaver had parked in a restricted area. What followed was contentious, but it was alleged that six black servicemen forced Irvine and Weaver from the jeep, took them into the nearby jungle, and then accosted and raped them. The alleged culprits, quickly identified and arrested, denied the charges. According to their account, they had refused sexual advances from Irvine and Weaver. Conversely, Flanagan and Havers contended that five of the accused had threatened to kill them if Irvine and Weaver did not agree to the black men's advances. Matters were confused further when Irvine and Weaver were initially unable to identify their attackers. Under further questioning, the two women's testimony invoked longstanding images of unchecked black sexuality that allegedly imperiled white women everywhere.[93]

---

[91] "Along the N.A.A.C.P. Battlefront," *The Crisis*, June, 1945, 174.

[92] Information on this case is scant. Walter A. Luszki's account is deeply flawed: he argues, for instance, that some women "invite rape" by dressing or behaving "in a teasing manner." Helpfully for the historian, however, he included records of the courts-martial, as well as copies of letters written by the six men executed. The quote is from Walter A. Luszki, *A Rape of Justice: MacArthur and the New Guinea Hangings* (Lanham, MD: Madison Books, 1991), xi.

[93] Jefferson, *Fighting for Hope*, 199–200.

Notwithstanding the contradictions between the various accounts of the incident at Milne Bay, the six black soldiers were found guilty of rape and carnal knowledge, and sentenced to death. Walter A. Luszki, commanding the Detention and Rehabilitation Center at Oro Bay, where the men were imprisoned and then hanged, subsequently outlined significant flaws in both the investigation of the alleged crimes and the quality of the defense counsel provided to the accused. If General Douglas Macarthur was aware of those issues, they did not sway his decision when he reviewed the case, as he was required to do as commander-in-chief of the Southwest Theater of Operations.[94] MacArthur's personal views toward African Americans were less than enlightened, and he concurred with the judgment of the court-martial that sentenced the six African Americans to hang.[95]

For their part, the condemned men were in no doubt that race was a telling factor in both their conviction and the sentence passed against them. The men's final letters to their families – rendered all the more poignant because some of the condemned were illiterate and were only able to dictate letters to Army chaplains – offer moving testimony to their plight, and their inability to confront the judicial authority or racist culture of the US military. Writing to his mother on the eve of his execution, Private Lloyd L. White assured her that he was "not rightly guilty of" the offences for which he had been convicted. The impending executions, he wrote, were partly attributable to "the color of our skin."[96] And while Private Arthur T. Brown admitted that he "was at the place" where the alleged crimes were committed, he insisted that he "never did any of them." But because he was black, he noted, his "word is no good."[97]

The execution of the six black men in New Guinea remained obscure until the publication of Walter Luszki's account in 1991. But another wartime allegation of African American sexual misconduct drew national attention during the Pacific War. While this case did not involve allegations that a white woman had been raped, it highlighted the enduring white fears of black sexuality. In early 1945, Samuel Hill, a noncommissioned

[94] Luszki, *A Rape of Justice*, 75–86.
[95] On MacArthur's willingness to enforce capital sentences against African Americans, see Luszki, *A Rape of Justice*, 107. On MacArthur and race, see William Manchester, *American Caesar: Douglas MacArthur, 1880–1964* (Boston, MA: Little, Brown, & Co., 1978), 431; D. Clayton James, *The Years of MacArthur, Vol. 2, 1941–1945* (Boston, MA: Houghton Mifflin, 1975), 257–8.
[96] Lloyd L. White to "Dear Mother," cited in Luszki, *A Rape of Justice*, 128.
[97] Arthur T. Brown to "Dear Father," cited in Luszki, *A Rape of Justice*, 129.

officer serving in New Guinea with the 93rd Infantry Division, was accused of raping a local woman, Baroe Banondi. As in previous cases where African Americans were accused of sexual crimes, the evidence against Hill was inconclusive. Although there were contradictions in the prosecution's case, and while Hill's commanding officers and two chaplains serving with the 93rd spoke in his defense, Hill was found guilty. His supporters, however, refused to accept the verdict. Arguing that the verdict was unreliable because the court-martial that had adjudged the case had been comprised solely of whites, and was therefore vulnerable to the charge that it was unrepresentative and perhaps incapable of fairly assessing Hill's guilt, his supporters appealed to the divisional commander, Major General Harry Johnson. While Johnson had a reputation for racial fairness, he refused to intervene. When further evidence was produced suggesting Hill's innocence the two Army chaplains who had spoken on his behalf – Captain Matthew Lowe and Captain S. McMaster Kerr – appealed to the Judge Advocate General's Office in Australia. By this point, word of the case had not only spread throughout the 93rd Division, but also to the African American community in the United States. The NAACP mobilized quickly to assist in Hill's defense. Under considerable public and political pressure, the Army recanted, and Hill was allowed to rejoin the service, albeit at a reduced rank.[98]

While we can only surmise that the relative leniency shown to Hill was a consequence of the fact that his victim was not a white woman, the fears of black sexuality underpinning each of these cases contributed to ongoing racial tensions among American troops throughout the Asia-Pacific. After touring the Pacific Theater in late 1945, Lester Granger, Executive Secretary of the National Urban League, concluded that women "cause most of the trouble between colored and white navy boys in the Pacific." Holding "island women" responsible for the "trouble," Granger conveniently absolved American servicemen of responsibility for their actions.[99] While other observers were more circumspect in blaming local women for racial rivalries among the US forces, they did agree that clashes between white and black servicemen – such as that which occurred on the island of Guam in late 1944 – were a consequence of what Walter White described as "sexual jealousy and rivalry."[100]

[98] See Jefferson, *Fighting for Hope*, 190–1, 203–9, 219–20.
[99] Granger, cited in Cherokee, "National Grapevine."
[100] Walter White, *A Man Called White: The Autobiography of Walter White* (London: Gollancz, 1949), 280.

Tensions over local women were particularly acute in the Philippines. The mutual familiarity between Filipinos and Americans, black as well as white, seemingly encouraged relations between servicemen and local women. These tensions arose almost immediately after the Allies had regained control of the Philippines. Frustrated by black troops' success in winning the attention of Filipino women, one white soldier lamented that "some of the nigger troops are making quite a hit with some of these Filipino women."[101] Referring to the "constant friction" between black and white troops in the Philippines – compounded by the willingness of the local Filipino press to publicize crimes supposedly committed by African Americans – in March 1945 a black serviceman described an incident at a local social club where African American troops were prohibited from dancing with Filipino women.[102] As the *Afro-American* reported in early 1946, the "sympathetic attention and care shown by the native girls to the colored men had been the cause of a lot of the jealousy of white boys." That jealousy, the paper contended, had given rise to an "anti-colored whispering campaign spread among the female population." "Not infrequently," the report noted, social functions had been marred by "frictions and fistic brawls over women."[103] Almost inevitably, African Americans bore the brunt of whites' frustration and anger. After a "white sailor had shot a Negro sailor over a Filipino girl," precipitating a riot among some of the African Americans stationed nearby, local commanders had begun "locking up all the Negro sailors." In response, Adolph Newton made his feelings clear: "A white sailor shoots a Negro, and they lock up all the Negro sailors – that's bullshit."[104]

A series of incidents between men of the 93rd Infantry Division and troops of the 31st Infantry Division highlight the tensions over Filipino

---

[101] APO 501, Headquarters, United States Army Forces in the Far East, Censorship Survey of Morale – Rumors, Propaganda. Issued by the Assistant Chief of Staff, G-2, March 1945, *Censorship Survey of Morale*, 38, RG 496, 496/290/47/27/7-, Records of the General Headquarters, Southwest Pacific Area and United States Army Forces, Pacific (World War II) Box 24, NARA.

[102] "Negro Troops Can't Dance with Filipinos," *Chicago Defender*, March 10, 1945. Robert M. Alexander recalled that he and several other African Americans stationed in the Philippines persuaded the editors of the *Manila Times* to give no more emphasis to crimes by black Americans than they did to those committed by white serviceman. See Robert M. Alexander, AFC/2001/001/12845, VHP-LoC. See also Jefferson, *Fighting for Hope*, 215; Maggi M. Morehouse, *Fighting in the Jim Crow Army: Black Men and Women Remember World War II* (Lanham, MD: Rowman and Littlefield, 2000), 146.

[103] Jesus V. Merritt, "1063 Filipino Girls Become Brides of Colored Soldiers," *Afro-American*, February 2, 1946. See also Jefferson, *Fighting for Hope*, 214.

[104] See Newton, *Better than Good*, 95.

women. The 31st, or "Dixie Division," was a National Guard unit, comprised principally of troops from the Deep South. While the men of the 31st had earlier complimented the 93rd for its role in assisting during a difficult amphibious assault, there had been subsequent clashes on the Indonesian island of Morotai. Relations soured again when the two divisions were stationed together in the Philippines. The white troops were especially angered by the friendly relations between African American soldiers and the local Filipino women. Certainly, the men of the 93rd were no less keen than their white compatriots to secure female company. Noting that the men of the 93rd had been oversees for "nineteen months without seeing any women to speak of," Walter Greene recalled that when the Division arrived in the Philippines the men "went hog wild." The major point of dispute between the white and black troops was over women. "The men of the Dixie Division," stated Greene, "couldn't stand the Filipino girls going for the Negro soldiers." As Nelson Peery explained, fighting "broke out when these Southern whites tried to Jim Crow the prostitution houses." Violence ensued, and a series of what Greene described as "small battles" soon escalated. Prohibited from fraternizing with the local women, some black soldiers took matters into their own hands, firing several shots at the tent used by the white officer who had issued that order. "Man," Greene recalled, "he came crawling out of that tent screaming bloody murder." Although the matter was settled soon after, when the order against black troops fraternizing with local women was rescinded, relations between white and African American servicemen remained tense.[105]

Peery's reference to "houses of prostitution" was not the only hint that sexual relations between American servicemen and Filipino women were frequently transactional, rather than romantic. Confirming that "white officers" stationed in the Philippines were determined to control any expression of African American sexuality, Alfred A. Duckett, wartime journalist and later collaborator with Reverend Martin Luther King, Jr., recalled that "the local sex workers had been told "all kind of horrible stories" about African Americans. "Some of the guys who wanted to negotiate with the prostitutes" – who he emphasized "were not white" – "were turned down."[106] Besides highlighting the degree to which

[105] Walter Greene, cited in Morehouse, *Fighting in the Jim Crow Army*, 149–50; Nelson Peery, *Black Fire: The Making of an American Revolutionary* (New York, NY: The New Press, 1994), 255, 278–80.

[106] Duckett, cited in Studs Terkel, *"The Good War": An Oral History of World War II* (1984; reprinted, New York, NY: Ballantyne Books, 1985), 370.

the commodification of sexual relations was commonplace, Duckett's account affirmed the underlying tensions between sex and race that characterized American military culture during the Pacific War.

US authorities' anxieties regarding these tensions were further reflected in their attitude toward black women's military service. African American women, rejecting the notion that their feminine identity would be compromised by military service, recognized that such service would extend their claims for full rights of citizenship. If those imperatives were common to all women, the burden of race rendered them all the more urgent for black women. Yet, while there is evidence that African American women would have welcomed the opportunity to serve in the Pacific Theater, US commanders were slow to recruit, train, and deploy black women. Moreover, defying black public opinion, and reflecting the wider under-utilization of "Negro womanpower," the Army refused to send African American women to the Pacific Theater. Defending that policy, the Army claimed that Pacific Theater commanders had made no requests for black WAC units. The twin imperatives of race and sex meant the deployment policies of other branches of the US military were similarly illiberal. It was not until 1945 that the Navy admitted black women.[107]

African American women were, however, deployed to the Pacific as nurses. Until January 1945 they served in segregated units, usually caring for black servicemen.[108] Few in number, black nurses serving across the Pacific Theater were concurrently confirming and challenging prevailing stereotypes regarding gender roles and women's capacities. On the one hand, the nursing profession enabled women to perform a nurturing role congruent with common views concerning women's appropriate place and responsibilities. Yet at the same time, nurses serving in a war zone were encroaching into a space that was traditionally defined as masculine.

---

[107] Anna Rosenberg, "Negro Womanpower is Still Untapped," *Cleveland Call and Post*, April 24, 1943. See also Barbara Brooks Tomblin, *G.I. Nightingales: The Army Nurse Corps in World War II* (Lexington: The University Press of Kentucky, 1996), 203; A. Russell Buchanan, *Black Americans in World War II* (Santa Barbara, CA: Clio Books, 1977), 111; Treadwell, *Women's Army Corps*, 601. Martha Putney has noted that even after the end of the war, Douglas MacArthur requested that African American women not be deployed to the Pacific. See Martha Putney, *When the Nation Was in Need: Blacks in the Women's Army Corps during World War II* (Metuchen, NJ: Scarecrow Press, 1992), 106.

[108] Melissa A. McEuen, *Making War, Making Women: Femininity and Duty on the American Home Front, 1941–1945* (Athens, GA; University of Georgia Press, 2010), 44. See also Judith L. Bellafaire, *The Army Nurse Corps: A Commemoration of World War II Service* (Washington, DC: U.S. Army Center of Military History, 1993), 8–9.

Inevitably, all women who served in a war zone were testing that boundary. But service in the Pacific War, with its unforgiving climate and terrain, meant that nurses stationed there were confronting challenges far more acute than those encountered by their counterparts in the European Theater. This already-difficult situation was further complicated by the fact that Allied women in the Pacific War zone faced the challenges of service among a male-dominated military in a region long associated with female sensuality.[109]

Quick to praise black WACs, nurses, and Red Cross workers, the African American press depicted black women's contribution to the war effort as evidence of their patriotic credentials and their rights of citizenship – and as part of the wider, transnational fight for democracy. Thus transformed into role models for all African American women, these black women were depicted as active contributors to the Double V campaign.[110] Frustrated by the Army's and Navy's continuing reluctance to deploy black women to the Pacific Theater, African American commentators hailed the contributions that black women nurses were permitted to make.[111] Through their care of white troops, and by their "unselfish performance of duty," black nurses were fulfilling an important role in "breaking down" barriers of race. Wounded soldiers, it was argued, cared "not whether" their "angel of mercy" had "a white or black face." Connecting black women's service in the Pacific War zone to the reform of race relations in postwar America, the *Chicago Defender* argued that when convalescing soldiers contemplated "the issues of democracy" confronting the United States, they would appreciate "the kind and skillful services" provided by African American nurses. Those nurses, the *Defender* suggested, were playing an important part in the "improvement in race relations" that would "carry over into civilian life."[112]

Extolling the services performed by black nurses, and connecting women's traditional virtues to notions of democracy, African American leaders relied on and celebrated stereotypical views of women. *The Crisis* regularly placed pictures of black nurses and African American servicewomen on its covers, and in February, 1943, editor Roy Wilkins wrote that "'our boys' will feel better" as soon as African American women

---

[109] See Brawley and Dixon, *Hollywood's South Seas and the Pacific War*, Chapter 6.
[110] See "WAACS Set pace as Model Soldiers: Win Friends, Influence People at Army Base," *Pittsburgh Courier*, December 19, 1942; Fowler Harper, "Negroes Get Better Deal in the Armed Services," *Philadelphia Tribune*, November 7, 1942.
[111] See "No Nurses Wanted," *Afro-American*, October 30, 1943.
[112] See "Negro Nurses and the Army," *Chicago Defender*, August 19, 1944.

"step off a boat somewhere on the other side of the world."[113] Although the editors of *The Crisis* applauded African American women's contributions to the war effort, by placing images of "these clear-eyed efficient young women" on the journal's covers, they were complicit in the "objectification" of black women.[114]

That process of objectification was also evident in black journalists' depictions of the handful of black women who served in the Pacific Theater. Inevitably, these women attracted the attention of black reporters and servicemen. While correspondents were careful to describe the handful of black women in the war zone in wholesome terms – emphasizing that "Miss Clara Wells" was "hardly a glamour girl type," Charles H. Loeb stressed that she had "the open friendliness that makes an instant hit with GI's wherever she goes" – the fact that so few African American women were sent to the Pacific War zone meant they attracted predictable attention of black servicemen.[115] The arrival of black Red Cross workers in wartime Australia also attracted the immediate attention of African American servicemen stationed there, many of whom "had not seen an American Negro woman in two years."[116] Further north, in the jungles of New Guinea, black servicemen also responded enthusiastically to the arrival of African American women. In early 1944 Joseph "Scoop" Jones enthused about the arrival of black female Red Cross workers in New Guinea. "Nobody knows," wrote Jones, "how much man can worship woman until he has witnessed the reaction of those who see one for the first time in months ... almost years." "There are six women here," he continued, "who could literally be classed as goddesses. To their throne come daily hundreds of GI's bearing gifts to get a glimpse of them and worship them." Jones gave credit to the Red Cross women – "morale commandos" as he labeled them – for giving "new life and vigor" to the African American troops.[117]

---

[113] Roy Wilkins, "Nurses Go to War," *The Crisis*, February, 1943, 44.

[114] McEuen, *Making War, Making Women*, 44. See also "Lovely Lassies in the Sepia Miss American Contest," *The Crisis*, July, 1944, 221; "Subject: Pinups in Bathing Suits," *New York Amsterdam News*, April 29, 1944; Maureen Honey, "Introduction," in *Bitter Fruit: African American Women in World War II*, ed. Maureen Honey (Columbia, MO: University of Missouri Press, 1999), 28–9.

[115] Charles H. Loeb, "Pacific Ablaze with 'Finish War' Activity," *Atlanta Daily World*, June 16, 1945.

[116] Enoch P. Waters, "Red Cross Worker in Australia Gets Hundreds of Proposals from Soldiers," *Chicago Defender*, October 30, 1943.

[117] "Scoop" Jones, "Women 'Morale Commandos' Reach Distant Outposts," *New York Amsterdam News*, January 8, 1944. See also "Scoop" Jones, "'Down Under' Diary," *Journal and Guide*, December 18, 1943.

Adolph Newton was one of the men described by Jones. When the men in Newton's unit learned "that there were some Negro women Red Cross workers" based nearby, they wasted no time in going to "check them out." To the men's delight, the rumor proved true. The three black women were "passing out coffee and doughnuts" to the African American troops. It "was a treat," Jones recounted, "just to hear their voices." The men drank their coffee, ate their doughnuts, and "just looked" at the women "for a while." Happy to "at least" be able to have "a look at an American woman" and exchange "a few words with her," Newton affirmed the positive impact that the presence of African American women had on the men's morale. Yet, while Newton could not understand immediately why armed guards accompanied the black women, military authorities were evidently worried that the men would behave inappropriately.[118] Such concerns were unfounded, but besides attesting to apprehensions regarding servicemen's inability to exercise restraint around women – specifically, "American" women – they also suggest that the military itself was implicated in the objectification of African American women, in the same way that it was implicated in the objectification of white women.

That process was evident elsewhere, too. Among those women most commonly objectified were female entertainers. To the chagrin of African American servicemen, black women performers were rare visitors to the Pacific Theater. Anne Lewis, an African American nightclub singer who toured the South Pacific in 1944 as part of a USO show – it is telling that the first all-black USO show did not reach the Pacific until mid-1944 – noted that the men "were so glad to see us." "[I]t was pitiful," she remarked.[119] After "not having seen any girls at all" for months on end, Daniel Davis relished the visit of female African American performers to his Aviation Engineering unit. Yet he also revealed that military commanders were anxious for the safety of the women performers. Although there was no suggestion that the women were in direct or imminent danger, Davis noted they were accompanied by armed guards.[120] As with Newton's account, it was unclear whether the precautions Davis described were to protect the women from African American troops, or from some other threat. But there could be no doubting that military authorities were determined to safeguard the women under their care.

[118] Newton, *Better than Good*, 51–2.
[119] E. B. Rea, "Encores and Echoes," *Afro-American*, November 4, 1944; "All-Negro Unit Scores with GIs in New Caledonia," *Pittsburgh Courier*, June 10, 1944.
[120] Daniel Davis, AFC/2001/001/64936, VHP-LoC.

The reception African American women received from many whites in the Pacific Theater often contrasted sharply to the warm reception they received from black servicemen. While some black nurses were surprised by the friendly reception they received from Australians – a subject explored in more detail in Chapter 4 – they were frequently treated with contempt by white American service personnel, women as well as men. For operational reasons – there were sometimes only a handful of women in a particular area, and it was logistically infeasible to provide segregated facilities – white and black women could find themselves in close proximity. Reporting from New Guinea in September, 1944, Conrad Clark described the close and spartan living conditions for African American and white Red Cross women. "All workers, both Negro and white," wrote Clark, "reside here and dine together. Four persons are detailed to a hut, and all privileges are the same for all."[121] Some white women coped with that early, if minor form of desegregation; others, however, were unimpressed. "We don't have too bad a time of it," recalled one white Army nurse, "except for" the presence of "a group of *colored* nurses." Alarmed that the African American women were "expected to eat with" the white women, the nurse described the "considerable unhappiness among the white girls." There was "a limit," she concluded, "to what you will accept war or no war."[122] If this nurse recognized the contradiction in her argument – while white servicewomen and nurses were themselves victims of a gender-based form of segregation, some were unwilling to abandon their own racist and segregationist values and habits – she left no record that she was prepared to modify her racist views. The lines of race and sex remained formidable.

Across the Pacific Theater, African American servicemen confronted numerous challenges. Racism, it seemed, was almost all pervasive, and was at its most potent when long-held concerns regarding African American sexuality shaped the military's racial policies and practices: for moral as well as supposedly military reasons, across a region often associated with images and ideas of sensual freedom, white authorities and servicemen were certain that black sexuality had to be contained. Wartime attempts to contain African American sexuality affected blacks' relationships with native women, with the white women who were part of the American

---

[121] Conrad Clark, "Life of GI Janes is Very Different," *New York Amsterdam News*, September 16, 1944.
[122] Cited in "Morale Report," September 15, 1942, File Theater Censor APO 926, GHQ, SWPA, 290/12/4–5, Box T-14533, RG 338, NARA.

military presence across the Pacific Theater, and with those European women associated with the colonial enterprise and who remained in the Asia-Pacific region. However, despite the constraints of military policy, and notwithstanding the frustrations arising from the paucity of women in the Pacific War zone, African Americans inevitably encountered and interacted with women. Those interactions were sometimes tolerated by military authorities – operational considerations meant that pragmatic concerns could outweigh the fears of black sexuality – but there were also instances when perceptions of black indiscretion brought the weight of American military justice to bear. African American servicemen's attitudes and experiences were shaped, too, by the tension between race and nationality. While their encounters with indigenous women highlighted the cultural chasm between the two groups, their encounters with white women confirmed that they remained on the margins of the nation with which they sometimes-reluctantly identified. As the next chapter reveals, those contradictions were further evidenced when African Americans encountered a nation whose own racial history appeared alarmingly similar to that of the American South.

CHAPTER 4

Nourishing the Tree of Democracy

Black Americans in White Australia

The African American presence in wartime Australia was a significant, albeit often overlooked aspect of the Pacific War. Alert to the connections between domestic and international manifestations of white supremacy, African Americans linked Australia's attempts to maintain racial purity through immigration restriction to the continuing mistreatment of the nation's indigenous population. Confronting this complex web of racism, black leaders described Australia's racial policies as antipodean analogs of the segregationism that relegated African Americans to the margins of American life. Australia, declared one black newspaper in March 1942, was "an outcast among the decent nations of the earth."[1] Labeling the White Australia Policy an affront to the democratic values for which the wartime Allies were supposedly fighting, African Americans believed their wartime mission Down Under entailed remaking, as well as saving, Australia. By "nourish[ing] the tree of democracy" in "the far-off ramparts of Australia" – and, by extension, elsewhere – African Americans were transforming the Double V campaign into a "Triple V" campaign: as they were struggling against racism at home and fascism abroad, they were also fighting racism among America's wartime allies.[2]

The approximately 100,000 African Americans who passed through or were stationed in Australia during World War Two were part of the

---

[1] "Australia: 'White Man's Country,'" *New York Amsterdam Star-News*, March 28, 1942.
[2] "Undemocratic Australia," *Chicago Defender*, April 4, 1942; "The Big Parade: MacArthur vs. Dixie. They Differ on Unity. Dixie Hates as Usual. Can't Fight Fascism," *Afro-American*, July 25, 1942; Sean Brawley and Chris Dixon, "Jim Crow Downunder: African American Encounters with White Australia, 1942–1945," *Pacific Historical Review* 71, no. 4 (2002): 614.

much larger movement of nearly a million Americans through a nation whose wartime population of just seven million, as one black newspaper pointed out, was smaller than that of the American state of Illinois. It is unsurprising, then, that Australian historians have given some consideration to the black presence in Australia between 1942 and 1945.[3] Inevitably, those analyses, relying primarily on Australian sources, have focused principally on the African American presence in terms of its significance for Australian history.[4] Perhaps equally inevitably, those analyses have explained African Americans' experiences in wartime Australia as being shaped initially by the legal, political, and cultural constraints of the White Australia Policy, and subsequently by the attempts of US military authorities to impose a form of segregation on black servicemen stationed in Australia.[5]

This chapter shifts the focus of analysis, to investigate African Americans' own understandings and experiences of the White Australia Policy. Exploiting a range of largely neglected black sources, this chapter gives voice to the hitherto-silenced African American servicemen who experienced the worst, and the best, of White Australia. If Australian historians have lapsed into historiographical parochialism in their analyses of the black presence in wartime Australia, American historians have largely ignored the subject.[6] While that neglect is curious –

---

[3] Anni P. Baker has noted that at "the height of the war effort, as much as 5 percent of Australia's population was American." See Anni P. Baker, *American Soldiers Overseas: The Global Military Presence* (Westport, CT: Praeger, 2004), 30. For a comparison of the populations of Australia and Illinois, see "Australia, Now Threatened, Much Like U.S.," *Atlanta Daily World*, March 21, 1942.

[4] Studies of Americans' experiences in wartime Australia include John Hammond Moore, *Over-Sexed, Over-Paid, and Over Here: Americans in Australia, 1941–1945* (St. Lucia: University of Queensland Press, 1981); John McKerrow, *The American Occupation of Australia, 1941–1945: A Marriage of Necessity* (Newcastle-upon-Tyne: Cambridge Scholars Publishing, 2013); E. Daniel Potts and Annette Potts, *Yanks Down Under: The American Impact on Australia* (Melbourne: Oxford University Press, 1985); Anthony J. Barker and Lisa Jackson, *Fleeting Attraction: A Social History of American Servicemen in Western Australia during the Second World War* (Nedlands: University of Western Australia Press, 1996).

[5] See, for example, Kay Saunders and Helen Taylor, "The Reception of Black American Servicemen in Australia during World War II: The Resilience of 'White Australia,'" *Journal of Black Studies* 25, no. 3 (1995): 338. See also Philip Bell and Roger Bell, *Implicated: The United States in Australia* (Melbourne: Oxford University Press, 1993), 100.

[6] The notable exception is the work of Travis J. Hardy. Daniel Kryder has mentioned, briefly, African Americans' wartime experiences in Australia. See Travis J. Hardy, "Strangers in a Strange Land," Paper presented to the 2017 Australian and New Zealand Studies Association of North America Conference, Washington, DC, February, 2017; Daniel Kryder, *Divided Arsenal: Race and the American State during World War II* (Cambridge:

Australia was the subject of widespread discussion in the black press during the aftermath of Pearl Harbor, and white Americans considered Australians' liberal treatment of African Americans as a racial crisis that threatened white masculine hegemony both at home and abroad – it is congruent with the wider neglect of the part played by African Americans in the Pacific War.

This analysis also complicates Travis J. Hardy's argument that the wartime alliance between the United States and Australia was predicated in part on "a common racial worldview."[7] African Americans, in concert with a significant section of the Australian populace, framed an alternative racial alliance, premised on the subversion of white supremacy. One of the ironies – or, more accurately, contradictions – of the Pacific War was that African Americans, often perceived as a threat to the racial and sexual codes upon which white Australians' notions of national identity and citizenship were predicated, arrived in early 1942 to save Australia from the "Yellow Peril."

Building on an earlier argument – which demonstrated that African Americans' experiences in wartime Australia were more positive than historians had previously assumed – and treating black servicemen as agents of their own destiny, rather than merely as victims of white racism, it is suggested herein that Australians' willingness to discard the racial assumptions underpinning the White Australia Policy offered a positive example for postwar race relations in the American South.[8] If the White Australia Policy was vulnerable to change, so too was Southern segregation, which was similarly depicted as both immutable and inevitable. Hence there was a symbiosis between African Americans' personal experiences in wartime Australia and their struggle for political and social equality in the United States. African Americans were self-consciously situating their confrontation with Australian racism within the context of their wider opposition to both American segregation and Western colonialism. The White Australia Policy, they concluded, was a racial anachronism which,

---

Cambridge University Press, 2001), 170, n.4. See also Gerald Horne, *Race War!: White Supremacy and the Japanese Attack on the British Empire* (New York, NY: New York University Press, 2004), 181–3.

[7] Travis J. Hardy, "Race as an Aspect of the U.S.–Australian Alliance in World War II," *Diplomatic History* 38, no. 3 (2014): 554.

[8] For an earlier revision of the orthodox interpretation of the white Australian reception accorded to African Americans during World War Two, see Brawley and Dixon, "Jim Crow Downunder," 607–32. See also Glenn A. Knoblock, *Black Submariners in the United States Navy, 1940–1975* (Jefferson, NC: McFarland & Co., 2005), 127–31.

if left untouched, would generate frictions that would precipitate another war across the Asia-Pacific region. Yet while blacks framed their quest for civil rights in terms of human equality, their attitudes toward Aboriginal Australians suggested a racial relativism – another expression of African American orientalism – that highlighted again the dilemmas confronting African Americans as they negotiated the tensions between racial and national identity.

At the outbreak of the Pacific War, with Japanese forces sweeping all before them, a nervous Australian government sought military assistance from the United States. This marked a dramatic change in Australia's strategic outlook, since defense planning had long centered around the nation's connections with Britain. But the demise of British power in the Far East – epitomized by the sinking of HMS *Prince of Wales* and HMS *Repulse* just three days after the Japanese attack at Pearl Harbor, and then by the fall of Singapore in February 1942 – demonstrated that the balance of power across Asia and the Pacific had shifted dramatically. As Australian Prime Minister John Curtin noted famously in late December 1941, "Australia looks to America."[9] Curtin's statement resonated among Australians, and the United States and Australia forged an enduring relationship based on many common values and principles. Yet the wartime relationship was not without differences. Although the presence of hundreds of thousands of American service personnel was a welcome bulwark against the widely feared Japanese invasion, it also precipitated significant political, social, and cultural tensions symbolized by the oft-repeated refrain that visiting Americans were "over-paid, over-sexed, and over here."[10]

Questions of race were at the center of these personal and political tensions.[11] Despite fears of a Japanese invasion, and notwithstanding the nation's embrace of American military power, the Australian government

---

[9] Melbourne *Herald*, December 27, 1941, at http://john.curtin.edu.au/pmportal/text/00468.html (accessed February 10, 2015).

[10] The *Christian Science Monitor's* Joseph C. Harsch, who arrived in Australia in February 1942, recalled hearing the phrase "overpaid, over-sexed, and over here" "very early" on during the American deployment. See Moore, *Over-Sexed, Over-Paid, and Over Here*, 100. For an analysis of Australians' continuing attachment to Britain during World War Two, see Richard Waterhouse, "Empire and Nation: Australian Popular Ideology and the Outbreak of the Pacific War," *History Australia* 12, no. 3 (2015): 30–54.

[11] "The American characteristic that most startled foreign observers," wrote Ken Coates and W. R. Morrison in 1990, "was racism." See Ken Coates and W. R. Morrison, "The American Rampant: Reflections on the Impact of United States Troops in Allied Countries during World War II," *Journal of World History* 2, no. 2 (1990): 210.

advised US authorities that it would prefer that African American servicemen were not deployed Down Under. In mid-January, 1942, the
Australian Government's Advisory War Council stated that it was "not
prepared" to "agree to [the] proposal that [a] proportion of United States
troops to be dispatched to Australia should be colored."[12] Even when the
nation's survival was apparently under threat, the racial principles encap-
sulated in the White Australia Policy remained sacrosanct. The Australian
Government was effectively seeking to superimpose the White Australia
Policy over its wartime alliance with the United States.

Confronting the bitter racial divide within their own military forces
only briefly – the prospect of "trouble" between black and white American
troops could not be discounted entirely – American policymakers and
commanders considered Australia's request.[13] Acknowledging that
Australia maintained a "sharp color line," and recognizing that neither
the Australian government nor people "desire the presence" of African
American servicemen, US authorities conceded that "under normal circumstances" it would be preferable to not send black troops to Australia.
The post-Pearl Harbor "emergency," however, rendered circumstances far
from normal. Consistent with policies implemented elsewhere (Britain's
preference to keep black servicemen out of the United Kingdom had been
overruled, for instance) and in an early indication that Australia and
the United States were "unequal allies," American authorities privileged
"military necessity" over Australia's racial anxieties.[14] While they assured

[12] Cited in Barry Ralph, *They Passed This Way: The United States of America, The States of Australia and World War II* (East Roseville, NSW: Kangaroo Press, 2000), 248. See also Ulysses Lee, *The Employment of Negro Troops* (Washington, DC: Office of the Chief of Military History, United States Army, 1966), 429; Kay Saunders, "Conflict between the American and Australian Governments over the Introduction of Black American Servicemen into Australia during World War Two," *Australian Journal of Politics and History* 33, no. 2 (1987): 39–46; E. Daniel Potts and Annette Potts, "The Deployment of Black Servicemen Abroad during World War Two," *Australian Journal of Politics and History* 35, no. 1 (1989): 92–6; Bryan D. Barnett, "Race Relations in Queensland during the Second World War – Pertaining to American Negro Regiments" (BA Honors disser- tation, University of Queensland, 1977), 22–9.

[13] "H.L.S.," Memorandum for the Chief of Staff. Subject: The Colored Troop Problem, March 23, 1942, Box 472, NM84, Entry 418, RG 165, Records of the War Department General and Special Staffs, National Archives and Records Administration, College Park, Maryland (NARA).

[14] Major General George V. Strong, Memorandum for the Assistant Chief of Staff, O.P.D. Subject: Utilization of Negro Troops in Friendly Foreign Territory, June 17, 1942, Box 472, NM84, Entry 418, RG 165, NARA. On the deployment of African American troops to Britain, see David Reynolds, *Rich Relations: The American Occupation of Britain, 1942–1945* (London: Harper-Collins, 1995), 217–18. Other studies of the American

their Australian hosts that African American servicemen would be stationed largely outside urban areas, and pledged that the black deployment to Australia would be limited in number, and would end as soon as the war was won, US authorities had begun dispatching black troops to Australia even before the end of 1941.[15] Unwittingly, by insisting that black troops would be deployed to Australia, normally racially regressive American commanders and policymakers were enabling African Americans to challenge white hegemony in countries such as Australia and Britain.

It was against that backdrop that African Americans and Australians contemplated each other cautiously during late 1941 and early 1942. Reflecting their lack of knowledge about African Americans, Australians expressed ambivalence about the arrival of thousands of black servicemen. African Americans had been infrequent visitors to Australia prior to World War Two. A handful of black sailors had been aboard the whaling vessels that had visited Australian shores from the eighteenth century, and some African Americans were attracted to the Australian colonies during the nineteenth-century Gold Rushes.[16] In the latter decades of the nineteenth century, African American entertainers were more regular visitors to Australia. Perhaps because they were still few in number, and perhaps because they were "more acculturated to white values and customs" than other nonwhites, black American entertainers reported that Australian racism was less virulent than that which they endured in the United States.[17]

Australia, however, was not throwing open its doors to African Americans. During the early decades of the twentieth century, fewer than twenty African Americans were typically granted visitors' visas each year by the Australian government – most were entertainers or sportsmen, permitted to stay only briefly. With black visitors still very much

---

presence in wartime Britain include Norman Longmate, *The G.I.'s: The Americans in Britain, 1942–1975* (London: Hutchinson, 1975), and Graham Smith, *When Jim Crow Met John Bull: Black American Soldiers in World War II Britain* (London: Tauris, 1987); David Reynolds, "The Churchill Government and the Black American Troops in Britain during World War II," *Transactions of the Royal Historical Society* 35 (1985): 113–33. The phrase "unequal allies" comes from Roger Bell, *Unequal Allies: Australian-American Relations and the Pacific War* (Carlton: Melbourne University Press, 1977).
[15] McKerrow, *American Occupation of Australia*, 151–2; Potts and Potts, *Yanks Down Under*, 14.
[16] E. Daniel Potts and A. Potts, "The Negro and the Australian Gold Rushes, 1852–1857," *Pacific Historical Review* 37, no. 4 (1968): 381–99.
[17] Richard Waterhouse, *From Minstrel Show to Vaudeville: The Australian Popular Stage, 1788–1914* (Sydney: New South Wales University Press, 1990), 148–9.

the exception, Australians' impressions of African Americans reflected long-standing racial stereotypes and the pedagogic power of Hollywood rather than an informed appreciation of black history and culture.[18] Visiting black sportsmen, lauded in the Australian press for their athletic prowess and physique, and African American entertainers, praised for their rhythm and musicality, evoked a measured admiration from Australian audiences. So long as African American visitors conformed to non-threatening racial "types," they were tolerated by Australians. As one black newspaper reported in March 1942, however, "colored scholars, scientists, and men of affairs were never welcomed" in Australia.[19]

Australians' admiration for African Americans was further tempered by apprehensions about black sexuality. Some black performers were barred from entering Australia and those who were admitted often had to pay a $500 bond to ensure their departure.[20] Others, like "Sonny Clay's Plantation Orchestra," had their apartments raided by the police before being charged with "disorderly conduct" and summarily deported with no recourse.[21] In the weeks following the expulsion of Clay's band in 1928, the real rationale for their deportation was provided by former Australian Prime Minister, William ("Billy") Hughes – and it was one that would have been both familiar and infuriating to African Americans. The musicians, Hughes explained, "had been too familiar with the white women since their arrival in Australia." Hughes depicted the Australian policy of deportation as a benign alternative to the American practice of lynching: "If that happened in the Southern" United States, Hughes noted, the culprits "would not be deported – they could not have lived overnight." Hughes thereby drew a comparison between the American South and Australia to which African Americans would refer during the Pacific War. Fueling Australians' racial and sexual concerns were fears that the nation might, as the Melbourne *Age* put it, "degenerate into a

[18] "American Dancers Invade Australia," *Chicago Defender*, November 13, 1926; "U.S. Thompson Is Still Hitting in Australia," *Chicago Defender*, May 1, 1937; "Australia A Haven for Colored Boxers," *Pittsburgh Courier*, November 13, 1926. See also Darryl McIntyre, "Paragons of Glamour: A Study of U.S. Military Forces in Australia" (PhD thesis, University of Queensland, 1989), 446–7; Rosemary Campbell, *Heroes and Lovers: A Question of National Identity* (Sydney: Allen and Unwin, 1989), 112–14.

[19] "Australia: 'White Man's Country,'" *New York Amsterdam Star-News*, March 28, 1942.

[20] "Must 'Be Good' and Have $500 to Enter Australia," *Chicago Defender*, December 7, 1929; "Race Actors Playing in Australia Bonded," *Philadelphia Tribune*, December 21, 1929.

[21] "Australia Enforces Color Line Bar: Efforts Made to Prohibit Alien Races, Deport U.S. Musicians in White Crusade," *Chicago Defender*, April 7, 1928.

miniature America."²² In the decades preceding World War Two, despite their increasing exposure to American culture, many Australians associated the United States with a racial and sexual discord that purportedly threatened Australia's nation's identity.

Australians' ignorance about African American culture and history persisted during World War Two. During the war the Australian military's "authorized education journal," *SALT*, published a number of pieces in which they sought to familiarize Australians with the Americans who were in the country in such large numbers. Between 1942 and 1945, however, just one essay in *SALT* was devoted to African Americans. At first glance, Lewis Sebring's May 1942 article appeared to contradict long-standing cultural and racial stereotypes regarding African Americans. Yet while he suggested that "Negroes Make Good Soldiers," Sebring – a correspondent for the *New York Herald Tribune* – presented an inadequate and distorted view of African Americans. Ignoring the period between the Civil War and World War Two, Sebring's potted history of black America implied that the struggle for civil rights had been won. African Americans, he claimed, "have taken their place in the life of the country, and many have become well known as business and professional men, as well as educators of their own race."²³

William Haymes's *The Aussies and the Yanks*, published in 1943, was no less problematic. The "American coloured boy," wrote Haymes, whether he be a "tractor driver, bulldozerman or just a labour unit boy, always remains the character we have established in our minds from the movie screen." Not content with investing Hollywood's depictions of African Americans with an almost documentary-like quality, Haymes reprised those stereotypes – physical, emotional, and intellectual. African Americans, he asserted, "walk in the same old way, a list to forward," with "arms dangling loosely." Insisting that "ninety-five per cent of the 'culud' boy cartoons" in his book were "fact," Haymes told his readers that African Americans' "irrepressible humour" never failed them, even when they were "scared." If that exercise in racial stereotyping was not

²² "Deport Musicians from Australia," *Philadelphia Tribune*, April 19, 1928; Melbourne *Age*, March 30, 1928, cited in Peter M. Sales, "White Australia, Black Americans: A Melbourne Incident, 1928," *Australian Quarterly* 46, no. 4 (1974): 79. See also "Australia Enforces Color Line Bar: Efforts Made to Prohibit Alien Races, Deport U.S. Musicians in White Crusade," *Chicago Defender*, April 7, 1928; "Australia Rejects Band," *Afro-American*, October 24, 1925.
²³ Lewis Sebring, "Negroes Make Good Soldiers," *SALT: Authorized Education Journal of Australian Army and Air Force* 3, no. 7 (May 18, 1942), 16–19.

sufficient confirmation of prevailing views of African Americans, cartoons included in *The Aussies and the Yanks* presented equally caricatured images, reiterating popular and unreconstructed misconceptions regarding blacks' alleged lack of courage and their inability to cope with the pressures of modern warfare.[24] While Haymes's book was written to entertain, Australians looked hard to find accurate and informed depictions of African Americans.

For their part, African Americans looked warily toward Australia. In the 1920s and 1930s the black press critiqued the White Australia Policy and race relations in Australia. As well as criticizing the treatment of Aboriginal Australians, black newspapers situated Australia's racial policies, domestic and foreign, within the context of Australians' fears of the Asia-Pacific region.[25] During the Depression, African Americans also linked Australia's racial attitudes to the nation's economic woes, which they argued were being compounded by a racially determined national indolence. Overturning stereotypes typically applied to African Americans, and reprising abolitionist and African American critiques of idle, slaveholding whites, the Baltimore *Afro-American* suggested that Australia's "impoverished condition" was exacerbated by the "general laziness of the white inhabitants, who are said to be chiefly interested in amusement and having an easy time."[26]

It is difficult to ascertain the extent to which the African American community was aware of the White Australia Policy prior to World War Two. But even if few African Americans knew about the policy prior to Pearl Harbor, the black leadership and press set about correcting that ignorance.[27] During late 1941 and early 1942, Australia figured prominently

[24] "Willo and Brillo" [William Haymes], *The Aussies and the Yanks: Frontline Fact, Fun and Fiction* (Sydney: F. Johnson, 1943), 4, 19.

[25] "Launch Desperate Attempt to Keep Australia White," *Chicago Defender*, July 11, 1925. See also "Australia Makes Fight to be White: Says America Taught Her a Few Things in Race Problem," *Chicago Defender*, March 25, 1922; "Australia Seeks White Supremacy: Dark Races Excluded by Rigid Rules, Students and Tourists Only Allowed," *Chicago Defender*, January 14, 1928; "Australia Bars All Black Folk Except Actors," *Afro-American*, September 19, 1924.

[26] "Australia, with 'White' Policy, is Bankrupt," *Afro-American*, September 13, 1930.

[27] The United States Army's official instructions for servicemen made no mention of the White Australia Policy. See Special Services Division, Army Service Forces, United States Army, *A Pocket Guide to Australia* (Washington, DC: War and Navy Departments, 1942). It is worth noting, too, that although African Americans occasionally conflated Australia and New Zealand – the *New York Amsterdam Star-News* held Australia's "brutal, bigoted persecutors" responsible for the extermination of "their 'coloureds' – the Mayoris" – they portrayed New Zealand's racial policies and values as a progressive and

in African American discourse as black editors, correspondents, and leaders contemplated both the reception African Americans would receive Down Under, and the significance of the White Australia Policy. African Americans' apprehensions melded individual, personal trepidations – how would they be received and treated by Australians? – with concerns regarding the prospect of helping to defend a nation with such a dubious record of race relations.

African Americans' misgivings about Australia, particularly as they were reflected in the well-founded suspicions that the Australian Government had sought to prevent the deployment of black servicemen to Australia, were articulated emphatically in the black press. "Australia's 'white soldiers only' edict," wrote the *Pittsburgh Courier* in March 1942, had "excited deep resentment among Negro leaders in the Capital."[28] That same month, as increasing numbers of African American troops began arriving in Australia, the *Chicago Defender* published a cartoon highlighting the contradictions associated with the Pacific War. A caricatured Japanese soldier approaches Australia, where a sign asserts "No Colored Races Allowed."[29] Aside from the obvious reference to a possible Japanese breach of the White Australian Policy, the *Defender's* cartoonist was alluding to the contradiction of African Americans fighting on behalf of a nation that during peacetime would have almost certainly refused them entry. That contradiction caused deep angst among African Americans. Condemning the paradox of "thousands of Negro soldiers" helping to defend "the white man's special preserve in the Pacific," black leaders contended that sending African Americans "to the defense of Australia" was "one of the most bitter experiences that any race may be called upon to face."[30] "What arguments," asked correspondent Lucius C. Harper,

---

dramatic contrast to those of neighboring Australia. As the *Afro-American* put it in 1943, "New Zealand both practices and fights for the democratic way of life." See "Australia's Bitter Pill," *New York Amsterdam News*, March 28, 1942; Mable Alston, "New Zealand Both Practices and Fights for the Democratic Way of Life," *Afro-American*, February 14, 1943. See also John Robert Badger, "World View: Colonies 'Down Under,'" *Chicago Defender*, April 21, 1945.

[28] "Australia Bans Race Fighting Men, Claim; Rumor 'White Only' Edict Given to U.S." *Pittsburgh Courier*, March 28, 1942.

[29] "So Sorry Please," *Chicago Defender*, March 14, 1942.

[30] "Australia: 'White Man's Country,'" *New York Amsterdam Star-News*, March 28, 1942; "U.S. Colored Troops in Australia," *New York Amsterdam Star-News*, March 21, 1942. See also Leslie Pinckney Hill, "What the Negro Wants and How to Get It: The Inward Power of the Masses," in *What the Negro Wants*, ed. Rayford W. Logan (Chapel Hill, NC: University of North Carolina Press, 1944), 79, and Roy Wilkins, "The Negro Wants Full Equality," in Logan, ed., *What the Negro Wants*, 114.

"can the democracies give the colored races that Australia must be saved?" (Figure 4.1).[31]

Recognizing, also, the international dimensions of the White Australia Policy, African Americans critiqued the ways in which the nation's racial policies had shaped its foreign relations. In August 1942, black journalist Louis Lautier contended that the Australian practice of "black birding" – whereby Pacific Islanders were tricked or kidnapped and taken to work on Australian sugar and cotton plantations – was a significant "obstacle" to Solomon Islanders' "acceptance of civilization."[32] Moreover, while Australians had ostensibly disavowed the role of a colonial power, African Americans recognized otherwise. In September 1943 *Afro-American* correspondent Vincent Tubbs criticized the Australian administration of Papua as "a benevolent dictatorship" designed to preserve the privileges of the "white governors"; later that year the *Pittsburgh Courier* used Australia's refusal to grant rights of citizenship to the widely valorized "Fuzzy Wuzzy Angels" – New Guinean natives helping Australian and American forces fight the Japanese – to lambast the White Australia Policy. Neither the indigenous peoples of New Guinea, who had sacrificed so much to help wounded Australian troops, nor "any other person of a non-white race," stated the *Courier*, could become a "citizen of Australia."[33]

Comparing Australia's racial policies to Southern segregation, and labeling Australia as the "whitest of the lily-whites" – a reference to the notorious Southern white Republicans who during the late nineteenth and early twentieth centuries had gained local control of the Party at the expense of African Americans – black leaders claimed that Australia's racially prescribed "immigration laws" matched "Dixie's worst."[34] The African American critique of the White Australia Policy extended beyond comparisons with the American South, as black leaders and correspondents

---

[31] Harper, "Dustin' Off the News: The Stronghold of White Supremacy is Facing Destruction," *Chicago Defender*, March 28, 1942.

[32] Louis Lautier, "Solomon Islands Populated by Dark Skinned Natives," *Pittsburgh Courier*, August 29, 1942.

[33] Vincent Tubbs, "Papuans Chop Up Tax Collector, Bake Him Slowly; Eat Him," *Afro-American*, September 25, 1943; "The British and the Darker Peoples," *Pittsburgh Courier*, December 11, 1943. On African American praise for New Guinea natives, see "They Call Them 'Fuzzy Wuzzy Angels' in New Guinea," *Cleveland Call and Post*, March 27, 1943.

[34] Samuel A. Haynes, "World Horizon," *New Journal and Guide*, April 11, 1942; "White-Supremacy Continent: Immigration Laws Match Dixie's Worst," *Pittsburgh Courier*, September 22, 1945. See also George Shuyler, "The Caucasian Problem," in Logan, ed., *What the Negro Wants*, 283.

"So Sorry Please"

FIGURE 4.1. "So Sorry Please": *Chicago Defender*, March 14, 1942. The *Chicago Defender* highlights the contradictions of Australia's racial policies
Reproduction with permission of the copyright owner. Further reproduction prohibited without permission.

denounced Australia's notorious "'white' policy" as "a symbol of the most brutal prejudices and vicious types of discrimination generally practiced in the United States and the Union of South Africa."[35] Most provocatively, they contended there was "no difference between sending a

[35] "Australia: 'White Man's Country,'" *New York Amsterdam Star-News*, March 28, 1942.

black man to fight on the side of Adolf Hitler to uphold his hellish racial and social theories and sending him to fight for the defense of Australia, which boasts that it is a 'white man's country.'"36 Suggesting that African American troops had "been assigned by Divine Providence to defeat Hitlerism in Australia before" they tackle "the bigger job of blasting the Nazi armies from the battlefields of Europe," and condemning Australia's "treatment of the African and Asiatic races," the *New York Amsterdam Star-News* contended that Australia must not be shielded "from the righteous consequences of her faithlessness to humanity."37

The transnational politics of race were never far from the surface as African Americans condemned Australia's wartime opportunism. Noting that "white Australians have lost all fear of the black man as a pack of yellow devils lounge [sic] at their island paradise," African Americans praised the "exploits" of black troops as "an eyeopener" to Australians "who up until the war were intent on keeping the country 'white.'"38 Recognizing that it was galling for Australia, "a vociferously self-asserting white man's country," to "accept protection and maybe salvation at the hands of colored soldiers," African Americans hoped that by liberating Australians from the thrall of racism they would extend democracy to "a distant outpost of white civilization."39

If that was a quintessentially American self-perception regarding the redemptive power of the United States, so too was the means by which African Americans imagined they would transplant their democratic vision on racially unreconstructed Australians. The black mission of racial liberation in Australia – a place where, as white author Pearl Buck prophesied in a letter widely republished in the black press, "white people" might be "made slaves by their conquerors" – was predicated on images of black military power.40 In April 1942 *The Crisis* juxtaposed a reference to suggestions that Japanese forces might encounter a more determined foe in Australia than they had encountered to date, with the news that "American Negro troops have already landed in Australia."41 Portraying black troops with weapons shouldered, marching proudly and confidently as they landed in Australia, a cartoon published in the

36 "U.S. Colored Troops in Australia," *New York Amsterdam Star-News*, March 21, 1942.
37 "Australia: 'White Man's Country,'" 1942.
38 Samuel A. Haynes, "World Horizon,'" *New York Amsterdam Star-News*, April 11, 1942; "Land Down Under Rebuilt by Our Engineer Units," *Philadelphia Tribune*, July 4, 1942.
39 "Australia's Bitter Pill"; "Undemocratic Australia," *Chicago Defender*, April 4, 1942.
40 "May Guide Way to Universal Freedom," *Afro-American*, March 7, 1942.
41 "White Man's War," *The Crisis*, April 1942, 11.

Chicago Defender depicted a masculine and martial image of African American servicemen challenging the racism of America's allies, as well as its adversaries.[42] Representing African Americans as rescuing not only those threatened by the Japanese, but also those suffering in racially discriminatory societies, the *Defender* asserted that African Americans were bearing "the spirit of freedom to distant parts." While "Uncle Sam" – a moniker which in this instance self-consciously included African Americans, and which suggested an African American appropriation of the notion of American exceptionalism – was willing to help maintain Australia's freedom from the Japanese, the *Defender* insisted that "keeping a FREE land 'WHITE' is not possible in this NEW, FREE AGE!" African Americans were, instead, embarking on a mission to "MAKE AUSTRALIA FREE."[43] The black warrior was also a black agent of transnational racial liberation (Figure 4.2).

Given the numerous critical references to Australia in the African American press during late 1941 and early 1942, it was unsurprising that black troops expressed apprehension regarding the reception they would receive in Australia. At first blush, those fears were well founded. Concomitant with various expressions of institutional and individual racism from Australians, black servicemen were generally not treated as well as their visiting white compatriots. African Americans were involved in a number of violent incidents, particularly in Queensland, where a majority of blacks were stationed. The records of the Queensland Police force, and those of their counterparts in other states, affirm that Australian authorities continued to fear the presence of African Americans. Police in Sydney, for instance, were accused of heavy-handedness in dealing with African Americans, and the black press accused Australian police forces of obsessing about any sign of intimacy between white Australian women and African American servicemen.[44]

---

[42] "To the Rescue," *Chicago Defender*, April 18, 1942.

[43] "They Bear the Spirit of Freedom to Distant Parts," *Chicago Defender*, April 18, 1942.

[44] Kay Saunders and Helen Taylor, Daryl McIntyre, Bryan Barnett, and – most recently – David J. Longley, have all described the discrimination and violence to which African Americans were subjected during their time in Australia. See Saunders and Taylor, "Reception of Black American Servicemen," 337–8; McIntyre, "Paragons of Glamour," 471–4, 482–3; Barnett, "Race Relations in Queensland," 44–56; David J. Longley, "Vincent Tubbs and the Baltimore *Afro-American*: The Black Press, Race, and Culture in the World War II Pacific Theater," *Australasian Journal of American Studies* 35, no. 2 (2016): 68–71. See also Jane Fidcock, "The Effects of the American 'Invasion' of Australia, 1942–45," *Flinders Journal of Politics and History* 11 (1985): 91–101. Keith Gilyard has suggested that Australians' friendly relations with African Americans were aresponse to white Americans' success in winning the affections of Australian

FIGURE 4.2. "To the Rescue": *Chicago Defender*, April 18, 1942. The black press celebrates African Americans' role in saving Australia

With the support of their American counterparts – who like some white American servicemen believed that Australians' naiveté regarding race relations could be attributed in part to the White Australia Policy, which had prevented Australians from learning how to "handle" the "colored people" – Australian authorities sought to impose a local form of segregation on visiting African Americans.[45] After transiting through Sydney,

---

women. Having "lost" that "battle," he contends, "Australians felt no need to help white Americans enforce U.S.-style discrimination against African American GIs." The problem with Gilyard's argument is one of timing: as African Americans' accounts make clear, black servicemen encountered a warm welcome from Australians as soon as the first black units arrived Down Under. See Keith Gilyard, *John Oliver Killens: A Life of Literary Black Activism.* (Athens, GA: University of Georgia Press, 2010), 59.

[45] Lieutenant A. E. Rogers to Mrs. A. E Rogers, July 26, 1942, Box T-1418, RG 338, NARA; Lieutenant C. F. Holloway to Mrs. C. E. Holloway, May 31, 1942, Box T-1418, RG 338, NARA.

Melbourne, or Brisbane, a majority of African American troops were deployed to remote areas of Australia. Meanwhile, many black servicemen, particularly those stationed in Brisbane, found themselves confined – "jim crowed" as the *Chicago Defender* put it – into specific, segregated parts of those cities.[46] It was no coincidence that the areas to which US authorities sought to restrict African Americans corresponded to those parts of the city to which Aborigines had historically been confined.[47]

Australian attempts to regulate and segregate African Americans were not the only manifestations of local racism. As late as November 1942, nine months after the arrival of the first detachments of African Americans, authorities were forced to deny a rumor among black servicemen that the Australian government had insisted that "a $500 bond had to be posted for each U.S. Negro soldier entering the country," to "guarantee their repatriation after the war." While the black press reported that those rumors were "probably spread" by mischievous "Axis agents," they were more likely informed by the knowledge that such bonds had routinely been imposed on African Americans visiting Australia during the interwar years.[48] Although a majority of the Australian press had revised their earlier unfavorable views of African Americans, some negative reporting continued. In particular, the misnamed *Truth* continued to publish incendiary stories alleging that black troops were a menace to local women.[49]

Many white Americans needed no persuading that African Americans were sexually predatory. Allegations of African American sexual violence prompted a sharp response from US authorities. Commenting on the forthcoming trial of Private Edward Joseph Leonski – a white American

---

[46] "Jim Crow Soldiers in Australian City," *Chicago Defender*, November 13, 1943. See also Lieutenant C. F. Holloway to Mrs. C. E. Holloway, May 31, 1942, Box T-1418, RG 338, NARA; McIntyre, "Paragons of Glamour," 466. See also Kay Saunders, "Racial Conflict in Brisbane in World War II: The Imposition of Patterns of Segregation upon Black American Servicemen," *Brisbane at War. Brisbane History Group Papers* 4 (1986): 29–34. Kate Darian-Smith has noted that while "some" of Melbourne's "brothels and others services" were "unofficially" labeled "'black only,'" the city "was never geographically segregated along racial lines." See Darian-Smith, *On the Home Front: Melbourne in Wartime, 1939–1945* (Oxford: Oxford University Press, 1990), 212.

[47] The deployment of African Americans in wartime Australia, noted Saunders and Taylor, prompted the reaffirmation and enlargement of "internal segregative practices." See Saunders and Taylor, "Reception of Black American Servicemen in Australia," 333.

[48] "Australians Spike Reports of Bonds for Negro Soldiers," *New York Amsterdam Star-News*, November 28, 1942.

[49] Fletcher Martin, "Army Refutes Charges that GI's are Menace," *Philadelphia Tribune*, July 29, 1942.

serviceman ultimately found guilty of, and executed for, the May 1942 murder of three Australian women in Melbourne – the *Chicago Defender* remarked that it was fortunate that there were no African American troops "near the scene of the killings." The *Defender's* comment spoke both to the ever-present fear among blacks regarding the "reprehensible methods" by which the American press and people would "play up" cases where it was assumed that African Americans were involved, and to the fear that rumors of black involvement in the Melbourne murders "might have fallen on willing ears since Australia had never admitted Negroes until this contingent of black troops arrived."[50] In spite of the convivial reception they were receiving from many white Australians, African Americans feared that Australians' friendly demeanor was precarious.

These concerns were exacerbated by a less well-known, but for African Americans far more troubling wartime case, in which four black soldiers and a black merchant seaman were found guilty of, and sentenced to hang for, the January 1944 rape of a white American Red Cross worker in Townsville, Queensland. This trial attracted widespread attention from the black press, and mindful of the apparent parallels with the earlier case of Frank Fisher and Edward R. Loury in New Caledonia, the National Association for the Advancement of Colored People (NAACP) paid close attention to the case against the black soldiers in Australia.[51] In the words of *The Crisis*, any black serviceman "faced with the average American white attitude toward an incident involving a Negro man and a white woman, simply" did "not get a fair trial."[52] As in the earlier case in New Caledonia, in defending the black men accused of rape, the African American press veered close to ascribing some of the responsibility for the alleged crime on the victim. As *The Crisis* put it, the victim "admitted she had been on a drinking party and was trying to hitch-hike to her quarters."[53] Such behavior, implied *The Crisis*, was a contributing factor to the incident that led to the conviction of the accused. The vexed relationship between race and sex across the Pacific Theater was never straightforward, but given the looming execution of the five black men, the priorities of the black press and leadership were clear. Eventually, following a sustained campaign in the African American press, vigorous

[50] "White Soldier Faces Trial in Australia Rape, Murder," *Chicago Defender*, June 13, 1942. On the Leonski case, see Potts and Potts, *Yanks Down Under*, 233–4; Ivan Chapman, *Private Eddie Leonski* (Sydney: Hale and Iremonger, 1982).
[51] "NAACP Probes Death Penalty of 5 Soldiers," *Philadelphia Tribune*, April 8, 1944.
[52] "Court-Martial for Rape," *The Crisis*, June, 1944, 185.
[53] Editorial: "Black and White Rape," *The Crisis*, July, 1944, 217.

lobbying by the NAACP, and a campaign by "Solicitor Williams," a civilian lawyer in Townsville, General Douglas MacArthur commuted the death sentences to life imprisonment.[54]

The racial crisis in the US military arising from the presence of black troops in Australia was further evidenced by a major outbreak of interracial violence in May, 1942. While the November 1942 "Battle of Brisbane," waged between Australian and visiting US troops, was a major incident in the history of wartime Queensland, and has become part of the popular Australian narrative regarding the wartime American presence, an earlier outbreak of violence in Townsville, 850 miles north of Brisbane, has been largely hidden from Australians' historical consciousness.[55] Although the "Townsville Mutiny" of May 1942 remains vague within Australian history and historiography, it received considerable attention from US military authorities during the weeks and months following the incident. Mindful that the Australian government had resisted the deployment of African Americans, who had only recently arrived in Australia, US authorities had an obvious motive for investigating the events in Townsville and ensuring they were neither repeated nor widely publicized. As *Time-Life* correspondent Robert Sherrod noted, the violence in Townsville was "one of the biggest stories of the war which can't be written – and which shouldn't be written, of course."[56]

While the "background of the incident" in Townsville was traced to "an accumulation of petty grievances," including "the monotonous life and hard labor," the catalyst for the riot was an assault by a white officer, Captain Francis H. Williams, commanding Company C of the 96th Engineers (Colored), on one of the men in his unit.[57] The Company, already disgruntled on account of Williams's poor leadership, was no

---

[54] "Australian Lawyer Asks NAACP Aid," *Philadelphia Tribune*, April 15, 1944; "5 Doomed Men Given Clemency by MacArthur," *Chicago Defender*, June 3, 1944.

[55] On the Battle of Brisbane, see, for example, Peter Thompson and Robert Macklin, *The Battle of Brisbane: Australians and Yanks at War* (Sydney: ABC Books, 2000); Kay Saunders, "Reassessing the Significance of the Battle of Brisbane," *Journal of the Royal Historical Society of Queensland* 15, no. 1 (1993): 70–3; John O. Killens, *And Then We Heard the Thunder* (New York, NY: Knopf, 1963), 441–85.

[56] Robert Sherrod, undated report, with processing note, "[Public activities-Biographical Information-Navy] Australia Material," Lyndon Baines Johnson Archives Collection, Lyndon B. Johnson Presidential Library, Austin, Texas. Townsville historian, Ray Holyoak, is continuing research into this episode.

[57] "Report of Riot at Townsville," Major General Julian T. Barnes to Chief of Staff, Southwest Pacific Area, 26th May 1942, RG 495, Box 992, Adjutant General, Formerly Classified General Correspondence, 1942–1944. 333–334.1, Records of Headquarters, United States Army Forces, Western Pacific, NARA.

longer willing to tolerate either his "rough and abusive language" or his ongoing mistreatment of his troops.[58] Convinced it was futile to seek redress for their grievances through the white-dominated military channels, the men of Company C concluded that the only way to remedy their situation was to kill Williams. Their plans, however, went awry, and the wounded Williams and another white officer were able to make their way from their camp into Townsville. Meanwhile, white officers from another American unit, their curiosity aroused by the sound of gunfire, had also been attacked by the mutineers. In desperation, one officer used petrol to ignite the base's ammunition dump, to prevent the mutineers from using its contents. Recognizing the seriousness of their actions, and having held the officers under siege for more than two hours, the mutineers ended their protest.[59]

The aftermath of the riot in Townsville reveals much about the US military's state of mind in mid-1942. In the relative privacy of his diary, Captain Hyman Samuelson, a white officer in the 96th, noted that he preferred to stay in New Guinea than take his troops to Australia, "where our troops would get in fights with white soldiers and" – he suggested obliquely – "in all kinds of other trouble."[60] Samuelson was not alone in seeking to avoid further problems. Although there can be no doubt regarding the depth of the institutionalized racism pervading the US armed forces, such was the strategic crisis at that stage of the war, that military circumstances took priority over the usual determination to keep African Americans in their place. And while initial enquiries suggested that the mutineers would be punished, identifying the guilty parties proved difficult. With nobody in Company C willing to testify against the mutineers, they went unpunished, and in June 1942, the month after the incident, the unit was transferred to New Guinea – where, it was reported soon after, its performance was "entirely satisfactory." In assessing the culpability of the men of Company C, moreover, Army authorities offered a rare acknowledgment of the factors underpinning the troops' riotous actions. Inexperience was a significant factor, with "the total length of

[58] Resume of Events in the Incident of May 23rd 1942, Concerning the 96th Engineers at Ross River Queensland, RG 495, Records of the Headquarters, United States Army Forces, Western Pacific (World War II), Entry 45, Box 185, File 291.2, 1; McKerrow, *American Occupation of Australia*, 160.

[59] McKerrow, *American Occupation of Australia*, 160.

[60] Samuelson, Diary entry March 16, 1943, in *Love, War, and the 96th Engineers (Colored): The World War Two New Guinea Diaries of Captain Hyman Samuelson*, ed. Gwendolyn Hall (Urbana, IL: University of Illinois Press, 1995), 159.

service ranged from considerably less than a year to about 14 months." Significantly, too, in explaining that a lack of camaraderie was key to the troops' violent reaction to their situation, the white investigative officers hypothesized that "colored soldiers may be expected to develop solidarity in military experience more slowly than white soldiers." Arguably, the reactions of the men of the 96th during, and subsequent to the events of May 22 – particularly the refusal of any of the men of Company C to testify against the mutineers – revealed precisely the opposite: they were exhibiting a degree of unit cohesion and loyalty that owed much to the particular circumstances they confronted as black troops in a white-dominated military hierarchy. Similarly, while the post-riot treatment of Williams potentially indicated a degree of racial enlightenment on the part of Army commanders – there were plans to court-martial him - military circumstances intervened, and the court-martial was "held in abeyance" – in effect, abandoned – as most of those involved in the riot soon found themselves deployed to New Guinea.[61]

More generally, however, when military circumstances were less urgent, the depth of white racism was affirmed by the violence – vigilante as well as official – against African Americans in Australia who transgressed acceptable forms of behavior.[62] Reports of violence against black troops in Australia – and elsewhere across the Pacific Theater – was one imperative behind the mid-1943 visit to Australia by Bishop John A. Gregg, of the African Methodist Episcopal Church.[63]

While Gregg's generally upbeat assessment of African Americans' situation in wartime Australia reflected a determination to present a positive image for the sake of morale, it is unlikely he would have glossed over serious racial problems had he found them, particularly given President Franklin D. Roosevelt's request for a candid assessment of racial issues

---

[61] "Notes on Staff Conference relating to Report of Inspector General and General Court Martial Charges arising out of the armed riot in Company 'C', 96th Engineer Separate Battalion, near Townsville, on May 22, 1942," June 28, 1942, RG 495, Box 992, Adjutant General, Formerly Classified General Correspondence, 1942–1944. 333–334.1, NARA See also McKerrow, *American Occupation of Australia*, 161.

[62] Some of the worst excesses against African American troops in Australia were perpetrated by US Military Police. Poorly trained, undermanned, and beset by the racist values that so thoroughly permeated the armed forces, white American MPs – there were few black MPs – had little hesitation in resorting to violence when dealing with African American troops. Ruth Danenhower Wilson noted that one battalion of African American MPs had been reassigned as "Port Companies," whose work comprised the "loading of ships." See Ruth Danenhower Wilson, *Jim Crow Joins Up*, Revised ed. (New York, NY: William J. Clark, 1944), 97.

[63] Enoch P. Waters, "MacArthur Welcomes Gregg," *Chicago Defender*, July 24, 1943.

FIGURE 4.3. Flanked by members of the 630th Ordnance Company, Bishop
John Andrew Gregg fondles a pet koala bear adopted by
Pfc. Sammy Hurt, July 21, 1943
Courtesy: National Archives 111-SC-180917.

in the Pacific Theater.[64] Indeed, the common assumption that Gregg
would present an unvarnished account of the black situation in Australia
prompted other concerns. Fearing that Gregg would incite rather than
merely report on black troops in Australia, for at least some of his time
there he was under surveillance by US military authorities. That those
authorities felt it necessary to monitor an individual of Gregg's reputation
and stature attests to their racial anxieties. Reporting on an address delivered by Gregg to black servicemen in the Queensland town of Cluden, it
was noted with some relief that Gregg had avoided provoking his audience and shunned any reference to recent racial disorders in either the
United States or Australia.[65]

---

[64] See E. F. Joseph, "Bishop Gregg Back from Tour of the Pacific," *Afro-American*, August
28, 1943.
[65] McKerrow, *American Occupation of Australia*, 163.

As Gregg's visit suggested, the black presence in wartime Australia prompted a range of responses from American and Australian authorities, and from African Americans themselves. Paying close attention to black sources complicates our understanding of the black experience in wartime Australia. Rather than focusing exclusively on the negative press reports, or the incidents involving African Americans, the more telling point – repeated in a range of published and unpublished primary sources – is that blacks were treated much better in "White" Australia than they had anticipated, and much better than they were treated in many parts of the United States. There was a significant disjunction between official Australian government policy and many Australians' interactions with African Americans. As the *Chicago Defender* noted, the friendly welcome accorded to black troops from the Australian people was in sharp contrast to Prime Minister John Curtin's declaration that his nation "would remain 'Free and White.'"[66] Further confounding matters, and perhaps leading some historians to overemphasize the negative aspects of the black experience in wartime Australia, African Americans incurred the wrath of white American servicemen stationed Down Under. Yet the cause of that wrath – many white Americans took great offense at the willingness of some Australian women to socialize with black Americans – provides the most compelling evidence that African Americans were welcomed warmly by Australians. To the irritation of their white compatriots, some blacks found themselves invited into Australian homes – and, on occasion, other more intimate places.

In their letters home, and in conversations with black correspondents, African Americans described "wonderful" relationships with their "hospitable and most congenial" Australian hosts, who "treated us better than we've been treated anywhere in the world."[67] Of his time in the Western Australian city of Perth, black Navy veteran Elvin Mayo recalled being "taken into people's homes – there was no prejudice."[68] Echoing black correspondent-turned soldier Jimmy Hicks's comment that white Australians "have absolutely no racial prejudices," and could

---

[66] "They Bear the Spirit of Freedom to Distant Parts," *Chicago Defender*, April 18, 1942.
[67] James Allan Strawder, AFC2001/001/72519, Veterans History Project Collection, American Folklife Center, Library of Congress, Washington, DC (VHP-LoC); "Soldier Praises Congenial Australians in Letter," *Atlanta Daily World*, October 29, 1942; Sam Lacy, "Back after Year of Jap War Service," *Chicago Defender*, May 1, 1943. See also Brawley and Dixon, "Jim Crow Downunder," 614–19; George Bracey, interview published in Knoblock, *Black Submariners*, 268.
[68] Elvin Mayo, interview published in Knoblock, *Black Submariners*, 320.

FIGURE 4.4. Nurses serving with the 268th Station Hospital in Australia receive
their first batch of mail, November 29, 1943
Courtesy: National Archives 111-SC-370740.

"not understand why our officers insist on their bi-racial policies," John
E. Hatcher reflected on differences in racial attitudes between white
Americans and white Australians. "Anywhere you wanted to go, or anything you wanted to do," he recalled, was permissible in Australia. Asked
if he felt freer in Australia, Hatcher was unequivocal: "Yes, yes, we did."[69]

---

[69] "Negro Troops Say Aussies 'Fine Folks," *Cleveland Call and Post*, September 12, 1942;
John E. Hatcher, AFC/2001/001/78373, VHP-LoC.

As Sergeant Alfred Covan Stevens noted in 1943, Australians treated him and "all the rest" of his "comrades as brothers."[70] If the language of black servicemen was effusive, and overlooked the continuing manifestations of white Australian racism, the interracial hospitality and fraternity they experienced during their time in Australia would have been unthinkable in many parts of the United States.

Few Australians were conscious that they were complicit in this war-time challenge to international racism. Although a number of churches and trade unions – who justified their longstanding support for the White Australia Policy on the grounds that it was a "political" response to an "influx of Asiatics and Orientals" taken to Australia for the specific purpose of providing cheap labor – offered their support to African Americans, Australians' enthusiasm for black Americans was usually instinctive, rather than self-conscious.[71] While African Americans were often viewed as anthropological curios – with "their jet black skin, white teeth and thick lips," the "Negroes" were "a strange sight," wrote Australian Army chaplain David Tratten – many Australians looked beyond their curiosity or misgivings about their black visitors.[72] In part, Australians' friendly response to the arrival of African Americans was pragmatic: with Australia's military resources stretched to breaking point, any American, regardless of their race or ethnicity, was welcome. During the early months of 1942, before Japan's defeats in the Coral Sea and at Midway, and before Australian forces had repelled the Japanese advance in New Guinea, previously held reservations regarding the presence of African Americans were abandoned without embarrassment. "We look upon Negro troops," noted Francis M. Forde, the Minister of War, "as part of the United States Army." In suggesting that the government "would not be so presumptuous as to place any bar against any form

---

[70] "Veteran of Pacific Fighting Experienced Many Thrills," *Pittsburgh Courier*, June 19, 1943. See also Bill Stevens, cited in *The Invisible Soldier: The Experience of the Black Soldier*, ed. Mary Penick Motley (Detroit, MI: Wayne State University Press, 1975), 75; Clarence Toomer, cited in Christopher Paul Moore, *Fighting for America: Black Soldiers– The Unsung Heroes of World War II* (New York, NY: One World/Ballantine, 2005), 64.

[71] "Australians Deplore Policy of U.S. Army," *New Journal and Guide*, November 28, 1943. On the trade unions and African Americans, see also Robert A. Hall, *Black Diggers: Aborigines and Torres Strait Islanders in the Second World War* (Canberra: Aboriginal Studies Press, 1997), 75; Brawley and Dixon, "Jim Crow Downunder," 620.

[72] David Tratten, undated diary entry, Private Papers of David Tratten, PR00218, Australian War Memorial, Canberra (AWM). On leave in Perth, black submariner William Allison "noticed that everyone was watching me. Many of the folks there had never seen a Black man." See William Allison, interview published in Knoblock, *Black Submariners*, 262.

of assistance to the defense of this country," Forde was at best disingenuous, given that just four months earlier the government of which he
was a part had lobbied actively against the deployment of black troops
to Australia.[73] But the government's hypocrisy was congruent with the
wider contradiction between Australians' enduring support for the White
Australia Policy and the friendly welcome given to black servicemen, particularly during the early months of 1942.

The significance of that friendly reception was recognized immediately by black correspondents and editors. "When U.S. Negro troops first
landed in Australia," noted the *New York Amsterdam News*, "they were
treated like human beings. They were freely invited to the Australians'
homes to dinner, [and] hospitably accepted in hotels, dance halls and other
public places."[74] African Americans' self-described mission of undermining the precepts of the White Australia Policy entailed more than a charm
offensive, however. In mid-1943 the *Afro-American* linked Australians'
friendly welcome to their respect for African Americans' courage and
battlefield acumen. Remarking that Australians were "inclined to ignore
race, creed and color in opening their doors to Americans," the *Afro-
American* reported that Australians valued the martial prowess of African
American troops. "[E]veryone," in Australia, wrote the paper, "considers
the colored troops more than a match for the Japs as jungle fighters."[75] At
a time when white American military commanders were endeavoring to
keep black troops away from the frontlines, some white Australians were
evidently willing to forego disparaging stereotypes regarding black people. Likewise, what is most significant about African American criticism
of those sections of the Australian press that did report unfavorably on
the behavior of visiting black servicemen – notably stories in *Truth* – is
that even in mid-1944, long after the novelty of the African American
presence had worn off, and long after Australians' fear of invasion
had subsided, such reports were "the exception rather than the rule in
Australian newspapers."[76] As noted in a November 1943 report in the
Philadelphia Tribune, Australians deserved praise for their attempts to
"accept and treat Negroes as their equals."[77]

---

[73] Edgar T. Rouzeau, "Australia Welcomes Our Boys," *Journal and Guide*, April 4, 1942.
[74] "Facts and Nonsense," *New York Amsterdam News*, June 12, 1943.
[75] Joseph, "Bishop Gregg Back from Tour of Pacific."
[76] "Australian Press Still Biased," *New Journal and Guide*, July 29, 1944.
[77] "Claim American Whites Insist Aussies Jim-Crow Race Troops," *Philadelphia Tribune*,
November 28, 1943.

Several imperatives underpinned the friendly reception accorded to black servicemen. Along with the part African Americans were playing in defending Australia, and the fact that they were sojourners rather than prospective immigrants, the social and cultural dimensions of African Americans' wartime presence were of immediate and lasting significance. When Australians looked at African Americans they emphasized the "American" in "African American" – or, as they would have said, "American Negro." Finally, Australians saw African Americans as exotic, and worldly – and a novelty, who, in the frugal atmosphere of wartime Australia could provide a welcome distraction from the tedium of daily life.[78] Besides being better paid than their Australian allies, black servicemen enjoyed spending what many Australians considered a generous salary following the privations of the Depression.

While Australians continued to be exposed to caricatured images of African Americans, they enjoyed a range of wartime performances, professional and otherwise, by black Americans. There was, according to a 1943 report in the *Chicago Defender*, "an especially noticeable demand" among Australians "for Negro showfolk."[79] The wartime black social clubs where many Australians enjoyed performances from, and socialized with, African Americans provide a fascinating microcosm of the complexities of race relations in Australia. Brisbane's "Dr. Carver Club," the "Booker T. Washington Club" in Sydney, and similar establishments in other cities, were very different from the segregated facilities that were commonplace in many parts of the United States.[80] Although these social spaces were

[78] See Brawley and Dixon, "Jim Crow Downunder," 627–8. The sight of four African American nurses on the streets of an unnamed Australian city in 1943 reportedly caused "bedlam" and "held up the traffic." The nurses, it was claimed, received an "ovation" befitting "a procession of queens." See Joseph "Scoop" Jones, "Soldiers Cheer as First Nurses Reach Australia," *Pittsburgh Courier*, December 11, 1943; "Nurses, Hospital Unit in Australia," *Afro-American*, December 4, 1943. See also Enoch P. Waters, "Pacific Patter," *Chicago Defender*, August 12, 1944.

[79] Tom Carrigg and Enoch P. Waters, "War Correspondent Goes Stage Because Australians Want News," *Chicago Defender*, December 4, 1943. During the war, formal and semi-formal groups of black performers, such as the "577th Glee Club," which sang at the "Brisbane City Hall before a Methodist congregation of 3,500," and an African American Army chorus that performed on the grounds of Sydney's Government House on Easter Sunday, 1944, proved popular with Australian audiences. See "577th Glee Club Pleases Aussies," *Afro-American*, September 9, 1944; Moore, *Over-Sexed, Over-Paid, and Over Here*, 213.

[80] "Australian Club Serves S.P. Men," *Afro-American*, September 30, 1944; "Scoop" Jones, "'Down Under' Diary," *Journal and Guide*, December 18, 1943. On the Booker T. Washington Club, see "Australians Rap Treatment of Race Troops," *Atlanta Daily World*, November 22, 1942. On black women visiting the Carver Club, see Lenore

often "out of bounds" to white American service personnel, Australians were frequent visitors.[81] Following an October 1943 visit to Sydney's Booker T. Washington Club, correspondent Enoch P. Waters was struck by Australians' willingness to socialize with African Americans. Australian servicemen, he noted simply, had "wandered in and joined in the fun."[82]

Notwithstanding these positive assessments of Australians' willingness to socialize with African Americans, the "huge influx" of black servicemen challenged personal relations and values in myriad ways.[83] As fears for the moral welfare of Australian women merged with concerns regarding morale among Australian servicemen, particularly those deployed far from home, it was the prospect of sexual relations between black servicemen and white Australian women that most sharply provoked Australians' anxieties. A December 1942 report from the Department of Defence confirmed that Australian authorities remained concerned that "Negro personnel" were both "highly sexed" and sexually predatory.[84] US authorities expressed these anxieties vigorously from early 1942. Nervous that relations between African American men and Australian women would strain the wartime alliance between the two nations, US commanders worried that any blurring of the color line, particularly as it pertained to interracial sex, might prompt violence among American forces. But their deepest fear was that wartime breaches of the strictures against interracial sex would foment problems in postwar America. Even the apparently innocuous perception that Australian women considered African American men to be "more appreciative of a kindness," and more friendly and courteous than their white compatriots, caused alarm, since such perceptions led some women to express "a preference for entertaining Negro soldiers."[85]

Unsurprisingly, given white Australians' and Americans' preoccupation with the issue of interracial sex, when the first groups of black servicemen arrived in Australia, attention was focused on their interactions with the

Lucas, "4 R.C. Workers Reach Australia," *Pittsburgh Courier*, August 21, 1943; Will V. Neely, "Five American Girls Arrive in Australia," *Pittsburgh Courier*, March 25, 1944.

[81] "Hot Spots Hit Australia, Race Troops Christen 3 Service Clubs," *Chicago Defender*, June 5, 1943.

[82] Enoch P. Waters, Jr., "Racial Mixtures Found Widespread in Australia," *Chicago Defender*, October 16, 1943.

[83] See Michael Sturma, "Loving the Alien: The Underside of Relations between American Servicemen and Australian Women in Queensland, 1942–1945," *Journal of Australian Studies* 13, no. 24 (1989): 4.

[84] Department of Defence, Minute Paper, December 28, 1942, 54, 506/1/1, AWM.

[85] Waters, "Racial Mixtures Found Widespread in Australia."

local women. Despite the best attempts of Australian and US authorities to limit liaisons between Australian women and black servicemen, significant numbers of white Australian women refused to respect prevailing conventions regarding relationships – platonic, sexual, and everything in between – that violated the color line. It is impossible to quantify the number of relationships, broadly defined, that developed between black servicemen and Australian women. While relatively few in number, such relationships were sufficiently common – and, most significantly, sufficiently public – to prompt the attention of Australians and Americans alike. Pacific War veteran James Allan Strawder spoke for many of his black compatriots: "I saw more mixed couples in Townsville and Sydney than I saw in all my life in New York City."[86]

Having braced themselves for a hostile reception Down Under, many blacks were surprised by the friendly welcome they received from some Australian women. As the *Atlanta Daily World* reported in early April 1942, black soldiers were sometimes seen "chatting" with Australian girls, and "thus far no trouble has been reported."[87] In fact, while there was some veracity to suggestions that Australians were "hastening" to initiate "all kinds of Jim Crow arrangements" to "prevent" African Americans from making what was euphemistically described as "social contact" with Australians, more notable was the friendly reception given to black troops.[88] If the public declarations of Australian interracial hospitality must be read cautiously, they are corroborated by other, more private sources.

Displays of interracial affection caused alarm among white American servicemen and their commanders. Affronted by scenes of African Americans liaising with white Australians, the apparent willingness of Australians to discard the racialist principles codified in the White Australia Policy caused great angst for white Americans, who articulated their anxieties in their private correspondence. As one military censor's report noted, "white troops" based in Australia "frequently objected to the association of colored soldiers with local women."[89] For Sergeant John F. Line, of the US Army Air Force, the sight of "negars (sic) and

[86] Strawder, AFC/2001/001/72519, VHP-LoC. See also "Facts and Nonsense," *New York Amsterdam News*, June 12, 1943.
[87] "Negro Troops Find 'White Law' Exists in Australia," *Atlanta Daily World*, April 1, 1942.
[88] "Undemocratic Australia," *Chicago Defender*, April 4, 1942.
[89] APO 501, Headquarters, United States Army Forces in the Far East, G-2: Office of the Chief of Counter-Intelligence; Theater Censor. Correspondence with Base Censors 1944–1945, RG 496, 496/290/47/27/7-, Records of the General Headquarters, Southwest Pacific Area and United States Army Forces, Pacific (World War II) Box 24, *Censorship Survey of Morale* (June 1943–August 1945), 14, NARA.

white girls" sitting around "necking" was "disgusting as heck."[90] Aghast at the spectacle of black men socializing in public with white Australian women, one white American serviceman reported that African Americans were running "hog wild."[91] "When they [African Americans] get back to the States," concluded another American serviceman, "we won't be able to do anything with them."[92] White officers expressed similar disquiet. Having witnessed African American servicemen socializing with white Australian women, Captain J. E. Schooley worried that because African Americans in Australia enjoyed "lots of privileges" that were denied them in the American South, there would be "a lot of trouble after the war, especially in the South."[93] And although Lieutenant Colonel Ivy A. Pelzman was appalled by the "terrible setup" at a "colored service club," where "white girls" were "dancing and loving up the darkies," he held African Americans responsible for such breaches of the color line, and was sufficiently persuaded by the charms of a local woman, Katherine ("Kitty") Jacobs, to marry her in January 1944.[94]

Australians' generally tolerant attitude toward African Americans prompted various responses from US military commanders and servicemen. Among the most telling evidence of American authorities' concerns were their efforts to censor word of Australians' liberal attitudes and behavior. Already worried that attempts to segregate black and white troops stationed in Australia would "accentuate a feeling of racial discrimination" in the United States, when dozens of American servicemen, white and black, reported that Australians were treating African Americans with respect and even affection, US authorities resolved to censor such correspondence. Inevitably, these attempts failed, as the black press reported the unexpectedly warm welcome African American servicemen were receiving from many Australians, and as black troops redeployed back to the United States provided first-hand accounts of their experiences Down Under.[95]

[90] Sergeant John F. Line to Mrs. J. F. Line, May, 1942, T-1418, RG 338, NARA.

[91] T. S. Hood to S. F. Hood, June 18, 1942, Office of the Base Censor, South West Pacific Theater, T-1418, RG 338, NARA.

[92] Private Cecil Tabor to Mrs. Tabor, February 24, 1943, T-1419, RG 338, NARA.

[93] Captain J. E. Schooley to Steve Corrigan, February 20, 1943, Office of the Base Censor, South West Pacific Theater, Box T-1419, Records of the United States Army Commands, RG 338, 290/45/12/2-3, NARA.

[94] A. Pelzman to Miss Margaret V. Walker, February 13, 1943, T-1419, RG 338, NARA; "Women and War Work," (Sydney) *Truth*, January 16, 1944.

[95] Censor's Report, appended to Travis Dixon to Fred Dixon, January 5, 1943, T-1419, RG 338, NARA; Brawley and Dixon, "Jim Crow Downunder," 608.

If censorship was not sufficient to avert a possible postwar racial crisis, there were other well-tried means of defending the racial and sexual order. Besides claiming that African Americans were sexually and morally degenerate, and were infected with venereal disease, some white Americans held Australian women responsible for the interracial relationships. Linking white Australian women's social and sexual behavior to the preservation of the racial unity upon which citizenship and the nation were predicated, and echoing Australian authorities' earlier hope that local women would understand and respect the "national white policy," Australian women who socialized with African Americans were labeled as deviant.[96] Referring to "white girls of the lowest class," some white American servicemen criticized the moral and social stature of those women who were carousing with black servicemen.[97] Not all white Americans were so judgmental, but it was widely recognized that Australian women were complicit in flouting the color line. After seeing a "beautiful white girl with a Negro," Private George L. Isaaks lamented that the "girls don't think anything of it."[98]

These criticisms of Australian women attracted the attention of NAACP Executive Secretary Walter White. Visiting Australia in early 1945, he noted that an Australian Red Cross worker – "a university graduate and a member of an excellent family" – had recounted the "insults she suffered from American officers" when they learned she was "working at a Red Cross club for Negroes."[99] Irrespective of such insults, some Australian women continued to defy the prevailing racial and sexual order. Writing three years after the arrival of the first groups of African American troops in Australia, White noted that although Sydney's Booker T. Washington Club was situated in "a slum and red light district," and while the police "vice squad" was looking to "pounce upon 'mixed' couples or parties," local women were continuing to socialize with their black visitors.[100] Another African American visitor to the Booker T. Washington Club, Enoch Waters, also defended the moral stature of those Australian women who mingled with black servicemen. Noting that the "demeanor

[96] "Troops in Australia Cause Alarm; Ask Respect for 'White Policy,'" *New York Amsterdam Star-News*, April 4, 1942. See also Brawley and Dixon, "Jim Crow Downunder," 621–2.
[97] T. S. Hood to S. F. Hood, June 18, 1942, Box T-1418, RG 338, NARA.
[98] George L. Isaaks to Norma Fay Cohn, July 27, 1942, Box T-1418, RG 338, NARA.
[99] Walter White to unnamed recipient, March 23, 1945, Reel 24, *Papers of the NAACP, Part 17: National Staff Files, 1940–1955*, Microfilm, eds. John Bracey and August Meier (Bethesda, MD: University Publications of America, 1992).
[100] Walter White to "Dear Folks," March 23, 1945, Reel 24, *NAACP Papers: Part 17*.

of the women, and the behavior of the men were of the highest order," he implied that black servicemen's and Australian women's interests in each other were platonic. Waters was perhaps simply naïve, or, more plausibly, his report was an attempt to persuade his black readership that black servicemen's moral virtue remained intact. In either case, his report was part of the African American press's broad endeavor to present black servicemen's international behavior as an affirmation of their entitlement to the rights of citizenship. Yet Waters's report was of deeper significance. In emphasizing that "white" girls in the Booker T. Washington Club outnumbered the "colored girls" – by "colored" he meant Aboriginal – he underscored the complex racial and sexual dynamics associated with the African American presence in wartime Australia.[101] Besides insinuating that white women were of a higher social status than their Aboriginal counterparts, he also implied that white women's willingness to socialize with African Americans was evidence of black servicemen's decorum and their status as ambassadors for their race. Finally, while more will be said regarding African Americans' perceptions of, and interactions with Aboriginal Australians, it is unlikely that many of the white Australian women who associated comfortably with African Americans would have so readily socialized with Aboriginal Australians – at least those they recognized as such.

The complexities of race relations in wartime Australia were further highlighted by marriages between black servicemen and Australian women. During and in the immediate aftermath of the Pacific War, 15,000 Australian women married American servicemen and migrated to the United States. The overwhelming majority of these women married white Americans, but a small minority – fifty women, according to a wartime report from correspondent Robert Sherrod – wed African Americans.[102] Although Sherrod almost certainly exaggerated the number of marriages, and while the historical record pertaining to marriages between African American servicemen and Australian women is predictably sparse, glimpses of such relationships can be found in a range of

[101] Waters, "Racial Mixtures Found Widespread in Australia."
[102] Robert Sherrod, "Australia Wants the GIs Back," *Life*, September 22, 1947, 16. See also Potts and Potts, *Yanks Down Under*, 369; Annette Potts and Lucinda Strauss, *For the Love of a Soldier: Australian War-Brides and Their GIs* (Sydney: ABC Enterprises, 1987), 63. On war brides, see also Robyn Arrowsmith, *All the Way to the USA: Australian WWII War Brides* (Mittagong: Robyn Arrowsmith, 2013). Victoria Grieves is conducting research into the children born of wartime relationships between Australian women and visiting American servicemen, including African American servicemen.

sources. Wartime black newspapers included occasional references to relationships between Australian women and black servicemen, and censored correspondence from white American servicemen included sharp, if predictable, criticism of marriages between African Americans and Australian women.[103]

Marriages – or even the prospect of marriages – between black servicemen and Australian women constituted a provocative and potent challenge to the cultural and legal bases of both the White Australia Policy and Southern segregation. Undoubtedly, these interracial marriages caused alarm among some Australians.[104] But they prompted a renewed racial and moral panic within the US military. "I am particularly distressed," wrote one American officer in mid-1944, "by the marriage of negro soldiers and Aussie women."[105] Not only did these marriages provoke the ire of American and Australian authorities, and not only did the Australian government make it clear that black servicemen would not be allowed to remain in Australia at war's end, but Australian women who married African Americans confronted significant legal and social challenges upon their arrival in the United States.[106] Despite the excitement of marriage and the novelty of moving to the United States, the bonds of romance were tested by pangs of homesickness and cultural unfamiliarity, and compounded by a racial imperative that meant interracial marriages were subject to widespread censure – and illegal in thirty of the forty-eight American states.[107] The handful of marriages between white Australians and African Americans therefore existed in a kind of legal limbo, or marital statelessness, since the legal codes of Australia and the United States restricted or even prohibited the citizenship and residential options for the married couple. In the words of Robert Sherrod, such marriages were "bound to fail."[108]

---

[103] See, for example, "Negro Sergeant Marries Aussie," *Chicago Defender*, June 26, 1943.

[104] See "Homecoming," *Time*, May 1, 1944.

[105] APO 501, Headquarters, United States Army Forces in the Far East, Censorship Survey of Morale – Rumors, Propaganda. Issued by the Assistant Chief of Staff, G-2, June 1944, RG 496, 496/290/47/27/7-, Records of the General Headquarters, Southwest Pacific Area and United States Army Forces, Pacific (World War II) Box 24, *Censorship Survey of Morale*, 49, NARA.

[106] McKerrow, *American Occupation of Australia*, 76–7.

[107] Reynolds, *Rich Relations*, 231.

[108] Sherrod, "Australia Wants the GIs Back." See also Hall, *Black Diggers*, 75–6; Michael McKernan, *All In!: Australia during the Second World War* (Melbourne: Thomas Nelson, 1983), 198.

At war's end, black correspondent Elder H. Russell reflected on the obstacles confronting African American servicemen and Australian brides, and the reception they would receive in postwar America. Enjoining his readers to "accept in good faith" servicemen's wives, even if "they are from another country or are of another race," he explained that US military authorities in Australia, including a "white base chaplain" who "did not believe" in "mixed marriages," had gone to considerable lengths to thwart such marriages.[109] That chaplain's anxieties were representative of those expressed by many of his white compatriots.

Some black servicemen, however, were undeterred by such concerns. In late 1943 – after a year negotiating his way through "red tape" – Lieutenant Hampson H. Fields became the first "Negro officer to crack the ice and marry an Australian girl." Anticipating an inevitable question, African American correspondent Joseph "Scoop" Jones noted that the bride, "Miss Norma Baptiste," was "of French and Australian descent." Reports of the wedding exuded optimism, and even the brief report in the Sydney *Truth* – which had done little to defuse tensions involving African Americans – identified Fields as being from the "U.S.A.," with no reference to his race.[110] By mid-1945, however, when the married couple arrived in Chicago, the tone of that city's black newspaper was more measured. While Norma Fields was optimistic that she would "like America," the *Defender* was less sanguine, noting in the title of the article that she would confront a "race problem." The editors did not elaborate on that "problem," but whether they were foreseeing individual expressions of racism against the Fields's interracial marriage, or whether they were alluding to the larger questions of African Americans' place in postwar America, the tone of the headline belied the hopeful expressions captured in the accompanying photograph of the young couple.[111] At war's end Hampson Fields stayed in the Army, serving in Korea and then Vietnam, and reaching the rank of Colonel. Whatever difficulties Hampson and Norma confronted – and it is easy to imagine the challenges they endured

[109] Elder H. Russell, "Will You Welcome Your Son's Foreign Bride?" *Afro-American*, September 29, 1945.

[110] "Scoop" Jones, "Took Year to Negotiate," *Afro-American*, December 4, 1943; "Scoop" Jones, "Ohio Officer First to Wed Australian Girl: Red Tape Cut for Romance," *Pittsburgh Courier*, December 4, 1943; "Women and War Work," (Sydney) *Truth*, January 16, 1944. See also "Cleveland's Lieut. Hampson Marries Australian Girl," *Chicago Defender*, December 4, 1943; "Aussie Girl Weds Officer," *Atlanta Daily World*, December 1, 1943.

[111] "Tan Yank Brings Australian Bride Home to Face Race Problem," *Chicago Defender*, July 7, 1945.

as the Army was desegregated during the late 1940s and 1950s – their marriage endured. Hampson Fields died in 1990 and buried next to him at Arlington National Cemetery is "Norma Kathleen, His Wife," who died in 2009.[112]

Marriages between Australian women and black serviceman raised questions regarding understandings of "race." Elder H. Russell emphasized that "in a majority of cases" Australian women who married African American service personnel were of "mixed parentage," and "could really be classed as colored." While he was perhaps hoping to assuage concerns regarding interracial marriages – presumably the fact that their complexions were closer meant such marriages would not attract the same opprobrium as those between "blacks" and "whites" – Russell's explanation served principally to highlight the ambiguities and complexities of "race" in both the United States and Australia.[113]

The marriage in August 1943 of Corporal Alfred Briscoe and Evelyn Bowles highlighted these complexities. While the story accompanying the photograph in the *Chicago Defender* of the newly married Briscoe and Bowles made no reference to Bowles' background other than to refer to Australia as her "native land," an article by Enoch P. Waters in the same edition of the paper provided a more detailed description of Bowles's ethnic and national origins. Pointing out that Bowles was the "granddaughter of an American Negro" who had "wandered to Australia years ago," Waters noted that apart from her grandfather, and her "white Australian grandmother," Bowles was "of Malayan stock."[114] As well as symbolizing the breakdown of racial, ethnic, and national boundaries that was accelerated by the Pacific War, the marriage between Briscoe and Bowles highlighted the challenges confronting those Australians intent on preserving the White Australia Policy.

The preservation of "white" Australia was also predicated on the oppression of the nation's indigenous population. This prompts questions pertaining to wartime interactions between African Americans and Australian Aborigines. US authorities' wartime decision to station black troops "in northern and northeastern Australia" was based not only on a desire to reduce opportunities for black servicemen to mingle with white Australian women, and avoid clashes between black and white

---

[112] "Grave Information for Hampson H. Fields," https://billiongraves.com/grave/Hampson-H-Fields/10188316#/ (accessed October 12, 2016)

[113] Russell, "Will You Welcome Your Son's Foreign Bride?"

[114] "Takes Australian Bride," *Chicago Defender*, September 2, 1943; Enoch P. Waters, Jr., "Australian Girl Is Bride of U.S. Army Corporal," *Chicago Defender*, September 2, 1944.

American troops, but also on an awareness that deploying black troops to the remote regions of Australia might facilitate "some association" with "the Australian Negro, commonly known as an aborigine."[115] Such an association, it was presumed, would be benign, and pose no threat to white hegemony. While US authorities fretted over the possibility of transnational racial activism in a range of contexts, they evidently did not fear collusion between African Americans and Aboriginal Australians.

Suggestions of such collusion rested on assumptions of shared racial identity between African Americans and Aborigines. During the period preceding World War Two, the black press had devoted column inches to the treatment of Australia's indigenous peoples. In 1928 the *Pittsburgh Courier* published an article referring to the Coniston Massacre, in which seventeen Aborigines were massacred in the Northern Territory; two years later, the Baltimore *Afro-American* charged that white Australians had treated the Aborigines "even worse than the Red Indian" had been treated in the United States.[116] During the Pacific War, African Americans expressed sympathy for the plight of Australia's indigenous population, and did not hesitate to criticize the "barbarous" means used by European colonists to "reduce the aboriginal population."[117] Additionally, in spite of reports that Aborigines were initially "terrified" by and "fled" from African Americans, the wartime black press highlighted friendly interactions between the two groups.[118] There were also occasions when African Americans connected the mistreatment of Aborigines to Australian authorities' attempts to prevent the deployment of African Americans to Australia. "The Australian ban against Negro soldiers fighting on the basis of equality with white soldiers," declared the *Pittsburgh Courier* in early 1942, was "a carry-over of the peace-time policy of excluding Negroes from the great sub-continent which was stolen from Negroid

[115] Colonel C. H Barnwell, 1943, cited in Walter A. Luszki, *A Rape of Justice: MacArthur and the New Guinea Hangings* (Lanham, MD: Madison Books, 1991), 90.

[116] "Race War in Australia," *Pittsburgh Courier*, September 29, 1928; "Australia, with 'White' Policy, Is Bankrupt," *Afro-American*, September 13, 1930. See also "Native Slaughter," Perth *Daily News*, November 13, 1928; "Says Australia's Aboriginal Dying," *Chicago Defender*, June 6, 1936; "Australia's Way of 'Justice' Is a Rank Travesty," *Chicago Defender*, July 11, 1936; "Fight Jim Crow Church Bars in Far Australia," *Cleveland Call and Post*, January 26, 1939.

[117] "Australia: 'White Man's Country,'" *New York Amsterdam News*, March 28, 1942.

[118] Lenore Lucas, "It's Corporal 'Farina' Now as Former 'Our Gang' Star Fights in Australia," *Chicago Defender*, May 22, 1943; "Making Friends in Australia, *Pittsburgh Courier*, May 23, 1942.

peoples."[119] This suggested a connection between African Americans and Aborigines, as did black journalist and historian Joel Augustus Rogers's statement that Australia was "the original black man's land."[120]

At first glance this analysis implied that African Americans and Aboriginal Australians shared common racial concerns, or even heritage. If US authorities did not fear an association between African Americans and Aborigines, the same was not true, however, of their Australian counterparts. Yet while Australian authorities' exaggerated fears of black sexuality led them to imagine that African Americans presented – in the words of a December 1942 Defence Department paper – a particular "menace near Aboriginal camps," such fears were largely ill-founded.[121] African Americans perceived urban-dwelling and often light-skinned Aboriginal women as very different from Aborigines living in remote regions, who had not had close contact with white society and hence considered to be culturally and linguistically distant. Such Aborigines were objects of sympathy, rather than equals in the transnational struggle against racism. Australia, claimed one wartime report in the *Chicago Defender*, was a country "where the colored people have not developed to the point they have in the [United] States."[122] Identifying a distinction between Aborigines "who have grown up around the larger cities and have a fair amount of education," and those "in the far North, [in] the bush country," African American soldier and correspondent Jimmy Hicks explained that whereas the former group "enjoy all the privileges of the white Australian," the non-urban Aborigine "really is a savage and lives in a savage habitat."[123]

There were parallels here with African Americans' perceptions of indigenes in other parts of the Asia-Pacific. Accordingly, while they expressed sympathy for Aborigines, and linked the White Australia Policy to the colonization of Australia, equally notable was African Americans' sense of difference from Aborigines.[124] Notwithstanding the aforementioned reports in the black press, African Americans were largely ignorant of

[119] "Australia Bans Race Fighting Men, Claim; Rumor 'White Only' Edict Given to U.S." *Pittsburgh Courier*, March 28, 1942.
[120] J. A. Rogers, "Colored Nations Draw Lines against Negroes," *Pittsburgh Courier*, January 4, 1941.
[121] Department of Defence, Minute Paper, December 28, 1942, 54, 506/1/1, AWM.
[122] Carrigg and Waters, "War Correspondent Goes Stage Because Australians Want News."
[123] "Negro Troops Say Aussies 'Fine Folks,'" *Cleveland Call and Post*, September 12, 1942.
[124] Robert Hall has suggested that African American "soldiers and Aborigines tended to associate, drawn together by their common experience of racism." See Hall, *Black Diggers*, 75.

the history and culture of Australia's indigenous peoples. A 1942 series of articles in the black press providing information about Aborigines served principally to confirm African Americans' sense of difference from Australia's indigenous peoples. While the *Pittsburgh Courier* referred to Australia's "Negro inhabitants," they did not mean to imply a cultural or even racial connection between Aborigines and African Americans; rather, the phrase "Negro" simply connoted dark-skinned peoples. Perpetuating a range of prevailing misconceptions, the *Courier* referred to the "250,000 aborigines who roamed the country before" it was "settled" by "the white man." Surviving Aborigines, continued the *Courier*, were "confined to reservations[s] and adjacent islands."[125] As an April 1942 report in the black press put it, "the Aborigines live in various stages of semi-civilization."[126] Perhaps most significantly, some African Americans concluded that Australia's Aborigines, "like the American Indian," seemed "to be a vanishing race."[127] In a range of ways, African Americans accepted prevailing Western views regarding the future of indigenous peoples in modern societies. Although they eschewed the notion of a hierarchy of race, which had long been a foundation of their own subjugation, African Americans themselves betrayed a sense of racial and cultural relativism. Paradoxically, that relativism reflected many of the assumptions regarding "civilization" and "savagery" which characterized white supremacist attitudes in the United States, and elsewhere.

As with so many aspects of African Americans' Pacific War experiences, their attitudes toward Aboriginal Australians reflected the complex relationship between issues of race and gender. Indeed, besides hinting at their sense of difference from indigenous peoples, the language used by African Americans to describe indigenous women betrayed the patriarchy that was commonplace in the black press and in military culture. James Allan Strawder, recalling that Aboriginal hostesses were hired to accompany African Americans on a cruise down the Brisbane River, was at pains to emphasize that the women were "lovely people," and that he had heard of an Aboriginal women – "Torins something" – who had achieved fame as an opera singer.[128] Similarly, one African American reporter, noting in 1943 that the "colored hostesses" he encountered in

[125] "Australia Still Wants 'Whites Only,'" *Pittsburgh Courier*, April 18, 1942.
[126] "Negro Troops Find 'White Law' Exists in Australia," *Atlanta Daily World*, April 1, 1942; "Australia, in Whose Defense Negroes Will Give Their Lives, Has Been for 'White Only' since 1900 and Won't Change," *Philadelphia Tribune*, April 11, 1942.
[127] Waters, "Racial Mixtures Found Widespread in Australia."
[128] Strawder, AFC/2001/001/72519, VHP-LoC.

the Carver Club were "Australian aboriginals," or "girls from the South Pacific islands," seemed almost surprised that that these "half-cast (sic)" women were both "well bred" and "charming."[129] His tone suggested that he anticipated otherwise.

The questions of racial and national identity implicit in such reports proved confounding, as African Americans grappled with the complexities of race and gender relations in a nation that had much in common with the United States, but which was disfigured by its own distinctive legacies of oppression. These tensions and contradictions were articulated in 1945, in a letter written by Walter E. Andrews, of the Sydney beachside suburb of Bronte, to the parents of an African American officer, Captain J. T. Brown, who had previously been stationed nearby. Emphasizing that the United States was "ever so much in front of us in practically everything," Andrews's letter highlighted wartime Australians' sense that America represented a form of modernity that contrasted to the staid conservatism of Australia. But it was on questions of racial identity and race relations that Andrews's letter was most revealing. Referring to the plight of Aboriginal Australians, he noted that "our coloured people are kept down and have little or no opportunity in their lives." Contrasting the degraded condition of Aborigines to the educated, relatively affluent African Americans he encountered during the war, and overlooking the fact that African Americans had been taken involuntarily to what became the United States while Aborigines were the indigenous peoples of Australia, Walters implied that the two groups occupied similar places in their respective nation's histories. That misunderstanding, or misrepresentation aside, Andrews recorded the significant role that African Americans had played in wartime Australia. Describing the blacks he met as "so nice," he summed up the impact of their presence: "We now understand that all men are equal."[130] While historians have demonstrated that Australian servicemen's wartime and postwar Asian encounters challenged the assumptions upon which White Australia was predicated, the African American presence also played a part in reshaping white Australians' racial consciousness.[131] As black correspondent Will V. Neely

[129] "Soldiers in Pacific Meet at Club Opening," *New Journal and Guide*, May 22, 1943.
[130] "'All Men Are Equal', Writes a Citizen of Australia," *Atlanta Daily World*, May 18, 1945.
[131] See Lachlan Grant, *Australian Soldiers in Asia-Pacific in World War II* (Sydney: NewSouth Publishing, 2014); Sean Brawley, *The White Peril: Foreign Relations and Asian Immigration to Australasia and North America, 1919–1978* (Sydney: University of New South Wales Press, 1995), 205–8.

wrote in early 1944, "the colored Yank" had proven "himself to be a true American." Australians, he wrote, were enjoying "getting a close up of one side of democracy at work."[132]

In John Oliver Killens's fictionalized account of the Pacific War the Battle of Brisbane is depicted – under the allegorical guise of the "Battle of Bainbridge" – as the culmination of the wartime tensions between white and black Americans stationed in Australia. During the aftermath of the conflagration in Bainbridge, Killens's "Solly" Saunders reflects on the deeper, global significance of the racial tensions between white and black Americans. While Solly was uncertain whether a "New World" would emerge from the "smoking ruins" of Bainbridge, and while he recognized the limits of Australians' racial enlightenment, his experiences in wartime Australia had provided compelling evidence that not all whites were imbued with the same racially venomous attitudes that characterized the American South and which the American military had sought to transplant to Australia.[133] Despite its tarnished racial record, in Killens's telling Australia represented hope, and the possibility of racial equality.

Killens was just one of many African Americans interested in Australia's racial policies. Apprehensive about Australians' racial attitudes, and conscious that the White Australia Policy was both a close cousin of Southern segregation, and inimical to the wartime Allies' stated democratic objectives, during late 1941 and early 1942 African Americans resolved to challenge their hosts' racial policies and practices. Yet while African Americans continued to fear that Australians were dreaming of a "'lily white' population" – that 1945 reference to white Southern racists of the late-nineteenth and early-twentieth centuries would not have been accidental – race relations Down Under proved more complicated than suggested by the White Australia Policy.[134] Not only did some black correspondents offer a sympathetic hearing to Australian politicians' explanations regarding the origins of the White Australia Policy, but – more significantly – African Americans' experiences in Australia

---

[132] See Neely, "Australia Not against Negro, Observers Say," *Atlanta Daily World*, February 2, 1944.

[133] Killens, *And Then We Heard the Thunder*, 485. See also Kay Saunders, "In a Cloud of Lust: Black GIs and Sex in World War II," in *Gender and War: Australians at War in the Twentieth Century*, eds. Joy Damousi and Marilyn Lake (Cambridge: Cambridge University Press, 1995), 182–4; Gilyard, *John Oliver Killens*, 59–60.

[134] "Australia Dreams of 'Lily White' Population," *Chicago Defender*, July 14, 1945.

demonstrated the possibilities of more enlightened racial practice.[135] Rather than clinging "tenaciously to the entrenched doctrines of racial pride and superiority," a significant proportion of the Australian population responded positively to the presence of African Americans in their midst.[136] By exposing the disjunction between the White Australia Policy on the one hand, and the attitudes and behavior of the Australian populace on the other, African Americans' experiences in wartime Australia provided a powerful example – for white and black Americans alike – of the possible fate of Southern segregation. And although Walter White's 1949 recollection of his wartime conversation with Prime Minister John Curtin – wherein Curtin pointed out that the positive impression created by African Americans in Australia had led him to favor a change to the White Australia Policy, which would allow African Americans to "settle" in Australia after the war – proved optimistic, blacks' interactions with Australians were one factor behind the broader social and cultural shift that led eventually to the abolition of the White Australia Policy.[137]

[135] See Enoch Waters's 1944 account of his meeting with Prime Minister John Curtin and other leading politicians. See Enoch P. Waters, "Pacific Patter," *Chicago Defender*, April 1, 1944.

[136] Kay Saunders, "The Dark Shadow of White Australia: Racial Anxieties in Australia in World War II," *Ethnic and Racial Studies* 77, no. 2 (1994): 338.

[137] Walter White, *A Man Called White: The Autobiography of Walter White* (London: Gollancz, 1949), 293.

CHAPTER 5

Behaving Like Men

Race, Masculinity, and the Politics of Combat

In 1944, the African American historian and educationalist Lawrence Reddick reflected on Hollywood's treatment of the racial issues which loomed so large in wartime America. Too often, Reddick explained, Hollywood either omitted black characters altogether, or perpetuated the negative stereotypes that were so deeply embedded in American culture. Reddick, however, identified a notable exception to those ongoing cinematic misrepresentations. At first blush, *Bataan*, released in 1943, was like any number of Hollywood's wartime paeans to American patriotism. Yet, while *Bataan's* tale of American heroism was in large measure an exercise in propaganda, intended to encourage wartime unity and reassure Americans of the righteousness of their cause, the film was distinctive in one significant respect. Pointing out that *Bataan's* characters "behave like men," Reddick emphasized that Private Wesley Epps, the movie's African American character, "was drawn as naturally and sympathetically" as his "companions."[1]

Praised by the National Association for the Advancement of Colored People (NAACP) as a "needed realistic picture," *Bataan* offered a glimmer of hope that white America was belatedly acknowledging African Americans' martial – and masculine – qualities.[2] But different views

---

[1] Lawrence Reddick, "Of Motion Pictures," in *Black Films and Film-makers: A Comprehensive Anthology from Stereotype to Superhero*, comp. Lindsay Patterson (New York, NY: Dodd, Mead, 1975), 19.

[2] Thomas Cripps, *Making Movies Black: The Hollywood Message Movie from World War II to the Civil Rights Era* (New York, NY: Oxford University Press, 1993), 76. See also Christopher Paul Moore, *Fighting for America: Black Soldiers – The Unsung Heroes of World War II* (New York, NY: One World/Ballantine, 2005), 145.

continued to prevail across the Pacific frontlines. In early 1945, *New York Post* correspondent and NAACP Executive Secretary Walter White queried General Douglas MacArthur regarding reports that black troops serving in New Guinea had broken under fire, and fled the battlefield. On the surface, MacArthur's response was unequivocal. Assuring White that race "has nothing whatsoever to do with a man's ability to fight," the general declared that "[a]ny man who says that another man's fighting ability can be measured by color" was "wrong." It was telling, however, that in repudiating a relationship between race and a martial spirit, MacArthur did not refer to African Americans. Indeed, while his declaration that one "of the greatest armies" he had "ever commanded was a Filipino one" was presumably intended to help maintain cordial relations with his Filipino allies, MacArthur's apparently enlightened assertions did not translate into US military policy toward African Americans, either in his area of command or elsewhere.[3] Underscoring the contradiction between the rhetoric associated with race relations in the United States and the lived experiences of African Americans, one black veteran of the Pacific War recalled that "anybody who thinks General MacArthur had any use for black troops had better take a second look at the treatment and use of black soldiers in that area."[4]

The Pacific frontlines were a world away from Hollywood. Yet like Reddick, MacArthur and his critics understood that questions of race and patriotism were linked ineluctably to notions of manhood and military valor. While the cultural derision of black masculinity was hardly new, as hundreds of thousands of African Americans joined the wartime rush of post-Pearl Harbor patriotism the "right to fight" assumed renewed urgency. And although *Bataan* challenged white Americans' expectations of black cowardice, enduring white assumptions regarding black passivity and timidity – codes, really, for a purported lack of manhood – underpinned the continuing mistreatment and marginalization of African Americans.

[3] General Douglas MacArthur, cited in *The Crisis*, May 1945, 143. The black press did note the late 1944 appointment to MacArthur's staff of Captain Frank Merith, who for two years fought a guerrilla campaign against the Japanese in the Philippines. See Fletcher Martin, "Negro Joins MacArthur's Staff in Pacific," *Cleveland Call and Post*, Merith was also identified as "Robert Merritt." See Enoch P. Waters, "American Negro Leads Filipino Guerrilla War," *Chicago Defender*, November 11, 1944. For more on Merith, see page 250.
[4] Bill Stevens, cited in *The Invisible Soldier: The Experience of the Black Soldier*, ed. Mary Penick Motley (Detroit, MI: Wayne State University Press, 1975), 75.

For African Americans the right to prove themselves in combat thus raised issues of deep cultural and political significance. Asked about being denied the opportunity to fight in combat, Robert Quarles, a veteran of the bloody campaign on Guadalcanal, replied bluntly: "We felt inadequate."[5] As Quarles's remarks implied, black servicemen's determination to take their place on the frontlines was in fact a dual struggle: as they sought to prove their worth to white America, they sought also to avoid internalizing pejorative stereotypes regarding black docility, timidity, and military incompetence.

African Americans realized the importance of all forms of military service. But combat duty was regarded as a quintessentially masculine endeavor, exemplifying the relationship between warrior and nation. Aware of these patriotic imperatives, white men had long defended their own political and cultural authority by refusing black men the opportunity to prove their manhood in combat. Indeed, given the close association between military valor, masculinity, and citizenship, denying African American men the opportunity to prove themselves in combat was a powerful means of denying them their rights as citizens of the United States. For their part, while African Americans recognized the contradiction of offering their lives on behalf of a country that denied them their rights, they hoped that disproving notions of black pusillanimity would enhance their claims for equal rights of citizenship. With their patriotism defined by race, as well as by nationality, African Americans knew that the "warrior image" – as Andrew J. Huebner has labeled it – was invested with a political significance that transcended the war against Japan.[6] In September 1941, the well-known black leader William Hastie had enunciated these racial and military imperatives to Henry L. Stimson, Secretary of War, for whom he was at the time serving as a civilian advisor:

> In the Army the Negro is taught to be a man, a fighting man; in brief, a soldier. It is impossible to create a dual personality which will be on the one hand a fighting man toward the foreign enemy, and on the other, a craven who will accept treatment as less than equal at home.[7]

[5] Robert Quarles, AFC/2001/001/80199, Veterans History Project Collection, American Folklife Center, Library of Congress, Washington DC (VHP-LoC).

[6] See Andrew J. Huebner, *Warrior Image: Soldiers in American Culture from the Second World War to the Vietnam Era* (Chapel Hill, NC: University of North Carolina Press, 2008). The question of black masculinity is a key theme in John Oliver Killens's *And Then We Heard the Thunder* (New York, NY: Knopf, 1963). See Jennifer C. James, *A Freedom Bought with Blood: African American War Literature from the Civil War to World War II* (Chapel Hill, NC: University of North Carolina Press, 2007), 19–20.

[7] See Hastie, "Survey and Recommendations Concerning the Integration of the Negro Soldier into the Army," Submitted to the Secretary of the Army, September 22, 1941, in

This tension was played out everywhere African Americans served during World War Two. However, given the central role of Pearl Harbor in framing wartime constructions of American patriotism, the black contribution to avenging Japanese perfidy at Pearl Harbor imbued black military service in the Pacific War with a particular significance. As well as avenging Japanese treachery, African Americans in combat across the Pacific Theater were putting their lives on the line in the contest over racial power across Asia and the Pacific. That contest was complicated and often contradictory. As they fought to prove themselves as warriors in a pitiless conflict to defend civilization, African Americans sought also to repudiate white stereotypes that depicted dark-skinned peoples as brutes – stereotypes that had as much currency as contradictory images of blacks as childlike and passive. Through all of this – and at the same time as they contemplated whether other nonwhite peoples could also assume the role of citizen soldiers – African Americans believed their battlefield sacrifices would ensure them a role in shaping the racial politics of the postwar Asia-Pacific. The black quest for the right to serve in combat – and to assert their masculine identity – was thereby joined to both their transnational quest to extend democracy, and to the US self-proclaimed role as a symbol of global freedom. The connection between race, gender, and international politics was hence explicit: black participation on the battlefields of the Pacific War was a tangible projection of African American power and a demonstration of the capacity of black men to challenge not just American racism, but also the racial values and practices associated with the old colonial order. African Americans were simultaneously projecting and redefining American power, domestically and internationally.

Across the Pacific Theater, African American combat service highlighted racial, political, and cultural imperatives central to the struggles for racial equality. Recognizing that white military and political authorities' efforts to circumscribe African Americans' combat roles was one part of the wider determination to disempower black men – as seen in Chapter 3, white attempts to control black sexuality across the Asia-Pacific Theater served a similar function – this chapter traces blacks' demands to serve on the frontlines, and considers the significance of combat service to black understandings of the Pacific War. Rather than providing a battle-by-battle account of blacks' contribution to the defeat of Japan, the

---

"Report of Judge William H. Hastie," Memo for Secretary of War, December 1, 1943, RG 165, Records of the War Department and Special Staffs, G-1, Personnel, Numerical File, 165/41/173, Box 173, National Archives and Records Administration, College Park, Maryland (NARA).

purpose here is to explore the meanings African Americans ascribed to combat service.[8] In demanding the right to fight, African Americans were striving to define and assert their own masculine identity, and claim the rights of citizenship so long denied to them.

Doris "Dorie" Miller was the first African American hero of the Pacific War, and of World War Two more generally. Yet, his feats were not recognized immediately. In the aftermath of Pearl Harbor, American attentions were focused on the Philippines, where US and Filipino forces provided valiant, if doomed, resistance to the invading Japanese. Only a relative handful of African Americans were involved in the struggle in the Philippines, but the black press ensured that their contribution was recognized, at least within the black community. Any expression of African American valor was valuable in making the case for blacks' right to participate as equals in the war, and claiming their rights as American citizens. Presenting an essentially integrationist message, in February 1942 the *Chicago Defender* valorized the black contribution to the defense of the Philippines. Under a headline "Black, White Die Together in the Philippines," the paper described the "death-defying courage" of those African Americans serving with the besieged garrison at Bataan. Reportedly fighting "as one" in their "valiant stand at Bataan," the "heroic soldiers" were "daily exploding the Hitler-inspired myths of race as they mingle their blood freely on this battlefield in the defense of American independence." The heroes of Bataan, proclaimed the *Defender*, were "demonstrating by their valor" that "regardless of race, creed, color or national origin, a united people can and will win this war."[9]

The *Defender's* headlines were premature. Although African Americans played a part in the Bataan campaign, and while those deeds were recognized in the black press, by keeping African American troops out of combat US commanders in the Philippines established a pattern that would be repeated time and again across the Pacific Theater.[10] Many

---

[8] Patrick K. O'Donnell's collection – purporting to provide "a complete yet deeply personal account of the war in the Pacific" – includes dozens of recollections by American combat veterans, none of whom are African American. See Patrick K. O'Donnell, *Into the Rising Sun: World War II's Pacific Veterans Reveal the Heart of Combat* (New York, NY: Free Press, 2002) (quote from back cover).

[9] "Black, White Die Together in the Philippines," *Chicago Defender*, February 14, 1942.

[10] The subsequent exploits of long-time Philippine resident, and former member of the 9th Cavalry, Captain James Coleman, were celebrated in the African American press. Coleman, who led a three-year guerrilla battle against the Japanese forces occupying the Philippines, claimed that his force of irregulars killed more than 1,000 Japanese. See Charles Loeb, "Guerrilla Leader Tells of 3-Year Battle with Japs," *Afro-American*,

white commanders remained convinced that African Americans were temperamentally and physiologically unsuited for combat. "The low average mentality of the colored soldiers," wrote Brigadier Neal Johnson in early 1943, "together with a lack of alertness and individual responsibility and initiative so necessary to modern combat," was deemed sufficient reason to keep black troops away from the frontlines. It was also notable that in referring to the challenges of "tropical conditions," Johnson pointed to the particular demands imposed by the geography and climate of the Pacific Theater. Most troubling for African Americans determined to prove their mettle in combat, Johnson seemed certain that blacks' inabilities were innate: "In my opinion this condition is almost impossible to correct to the point where they can be considered first class offensive troops."[11] White notions of African American passivity proved difficult to shake.

African American frustration at the way in which black military personnel were disproportionately relegated to service roles has been noted in Chapter 2. That frustration was most pronounced when African American combat units were held back from frontline duties, or were split up and deployed separately.[12] For the soldiers of the 24th Infantry Regiment and the 93rd Infantry Division, the continuing disappointment of being restricted to noncombat duties was compounded by the scrutiny to which they were subjected, even during the extended periods when they were far removed from the frontlines. Any failure, or even perception of failure, would be pounced upon as proof of African Americans' unsuitability for combat and as a failure of black manhood. Black performance

June 2, 1945. See also "'Pop' Coleman, Pride of the Philippines," and "Japanese Offered 5,000 Peso Reward for Coleman's Head," *Ebony* 15, no. 5 (1960): 78–80, 82.

[11] Memo: Brigadier Neal C. Johnson to Commanding General, USAFISPAC, January 11, 1943, Subject: "Combat Efficiency, Employment and Command of the 24th Infantry," RG 407, Records of the Adjutant General's Office, 1917-, World War II Operations Reports, 1941–8, Box 16958, Entry 427, 407/270/61/1/2, NARA. Benjamin O. Davis, Jr., commander of the all-black Tuskegee Airmen, recalled that on the eve of Pearl Harbor US military authorities continued to regard African Americans as "totally inferior to whites" and "incapable of contributing positively to its combat mission." See Benjamin O. Davis, Jr., *Benjamin O. Davis, Jr., American: An Autobiography* (New York, NY: Plume, 1992), 69. On these racially based preconceptions, see also Sherie Mershon and Steven Schlossman, *Foxholes and Color Lines: Desegregating the U.S. Armed Forces* (Baltimore, MD: Johns Hopkins University Press, 1998), 13–19.

[12] See Ruth Danenhower Wilson, *Jim Crow Joins Up*, Rev. Ed. (New York, NY: William J. Clark, 1944), 97. See also "Many Negro Combat Units Being Broken Up," *Pittsburgh Courier*, October 30, 1943. For an excellent summary of the wartime deployments of the 24th Infantry and the 93rd Division, see Ulysses Lee, *The Employment of Negro Troops* (Washington, DC: Office of the Chief of Military History, United States Army, 1966), 497–517.

in combat was thus invested with a racial and political significance that transcended the immediate task of defeating Japan.

Across the Asia-Pacific Theater, black correspondents reflected on these issues. Underscoring the significance of frontline military service, the African American journalist Billy Rowe linked the men of the 93rd Division to the long tradition of the citizen soldier. "These men out here," he explained in late 1944, "are not really soldiers as such, but civilians in uniforms." Like generations of citizen soldiers before them, the African American troops of the 93rd had "laid aside their books and pencils, typewriters and adding machines, shovels and ploughs, wagons and trucks, shears and needles and all other implements of modern labor to man a gun." Deliberately and very explicitly connecting black combat duty in the Pacific War to the model of martial masculinity first celebrated by Americans during the war that had established the United States, Rowe applauded the African American soldiers of the 93rd Division as "the minute men of our generation."[13] And although Rowe emphasized that black combat troops' "interpretation of what they were fighting for" was "different from that of the politician" – the soldiers' definition of "democracy" was centered "around a mother, a sweetheart, a home and all that goes with it" – the image of martial manhood he described was a familiar one in American culture. Frontline military service was thus depicted as a public duty to defend the feminine, domestic sphere. At the same time, Rowe made clear the long-term political consequence of black combat service. The successful prosecution of such duty, he averred, would provide a "chance" for African Americans "to get away from the squalid ugliness of poverty and be fully integrated into the American form of life."[14] Another African American correspondent, Edgar T. Rozeau, further reflected on the long-term political significance of black combat service. Fearing that a "future generation of whites" might refuse to grant civil rights to African Americans, on the grounds that "the sacrifices made by Negro soldiers in this war were not enough to procure the same brand of democracy for which the white man paid with his life," Rozeau urged blacks to put their apprehensions and doubts to one side – in other words, to behave as men – and demand the right to fight.[15]

---

[13] Billy Rowe, "93rd Still Waiting ... for Big Test: Ready and Willing to Take Positions on Pacific Fronts," *Pittsburgh Courier*, December 23, 1944.
[14] Rowe, "93rd Still Waiting ... for Big Test: Ready and Willing to Take Positions on Pacific Fronts."
[15] Edgar T. Rozeau, "'Insist on Combat Duty' – Rozeau: Unable to Find Negroes Manning Gun on Frontline," *Pittsburgh Courier*, January 1, 1944.

In January 1944, the same month that Rozeau's article was published in the *Pittsburgh Courier*, the 93rd Division was deployed to the Pacific Theater. Established during World War One, and reactivated in April 1942, the 93rd underwent extensive – and in the eyes of many black commentators, excessive – training, first in Louisiana, and then at Fort Huachuca, Arizona. Meanwhile, the 24th, an independent regiment with a history stretching back to the Indian Wars of the postbellum period, had been sent to the Pacific Theater in April 1942.[16] For different reasons, the timing of both units' deployment was criticized. In the case of the 24th, it was claimed that the unit's departure from Fort Benning, Georgia, in early 1942, was "truly a sad occasion." With a "majority of the men" regarded as "little more than raw recruits," it was widely agreed that the regiment "was not ready for combat."[17] By contrast, many African Americans were sure that the 93rd Division was kept too long in the United States by white military and civilian leaders unwilling to commit even highly trained black troops to combat. Sergeant Donald McNeil summed up the frustration of many of his comrades in the 93rd Division. Fourteen months after enlisting in the Army he was "still in the States." "[T]ired of the routine," he felt "over trained and getting nowhere."[18]

In part, the frustrations articulated by black combat troops reflected the nature of the Pacific conflict. Fought over vast distances, with relatively few personnel committed to frontline combat, the Pacific War was in large measure a contest over logistics. Unsurprisingly, at some point most infantrymen, white and black, found themselves relegated to labor duties. Official denials to the contrary, however, black combat troops spent a disproportionate amount of their time performing such tasks.[19] While the 24th Regiment saw some frontline action soon after it reached the Pacific war zone, the men of the unit spent much of their time performing laboring duties. Consequently, the Regiment's experiences differed significantly from those of other combat units: while many

---

[16] On the early history of the 24th, see William T. Bowers, William M. Hammond, and George L. MacGarrigle, *Black Soldier, White Army: The 24th Infantry Regiment in Korea* (Washington, DC: Center of Military History, United States Army, 1996), 3–18; William G. Muller, *The Twenty-Fourth Infantry: Past and Present* (1923; reprinted, Fort Collins, CO: Old Army Press, 1972).

[17] L. Albert Scipio, *Last of the Black Regulars: A History of the 24th Infantry Regiment (1869–1951)* (Silver Springs, MD: Roman Publications, 1983), 67.

[18] McNeil, World War II Veterans Survey. 93rd Infantry Division. Box 1, File 6684, United States Army Military History Institute, United States Army Heritage and Education Center, Carlisle, Pennsylvania (USAHEC).

[19] Nelson Peery, *Black Fire: The Making of an American Revolutionary* (New York, NY: The New Press, 1994), 233.

American units were ill-prepared for combat during the early stages of the conflict, white troops were subsequently provided with additional training, and given further opportunities to prove themselves in battle.[20]

The experiences of the 93rd Division were no less frustrating than those of the 24th Regiment. Exacerbating the irritation of many African Americans, not only were the men of the 93rd used as laborers, but the Division's three regiments were long denied the opportunity to fight as a coherent, unified division. Bill Stevens, a veteran of the 93rd, articulated a blunt and common complaint among black veterans of the Pacific War. Besides being subjected to incessant and demeaning treatment from white servicemen and officers – in the words of another veteran the 93rd, Sergeant Willie Lawton, the Division "was a discriminatory, bigoted organization from the lowliest white lieutenant right up to the commanding general, H. H. Johnson" – Stevens contended that African American "combat troops in the Pacific," were "totally misused and humiliated." The 24th Infantry Regiment, he recalled, "did so much work as labor battalions that" he "wondered why they did not designate them as the 24th stevedores." The implications of the exclusion of African Americans from combat were obvious to Stevens: "the lie goes merrily along, perpetuated by whites, that the black man is a big zero as a fighting man; he is a coward." "From where I sat," noted Stevens, African Americans "weren't going to get a chance" to fight, "even if it caused the death of every cracker in the Pacific to keep it that way. The glory boys had to be white!"[21] Decrying the misuse of African American combat troops, black veteran Albert Evans contended that using the men of the 93rd Division as stevedores "was a true morale destroyer."[22] As these men's testimony suggests, while black servicemen in a range of military units expressed their frustration at their relegation to stevedoring and similar duties, those troops trained and prepared for frontline duty regarded laboring tasks as particularly demeaning: willing to wage war on behalf of their nation, and conscious of the political and cultural significance of African American combat service, they regarded other duties as an affront to their masculine pride and racial sensibilities.

---

[20] Bowers, Hammond, and MacGarrigle, *Black Soldier, White Army*, 21; Moore, *Fighting for America*, 76.

[21] Bill Stevens, cited in Motley, ed., *Invisible Soldier*, 76–7; Lawton, cited in Motley, ed., *Invisible Soldier*, 103. See also Jean Byers, *A Study of the Negro in Military Service* (Washington, DC: Department of Defense, 1950), 119.

[22] Evans, cited in Motley, ed., *Invisible Soldier*, 99.

The ongoing misuse of black combat units drew sustained criticism in the African American press and among black leaders who were convinced that the Army's policies reflected racial, rather than military priorities. In early 1944, nearly two years after the 24th Regiment was deployed to the Pacific, Hamilton Fish, III, a black member of the House of Representatives, complained to Secretary of War Henry L. Stimson that the 24th was being held back from combat duties. Referring to newspaper reports that the 24th – "fully equipped and prepared for any eventuality" in the Pacific Theater – was "performing service duties at docks and supply dumps," "Fish lamented that breaking up African American combat units, and transferring "personnel" into service units was "demoralizing to Negro soldiers" and "to Negro people generally."[23] Stimson, conceding that some black combat units had been deployed to noncombat roles, claimed nonetheless that such procedures reflected the need to match resources to demands across the theater, rather than a deliberate policy of keeping African American combat troops away from the frontlines. White units, asserted Stimson, were subject to similar procedures "in order to obtain maximum manpower value."[24]

Black leaders refused to be placated, however. The Army's refusal to deploy and make effective use of the 93rd Division became a *cause célèbre* within the African American community. "Why," demanded the *Pittsburgh Courier* in November 1943, "during the hour of decision," is "this highly trained combat unit being used to guard warehouse and tool sheds."[25] Unpersuaded by Stimson's explanation for the non-deployment of black combat units, William H. Hastie, who in January 1943 had resigned as an aide to Stimson in protest against the military's segregationist policies, declared in February 1944 that the "truth of the matter" was that "Negro combat units" had "been the problem children of the Army for more than two years." The difficulty, Hastie argued, was not that units such as the 24th Regiment and 93rd Division "were incompetent," but rather that "no one wanted them." Fearing the consequences of adding "a 'racial problem' to other headaches in the theater of war," commanders in

[23] Hamilton Fish to Henry L. Stimson, February 1, 1944, Box 1065, RG 407, 291.2 Race, Records of the Adjutant General's Office, NARA.
[24] Henry L. Stimson to Hamilton Fish, February 19, 1944, Box 1065, 291.2 Race, RG 407, NARA. In late 1944 Fletcher P. Martin noted that while there were perhaps sound operational reasons why African American Marines had not been committed to combat, those reasons remained obscure. See Fletcher P. Martin, "Negro Marines Removed from Combat Duty: Perform Service Tasks in Pacific," *Pittsburgh Courier*, October 28, 1944.
[25] "The Mystery of the 93rd Division," *Pittsburgh Courier*, November 27, 1943.

the field, with the support of their superiors in Washington, were unwilling to risk sending black troops to the frontlines. "Nurtured on the myth" that African American troops could not "be relied upon in combat," they preferred instead to maintain the racial status quo. Seeking to justify theater commanders' reluctance to utilize African Americans in combat roles, military authorities acknowledged "the deadening difference of inequality of background and opportunity." Yet, Hastie, and others, insisted that blacks be given opportunities to fight. "Nothing," Hastie wrote, could "do more to improve the often unsatisfactory relations between white and colored soldiers than the sharing of common experience on the field of battle." Linking battlefield experiences to a postwar transformation of race relations in the United States, Hastie foreshadowed the long-term consequences of shared battlefield experiences. "The veterans of this war," he insisted, "will be the greatest force for racial good or for racial enmity in America." Confident there would be "no place" for "[p]rejudice and intolerance" in "the hearts and minds of comrades in arms" who had "fought and bled and conquered shoulder to shoulder," Hastie appealed also to the self-interest of white America: the "great combat potential of the Negro soldier," he argued, was "a valuable asset in the winning of the war."[26]

The black press maintained pressure on US military and civil authorities to make better use of black combat units. Speaking on behalf of the NAACP, *The Crisis* was sharply critical of the Secretary of War's justification for the non-deployment of African American combat troops. Denouncing Stimson's explanation as "probably the most inept letter of the war," in April 1944 the editors of *The Crisis* complained that the 24th Regiment "had been in the South Pacific for twenty-one months doing stevedoring work."[27] Similarly, the men of the 93rd Division, having been given belated opportunities to prove themselves in the fighting on Bougainville, were subsequently frustrated to be omitted from the forces

[26] William H. Hastie to Henry L. Stimson, February 29, 1944, Box 1065, RG 407, 291.2 Race, NARA; *Armed Services Forces Manual M5: Leadership and the Negro Soldier*, October 1944 (Washington, DC: General Reference Branch, Center of Military History) in *Blacks in the Military: Essential Documents*, eds. Bernard C. Nalty and Morris J. MacGregor (Wilmington, DE: Scholarly Resources, 1981), 129. On Hastie's resignation from the War Department, see Gilbert Ware, *William Hastie: Grace under Pressure* (New York, Oxford University Press, 1984), 130–2; Phillip McGuire, *He, Too, Spoke for Democracy: Judge Hastie, World War II, and the Black Soldier* (New York, NY: Greenwood, 1988), 83–6.
[27] "Army Labor Battalions," *The Crisis*, April, 1944, 104. See also "'All Negro Troops Ask Is a Chance:' Waters," *Chicago Defender*, December 16, 1944, NY

liberating the Philippines. In the words of black correspondent Charles H. Loeb, the men of the 93rd were "champing at the bit" to see more action.[28]

Criticism of the Army's reluctance to deploy black troops to combat came from many quarters. Disappointed to learn "that Negro combat units were not wanted overseas," in September 1943 Mack C. Spears, a World War One veteran and National Treasurer of the National Council of Negro Veterans, expressed frustration that the fully trained 93rd Division was being "split up and stationed in various camps."[29] The following month, William S. Braddon, Pastor of the Berean Baptist Church in Chicago, criticized the "utter" failure of the "War Department to activate" African American combat troops. Connecting his congregation's concerns to wider, national debates, Braddon noted that "13,000,000 other Negro patriots" were "demanding" that their "state and national representatives" explain "why the apparent discrimination, waste of manpower, prolongation of this war, sacrifice and disruption of our normal mode of life" was allowed to continue.[30] Angry at being denied the opportunity to serve in combat, one black soldier explained the contradiction in US policy: "How can we truly say," he asked the Secretary of War, "that we are fighting for freedom for all? How can we tell the world that we believe in Democracy when you[,] the head of our army[,] do not practice it in your army[?]"[31]

The African American leadership pressed that point emphatically. Walter White, with his attention fixed firmly on the American role in shaping the postwar world, described the "bewilderment" being "created throughout the Pacific" as a consequence of the United States sending "two armies – one white and one Negro – to fight" a war "against the racial theories of Hitler and Japan."[32] For White, ever attuned to any transnational expression of racism, US military authorities' reluctance to deploy black troops to combat, along with politicians' timidity in exerting their authority over military commanders, were prompting America's

---

[28] Charles H. Loeb, "93rd Champs at Bit for Pacific 'Big Show,'" *Atlanta Daily World*, January 16, 1945.

[29] Mack C. Spears to the War Department, September 25, 1943, Box 1066, RG 407, 291.2 Race, NARA.

[30] William S. Braddon to War Department, October 11, 1943, Box 1066, RG 407, 291.2 Race, NARA.

[31] Roy W. Thompson to Henry L. Stimson, March Henry L. Stimson, March [?], 1944, RG 407, Box 1065, 291.2 Race, NARA.

[32] Statement by Walter White, April 9, 1945, Reel 13, *Papers of the NAACP, Part 14: Race Relations in the International Arena, 1940–1955*, Microfilm, eds. John H. Bracey, Jr., and August Meier (Bethesda, MD: University Publications of America, 1993).

nonwhite allies to question the US commitment to the democratic principles for which the war was supposedly being fought. By implying that the United States and its black population should be role models for colonized peoples around the world, White was not only endorsing the idea of American exceptionalism, but also articulating a form of African American exceptionalism.[33] Equally significantly, he suggested, limiting African Americans to noncombat roles – and denying them their masculine identity – was undermining the US claim to be the archetype of democratic and enlightened values.

That claim was further compromised by the racial policies of the Marine Corps. Indeed, while the frustration that many African Americans expressed when they were not allowed to take their place in the battle zone was evident in each of the branches of the US armed forces, that frustration, and the racialized and gendered tension between black passivity and black manhood, was particularly stark in the Marine Corps. The Marines' credo – "every Marine a rifleman" – meant that the Corps' leadership, unlike their counterparts in the Army and Navy, could not easily enlist African Americans only to then relegate them to service roles. Even amid the military buildup of the late 1930s and early 1940s, as the Corps confronted the contradiction between its refusal to accept black recruits and the need for more manpower, Marine commanders remained racially recalcitrant. After asserting in January 1941 that "there would be a definite loss of efficiency" if the Marines was forced to "take Negroes," the Corps' Commandant, Major General Thomas Holcomb, later spoke candidly to the Navy's General Board regarding the prospect of expanding the Corps. "If it were a question of having a Marine Corps of 5,000 whites or 250,000 Negroes," Holcomb preferred to "have the whites." While his public language was more circumspect, he was resolute in his conviction that the Marine Corps should remain white.[34]

Holcomb's views reflected the prevailing racial culture within the Corps. Within a few months of Pearl Harbor, however, political pressure

---

[33] "Empire Colonial Policy in Pacific is Seen in Danger," *Pittsburgh Courier,* April 21, 1945.

[34] Holcomb, cited in Michael Lee Lanning, *The African-American Soldier: From Crispus Attucks to Colin Powell* (Secaucus, NJ: Birch Lane Press, 1997), 211; Holcomb, Navy General Board, "Plan for the Expansion of the USMC," 18 April, 1941 (No. 139), Records of the General Board, Op Navy Archives, cited in Morris J. MacGregor, Jr., *Integration of the Armed Forces, 1940–1965.* Washington, DC: Center of Military History, United States Army (1981), 100. For a sympathetic account of Holcomb's views, see Robert K. Culp, *The First Black United States Marines: The Men of Montford Point* (Jefferson, NC: McFarland & Co., 2007), 20–1.

from the White House, and from liberal Republicans, compelled the Marines' leadership to accept black recruits.[35] In May 1942 Holcomb announced that from the following month the Corps would recruit African Americans for service "in a combat organization."[36] Yet the Marine leadership agreed that that unit would be strictly segregated, and while some officers called for "the maximum practicable number" of blacks to be assigned to "combat units," many others remained adamant there would be "very few" African Americans of "sufficient intelligence to be of much use to combat organizations."[37]

Intent on refuting such assumptions, African Americans' determination to serve in the Marine Corps was part of the wider challenge to racial segregation. Roland Durden's motivation for enlisting in the Corps – "I wanted to join the Marines to become a man" – was a typically youthful affirmation of the role of frontline military service in establishing masculine self-identity.[38] But the Marines' enduring reputation for their martial spirit, and the positive wartime publicity they were receiving for their role in fighting the Japanese, rendered black service in the Corps especially significant. For some black men, the Marines' formidable reputation was incentive enough. Having "heard that the Marine Corps was the toughest outfit going," and confident that he "was the toughest," Edgar R. Huff joined the Corps because he "wanted to be a member of the best organization."[39] Put simply, the Marines were seen to embody the most valorous and masculine virtues of American military culture.

African Americans who did succeed in joining the Marine Corps encountered a racist culture that often seemed intractable. Although some Marine officers boasted there was "no racial problem" among their

---

[35] Henry I. Shaw and Ralph W. Donnelly, *Blacks in the Marine Corps* (Washington, D.C: History and Museums Division, Headquarters, U.S. Marine Corps, 1975), 1. See also Byers, *Negro in Military Service*, 248.

[36] Bernard C. Nalty, *The Right to Fight: African-American Marines in World War II* (Washington, DC: Marine Corps Historical Center, 1995), 2–3.

[37] *Memorandum, Commandant US Marine Corps, to Distribution List, 20 March , 1943, Subject: Colored Personnel*. Reference Section of the Director of Marine Corps History and Museum, Washington, DC, and *Memorandum, Director of Plans and Policies to Director, Division of Plans and Policies, 26 December, 1942, Subject: Colored Personnel*, Reference Section, Office of the Director of Marine Corps History and Museums, Washington, DC, both reprinted in the Epilogue of Perry E. Fischer and Brooks E. Gray, *Blacks and Whites Together through Hell: U.S. Marines in World War II* (Turlock, CA: Millsmont Publishing, 1994).

[38] Roland Durden, cited in Melton A. McLaurin, *The Marines of Montford Point: America's First Black Marines* (Chapel Hill, NC: University of North Carolina Press, 2007), 27.

[39] See Edgar R. Huff, cited in Shaw and Donnelly, *Blacks in the Marine Corps*, 3.

FIGURE 5.1. Howard P. Perry, the first African American to join the Marine Corps.
Courtesy: National Archives 208-NP-10KK-1.

African American units, and told white Marines they were "not to think of each other as black or white," deep-seated racial divisions persisted within the Corps.[40] That racism was highlighted by the Marines' aversion to accepting and training African Americans as officers. It was not

[40] Wilson, *Jim Crow Joins Up*, 58–9.

until 1945 that blacks were recruited as officers to the Corps as officers, and while the African American press celebrated that achievement, the Marines' reputation for racial intolerance persisted.[41] The two black Marine defense battalions that were trained for combat during the Pacific War – the 51st and the 52nd – constituted only a small proportion of the African American recruits who passed through the Marine Corps training center at Montford Point, North Carolina. Instead, the overwhelming majority of black Marines were trained as messmen and stewards, or for ammunition and depot companies. Having endured the travails of training, when black Marines were deployed to the Pacific, they encountered white Marines who remained convinced that African Americans lacked the fighting spirit or aptitude required for combat. Black Marines typically found themselves performing menial tasks – albeit occasionally close to the frontlines. As Private John R. Griffith, of the 52nd Defense Battalion put it, rather than "being a Defense Unit," the 52nd "turned out to be nothing more than a working battalion."[42] A "large proportion" of the "sixteen thousand" African American Marines, complained one commentator in 1944, were "being used overseas only as labor units."[43]

In the face of the sustained black criticism at the misuse of African American combat personnel, by mid-1944 civil and military authorities in the United States were assuring their critics that black units were being deployed to the frontlines. The 24th Infantry Regiment and the 93rd Infantry Division, it was noted, had been sent to the combat zone.[44] While Nelson Peery subsequently recalled that committing the 93rd Division to battle was a "political gesture of little military significance," during the war the decision was widely celebrated by African Americans.[45]

---

[41] "Three Train as Officers in Marine Corps," *New Journal and Guide*, April 21, 1945.
[42] Griffith, cited in Shaw and Donnelly, *Blacks in the Marine Corps*, 27. See also Gail Buckley, *American Patriots: The Story of Blacks in the Military from the Revolution to Desert Storm* (New York, NY: Random House, 2001), 312; Charles D. Melson, *Condition Red: Marine Defense Battalions in World War II* (Washington, DC: History and Museums Division, Headquarters, U.S. Marine Corps, 1996), 24.
[43] Wilson, *Jim Crow Joins Up*, 97–8. See also Fletcher P. Martin, "Negro Marines Removed from Combat Duty: Perform Service Tasks in Pacific," *Pittsburgh Courier*, October 8, 1944.
[44] See John J. McCloy, Assistant Secretary of War, to Roy Wilkins, April 5, 1944, Box 1065, RG 407, 291.2 Race, NARA; Maggi M. Morehouse, *Fighting in the Jim Crow Army: Black Men and Women Remember World War II* (Lanham, MD: Rowman and Littlefield, 2000), 130–1.
[45] Peery, *Black Fire*, 241.

FIGURE 5.2. Self-defense training: Marine Corporal Arvin Lou Ghazlo instructs Private Ernest C. Jones, Montford Point Camp, NC. April 1943.
Courtesy: National Archives 127-N-5334.

After the long African American struggle to win the right to serve on the frontlines, the men of the 93rd Division, like their counterparts in the 24th Regiment, quickly recognized the perils of combat. They were of course far from alone, however, in understanding those perils. During the Pacific War, black service personnel in a range of ostensibly noncombat units found themselves under fire. Here, the specific geographic and military context of the Pacific War was significant: notwithstanding parallels between combat experiences in the different theaters of World War Two, the ruthless nature of the war across the Asia-Pacific – where few prisoners were taken, and where the conflict was often fought across indistinct and porous "frontlines" – rendered combat there different from that typically experienced by the Western Allies in the European Theater. Moreover, given the ability of both sides to project naval and air power over long distances, and given that Japanese stragglers could threaten the security of Allied personnel far removed from the frontlines, servicemen in noncombat roles could find themselves close to danger. Black newspapers recounted numerous examples of black noncombatants in the Pacific Theater taking up arms when circumstances demanded. In December 1943, the *Chicago Defender* reported that Steward's Mate Elbert H. Oliver had "seized the controls of a gun" and started firing at Japanese planes attacking US ships. Awarded a Purple Heart and a Silver Star for his gallantry, Oliver's exploits were compared to the legendary feats of Dorie Miller.[46]

Yet, while popular memory emphasizes black servicemen's determination to take the field of battle, and although the significance of frontline military service was well understood by African American troops, collective racial politics were complicated by concerns for individual, personal welfare. Although many black servicemen insisted they were keen to fight – "most of us," wrote a member of the 93rd Division, "welcome the opportunity to prove that we are a fighting unit second to none" – others were relieved to avoid frontline duty.[47] Morris Owen Pasqual, Sr., recalled that avoiding combat "didn't bother" him "too much," while Howard Hickerson, serving with the 93rd Division, spoke unambiguously: "We were glad we were not being sent up to the main line of fighting. We wanted to survive … None of my friends volunteered or wanted to go up to the front part." Furthermore, while some men resented the frequent assignment of African American troops to menial tasks, Hickerson reiterated a sentiment articulated regularly by noncombatant black servicemen. Repairing and setting up communications equipment, carrying supplies, and assembling tanks and other weapons, he insisted, were tasks "of utmost importance."[48]

---

[46] Enoch P. Waters, "Sailor Wins Silver Star; Hero in S. Pacific Battle," *Chicago Defender*, December 4, 1943.

[47] See "Quarterly History," January – March 1944, HQ and Hq Battery, 93rd Infantry Division Artillery, Box 11333, RG 407, NARA.

[48] See Pasqual, AFC/2001/001/48929, VHP-LoC; Hickerson, cited in Morehouse, *Fighting in the Jim Crow Army*, 158.

Distinguishing these views of African American servicemen from the statements of the wartime black press and leadership yields a more nuanced reading of black attitudes to the prospect of combat duty. Recalling Walter White's eagerness to persuade commanders to commit black troops to battle, Bill Payne remembered "feeling at the time … why don't you just get your little tail right on back to the United States and leave us alone."[49] Echoing Marine Walter Maddox's criticism of the Baltimore *Afro-American's* campaign to persuade military authorities to deploy blacks to combat, Nelson Peery recalled that African American infantrymen "did not trust" the black newspapers. Nobody, he said, "wants to go into a war and get killed."[50] Peery's skepticism toward the African American press's campaign to see black troops assigned to combat was confirmed by *Chicago Defender* correspondent Enoch P. Waters. Angered by the *Defender's* criticism of the Army's policy of assigning African Americans to service units, one black serviceman berated Waters: "Why should we volunteer our lives to fight for a Jim Crow country?"[51]

While African American servicemen remained alert to that contradiction, and although the racial imperative complicated their efforts to merge their role as warriors with the image of the citizen soldier, thousands of black servicemen self-consciously set about proving themselves in combat. The transformation of combat from abstraction to reality could prove disillusioning as well as terrifying. There was nothing unique about that process – the first moments of battle have shattered the optimistic illusions and patriotic fervor of millions of young soldiers. Congruent with the broader image of the self-deprecating World War Two veteran – an intrinsic element of popular constructions of the Greatest Generation – African American veterans frequently eschewed gung-ho or self-aggrandizing descriptions of their wartime roles. Nevertheless, black servicemen's determination to prove themselves on the battlefield reflected masculinist as well as racial imperatives. For Donald McNeil, the importance of proving his valor – an almost-universal aspiration among untested combat troops – highlighted the explicitly racial dimension of

[49] Payne, cited in Morehouse, *Fighting in the Jim Crow Army*, 157.

[50] Walter Maddox, cited in McLaurin, *Marines of Montford Point*, 120–1; Peery, cited in Morehouse, *Fighting in the Jim Crow Army*, 157. There were occasions when black newspapers recognized that not all African American combat troops were "clamoring" for battle. See "First Colored Marine Unit Is Ready to Fight," *Afro-American*, November 27, 1943.

[51] Enoch P. Waters, *American Diary: A Personal History of the Black Press* (Chicago, IL: Path Press, 1987), 390.

black military service. Asked what he was thinking and experiencing during combat, McNeil recalled that he wanted to do his "best." It was important, he remembered, to have "confidence" that he and the men of his unit "were good" at making war.[52]

Courage, and expectations of courage, were widely valorized. Yet many black troops – like their white compatriots – admitted their anxieties. Some men betrayed their fears long before they encountered the enemy. James E. Davis, a veteran of the 93rd Division, recalled that when his unit sailed from San Francisco, and the troops were struck by the reality that they were "going overseas," some "started crying."[53] And while Donald McNeil did "not remember being afraid," he admitted to be being "numb with anticipation."[54] For many servicemen, the reality of battle caused uncontrolled, gut-wrenching fear. When Frank Douglas's Marine unit landed at Guadalcanal, he thought "this is the end."[55] Henry William Fleming, asked many decades after the war's end how he reacted when he heard an air-raid siren, made no effort to disguise his fear: "Oh, Lord, it's the end of the world."[56]

Combat troops were not the only ones to express these anxieties. In October 1943, Herman A. Bing, of the 756th Sanitation Company, wrote home from Fort Pickett, Virginia:

> [F]or the first time since I've been in the Army I feel that I won't see any of you again and that's a helluva feeling to have. I am not scared but it hurts me to think I really never have accomplished enough to be willing to quit the scene.[57]

Juxtaposing his denial of fear alongside his apprehensions that he would never again see his family, and that his accomplishments amounted to little, Bing captured many of the emotions experienced by young men bound for war. As it turned out, Bing survived the war, and his subsequent letters suggested that he largely avoided the stresses experienced by combat troops. Yet when he noted in May 1945 that Japanese "snipers are all over," he affirmed that even for troops in noncombat roles, serving

---

[52] McNeil, World War II Veterans Survey. 93rd Infantry Division. Box 1, File 6684, USAHEC.
[53] James E. Davis, AFC/2001/001/56158, VHP-LoC.
[54] McNeil, World War II Veterans Survey. 93rd Infantry Division. Box 1, File 668, USAHEC.
[55] Frank Douglas, AFC/2001/001/86594, VHP-LoC.
[56] William Henry Fleming, AFC/2001/001/13308, VHP-LoC.
[57] Sergeant Herman A. Bing to Elnora Williams, October 18, 1943, Box 1, MG429, World War II Letters from African American Soldiers, Schomburg Center for Research in Black Culture, New York Public Library, New York City.

in areas apparently liberated from the Japanese, personal safety could be precarious.[58]

In the heat of battle, motivations varied widely. African American servicemen were determined to repudiate white stereotypes regarding black passivity, but at the point of battle, emotions and responses were more often impulsive than planned, as patriotic and racial imperatives gave way to individual fear, frustration, and fury. Vengeance could be a powerful motivation. Describing the response of black servicemen to Japanese air raids, Enoch Waters noted that actions could be "instinctive, rather than reasoned." The exasperation "of being unable to counterattack," he wrote, could provide the motivation to "transfer the hatred of racism at home to the Japanese." That motivation could be intensely personal, as some servicemen, rather than seeking to defend their country, sought "to even a personal score."[59] Waters's account suggested that Japan's attempt to forge a transnational alliance among nonwhites had failed to engender support among African Americans serving on the frontlines.

Such an alliance was made even more unlikely by African Americans' commitment to their Christian faith. Nowhere was that faith more keenly felt than in combat. Just as fear was a universal sentiment on the battlefield, there were few atheists in foxholes. When Henry William Fleming recalled that in battle "you call to God," he spoke for millions of soldiers, of all nationalities and all races, who experienced the unbridled fear of combat.[60] These emotions could be experienced by service personnel in all branches of the military. During torpedo and bombing attacks on the USS *Harrison* Calvin C. Miller remembered reciting the 27th Psalm: "That's how I made it without going crazy."[61] Although spiritual and patriotic faith could be challenged by the brutalizing and disillusioning experiences of combat, and its often-gruesome aftermath, many black servicemen remained confident, as Private George Ruth, Jr., put it, that "God was with us."[62] That faith could be profoundly cathartic. Nelson Peery recalled the scene following the death in battle of "Lonnie," a much-loved and valued comrade. Peery's grief – compounded by the knowledge that Lonnie's death was "unnecessary," after their squad was sent on a needless mission – was assuaged partly by the shared expressions of religious

---

[58] Herman A. Bing to Elnora Williams, March 13, 1945, Box 1, World War II Letters, Schomburg Center.

[59] Waters, *American Diary*, 373.

[60] Fleming, AFC/2001/001/13308, VHP-LoC.

[61] Calvin C. Miller, AFC/2001/001/74496, VHP-LoC.

[62] Ruth, World War II Veterans Survey. 93rd Infantry Division. Box 1, File 668, USAHEC.

faith as the men in Peery's platoon remembered their fallen friend. While the service held in memory of Lonnie resembled those held by servicemen of all races, in all armies, Peery's description of the "melancholy of taps" mingling "with the frustrations" that they, "as Negro soldiers bore in silence," along with the men singing and reading aloud from the Bible, lent the ceremony a distinctly African American tone and form.[63]

Military authorities encouraged servicemen to meld their religious faith with patriotism. But such beliefs alone were not sufficient to forge combat discipline: rigorous training and effective leadership were essential. In the case of the 93rd Division, the preparation had been particularly – and for many African Americans, frustratingly – thorough. Given, also, that the Division was subsequently deployed to the jungles of the Asia-Pacific Theater, the lengthy period spent preparing in California and Arizona – following a period of training in Louisiana – was curious.[64] Similarly, Private James Trout, of the 24th Infantry Regiment, and a veteran of the Guadalcanal campaign, explained that while American troops had been "trained to cope with modern warfare, which stresses speed," fighting in the jungles of the South Pacific meant moving "slowly and with extreme caution." "There were times," he recalled, when he had been "compelled to lay in one position for nine and ten hours without moving."[65]

The adverse conditions described by Trout were commonplace throughout the Asia-Pacific Theater. In such circumstances unit cohesion and battlefield performance depended in large measure on good leadership. As in all armies, the quality of leadership was instrumental in determining the combat performance of African American units. On this issue, the intersection of racial and military politics undermined black combat performance and caused untold aggravation for black servicemen. The fact that most of their officers were white was a constant source of discontent for black troops, and an issue prompting sharp criticism in the African American press. Many white officers, from newly commissioned second lieutenants to the most senior generals and admirals, remained skeptical about African Americans' capacity for combat. Among the most telling evidence of the white military establishment's continuing low regard for

---

[63] Peery, *Black Fire*, 238–9.
[64] *93rd Infantry Division: Summary of Operations in World War II*. Prepared by the Historical Section, 93rd Division, March, 1946, 2–3, in RG 407 Records of the Adjutant General's Office, 1917. 407/270/57/26/1-2, World War II Operations Reports, 1941–1948, 93rd Infantry Division, Entry 427, Box 11329, NARA.
[65] Sam Lacy, "Army Vet at 23, Chicagoan Tells Thrilling War Tales," *Chicago Defender*, September 18, 1943.

African American combat performance is that blacks received none of the 294 Medals of Honor awarded during the World War Two. Even recognizing that relatively few African Americans were assigned to combat roles, their exclusion from the list of Medal of Honor recipients is a telling indicator of white officers' jaundiced view of black servicemen. In a sign, too, of the ongoing exclusion of African Americans from the dominant narrative of World War Two, it was not until the 1990s that the Medal of Honor was belatedly awarded to seven African Americans – only one of whom was still alive – for their service during World War Two. Of those seven black recipients of the Medal of Honor, only one – George Watson, of the 29th Quartermaster Regiment – had served in the Pacific.[66]

Further evidence of the white military establishment's contempt for black combat units was the frequent rotation of officers and non-commissioned officers through African American units. This refusal to provide cohesive and stable leadership adversely affected both the 24th Regiment and the 93rd Division. Disappointed that white officers who "disagreed with anti-negro policies" were often deployed only briefly to African American units, black troops also criticized the frequent changes of leadership. Unconvinced by military authorities' explanation that the seemingly constant flow of black non-commissioned officers (NCOs) from the 93rd was a consequence of the need to build leadership capacity in other black units, African Americans regarded the practice as a deliberate attempt to weaken the Division and leave it unprepared for combat.[67]

In spite of those problems of leadership, and the persistent doubts of their detractors, black combat troops showed courage and resourcefulness on the field of battle. After their early difficulties, when the men of the 24th Regiment were given opportunities to do so they performed well in combat and received official, if limited recognition for their services.[68]

---

[66] See Elliot V. Converse, III, et al., *The Exclusion of Black Soldiers from the Medal of Honor in World War II. The Study Commissioned by the United States Army to Investigate Racial Bias in the Awarding of the Nation's Highest Military Decoration* (Jefferson, NC: McFarland and Co, 1997), 4–5, 16; Center of Military History, "African American Medal of Honor Recipients," https://history.army.mil/moh/mohb.html (Accessed October 20, 2017). For further critique of the continuing reluctance of the US military and political establishment to acknowledge African American demonstrations of valor during World War Two, see Linda Hervieux, *Forgotten: The Untold Story of D-Day's Black Heroes, at Home and at War* (New York, NY: Harper, 2015).

[67] See General George S. Marshall, Memorandum to General Douglas MacArthur, March 1, 1945, 165/15/6, RG 165, Box 06, NARA.

[68] Bernard C. Nalty, *Strength for the Fight: A History of Black Americans in the Military* (New York, NY: Free Press, 1986), 171; Bowers, Hammond, and MacGarrigle, *Black Soldier, White Army*, 22.

The battlefield successes of the 24th Regiment were celebrated widely in the black press. Praising the way in which the troops of the 24th "completely routed" the Japanese in an April 1944 battle near the Mavavia River, in New Guinea, Fletcher P. Martin emphasized that the encounter had involved an amphibious landing – a complex feat of arms requiring careful planning and precision – and that the Regiment's black infantrymen had worked in concert with flame-throwing and armored units. Defying earlier assertions that African Americans lacked "the skill and intelligence" to handle "machinery and mechanical appliances," Fletcher contended that black troops were capable of successfully executing complicated military maneuvers.[69] That capacity set them apart from indigenous troops of the Pacific Islands: while the natives' courage was recognized by African American reporters, their commendable combat record was often considered to be a consequence of inherent bravery, rather than a capacity to manage the complexities of the modern battlefield.

The battlefield record of the 93rd Division was mixed. While this patchy record was attributed in part to the Division's protracted deployment to the Pacific Theater, and to the subsequent separation of its three regiments, African Americans were especially frustrated by persistent rumors that the Division's troops – and, by extension, all blacks – were cowardly.[70] The failings of Company K, of the 25th Infantry Regiment, were used to tarnish the reputation of the entire Division. On April 6, 1944, Company K set out to ambush Japanese forces near the Torokina River, on the New Guinea island of Bougainville. The operation, however, did not go as planned. Following an ambush by Japanese troops, elements of Company K broke ranks and retreated – some reports said fled – from the battlefield. Seventeen Americans were killed. This episode fueled a rumor that the 93rd Division had "broken under fire." By contrast, when white units ran from battle – as happened on several occasions, especially during the early stages of the Pacific campaign, and particularly when units were first exposed to major combat – they were typically described as merely "inexperienced."[71]

[69] Fletcher P. Martin, "24th Infantry Routs Japs in Swift, Surprise Attack," *Philadelphia Tribune*, May 6, 1944. Major Cornelius DeW. Willcox, cited in Nalty, *Strength for the Fight*, 89. See also Fletcher P. Martin, "24th Patrols Rout Small Enemy Bands," *Pittsburgh Courier*, April 22, 1944.
[70] Morehouse, *Fighting in the Jim Crow Army*, 135.
[71] Robert F. Jefferson, *Fighting for Hope: African American Troops and the 93rd Infantry Division in World War II and Postwar America* (Baltimore, MD: Johns Hopkins

FIGURE 5.3. Sergeant John C. Clark and Staff Sergeant Ford M. Shaw, 25th Combat Team, 93rd Division, clean their rifles, Bougainville April 4, 1944. Courtesy: National Archives 111-SC-364565.

The incident involving Company K attracted widespread, critical attention from military commanders and the press: for the critics of black troops, here was evidence of African Americans' inability to coordinate and execute tactical maneuvers under fire, and their innate incapacity to withstand the stresses of battle. Within the 93rd Division there was considerable reflection regarding Company K's battlefield failure. While senior officers conceded the skill of the Japanese ambush, they also acknowledged that more experienced soldiers would have been better prepared for combat.[72] The question of leadership was central. Realizing

---

University Press, 2008), 177–9; Nalty, *Strength for the Fight*, 170; Harry A. Gailey, *Bougainville, 1943–1945: The Forgotten Campaign* (Lexington: University Press of Kentucky, 1991), 178–81. A. Russell Buchanan has noted that when African American units "went into action in the Pacific" they "reacted as did other newly trained units." See A. Russell Buchanan, *Black Americans in World War II* (Santa Barbara, CA: Clio Books, 1977), 94–5.

[72] See the extensive correspondence included in the Papers of General Leonard Russell Boyd, Box 1, Hoover Institution Archives, Stanford University, Stanford, California

that inexperienced, or "green," soldiers could only perform in battle if they were well led, the Division's officers renewed their efforts to ensure that the men under their command received adequate training, support, and leadership.[73]

The various elements of the 93rd subsequently redeemed themselves, but as Colonel E. M. Yon, commanding officer of the 25th Infantry Regiment, admitted, there were other, albeit isolated instances when units of the 93rd did not demonstrate the required combat awareness or spirit.[74] For many white Americans, civilians and military alike, stories of black troops' cowardice – apparently confirmed by the incident involving Company K – justified their preconceptions regarding African Americans' alleged inability to cope with the pressures of twentieth-century warfare.[75] Units of the 93rd Division were frequently restricted to mopping-up duties, and were censured for lacking the requisite spirit to conduct large-scale offensive operations.

Dismayed by the rumors and innuendo regarding African Americans' battlefield performance, black leaders and correspondents sought to counter the negative perceptions of the 93rd Division. Denouncing "a widespread and apparently deliberate attempt on the part of certain persons to brand Negro combat troops as failures and cowards" as "one of the most shameful episodes of the Pacific War," Walter White extolled the Division's achievements.[76] Suggesting some military commanders had deliberately disparaged the 93rd, White assured President Franklin D. Roosevelt that despite confronting serious difficulties in terms of deployment, training, and on occasions leadership, the Division had performed well when given opportunities to do so.[77] White's assessment of the 93rd mirrored that of Major General Raymond G. Lehman, who commanded the Division from

(Boyd-Hoover). See also Jefferson, *Fighting for Hope*, 179–83; Gerald Astor, *The Right to Fight: A History of African Americans in the Military* (Novato, CA: Presidio, 1998), 240–1.

[73] See "Lessons Learned from Bougainville," Col. Edwin M. Yon to Commanding General, Provisional Brigade, 93rd Infantry Division, May 30, 1944, Bougainville File, Box 1, Boyd-Hoover.

[74] Colonel Edwin M. Yon, "Policies Relating to Officers and Non-commissioned officers of the 25th Infantry," June 7, 1944, Box 2, Boyd-Hoover.

[75] On the rumors surrounding the alleged failures of the 93rd Division, see Gailey, *Bougainville, 1943–1945*, 182.

[76] See Walter White, correspondence from Hollandia, Dutch New Guinea, February 12, 1945, Bougainville File, Box 1, Boyd-Hoover.

[77] See General George S. Marshall, Memorandum to General Douglas MacArthur, March 1, 1945, 165/15/6, RG 165, Box 06, NARA; Walter White, "Memorandum to the President," February 12, 1945, Reel 24, *Papers of the NAACP, Part 17, National Staff*

May 1943 until August 1944. Declaring that his Division had proved itself in battle, and stating that the men under his command were "quick to learn and eager to perform," Lehman contended that African American troops "have the same courage, the same fear and fighting spunk as any other soldiers." The troops of the 93rd, he concluded, were "about the best disciplined men in the Army."[78] While Lehman's remarks undoubtedly reflected a desire to highlight his own qualities of leadership, they were also an emphatic repudiation of prevailing white criticisms of African Americans' capacity for combat operations.

The 93rd Division and the 24th Regiment became sources of immense pride for African Americans. John David Jackson, serving in a quartermaster unit, remembered the 93rd succinctly but unequivocally: "They were good."[79] Thomas W. Davis, of the 1865th Engineering Aviation Battalion, recalled that the "troops of color" in his unit were "very proud of" of the 24th Regiment. Linking the Regiment's combat prowess and its martial, masculine spirit to a refusal to be bullied by white troops and Military Police, Davis noted that the men of the 24th "had been in combat and they knew what they were doing and they had this flair about them." "They were superior," he stated, "and they had a superiority complex." Accordingly, while he admitted that the soldiers of the 24th were "troublemakers," he emphasized that they were "proficient and efficient." Most importantly, he suggested that their "history" meant they were unwilling to accept the racism commonplace in military culture.[80] Of course, that spirit of defiance was precisely what many white commanders had feared.

The 19,000 African Americans who served in the Marines Corps also confronted that racist military culture.[81] Black Marines – such as the men of the 3rd Ammunition Company, whose exploits during the invasion of Saipan led the Corps commandant, General Alexander Vandegrift, to announce that "Negro Marines are no longer on trial. They are Marines" – eventually served with distinction in combat. In response, the African American press wasted no time in celebrating the courage and composure of black Marines who found themselves in combat. Yet segregative

Files, 1940–1955, Microfilm, eds. John H. Bracey, Jr., and August Meier (Bethesda, MD: University Publications of America, 1994).

[78] "Tan Yanks," *Time*, May 29, 1944.

[79] Jackson, AFC/2001/001/38452, VHP-LoC. See also "Patrol of 93rd Cuts Jap Lines," *Norfolk Journal and Guide*, September 30, 1944.

[80] Thomas W. Davis, AFC/2001/00/76550, VHP-LoC.

[81] Perry E. Fischer, "Epilogue" to Fischer and Gray, *Blacks and Whites Together*.

practices persisted, and the Corps' racially determined deployment policies remained a lasting source of frustration for African Americans.[82] Condemning the twenty-one-month deployment of the 51st Marine Defense Battalion to the island of Eniwetok , in the "desolate wastes in the middle of the Pacific Ocean," at war's end black journalist Harry McAlpin expressed frustration at the Corps' refusal to make proper use of trained African American units.[83]

No less galling for black Marines was the Corps' custom – following the practice of the Army – of not placing African Americans in command of whites.[84] This compounded an already-tense situation. Despite claims that white officers "assigned to" lead black Marines "were scrupulously screened to assure that, as much as possible, they were free of racial bias," racism persisted. Moreover, in asserting that "[o]nly a foolhardy White NCO or Officer," who was "not serious about his career," would "jeopardize his future by openly displaying prejudice," the key point was the reference to *open* displays of prejudice: unwittingly, the authors were conceding that more subtle forms of discrimination remained commonplace in the Marine Corps.[85] As one African American Marine veteran recalled, "segregation and discrimination" were "very complete" during the war.[86]

Battlefield relations between black and white servicemen underscored the disjunction between the wartime rhetoric of equality and the realities of race relations. African American reporters and veterans presented two, contradictory messages regarding battlefield relations between black and white Americans. Echoing those white servicemen who contended that distinctions of race diminished "the closer you get to combat," some reports emphasized the degree of cooperation between white and black servicemen.[87] Headlining a report from Fletcher P. Martin, who had earlier

[82] Jack D. Foner, *Blacks and the Military in American History: A New Perspective* (New York, NY: Praeger, 1974), 173. See also Fletcher P. Martin, "Commanding of Work of Marines," *Pittsburgh Courier*, January 1, 1944; "Colored Marines in Thick of Southwest Pacific War," *Afro-American*, March 4, 1944; "Marines under Attack from Air Constantly," *Norfolk Journal and Guide*, March 4, 1944; "Jap-Nemesis," *Chicago Defender*, May 19, 1945.
[83] Harry McAlpin, "First Negro Marine Outfit Sidetracked," *Cleveland Call and Post*, October 20, 1945.
[84] Nalty, *The Right to Fight*, 4.
[85] See Fischer and Gray, *Blacks and Whites Together*, 5. Distancing himself from racist practices and values, Perry Fischer, one of the authors pointed out that as a Jew, he, too, "was a minority." See Fischer and Gray, *Blacks and Whites Together*, 10.
[86] Jonas E. Bender, AFC/2001/001/49670, VHP-LoC.
[87] "White Soldier Tells How True Democracy Works on Pacific Isle," *Pittsburgh Courier*, April 22, 1944. See also Vincent Tubbs, "Survivor Tells of Sinking of U.S. Transport

described how "[h]ard-bitten U.S. Marines" had, "watched admiringly" as two "Negro mess attendants" had manned machine guns to fight off a Japanese air attack, the *Atlanta Daily World* declared in October 1944 that "Negro and White Marines Unite to Subdue Japs."[88] While racial antagonisms certainly did not disappear in combat, the heat of battle – or other times of crisis, such as when survivors of ships sunk in combat were awaiting rescue – could generate a greater degree of racial cooperation and mutual recognition of the other's battlefield contribution than was case when the enemy was at a distance.[89] Reuben McNair, one of the first African American Marines, recalled that a group of white Marines labeled his unit "black angels," in recognition of their battlefield service.[90] In particular, the handful of African Americans who served aboard submarines emphasized that racial tensions were frequently diminished by the shared stress of undersea service. "I had no problems with my color on *Devilfish*," recalled Jesse Allen. "We all had to work together and had no time for shit like that."[91] Elsewhere, even Nelson Peery, an eloquent and unwavering critic of American racism, noted that a white Marine had taken the time to offer friendly advice when Peery's unit reached the frontlines in the Solomons.[92] And in January 1945, the *Chicago Defender* reported that African American engineers had dropped their "shovels" and "joined white soldiers in battle" on Leyte Island in the Philippines.[93]

    Ship," *Afro-American*, January 1, 1944; Charles H. Loeb, "Thrilling Stories of Undersea Fleet Reveal Navy Negro Heroes," *Atlanta Daily World*, August 31, 1945. The Pacific War experience of African Americans contrasts with some scholars' accounts of the desegregated military of the 1960s. It has been asserted that during the Vietnam War, although relations between blacks and whites were frequently tense in areas away from the frontlines, in the heat of combat the lines of race were less distinct. See Herman Graham, III, *The Brothers' Vietnam War: Black Power, Manhood, and the Military Experience* (Gainesville, FL: University Press of Florida, 2003), 45–7, 63–6.

[88] Fletcher P. Martin, "Sailors Grab Machine Guns: Fight off 15 Jap Bombers," *Chicago Defender*, March 4, 1944; "Negro and White Marines Unite to Subdue Japs: Supply Units Rapidly Turned into Combat," *Atlanta Daily World*, October 13, 1944.

[89] Describing relations between blacks and whites aboard a lifeboat following the sinking of the USS *Gregory*, in September 1942 Steward Ray Carter noted that "Brotherly love just oozed all over the place." See Gregory, in Motley, ed., *Invisible Soldier*, 108.

[90] Reuben McNair, cited in McLaurin, *Marines of Montford Point*, 127–8.

[91] Jesse Allen, interview, in Glenn A. Knoblock, *Black Submariners in the United States Navy, 1940–1975* (Jefferson, NC: McFarland & Co, 2005), 260.

[92] Peery, *Black Fire*, 242.

[93] Fletcher P. Martin, "Tan Yanks Rout Jap Chutists: Thwart Nippon Stab at Key Leyte Airfield," *Chicago Defender*, January 13, 1945. For an earlier example of black engineers assuming a combat role, see "Labor Troops Drop Shovels, Man Guns in New Guinea Push," *Norfolk Journal and Guide*, November 28, 1942.

If those black engineers were not quite turning ploughshares into swords, the implication was clear: as well as cooperating with white soldiers on the battlefield – in other words, where it mattered most – they were also proving that when given the opportunity black noncombatants could play their part on the frontlines.

Reports of battlefield cooperation between black and white service-men were not without foundation. Yet, even after African Americans had proved themselves in combat significant numbers of white servicemen continued to belittle the combat proficiency and masculine valor of black troops. Indeed, there is evidence that as the Allies advanced toward Japan during 1944 and 1945, the deployment of African Americans to com-bat roles exacerbated rather than diminished white anxieties. Censored correspondence from early 1945 suggests that white servicemen's racial anxieties were underpinned by sexual anxieties and a concern for their own masculine identity.

Tensions between white and black servicemen stationed in the Philippines have been described in Chapter 3. But these tensions are also significant for what they reveal about the connections between notions of martial prowess and masculinity. The complex racial situation in the Philippines, where white and black American troops vied for the company of local women, was exacerbated by reports that in trying to "get Filipino girls," African Americans were describing themselves as "night raiders," or "night fighters." Significantly, too, blacks were allegedly claiming to be "American Indians." That rumor had been spread earlier in the war by white American troops in Australia, and elsewhere, to disparage African Americans. But in this white serviceman's telling, the imagined confusion between African Americans and Native Americans was serving a differ-ent purpose: in their effort to persuade Filipino women of their mar-tial qualities, black troops were representing themselves as Amerindians. This serviceman's account reveals much about his own racial perceptions. But it also suggests that African Americans themselves were prepared to exploit, and perhaps accept, common stereotypes regarding Native Americans' fighting qualities. While it is unclear whether the white ser-viceman in question shared those views concerning Native Americans, his assessment of the combat proficiency of their African American com-patriots was blunt: the "niggers" were "afraid of their own shadow at night." Concluding that military authorities "ought to take them black so and sos," and "put them on the front line and get rid of some of them," his assertion that African American troops were not "much good for any-thing" was unsurprising in the context of a military culture that continued to demean African Americans.[94] However, the fact that he continued to feel empowered to restate those assertions – so near the end of a war in which hundreds of thousands of African Americans had taken part, and which was purportedly being fought on behalf of universal principles of equality – highlighted the enormity of the task ahead for blacks striving for civic and political equality.

The persistence of white racism in the battle zone was stark evidence of the imperfections of American civilization. Yet black combat troops saw themselves, and were depicted by the African American press, as standing in the vanguard of the global fight for civilized values. This raised questions regarding the battlefield behavior of black troops. Confronting an enemy apparently unrestrained by the conventions of "civilized" warfare, black servicemen sought to maintain their dignity under the most adverse circumstances. This issue was further complicated because African Americans' service on the battlefield was considered a test of their masculine credentials. Servicemen of all races experienced these often-conflicting imperatives. But as blacks were frequently reminded, they were exemplars of their race, whose battlefield performance – the key measure of military conduct – was subject to the highest standards and constant comparison with their white compatriots.

Frequently appalled by the brutality they encountered across the Asia-Pacific Theater, black servicemen recognized that modern warfare, particularly when fought amid the alien and even primordial jungles of the Asia-Pacific, was the antithesis of the honorable, manly endeavor some had imagined. While some claimed that "a lot of Japs will be allowed to live due to the fact that we are a civilized people," others spoke of the need to not merely subdue, but – borrowing language used widely in wartime America – "exterminate" the Japanese. Many African Americans, like their white counterparts, believed that the moral imperatives of "civilized" warfare had been undermined by Japanese atrocities. "Reports of Jap cruelty to captured prisoners," noted one black serviceman, had "caused every fighting American to realize he is up against one of the lowest type of barbarian."[95]

---

[94] APO 501, Headquarters, United States Army Forces in the Far East, Censorship Survey of Morale – Rumors, Propaganda. Issued by the Assistant Chief of Staff, G-2, *Censorship Survey of Morale*, 38, March 1945, RG 496, 496/290/47/27/7-, Records of the General Headquarters, Southwest Pacific Area and United States Army Forces, Pacific (World War II) Box 24, NARA.

[95] See Andrew J. Bowler, "The Inquiring Reporter," *New Journal and Guide*, February 12, 1944.

Both sides – and all races – bore varying degrees of responsibility for the descent into ferocity that culminated with the atomic bombing of Hiroshima and Nagasaki. Although African American blues singer Lonnie Johnson's plaintive call to his sweetheart – "wait for me" – reflected the fears of lovesick soldiers everywhere, his declaration that if he could not bring his lover "a Jap," he would bring her "back a head or two" went much further in joining love and patriotism to the savagery of the Pacific War.[96] Hinting at what was in store for black troops in the Pacific Theater, Johnson anticipated – and contributed to – the desensitization of the enemy, which was a prerequisite for the mutual brutalization associated with the Pacific conflict. Bill Stevens, a veteran of the 93rd Division, emphasized that the well-earned Japanese reputation for cruelty had to be seen alongside Americans' capacity to transcend the boundaries of acceptable battlefield behavior. Unlike the aforementioned African American troops who had apparently been willing to utilize Native Americans' reputation for cruelty to emphasize their own martial qualities, Stevens referred to Native Americans more critically, emphasizing instead their alleged penchant for cruel and macabre behavior. "I saw souvenirs in the hands of our men, or on their belts," he noted, "that would have curled the scalplock of Pontiac." Just as significantly, he suggested that Americans had also committed sexual crimes. "There were Japanese women on many of those islands; need I say more?"[97] Such displays of battlefield cruelty and sexual violence, Stevens implied, rendered military service a betrayal, rather than a fulfillment of masculine virtue.

While historians ponder the cycle of violence that made the Pacific War such a ruthless contest, African Americans recognized the consequences of that savagery for Pacific Islanders. Notwithstanding Western – and African American – ambivalence about whether the prewar Pacific represented savagery, or an idyll, there was no question of the terrors and violence unleashed by World War Two. As Fletcher Martin contemplated that violence, and sought to explain Islanders' determination to avenge Japanese cruelty, he turned to notions of innocent, childlike natives. Juxtaposing "a group of woolly headed people who had nothing to do with what goes on today in the world" against the horrors of wartime occupation, Martin suggested that the Islanders' innocence made Japan's atrocities all the more deplorable. Japanese behavior, he contended, was

[96] Guido van Rijn, *Roosevelt's Blues: African-American Blues and Gospel Songs on President FDR* (Jackson, MI: University Press of Mississippi, 1997), 154.
[97] Stevens, cited in Motley, ed., *Invisible* Soldier, 77–8.

the "foundation" for the Islanders' "hatred," which filled some – such as "Lumbo, a native boy" from the Solomons, who sought to avenge the rape and murder of his girlfriend at the hands of the Japanese – with a "burning desire to kill and kill."[98]

Black servicemen, therefore, expressed sympathy for the victims of Japanese tyranny. Yet they also recognized Asians and Pacific Islanders as active agents in determining their own future, partly through the logistical and intelligence support they provided to Allied forces, but also through their contribution on the field of battle.[99] This was an issue of long-term significance, as African Americans' perceptions of the fighting qualities of Pacific Islanders and Asians resonated beyond the wartime battlefields and played a part in shaping their understanding of the postwar world. Battlefield valor was not only a means by which African Americans could assert their place in the American polity; given the long association between military service, masculinity, and the rights of citizenship, it was also a means by which Pacific Islanders could repudiate racial assumptions upon which the colonial enterprise was based.

Black servicemen accepted many of the stereotypes associated with Pacific Islanders. One of those stereotypes was that native peoples were passive, even childlike – characteristics also widely attributed to African Americans. Without resorting to very different pejorative stereotypes of native peoples – that they were innately violent, or even savage – African Americans used Islanders' capacity to wage war to challenge assumptions of native passivity. Writing in early 1944, black journalist John Robert Badger explained that Fijian commandos who had displayed their valor and combat prowess in the Solomon Islands were not "the kind of native soldiers" seen in "cheap picture magazines and cheaper Hollywood thrillers." Rather than the "bare-footed, bare-waisted, calico skirted people with grease-paint smeared over their bodies," armed only "with spears and shields" – as they were commonly depicted in Western culture – the native troops he described exhibited all the traits of a modern army.[100] Just as African Americans used military service to press their claims for citizenship, they suggested that Pacific Islanders' ability to wage war was an essential element of their claims for independence.

[98] Fletcher P. Martin, "Tulagi Native Lives for Day of Revenge," *Philadelphia Tribune*, March 18, 1944.
[99] Fletcher P. Martin, "24th Infantry Locks Horns with Japs on Bougainville," *New York Amsterdam News*, April 8, 1944.
[100] John Robert Badger, "World View," *Chicago Defender*, January 29, 1944.

Notions of masculine bravery were key to that process. Black reporters stationed in the Pacific Theater referred often to the masculine valor of their nonwhite allies. In the process they both repudiated and reinforced stereotypical views of Pacific Islanders – and, by extension, other nonwhite peoples. While the *Philadelphia Tribune* noted that "Native Fiji Islanders" had demonstrated their capacity to make effective use of the "modern weapons" with which they were now equipped, the paper also reported that those Fijians had been fighting "alongside American and Australian troops" and had been led by New Zealand officers."[101] If that was ambivalent praise for the Fijian troops, there were occasions when African Americans expressed unambiguous admiration for the fighting qualities of indigenous troops. Acclaiming the Fijians as "effective allies," reports in the black press emphasized the heavy toll they inflicted on enemy forces. During a series of bloody encounters in early 1944, the "fierce warriors from the Fijis" reportedly accounted for "at least 179 Japanese" for the loss of just "one killed and three wounded."[102] Fletcher P. Martin also lauded the Fijians' martial qualities. Describing the "toughest" and "deadliest" soldiers in the South Pacific, Martin assured his readers that Fijian soldiers represented "the island's best in manhood." Although it was unsurprising that African American constructions of masculinity emphasized battlefield courage, Martin offered a more nuanced view of ideal manhood. Declaring that the Fijians were the "most feared by the Japanese," he referred also to their happy and "warm demeanor," and emphasized they were well-liked by their allies.[103] Forgetting, perhaps, that those images of happy natives echoed stereotypes of contented African American slaves, Martin's account transformed longstanding Western assumptions regarding primitive or even savage Islanders into images of willing soldiers whose battlefield deeds were matched by their ability to work harmoniously with their American allies – black and white.

African Americans also paid tribute to the fighting qualities of Tongans and New Guineans. Proving themselves "invaluable as snipers, guerrilla fighters and in mopping up operations," a unit "composed of natives

[101] "Native Fijian Troops Use Modern Arms," *Philadelphia Tribune*, April 22, 1944.
[102] "Fijian Natives Use U.S. Arms," *Chicago Defender*, April 22, 1944. See also "Fijians to Lead Fight on Nippons," *Pittsburgh Courier*, June 19, 1943.
[103] "Fijian Soldiers Toughest, Deadliest in South Pacific," *Afro-American*, October 9, 1943; Fletcher Martin, "Fijians Gain Respect of Enemies and Allies," *Philadelphia Tribune*, May 27, 1944. See also Rudolph Dunbar, "Fijians on Battlefield Praised as 'Finest Jungle Fighters,'" *Cleveland Call and Post*, July 10, 1943.

from practically every tribe on the island" of New Guinea had reputedly "attained a splendid reputation for its record in jungle fighting." "[I]ntensely proud of being soldiers," these troops were described as "unsurpassed" in "the particular type of warfare" in which they were engaged.[104] And while correspondents such as Martin noted an occasional "bad one" among the "remarkable" natives of New Guinea – such as "Embogi," whose lust for power led him to commit various atrocities among his own peoples – even in those cases African American depictions of natives could conclude on a positive note, as suggested by Embogi's repentance, moments before his execution.[105]

Moreover, while African American commentators referred to Pacific Islanders' propensity for sometimes-excessive battlefield behavior, those remarks must be seen in the wider context of the uncompromising nature of the Pacific War. Fletcher Martin's comments are again instructive. Expanding on earlier reports that "military experts" who had "seen the Fijians in action describe them as probably the finest jungle fighters in the world," he presented a more explicit account of the Fijian Scouts' enthusiastic approach to warfare: "one patrol," he noted, returned with nine enemy "skulls."[106] Protagonists from all sides in the Pacific War were guilty of gathering gruesome trophies of war, and Martin's depictions of the Fijians' uncompromising battlefield conduct was characteristic of what became known as "total war." That concept has sometimes been associated with the technology of modernity. But in describing the Fijians' eagerness for bringing back the skulls of their enemies, Martin touched on longstanding Western perceptions of head-hunting Pacific Islanders, and implied that supposedly primitive and uncivilized indigenes were the most effective exponents of total war amid the jungles of the Asia-Pacific.

Experiences of combat also shaped African Americans' views of their enemy. Exploring blacks' prewar views of Japan, and emphasizing the possibilities of an Afro-Asian challenge to the white racial order, scholars have identified – and, as shown earlier, perhaps exaggerated – a sympathy

---

[104] "Papuan Natives Excel in Jungle Fighting; Feared by Japs," *Cleveland Call and Post*, June 5, 1943. See also Fletcher P. Martin, "Martin Praises Heroism of Guinea Scouts," *Atlanta Daily World*, December 10, 1943; "Returned War Veteran Praises 24th Infantrymen," *Norfolk Journal and Guide*, November 25, 1944.

[105] Fletcher Martin, "Wanted to Be King: Bad Native Hanged," *Philadelphia Tribune*, December 18, 1943. See also "Allied Party Butchered by Jap Soldiers," *Cleveland Call and Post*, May 22, 1943.

[106] Dunbar, "Fijians on Battlefront Praised as 'Finest Jungle Fighters'"; Fletcher Martin, "93rd Division Pushes on to Conquer Japs," *New York Amsterdam News*, April 29, 1944.

within the wartime black community for Japan's anticolonial stance. There has been scant analysis, however, of black servicemen's views of their Japanese adversaries. If African Americans shared the broader Allied wartime view of the Japanese as uncivilized, or even barbaric, it complicated the prospects of an Afro-Asian alliance against white racism and colonialism, and portended significant obstacles standing in the way of a postwar transnational challenge to white authority.

Americans' wartime views of the Japanese were shaped by perceptions of duplicity at Pearl Harbor and by Japan's contempt for the conventions of military conduct. Borrowing the language of long-held Western stereotypes of Asians, a 1943 news report described the Japanese as a "race of inscrutable men," whose wartime behavior "cannot be based on the ordinary human standards."[107] Despite viewing this virulent anti-Japanese sentiment through distinctly African American eyes, a majority of black servicemen concluded that the Japanese were a savage, deceitful foe.[108] Black servicemen's critique of Japan's wartime excesses was informed by, and in turn contributed to, the underlying black skepticism regarding Japanese claims to be acting on behalf of an Afro-Asian alliance. Conscious of the colonial and racial dimensions of the Pacific War, African American servicemen's attitudes contrasted to the prewar views of black editors and writers who had expressed sympathy for Japan's self-proclaimed role as the nemesis of white colonialism.

Interviewed in 1945, Private Charles Nelson urged African Americans to make "no mistake about the Japanese soldiers and their feelings 'on the brother.'" The Japanese, he insisted, "figure we're all Americans, regardless of color, so they're as cruel to the Negro as they are to the whites. They don't mean us any good." "[S]ome Japs I've talked to," he noted, "make fun at us and refer to us as cotton-pickers."[109] An awareness of

---

[107] "How Japs Fight," *Time*, February 15, 1943. See also John Dower, *War Without Mercy: Race and Power in the Pacific War* (New York, NY: Pantheon, 1986), 48–53; Emily Rosenberg, *A Date Which Will Live: Pearl Harbor in American Memory* (Durham, NC: Duke University Press, 2003), 54–5.

[108] My conclusions accord with Michael Cullen Green's analysis of the black presence across postwar Asia. Of the hundreds of thousands of African American soldiers serving in Japan and South Korea during the 1940s and 1950s, Cullen suggests, only a few "reached harmonious conclusions about Afro-Asian solidarity." The "domestic Cold War environment," he continued, "was rarely if ever the most important factor shaping the attitudes, interpretations, and goals of black servicemen." See Green, *Black Yanks in the Pacific: Race in the Making of the American Military Empire after World War II* (Ithaca, NY: Cornell University Press, 2010), 3.

[109] "Returned Soldier Says Home World's Best Place to Him: Talks about War in the Pacific," *New York Amsterdam News*, February 24, 1945.

those Japanese views made wartime reports of Japanese mistreatment of African Americans all the more plausible. Nelson Peery detailed the fate of one black serviceman who fell into Japanese hands: "the missing soldier" was found "hanging by his thumbs from a banyan tree, his body pierced by fifty bayonet wounds." While Peery admitted that his African American comrades also betrayed vicious instincts – the "scent of victory," "the blood lust," and "the savage instinct to kill, to hate, to destroy," had "become a material force" – in noting that the men in his unit were seeking to avenge their dead friend, he suggested that in that instance it was the Japanese who had initiated the cycle of violence.[110]

Japanese commanders and propagandists, seemingly oblivious to the consequences of their nation's wartime behavior, continued in their efforts to exploit what they described as "an ever present conflict of feeling" between "Caucasians and the Negroes."[111] Bill Downey, stationed on the tiny, nondescript island of Funafuti, recalled the taunts of Tokyo Rose. "I beseech you black men of the Marines to listen to me. Don't you know you are being used? They make you do the menial work and fill your head with lies about the Japanese people being your enemies." Frustrated that his unit had been "dumped" in a relatively insignificant corner of the Pacific conflict, Downey remembered Tokyo Rose's mocking reference to the fact that black Marines continued to be used "as stevedores for the whites."[112] Notwithstanding their professions of sympathy for African Americans, however, and despite judging the "abilities of the American Negro" as "relatively outstanding," the Japanese remained ambivalent about the capacities of African Americans. Having noted that blacks were "unsuitable officers," Japanese analysts concluded that African Americans were generally "indolent," had "little willpower," and "were inclined to be cruel." Perhaps most significantly, the Japanese report suggested the African Americans lacked a "spirit of unity."[113]

All military forces prize that spirit of camaraderie, but Allied commanders recognized that the Japanese attached an almost-mystical faith

[110] Peery, *Black Fire*, 246.

[111] Military Attaché Report for the Military Intelligence Division of the War Department General Staff, October 10, 1944. Subject: Japan-Japanese Intelligence Report on U.S. Negro Troops, Box 443, Entry 43, File 291.2, RG 165, NARA. See also Gerald Horne, *Race War!: White Supremacy and the Japanese Attack on the British Empire* (New York, NY: New York University Press, 2004), 227–8.

[112] Downey, cited in Buckley, *American Patriots*, 318.

[113] Military Attaché Report for the Military Intelligence Division of the War Department General Staff, October 10, 1944. Subject: Japan-Japanese Intelligence Report on U.S. Negro Troops, Box 443, Entry 43, File 291.2, RG 165, NARA.

in their servicemen's devotion to the national cause. During the early stages of the Pacific War, these Allied perceptions informed their analysis of the unanticipated Japanese battlefield successes. Within a few months of Pearl Harbor, African American commentators were suggesting that the Japanese – previously denigrated as "little brown fellows" by many Americans – were "more dangerous than Hitler's Nazis."[114] The initial Allied scorn for the fighting qualities of the Japanese had been replaced quickly by a racially informed sense that Japanese troops were imbued with an innate capacity to wage war amid the hostile terrain of the Asia-Pacific. Japanese "foot soldiers," noted one correspondent in 1942, "slithered through the dark jungles of New Guinea like drops of mercury spilled on a door mat."[115] As the war continued, the Allied assumption that the "tricky" Japanese fought "differently" was evidenced by their obdurate refusal to surrender.[116]

As African Americans contemplated the fighting qualities of Japanese troops, they also pondered the relationship between race and masculinity in the United States. One black veteran, Bill Stevens, used his forthright assessment of the Japanese fighting spirit to deride the white masculinist warrior tradition. Pointing out that the Japanese had often been derided as "the little 'monkey man,'" he recalled that "the big bad American Marines were going to kick their asses properly and put them in their place." Contrary to Americans' expectations, however, that "inferior breed," proved to be "excellent soldiers," who "beat the shit out of our legendary Marines." Japanese bravery and resourcefulness, Stevens continued, were complemented by a capacity to conduct a form of psychological warfare, as they "took the great white American ego and used it as a weapon against him." By constantly "demoralizing" front-line American units, and by waging "psychological warfare on a scale" that the Americans "had never dreamed possible," the Japanese "kept our men tied in knots."[117]

---

[114] "How Many More Mistakes Can We Afford to Make?" *Afro-American*, September 26, 1942.

[115] "Pause at Kokoda," *Time*, August 10, 1942.

[116] "Negro Marines Board Transport on First Leg of Voyage to Battle Tricky Japanese," *Cleveland Call and Post*, February 12, 1944; "How Japs Fight," *Time*, February 15, 1943. One black veteran, perhaps confusing his Japanese enemies with stereotypes widely associated with the Chinese, claimed that Japan's wartime fanaticism was fueled by their use of opium. See Simeon Booker, "God Helped Me to Get Home – Wounded Vet: Sgt. Clarence Newton," *Afro-American*, December 4, 1943.

[117] Stevens, cited in Motley, ed., *Invisible Soldier*, 77–8.

While Allied servicemen across the Pacific Theater continued to be impressed by their enemy's tenacity during 1944 and 1945, the combat performance and offensive spirit of Japanese forces deteriorated significantly. Some black servicemen, such as Marke Toles, encountered debilitated Japanese troops whose morale was poor. "Many of the Japanese soldiers were starving," Toles recalled, "and wouldn't attack us unless we attempted to ambush them."[118] As Allied forces secured battlefield ascendancy, Japanese forces resorted to ever more desperate measures – which served only to affirm perceptions that they were in some respects subhuman. Nelson Peery described the terrors associated with fighting Japanese "suicide units." "It's a really nasty business," he recalled, "hunting them down like dogs and killing them."[119]

Peery's language suggested the extent to which African American servicemen regarded themselves as very different from – and superior to – their Japanese adversaries. These differences were also evident when black troops considered the limits of their foes' tactical nous and battlefield imagination. Reflecting common Allied perceptions, Bill Payne described the Japanese as "really tough fighters" who "could maneuver through the jungle and the trees and the caves better than we could." Yet while it was "nearly impossible" to force the Japanese from caves, and other well-protected defensive positions, Payne suggested that "their imagination was limited." "They took orders," he wrote, "and followed them, and that was that." Payne's reflections on Japanese soldiers' willingness to follow orders, without question or challenge, said much about the two competing military cultures. Japanese soldiers, he wrote, "took orders to the letter," and "followed them, and that was that." "There was no individual thinking," he said. American troops, by contrast, were "trained to think for themselves," and if "they got into a situation, they could find a way out." And even for African American troops, who were at the bottom of the American military hierarchy, and whose military aptitude was the subject of almost-constant white derision, there were instances when orders were not sacrosanct. "We were taught to follow orders," Payne concluded, "but we were also taught to go beyond that from time to time."[120]

Payne's account affirmed the complex racial dynamics associated with the Pacific War. These complexities were further evidenced by reports that frontline Japanese forces, building on their government's aforementioned

[118] Toles, cited in Jefferson, *Fighting for Hope*, 170.
[119] Peery, cited in Morehouse, *Fighting in the Jim Crow Army*, 141.
[120] Payne, cited in Morehouse, *Fighting in the Jim Crow Army*, 143.

attempts to woo African Americans, were treating black Americans differently from their white compatriots. In May 1943 Vincent Tubbs referred to "stories that the Japs do not strafe lifeboats in which there are colored seamen."[121] But such stories were almost certainly apocryphal, and although Tubbs's report was suggestive of the distinctive African American understanding of the racial dimensions of the Pacific War, the black press also reported widely on Japanese atrocities against Allied troops, white and black.[122]

While African Americans found many reasons to condemn "Jap tactics and atrocities," the most graphic expression of Japanese savagery was the mistreatment of Allied prisoners-of-war (POWs).[123] There were relatively few POWs taken by either side during the Pacific War, and although the treatment of black POWs depended in large measure on the whim of individual Japanese camp commanders, there was obvious propaganda potential in convincing African American POWs to turn against the United States. Treating black POWs humanely was a first step in that process. The Japanese record in this regard was mixed, however. John Dushek, a black seaman imprisoned by the Japanese, reported that the commander of the camp in which he was imprisoned had given preferential treatment to a group of "wealthy white industrialists" who were prisoners in the same camp.[124] Conversely, Dr. Robert T. Browne, interned by the Japanese when they captured Manila in early 1942, described Japanese attempts to challenge racial hierarchies among the American internees. The Japanese, he reported, "insisted there should be no discrimination or segregation within the camp."[125] Captain Chester Sanders, one of just six

[121] Vincent Tubbs, "Too Far Out to Swim Back," *Afro-American*, May 8, 1943.
[122] See "Japs Shot Yanks in Pacific Ocean," *New Journal and Guide*, December 11, 1943.
[123] "Action-Packed Film of Jap Atrocities," *Cleveland Call and Post*, May 15, 1943.
[124] Jonathan Richards, "I Was a Jap Prisoner," *Afro-American*, January 8, 1944.
[125] Louis Lomax, "N.Y. Man Describes 3 Years of Life in Jap Prison Camp," *Afro-American*, June 2, 1945. See also "Japanese Try Jim Crow Rule against Whites," *New York Amsterdam News*, September 22, 1945; Horne, *Race War!*, 220–1. Recollecting his Pacific War experiences African American Navy veteran Eddie Will Robinson described his imprisonment by the Japanese following the sinking of the submarine on which he served. In those recollections, Robinson depicted himself as a feisty, assertive young man, willing to defy Japanese authority, and, in order to secure his safety and that of his fellow prisoners, play an almost caricatured role that apparently confirmed Japanese preconceptions of African Americans. Robinson's recollections, however, are inaccurate – and perhaps suggest more about the racial politics of the 1970s, when he was interviewed, than they do about his wartime experiences. While Robinson did serve aboard the USS *Thresher*, and – just possibly, as he claimed, briefly aboard the USS *Flying Fish* – neither submarine was sunk by the Japanese. He is recorded as having joined the crew of the *Thresher* in March, 1944, serving there until the end of the war.

black survivors of the Bataan Death March, noted that black POWs had been treated less harshly than white prisoners. Yet while he was spared the beatings to which other POWs were routinely subjected, when his Japanese captors recognized Sanders's status and rank they "sought to force information from him by placing him in solitary confinement without light, without a bed." By war's end Sanders had reportedly "lost 112 pounds."[126] In another sign of the limits of Japanese compassion toward African Americans, Sanders's wife, imprisoned from late 1941 until 1945, endured numerous hardships and cruelties. During the final stages of the war, she reported, the prisoners were starving.[127]

At the same time as African American commentators and servicemen condemned Japanese cruelty, the dual imperatives of the Double V campaign remained significant. Contemplating whether the Japanese were any more savage than white Mississippians, black World War One veteran and journalist P. L. Prattis concluded in late 1942 that in terms of "pure savagery, what is there to compare with the slaughter of blacks at Fort Pillow by General Forrest in our own Civil War?"[128] Criticisms of American racism also underpinned black servicemen's expressions of humanity toward their Japanese adversaries. Recalling the sight of dead Japanese on Okinawa, Russell Taylor McCabe explained that the "one thing that really disturbed him" was seeing "a lot" of American soldiers removing "gold teeth" from Japanese corpses.[129]

Robinson is included in two photographs, taken in 1945, of the crew of the *Thresher*. And while Glenn A. Knoblock's carefully collated list of African American submariners includes a reference to an "Elrey" Robinson serving aboard the *Flying Fish*, it is unlikely that was a mistranscription of "Eddie." See Robinson, in Motley, ed., *Invisible Soldier*, 111–14; Knoblock, *Black Submariners*, 74, 96, Appendix (unpaginated).

[126] "First Freed Jap Prisoner in Frisco; Lost 112 Pounds," *Afro-American*, April 14, 1945. It was estimated there were approximately 250 African Americans among the tens of thousands of American troops left on the Philippines. Most were serving in "engineering, quartermaster, trucking, ordnance, laundry, and kitchen details." See Moore, *Fighting for America*, 47.

[127] See "Mrs. Millie Sanders Home, Says She Faced Starvation by Japs," *Afro-American*, May 5, 1945. See also E. F. Joseph, "Negro Captain, Jap Prisoner, Loses 112Lbs," *Philadelphia Tribune*, April 14, 1945; Charles H. Loeb, "Jap Held Negro Prisoners Set Free in Philippines," *Chicago Defender*, February 24, 1945; Reginald Kearney, *African American Views of the Japanese: Solidarity or Sedition* (Albany, NY: State University of New York Press, 1998), 121.

[128] P. L. Prattis, "The Horizon: Are Japanese More Savage than Mississippians?" *Pittsburgh Courier*, November 14, 1942.

[129] Russell Taylor McCabe, AFC/2001/001/7757, VHP-LoC. See also "Sergeant Fetches Japs' Gold Teeth from Guadalcanal," *Afro-American*, May 1, 1943; Horne, *Race War!*, 226.

Adolph Newton's description of the treatment of a Japanese pilot – and the desecration of his corpse – was a revealing commentary on the wartime descent into barbarism across the Asia-Pacific. Emphasizing that the pilot's "hands were tied behind his back" and his legs "tied at the ankles," Newton catalogued the brutalities inflicted by the triumphant Americans. This was no exhibition of honorable manhood. Convinced that the pilot "had been alive when" he had been "pulled from the bay," Newton noted there "were three bullet holes in his face." The "way the guys on the boat were smiling only strengthened" Newton's belief that the pilot had been killed after being captured. Compounding matters, after the "white fellows" started "to curse" him, "someone pulled out a dirk and plunged the blade into the lifeless body." Driven by bloodlust, other Americans joined in "to stab the body." Newton did not condemn the killing of the pilot, who just "the night before" had slain some of Newton's "shipmates." He was, however, troubled deeply by the "way they treated his body." "Not only did they stab it repeatedly," he recalled, "but someone pulled the teeth from the body, and they called him awful names." Revolted by the treatment of his enemy, Newton realized that similar treatment could be inflicted upon him, albeit not by the Japanese. As he stood watching the defilement of the pilot's corpse, Newton "wondered if they would do that to me." "From somewhere," he wrote, "came the answer: Yes!" The treatment of the dead Japanese, he realized, reminded him "of some of the pictures" he "had seen of the lynching of Negroes in the southern part of the United States." Later, after learning that a group of white servicemen had plotted to murder African Americans who had established relationships with Filipino women, Newton reflected that "the answer to the question I had asked myself when they brought in that Japanese pilot had been confirmed."[130] For Newton, the cruelty shown by white Americans during the Pacific War was indivisible from the racism of the American South.

African Americans on the frontlines in the war against Japan were few in number. Yet the political and cultural significance of their service should not be discounted. While they expended as much energy fighting discrimination within the US armed forces as they did fighting the enemy, African Americans' presence in the war zone attracted significant attention from the black community, from the American military establishment, and from civil and political leaders in the United States. Black service on the

---

[130] Adolph Newton, *Better than Good: A Black Sailor's War, 1943–1945* (Annapolis, MD: Naval Institute Press, 1999), 64, 77.

battlefield was at once a powerful symbol of African American defiance and manhood, and a portent of the rising tide of black militancy, which contributed to both the civil rights struggle within the United States and the international fight against colonialism and racism. African Americans understood well the significance of black combat: the blood they spilled had earned them the right to play their part in reshaping the postwar world, both at home and abroad. African Americans' presence on the battlefield, moreover, was a significant factor in shaping their views of the postwar Asia-Pacific. Although the black leadership was impressed by the possibility of Japan's anticolonial stance, and notwithstanding the common understanding within the black community that the Pacific War was substantially about race, a majority of African American service personnel concluded that Japan's claim to be leading a transnational struggle against racism and colonialism was fatally compromised by the savagery with which the Japanese conducted the war. African Americans also understood the significance of Pacific Islanders' battlefield contributions. Like African Americans, Pacific Islanders were variously stereotyped as savage brutes or as passive, demasculinized victims of white colonialism; like African Americans, too, they were caught up in the violence of a total war. The cycle of brutality that characterized the Pacific War reached its nadir with the atomic bombing of Japan. As the final chapter explains, blacks' meditations on the use of atomic weapons was one aspect of their wider contemplation of the transformation of the Japanese from hated foe to vanquished adversary.

CHAPTER 6

Liberators and Occupiers

African Americans and the Pacific War Aftermath

In May 1944, Staff Sergeant Ernest Brown of the 93rd Infantry Division ruminated on the long-term significance of his experiences in wartime New Guinea. By enabling white and black Americans to come together to defeat the "common enemy," the Pacific War was laying the foundations for a postwar racial order free of the discrimination and inequalities that had hitherto tarnished the United States. Invoking the memory of Abraham Lincoln – and putting to one side Lincoln's tardiness in both issuing the Emancipation Proclamation and allowing African Americans to join the Union Army – Brown emphasized that black and white American troops were living proof of the Great Emancipator's warning that "[u]nited we stand and divided we fall." As white and "colored men of arms" fought alongside each other, he wrote, they were building "something" that would "add greatly to the peace that must come some day." This "was a spirit," Brown concluded, that all American soldiers hoped to find when they returned home.[1]

Five months later, in October 1944, following a visit to a military hospital in New Guinea, the African American correspondent Conrad Clark offered an equally buoyant assessment of postwar race relations. Observing "Negro soldiers playing games with white American and Australian fellow soldiers," and concluding there was "no Jim Crow" among the wounded troops, or their white doctors and nurses, Clark was heartened by the spectacle of "Negro soldiers exchanging post-war views with white soldiers." The hospital, he concluded, was an "example of

[1] See Billy Rowe, "Spirit of Lincoln Exists as Yanks Battle Japanese in Mire," *Pittsburgh Courier*, May 20, 1944.

democracy."[2] In Clark's telling, these recuperating servicemen – black and white – represented an idealized, racially integrated image of democracy at work, whose foot soldiers were not only actively engaged in winning the war; they were also planning a postwar world free of the discrimination and prejudices that had marred the old order.

The optimistic images of interracial harmony presented by Clark and Brown were largely illusory, however. While their expressions of confidence in a racially enlightened future reflected a characteristically American sense of possibility, other African Americans were less sanguine. Amid disquieting signs that Southern segregation and racial violence remained ascendant at home, and skeptical of American policymakers' commitment to the universal principles of human rights to global peace and prosperity articulated at the recently completed United Nations (UN) Conference on International Organization, black leaders such as Walter White conveyed the disenchantment among African Americans. In July 1945, as the Pacific War reached its furious apogee, White was lamenting the "despair and disillusionment of Negro soldiers in the Pacific." Black servicemen's despondence, he explained, was a consequence of the "perpetuation of the same racial theories" that African Americans were "supposed to be fighting to eliminate in other parts of the world." Linking the persistence of American racism to the US global mission, White prophesied that the decade following the war would "unquestionably be the most critical in human history." The issues at stake, he averred, allowed no compromise. Endorsing the anticolonial and antiracial principles outlined in the April 1945 "Colonial Conference," organized by W. E. B. Du Bois and attended by delegates from Asia, and other colonized regions, White asserted that Americans would "have to demonstrate" whether they were "in earnest in pledging" that "there shall be no discrimination on account of 'race, religion, language or sex.'"[3]

Despite presenting contrary images of African American attitudes during the latter stages of the Pacific War, Brown, Clark, and White, were similarly determined to hold the United States accountable to the promise of its wartime rhetoric. Black leaders and editors were also unanimous

---

[2] Conrad Clark, "New Guinea Hospital Example of Democracy," *New York Amsterdam News*, October 21, 1944.

[3] "White Warns Prejudice May Void UNCIO," *Atlanta Daily World*, July 8, 1945. See also Thomas Dyja, *Walter White: The Dilemma of Black Identity in America* (Chicago, IL: Ivan R. Dee, 2008), 167. On the 1945 Colonial Conference, see Carol Anderson, "From Hope to Disillusion: African Americans, the United Nations, and the Struggle for Human Rights, 1944–1947," *Diplomatic History* 20, no.4 (1996): 534.

in the view that African Americans' military service had earned them the right to play their part in remaking the world. As the *Philadelphia Tribune* reported at war's end, the role of black troops was nothing less than to "return peace to the whole world."[4] African American veterans concurred with the *Tribune's* assessment. While many were concerned principally with navigating their way through the convoluted points system that determined when individual servicemen could return home – a system which also frustrated white military personnel, but which black troops believed was being used to deliberately delay their return to the United States – African American servicemen were conscious of the transnational political implications of their military service.[5] William Anderson, Jr., spoke for many of his fellow black veterans. By playing their part in winning the war, he suggested, African Americans had helped put the United States "on top of the world."[6] Black military service was again being linked to principles of American exceptionalism and the rise of American global hegemony.

Beginning with an examination of African Americans' attitudes toward the end of the Pacific War – including the use of atomic weapons on Hiroshima and Nagasaki – this chapter considers blacks' views of, and interactions with, their erstwhile enemy, who within a few years would become an important Cold War ally. Attention then turns to the broader question of black perceptions of the postwar Asia-Pacific, where the war had disrupted and in many cases overturned colonial hierarchies. African Americans spoke enthusiastically about a postcolonial Asia-Pacific, yet they continued to carry many of the racial and cultural assumptions that had characterized the colonial enterprise. And although they opposed a postwar return of the European colonial powers throughout the Asia-Pacific, the Cold War would soon place African Americans in an awkward position, since the reinstatement of colonial authority was often presented as the only feasible alternative to the chaos of communist-led nationalist forces.[7] After fighting – again – to establish their loyalty to

---

[4] "Victory in the Pacific: Record of Negro Achievement in the War against the Japs," *Philadelphia Tribune*, September 8, 1945.

[5] On African American troops' continuing frustration with the military bureaucracy, see, for example, the correspondence included in "Soldier Complaints," Records of the National Association for the Advancement of Colored People, Group II, Box G15, Manuscript Division, Library of Congress, Washington, DC (NAACP-LoC).

[6] William Anderson, Jr., AFC/2001/001/73387, Veterans History Project Collection, American Folklife Center, Library of Congress, Washington, DC (VHP-LoC).

[7] See James L. Roark, "American Black Leaders: The Response to Colonialism and the Cold War, 1943–1953," *African Historical Studies* 4, no. 2 (1971): 258.

the United States, for African Americans the postwar period presented renewed tensions between racial and national loyalties: while black servicemen, and those who spoke on their behalf, repudiated American racism, they continued to identify as Americans. As they fought for freedom at home and abroad, African Americans contemplated – again – the meanings they ascribed to "America."

African Americans' interest in the 1945 deliberations in San Francisco that led to the establishment of the United Nations reflected long-standing concerns.[8] Even before US entry into World War Two, the tumult arising from the European conflict had prompted black leaders to advocate collective action among persecuted peoples. Invoking the "Four Freedoms" identified in the Atlantic Charter, black journalist Marjorie McKenzie contended in mid-1942 that there was hope for a democratic and racially liberal "post-war world" if African Americans joined with other "oppressed" and "minority groups."[9]

That spirit of transnational racial collectivity underpinned African American wartime calls for a "Pacific Charter." Transposing the principles of self-determination articulated in the Atlantic Charter to the Asian-Pacific context, black leaders anticipated that a postwar Pacific community would overturn colonial and racial hierarchies. In a 1942 message drafted but not sent to the Japanese people, Walter White suggested that a Pacific Charter would "guarantee in absolute terms the four freedoms to *all* the peoples of the earth."[10] Once again applying a phrase associated with unreconstructed Southern racism to the international arena, Lewis K. McMillan contended that by disempowering the "handful of arrogant, greedy trouble-making lily whites" who wielded disproportionate and often-ruthless authority, a Pacific Charter would enable the Asia-Pacific region to "thrive" and "bless the whole world with civilization."[11] Yet while African Americans condemned

---

[8] On African American responses to the United Nations meeting in San Francisco, see John Hope Franklin and Alfred A. Moss, Jr., *From Slavery to Freedom: A History of African Americans*, 8th edn. (New York, NY: Alfred A. Knopf, 2000), 499–502.

[9] Marjorie McKenzie, "Pursuit of Democracy: There Is Hope for Us in the Post-War World If We Join with Other Minority Groups," *Pittsburgh Courier*, July 4, 1942.

[10] See Walter White, "Message to the People of Japan," Draft, 1942, Reel 13, *Papers of the NAACP, Part 14: Race Relations in the International Arena, 1940–1955*, Microfilm, eds. John Bracey and August Meier (Bethesda, MD: University Publications of America, 1993). See also Kenneth Robert Janken, *Walter White: Mr. NAACP* (Chapel Hill, NC: University of North Carolina Press, 2006), 280.

[11] Lewis K. McMillan, "Is World War II Another Scramble for Plunder: How Will the Colored People Fare?" *Cleveland Call and Post*, October 23, 1943.

white racism, at war's end their views of "civilization" remained centered on assumptions regarding the superiority of Western – specifically American – values. These values were also significant in distinguishing African Americans' vision of a Pacific Charter from Japan's rhetorically similar vision of a Greater East Asia Co-prosperity Sphere.[12]

African Americans were not alone in pondering these questions. Having experienced Japan's dismantling of the colonial order, Pacific Islanders and Asians were more than passive bystanders to the wartime turmoil that had surrounded them. Wary of unfulfilled promises, and referring explicitly to Allied wartime rhetoric, they questioned whether the principles of democracy and universal human freedoms that underscored the Allies' mission of liberation would extend to the nonwhite nations of the world. As the Filipino General Carlos Romula remarked in 1945, the colonized subjects of Asia wondered whether "the Atlantic Charter" applied also "for the Pacific?"[13] Conversely, the prospect of a Pacific Charter based on the principles enshrined in the Atlantic Charter was deeply troubling for European powers hoping to restore their colonial authority.

From 1945, there was thus a multiracial, multinational contest for authority across the Asia-Pacific. Japan had presented itself as the nemesis of Western colonialism, and the demise of Japanese power at the end of World War Two presented opportunities for the United States. Although the United States was ascendant, however, it was not omnipotent. Confronting the limits of its power, America's international mission continued to be complicated by the politics of race, at home as well as abroad. African Americans were part of the international conversation regarding the future role of Japan, and their postwar experiences in Japan were more than a coda to their wartime experiences: they were a significant aspect of African Americans' perceptions of the postwar Asia-Pacific.

While the tide of battle turned against Japan by mid-1942, during 1944 and early 1945 few Americans believed the Japanese would succumb quickly to the onslaught of Allied power. As Allied troops paid a bloody price for each island or territory reclaimed from the Japanese, and

[12] Etsuko Taketani has contended that Walter White's vision of a postwar Pacific "accorded eerily with the design for the Greater East Asia Co-prosperity Sphere projected by the Japanese propaganda machine." See Etsuko Taketani, *The Black Pacific Narrative: Geographic Imaginings of Race and Empire between the World Wars* (Hanover, NH: Dartmouth College Press, 2014), 187.
[13] Cited in Thomas Borstelmann, *The Cold War and the Color Line: American Race Relations in the Global Arena* (Cambridge, MA: Harvard University Press, 2001), 29.

with enemy troops fighting ever more tenaciously as they were forced back toward the Japanese homeland, "the Golden Gate in '48" was a popular refrain among many American servicemen, black and white.[14] The atomic bombing of Japan in August 1945, however, brought the Pacific War to an unexpectedly rapid conclusion. African American servicemen and reporters who saw the destruction inflicted on Hiroshima and Nagasaki contemplated the significance of what black Navy veteran Charles Watford described as the "devastating" power of the atomic bombs.[15] Air raids on Tokyo, and other Japanese cities had killed hundreds of thousands of people and wrought almost unimaginable devastation. Yet the unprecedented destruction caused by the atomic attacks on Japan - a consequence of an attack not by hundreds of bombers, but by a single aircraft - raised questions regarding the underlying reasons for Japan's defeat. Witnessing first-hand the consequences of the "terrific" power unleashed by the atomic bombing of Hiroshima, black correspondent Charles H. Loeb reflected on the "plight of these little people who weren't quite westernized enough to tackle the greatest free nation on the Globe." While he acknowledged that "caste, class industrial exploitation, peonage and regimentation" weakened "America's gigantic structure," such divisions had a much more deleterious impact on the Japanese, who Loeb regarded as "too immature" to deal effectively with such handicaps. Loeb's condescension toward the Japanese – "a second class Nation of regimented people" whose best "fighting men were no match for" the US "enormous resources and aroused fighting spirit" – was paralleled by his apparent acceptance of the premises of American exceptionalism.[16]

African American servicemen contemplated the significance of the nuclear attacks on Hiroshima and Nagasaki. In the immediate aftermath of the war, most black servicemen expressed relief that the atomic bombs had ended the war. Many shared the wider view that the United States was entirely justified in using whatever weapons it had at its disposal to defeat an enemy who had scorned the conventions of "civilized" warfare. Adolph Newton's ignorance about the bomb – "we believed anything that was said about it" – was commonplace among black servicemen,

---

[14] "Golden Gate in '48' Is Motto of Pacific Yanks, Nurse Says," *Chicago Tribune*, September 28, 1944.

[15] Charles Watford, AFC/2001/001/64373, VHP-LoC.

[16] Charles H. Loeb, "Loeb Reflects on Atomic Bombed Area," *Atlanta Daily World*, October 5, 1945; Loeb, "Surrender Rites Find Negro Well Represented," *Atlanta Daily World*, September 4, 1945.

FIGURE 6.1. August 14, 1945: Enlisted men aboard the aircraft carrier USS *Ticonderoga* celebrate the news of Japan's surrender
Courtesy: National Archives 80-G-469544.

but it did not diminish the euphoria regarding the end of the war.[17] Long-serving Navy veteran William Henry Harvey – he had arrived in Hawaii just two days before Japan's attack in December 1941, and remained in the Navy long enough to play his part in the Vietnam War – remembered being "glad" about the bombing of Hiroshima. "We were so happy it was all over," he noted.[18]

Black combat troops' views of the atomic bombs were particularly stark. Many feared that white military commanders, anticipating a long and costly battle to subdue Japan, would yield to pressure from African American leaders and editors to make better use of black combat troops. Marine Mortimer Augustus Cox, conscious that some historians continue to "second-guess" President Harry Truman for his decision to use atomic weapons, and aware that an invasion of Japan would have been

[17] Adolph Newton, *Better than Good: A Black Sailor's War, 1943–1945* (Annapolis, MD: Naval Institute Press, 1999), 85.
[18] William Henry Harvey, AFC/2001/001/27509, VHP-LoC.

both bloody and protracted, remained grateful for Truman's decision.[19] Many men of 93rd Infantry Division, recognizing that the division had been one of the last combat units deployed to the Pacific, believed they would be assigned an important role in the planned invasion of Japan. Considering the bloody fighting that had taken place on Okinawa and other islands close to the Japanese homelands, and given that Japanese civil and military leaders were vowing to exact a bloody toll from the invading Allied forces, it was unsurprising that black combat soldiers expressed few scruples – at least initially – regarding the death toll associated with the atomic bombing of Hiroshima and Nagasaki. William Earl Lafayette recalled that "the troops generally thought" the bombing of Hiroshima was "a good thing."[20] Another member of the 93rd Division, Donald McNeil, spoke for many of his black compatriots. Cautioned that his unit "would be in the invasion of Japan," and warned that up to "two million casualties" could be expected among the invading Allied forces, McNeil was "very happy" that the decision was made to use nuclear weapons to end the war. Articulating a sentiment common among Allied service personnel, McNeil opined that since "we did not start the war, I would rather they be killed than us."[21] The lines between Japanese civilians and military personnel, and between the Japanese public and their leaders who had decided to go to war against the United States, were as indistinct for McNeil as they were for millions of his compatriots. African Americans' responses to the atomic bombing of Japan affirmed they were not immune to the brutalization associated with the terrors of total war.

Yet the nuclear attacks on Japan did lead some African American servicemen – particularly those who witnessed first-hand the devastation caused by the atomic bombs – to reflect on the dehumanization associated with war. This was the case even for servicemen who had served in combat units. Bill Payne, a Marine, expressed sentiments common among black servicemen. When the men in Payne's unit learned about the bombing of Hiroshima and Nagasaki, they were "just elated that the war was over." But he also noted that they "didn't know the magnitude of the

---

[19] Mortimer Augustus Cox, AFC/2001/001/43735, VHP-LoC.

[20] William E. Lafayette Collection, AFC/2001/001/43118, VHP-LOC.

[21] McNeil, cited in Maggi M. Morehouse, *Fighting in the Jim Crow Army: Black Men and Women Remember World War II* (Lanham, MD: Rowman and Littlefield, 2000), 183; Donald McNeil, World War II Veterans Survey, 93rd Infantry Division, Box 1, File 6684, 28, United States Army Military History Institute, United States Army Heritage and Education Center, Carlisle, Pennsylvania (USAHEC).

thing until later."[22] For Charles Berry, of the 24th Infantry Regiment, seeing the destruction at Nagasaki led him to consider "how cruel war is and that there are no winners."[23]

For some black servicemen, the aftermath of the atomic bombing of Japan was personally transformative. Archibald Mosely – who in 2011, along with the other members of the first group of black Marines, was belatedly awarded the Congressional Gold Medal – used familiar American images to convey the horror he encountered in Nagasaki:

> You should have seen that area at that time, because the atomic energy had just ... As a Boy Scout, after roasting wieners and marshmallows, we would kick out the fire, leaving scorched, ash-covered earth behind. That's what the entire landscape was like in those cities. I often wondered how long it was going to be before the good Lord could heal the earth to a place where it would be fertile again.

Convinced that "war is hell," Mosely's encounter with the human and physical devastation in Nagasaki was instrumental in encouraging him to enter the ministry.[24]

Far removed from the frontlines, the editors of *The Crisis* also contemplated the racial and moral issues raised by the atomic bombing of Hiroshima and Nagasaki. Noting that the "problems of peace may be more vexing than the problems of war," *The Crisis* asked whether the United States was justified in using nuclear weapons against Japan. Agreeing that the atomic bombs signaled a new and horrific extension of technological warfare, *The Crisis* reflected more deeply on the racial dimensions of the cruelty associated with the Pacific War. It was incongruous, the editors noted, for Americans, who claimed to be "civilized," and who judged the Japanese as "lower than humans," to "use flame-throwers" to roast "human beings alive." "Why," the editors continued, "did we use the atomic bomb, a weapon so terrible that we, ourselves, feared that its use might obliterate us and all civilization?"[25] Identifying a racial imperative behind the atomic bombing of Hiroshima and Nagasaki, and referring to an issue that figures in the continuing historiographical

---

[22] Payne, cited in Morehouse, *Fighting in the Jim Crow Army*, 183.

[23] Charles Earnest Berry, AFC/2001/001/5950, VHP-LOC.

[24] Stephen Rickerl, "Mosely Accepts Overdue Honor," *The Southern Illinoisan*, November 13, 2011; Archibald Mosley cited in Melton Alonza McLaurin, *The Marines of Montford Point: America's First Black Marines* (Chapel Hill, NC: University of North Carolina Press, 2007), 154.

[25] "The Atomic Bomb," *The Crisis*, September, 1945, 249.

debates concerning the decision to use nuclear weapons against Japan, black correspondent Alfred Duckett noted that some African Americans did not "believe the atom bomb would have been dropped on Hiroshima had it been a white city."[26]

For some black servicemen, the nuclear attacks on Japan were further racialized, as they encountered Japanese civilians who blamed African Americans for the attacks on Hiroshima and Nagasaki. Recalling considerable animosity from the Japanese he encountered while on occupation duty in Tokyo, Rollins Edwards noted that the men in his unit had been compelled to carry their "loaded and cocked" rifles to discourage acts of violence from the locals, who had been told that African Americans were "responsible for the atomic bomb." As Edwards further explained, the Japanese also believed that "radiation from the bomb" had "turned" him and his men "black."[27]

African Americans' reflections on the use of atomic weapons was one aspect of their wider contemplation of the transformation of the Japanese from a detested foe to Cold War ally. More significant in that process were blacks' first-hand encounters with their defeated adversaries. To the chagrin of many African Americans, who like their white compatriots hoped to return to the United States as soon as possible following the cessation of hostilities, black service personnel were included in the Allied occupation forces that served in Japan at the end of the war.[28] By late 1945 it was estimated that nearly 15,000 African Americans were serving in the Tokyo area, with many thousands more serving elsewhere throughout Japan.[29] Black participation in the Allies' postwar occupation of Japan can be read as more than a pragmatic deployment on the part of US military commanders. It was also one manifestation of African Americans' belief that their contribution to Allied victory, in conjunction with their unique insights and experiences, qualified – or even obliged – them to shape a postwar world turned upside down by the global challenges to white authority. *Chicago Defender* columnist John Robert Badger, anticipating in April 1945 that the Allied occupation would be "very complicated as well as long," cautioned of a "very great

---

[26] See Duckett, cited in Studs Terkel, *"The Good War": An Oral History of World War II* (1984; reprinted, New York, NY: Ballantyne Books, 1985), 370.

[27] Rollins Edwards, AFC/2001/001/68079, VHP-LoC.

[28] Frank Bolden, "Peace Means These GIs Can Leave the Jungle," *Pittsburgh Courier*, September 1, 1945.

[29] Vincent Tubbs, "Reveal 14,866 Tan GI's in Tokyo Area," *Afro-American*, December 15, 1945.

danger" if the occupation was left to "white forces alone." Japanese anger and frustration at their defeat, he worried, might "be transformed into actual guerrilla warfare and assassinations." Japan's "racial mythology," based on "anti-Caucasian hatred," coupled with an ongoing conviction that Japan had fought the war to liberate oppressed peoples from white domination, meant that white occupation forces might antagonize the defeated Japanese. Based on conversations with representatives of America's Asian allies, Badger concluded that the occupation forces "should include Chinese, Filipino, Siamese, Indian and other troops from Asiatic countries." Here was an explicit African American enunciation of support for a transnational union of nonwhite peoples. Yet the postwar politics of race were more nuanced than suggested by a bifurcated division between whites and nonwhites. Recognizing that the "United States does not intend to play second fiddle to any other power in the control of Japan," Badger understood that a significant proportion of the occupying forces would be American. With those two imperatives in mind, and apparently accepting the exceptionalist principles implicit in American leadership of the occupation forces, Badger foreshadowed "that our [African American] boys are going to get the tough and important job of occupying the Japanese Islands." An African American occupation force, he suggested, would "cut the ground from under" Japanese "militaristic propaganda that this is a race war."[30]

Determined that African Americans would play a tangible, active role in the postwar Asia-Pacific, Badger's hypothesis is instructive. Although he appeared to be contesting Japan's analysis of the racial dimensions of the Pacific War, his own analysis revealed that African Americans continued to view the conflict as a "race war." In addition, his suggestion that black troops could mollify those Japanese frustrated at their nation's defeat implied common ground between African Americans and Japanese – and perhaps a return to prewar and wartime discussions regarding links between the two groups. Besides affirming the disjunction between African American and Japanese interpretations of "race war," Badger's remarks suggested that the relationship between notions of "race" and "nationalism" remained complex and frequently contradictory.

Occupation proved a complicated task. While "much of what makes Japs tick" remained "unknown" to Americans, direct contact with the beaten enemy broke down many of the barriers between Japanese and

[30] John Robert Badger, "World View: The Occupation of Japan," *Chicago Defender*, April 7, 1945.

African Americans.[31] Among the most significant of those barriers was an Allied perception that the Japanese placed a different – in practice that meant lower – value on individualism, and the individual, than Westerners. In stating that "Japanese Joe is no individualist," Charles Loeb used vernacular language to raise an important distinction between occupiers and occupied.[32] To refer to an obvious, albeit for black servicemen important example, although they had served willingly in the US military, at war's end a majority African Americans were impatient to return to what Loeb described as "their own individualities."[33] While the tension between individualism and communalism was complicated by questions of race, African Americans' experiences in postwar Japan also underscored the connection between individualism and democracy. As Loeb put it, Japanese were "first the subject of the Emperor, then the son of his father, then, and only last, himself." Such a system, Loeb explained, "was a natural reverse on the American pattern." "How we ever expect to make a 'democrat' of him," Loeb argued, "is beyond comprehension."[34]

As was the case with their wartime encounters elsewhere across the Asia-Pacific, African Americans' views of their former enemy were shaped by Japan's physical, as well as human geography. The Japanese landscape intrigued some African Americans. For Charles Berry, Japan's "very beautiful" physical landscape, with its "castles and architecture" was an "absolutely fascinating" contrast to the United States. Many servicemen concurred with Private Willie Carter's assessment. Writing from Yokohama, Carter conceded that "I don't know what I was expecting Japan to be like, but it wasn't this." Black reporter Enoch P. Waters explained that black troops were surprised by Yokohama's homely and even familiar feeling, and – notwithstanding the devastation caused by the war – by the extent to which the city was "westernized."[35] Like other visitors to Japan, African Americans were struck by the unique Japanese melding of tradition and modernity. Arriving in Yokohama after traveling though the Japanese countryside, Loeb noted that "feudalism suddenly

[31] Vincent Tubbs, "Many Jap, African Customs Alike: Both Peoples Use Same Primitive Farm and Selling Methods," *Afro-American*, October 13, 1945.
[32] Charles Loeb, "Inside Japan," *New Journal and Guide*, October 27, 1945.
[33] Charles Loeb, "Troops in Tokio Face Same Jim Crow Pattern; Disgruntled GI's Wonder if Sacrifice was in Vain," *Philadelphia Tribune*, September 15, 1945.
[34] Charles Loeb, "Inside Japan."
[35] Charles Earnest Berry, AFC/2001/001/5950, VHP-LOC; Enoch P. Waters, "'Hominess' of Yokohama Surprises Yanks," *Chicago Defender*, September 22, 1945.

became transformed into modernity."[36] Japan was in this regard a contrast to what African Americans had encountered elsewhere in Asia and the Pacific.

Like their white compatriots, African Americans reacted in various ways toward the Japanese. Some continued to consider the Japanese as vicious, even sub-human, and undeserving of sympathy. Others, however, expressed pity for the plight of the conquered Japanese – particularly the civilians – who endured hardship and deprivation long after the war's end. Like other Americans, blacks' initial interactions with Japanese reflected common Western assumptions regarding Asians: Loeb suggested in September 1945 that the Japanese were "accepting their defeat" with "characteristic Oriental resignation."[37] African Americans' views of the Japanese – whether they be a savage enemy, or a defeated foe who accepted their fate without protest – were predicated on essentialist views of an Oriental "type" that reflected longstanding Western views of Asia and Asians. Such views were predictable, but they served nevertheless as a reminder of the hierarchical nature of African Americans' vision of a transnational alliance of nonwhite peoples that would overturn white supremacy.

Loeb's language, like Vincent Tubbs's reference to the "peculiar Oriental shell into which Japan" retreated at war's end, hinted at the persistence of racially based stereotypes among African Americans. Tubbs's response to his encounters with the Japanese, and his racial views, were no less revealing than Badger's. While he reported that certain Japanese habits – including their "markets, street vendors and numerous other customs" – "almost provoked" him into penning a "piece comparing them with equatorial Africans," he concluded that such a comparison "wouldn't be fair to the Africans." Yet at the same time as he restated a hierarchy among nonwhite peoples, in proclaiming that the Japanese and Africans "have a culture and type of civilization hundreds and even thousands of years older than the Western civilization the world now seeks to impose upon them," Tubbs suggested that the virtues of US democracy would not be obvious to non-Americans. Having been advised by Americans to consider the advantages of "universal suffrage," the Japanese were undoubtedly puzzled by the American democratic system, where racist politicians used poll taxes and "other political subterfuges" to prevent

---

[36] Charles H. Loeb, "Yokosuka and Yokohama Become More Than Names as Loeb Travels in Japan," *Cleveland Call and Post*, October 20, 1945.
[37] Charles H. Loeb, "'Correspondent Finds Japanese Glad War Over," *Atlanta Daily World*, September 2, 1945.

African Americans from voting.[38] Consequently, although black commentators such as Tubbs continued to betray their faith in the merits of Western civilization, they insisted that the realities of racial segregation undermined America's claims of moral superiority. Domestic racism continued to compromise America's global mission.

For black reporters such as Tubbs, the occupation of Japan was an immediate, racially charged aspect of that global mission. While African American observers noted that many Japanese appeared to be resigned to their fate, they also suggested that the task of occupation was made more difficult by what some African Americans regarded as the inherently warlike nature of Japanese society. The contradictions that characterized African Americans' views of other nonwhite peoples they had encountered across the Asia-Pacific were evident in their postwar analyses of the defeated Japanese. Given the horrors of the Pacific War, where violence was underpinned by racially inscribed notions of Japanese savagery, and where Allied prisoners-of-war had routinely suffered at the hands of their Japanese captors, it was unsurprising that many African Americans continued to subscribe to such stereotypes. Furthermore, black suspicions regarding Japan's international aspirations, and its professed allegiance to other nonwhite peoples, persisted peoples, persisted after Japan's surrender. As the *Chicago Defender* reporter Homer Smith (writing under the pseudonym "Chatwood Hall") noted in September 1945, "Japanese war lords" had "built up a vast colored slave empire" across Asia.[39] Smith's invocation of slavery to condemn Japanese imperialism was a powerful testament to African Americans' skepticism concerning Japan's claims to be acting on behalf of colonized and otherwise oppressed nonwhite peoples.

Some African American commentators, distinguishing between black and white Americans' perceptions of the Japanese, suggested African Americans were imbued with a deeper capacity for empathy, and an ability to transcend their immediate political and national milieu. In early 1945 it was reported that whereas 62 percent of Americans surveyed agreed that "the Japanese people will always want war," the comparable figure among the African American population was 51 percent. Rather

---

[38] Tubbs, "Many Jap, African Customs Alike: Both Peoples Use Same Primitive Farm and Selling Methods." On Tubbs's views of the Japanese, see also David J. Longley, "Vincent Tubbs and the Baltimore *Afro-American*: The Black Press, Race, and Culture in the World War II Pacific Theater," *Australasian Journal of American Studies* 35, no. 2 (2016): 61–80.

[39] Chatwood Hall, "Jap Empire Built on Slavery for Darker Races," *Chicago Defender*, September 8, 1945.

than suggesting that African Americans' more moderate views of the Japanese were a consequence of Japan's efforts to woo black Americans to an alliance of nonwhite peoples, some commentators implied that African Americans were better able to appreciate and understand their enemy. And although many blacks continued to harbor doubts about Japanese intentions – in October 1945 Tubbs warned Americans to "not forget too quickly" the terror that Japan had inflicted on the peoples of the Asia-Pacific – others separated the wartime behavior of the Japanese nation from the suffering of individual Japanese. As Tubbs himself noted, even "battle weary" black veterans "were filled with compassion" when they witnessed the deprivations suffered by Japanese civilians in the aftermath of the war. "God, I feel sorry for them," Private Alfred Moore told Tubbs, "we ought to do something to relieve their suffering."[40] These qualities of empathy and compassion would presumably be vital as the United States sought to forge new alliances from the wartime destruction across the Asia-Pacific.

As had been the case with African Americans' encounters across the Asia-Pacific war zone, individual experiences informed collective understanding of the Japanese. Perhaps reflecting the longer-term African American interest in Japan, some blacks who participated in the Occupation endeavored to learn more about the culture and history of their former adversaries. Linguistic differences – which had also impeded interactions between African Americans and Pacific Islanders during the course of the war – were a significant obstacle to such exchanges. Although "few Americans" would "feel called upon to study" the Japanese "seriously," noted Charles Loeb, the "first barrier for those of us who wish to return home with an unbiased view of Japanese life and thought" was "the language, with its thousands of intricate Chinese characters."[41] There are no statistics regarding the number of African Americans who learned to speak or read Japanese – the "funny lingo" as black correspondent Enoch P. Waters condescendingly described it – but it can be safely assumed that only a relative handful did so.[42]

[40] "Japs will Always Want War Say Americans," *New Journal and Guide*, February 17, 1945; Vincent Tubbs, "Jungle-Weary Tan Yanks Feel Sorry for the Japanese," *Afro-American*, September 29, 1945.
[41] Loeb, "Inside Japan."
[42] Enoch P. Waters, "Musical GI Masters Okinawa Japs, Then Their Language," *Chicago Defender*, July 21, 1945. See also the recollections of Ellis Cunningham, cited in McLaurin, *The Marines of Montford Point*, 154.

While the profound cultural differences between African American occupiers and occupied Japanese could be manifested with hostility, tensions between African Americans and Japanese frequently dissipated as the two groups became better acquainted.[43] As Rollins Edwards put it, when the Japanese learned African Americans were not responsible for the decision to use nuclear weapons on Japan, and were not as they had been depicted by white Americans, they "really treated" blacks "well."[44] Even in instances that suggested Japanese hostility toward African American troops, a closer examination indicated race was not the only factor shaping the reception accorded to black servicemen in Japan. In late 1945 it was reported in the African American press that a number of black Occupation troops had died after drinking "poisonous liquor." Yet although the African American correspondent Peyton Gray noted that the liquor had been sold to black troops by Japanese, he also pointed out that "poisoned liquor" had found its way into Army camps "in all but a few Pacific islands."[45] There was no reason to believe, Gray suggested, that the servicemen's deaths were a consequence of an underlying Japanese hostility toward African Americans. What Gray did not say was that the victims of poisoned alcohol bore some responsibility for their own demise.

Replicating a pattern common across the Pacific Theater, the animus experienced by some African Americans stationed in postwar Japan could be a consequence of their white compatriots' attempts to provoke trouble between themselves and black troops, and between African Americans and the "other" – in this instance the Japanese. Possibly, too, white servicemen were reflecting the well-established fears of a racially-based collusion between African Americans and Japanese. As one black veteran of the Occupation recalled, "a lot of [the] time" white servicemen succeeded in practicing "the prejudice" that was commonplace in the United States.[46] Therefore, while the aforementioned linguistic differences between Japanese and Americans made it more difficult for white Americans to "propagandize" against African Americans, white Americans sometimes succeeded in spreading the "virus of race

[43] Charles Loeb, "Japs Disinterested in JC Ideas – GIs," *Afro-American*, October 13, 1945.
[44] Rollins Edwards, AFC/2001/002/68079, VHP-LoC.
[45] Peyton Gray, "Jap Liquor Kills 6 GI's; 4 in Peril," *Afro-American*, November 10, 1945. See also Peyton Gray, "Poisoned Liquor Kills GI in Japan," *Afro-American*, October 13, 1945.
[46] Charles Berry, AFC/2001/001/5950, VHP-LoC.

prejudice" among the Japanese.[47] That prejudice was manifested by whites' demeaning depictions of African Americans, and by attempts to impose segregationist practices in Japan. Along with restrictions placed on black servicemen's freedom of movement – some were confined to their "bivouac areas," for instance – the now-familiar stories that African Americans had tails were reprised in postwar Japan.[48] Racial segregation and derogatory stereotypes were again complementary halves of white men's attempts to preserve their own authority.

Emboldened by their wartime experiences, and conscious of the transnational nature of the struggle against racism, African Americans challenged white Americans' attempts to cast blacks stationed in Japan as disruptive troublemakers. Countering white attempts to foment racial trouble, black reporters focused on positive interactions between African American troops and their Japanese hosts. In October 1945, soon after the first contingents of African Americans began arriving in Japan, Charles Loeb reported that relations between the Japanese and black occupation forces were becoming more friendly. The experience of working together – Loeb referred specifically to Japanese stevedores working under the direction of African Americans – was fostering closer understandings and relations. "We have encountered not the slightest sign that Japanese regard us as anything but Americans," one black serviceman told Loeb.[49] Yet Loeb's story, and the language he used to describe relations between African Americans and Japanese, betrayed more than he probably intended. Given that many black servicemen had resented being used as stevedores, their willingness to assign such tasks to the defeated Japanese, and to assume supervisory roles, hinted at the complex racial and national hierarchies arising from African American participation in the Allied Occupation.

The questions of race and nationality arising from the black presence in postwar Japan were further complicated by the romantic and sometimes intimate relations that developed between occupiers and occupied. Paralleling a pattern evident elsewhere across the Asia-Pacific Theater, blacks' postwar relations with Japanese and Okinawan women (African Americans frequently did not distinguish between the two groups) were complex and contradictory. Sleeping with a former enemy is inevitably

[47] Robinson, cited in McLaurin, *Marines of Montford Point,* 102; Charles Loeb, "Jap Friendliness to GIs Increases," *Afro-American,* October 13, 1945.
[48] Charles Loeb, "Troops 'Take' Tokyo," *New Journal and Guide,* September 15, 1945; Rollins Edwards, AFC/2002/001/68079, VHP-LoC.
[49] Loeb, "Jap Friendliness to GIs Increases."

contentious, but many white Americans' abiding fears of black sexuality – in any guise – led them to condemn any form of intimacy between African American servicemen and Japanese women.

African Americans expressed a range of views regarding sexual relations with Japanese women. Black reporter and activist Irene West believed that Japanese women were characterized by feminine traits that were both laudable, and likely to appeal to American, including African American men. "In time," she suggested, Japanese women's "sweet and docile" nature would win the "passion and love" of many servicemen.[50] West's essentialist depiction of compliant Japanese women was predicated on an unspoken contrast with their purportedly feistier American counterparts. Many servicemen, she implied, preferred the more demure version of womanhood exemplified by Japanese women. West's views of Japanese women rested on racially determined stereotypes which seemingly resonated as strongly among black as they did among white Americans. Cultural and national differences could transcend imagined bonds of womanhood across ethnic and racial boundaries.

African American servicemen also betrayed the influence of prevailing racial stereotypes concerning Japanese women. Those stereotypes left some black servicemen uninterested in, or even repelled by, the prospect of intimate relations with Japanese women. Stationed on Okinawa at war's end, William B. Rice, Jr.'s reference to the women he encountered there as "native women" suggests he did not differentiate Okinawan women from the women encountered by African American servicemen on Pacific islands. While the Okinawans would almost certainly have rejected such a comparison, Rice's statement hinted at servicemen's habit of regarding Asians and Pacific Islanders as an indistinct "other." Rice's views, and his wariness, also reflected his knowledge that a number of his compatriots who had been "fooling around" with the local women had contracted "some kind of venereal disease."[51] Some African American servicemen, themselves so often depicted as sexually impure, remained apprehensive about the prospective consequences of cross-racial carnal contacts.

In spite of those risks, and notwithstanding African American expressions of disdain for the Japanese and Okinawans, intimate relations developed between some black servicemen and Japanese women. Perhaps attracted by the traditional feminine traits Irene West ascribed to Japanese women, some servicemen hoped to forge long-term relationships. Stationed

[50] Irene West, "Japs will Bear Strange Fruit," *Afro-American*, September 15, 1945.
[51] William B. Rice, Jr., AFC/2001/001/47130, VHP-LoC.

in Fukuoka after the Japanese surrender, Charles Berry remembered "having fun with the Japanese girls," who he recalled were "real nice." Evidently his intentions became more serious, as he proposed and became engaged to a Japanese girl. Whether the marriage would have taken place remains uncertain as his fiancée died after contracting pneumonia.[52]

Other servicemen's interests were more short term, and carnal. While black servicemen were surprised to find that Tokyo was "very modern," it was their determination to consort with Japanese women plying the world's oldest profession that attracted the attention of Charles Loeb. Characterizing the American occupation of Japan as "the goofiest occupation in history," Loeb stated that black troops were showing "characteristic GI ability to locate the most isolated brothels with uncanny instinct." Loeb's tone was flippant, but he stressed that his subject matter was of serious concern to commanders. US military authorities, "alarmed by the promiscuous 'fraternization' going on," were "not likely" to criticize Japanese attempts to regulate the sex trade.[53] As elsewhere across the Pacific Theater, the prospect of sexual relations between African American servicemen and local women prompted deep anxiety among American commanders.

White enlisted servicemen expressed similar anxieties. Racial tensions between US servicemen stationed in Japan were frequently a consequence of rivalry for the affections of local women – including those paid to provide such affections. Accordingly, where Charles Loeb used humor to discuss black Americans' liaisons with Japanese sex workers, his fellow reporter Billy Rowe emphasized a different aspect of the trade. During the initial stages of the Occupation, Rowe explained, black and white troops alike had sought and secured their "own pleasure" in an area known as "Cherry Blossom Lane," on the outskirts of Tokyo. While some brothels were off limits to black troops, African Americans and whites had visited those establishments and "departed without trouble." The arrival of the First Cavalry Division, however, dramatically changed relations between white and African American troops, as the cavalrymen insisted that a form of segregation be imposed to regulate black troops' access to Japanese brothels. Inevitably, racial tensions increased, as the white troops succeeded in imposing "the first form of discrimination to rise in Japan."[54]

---

[52] Charles Earnest Berry, AFC/2001/001/5950, VHP-LOC.
[53] Loeb, "Yanks Find Tokyo 'Very Modern.'"
[54] Billy Rowe, "G.I. Bigotry Threatens U.S. Plan in Japan," *Pittsburgh Courier*, October 27, 1945.

Not only was the intersection between race and sex proving as vexing after the war as it had been during the conflict, but the apparent willingness of African American commentators to accept that black servicemen would take advantage of the easy access to prostitutes revealed much about the sexual mores of the period. No doubt, part of the nonchalant rationalization of such behavior owed much to "traditional" views concerning masculine sexual desire, particularly within a still-predominantly masculine military system and culture. But it also was also suggestive of the complex racial dynamics at play between white and African American servicemen on one hand, and vanquished, disempowered Japanese women on the other. That disempowerment – not dissimilar to explanations that Japanese women resorted to prostitution in order to protect their families from material hardship – was the most plausible explanation for the purportedly demure Japanese femininity identified by Irene West. Yet few servicemen, black or white, discerned such distinctions. Relations between Japanese women and black servicemen could be affectionate and intimate, but they were inherently unequal, and as Rowe had reiterated, linguistic differences were a significant obstacle. Finally, Rowe's reporting of sexual transactions between black troops and Japanese women, and the willingness of his editors to publish those reports, challenged widely repeated wartime assertions concerning the moral stature and purity of African American servicemen abroad.[55]

African Americans' relations with the Japanese were one part of their wider interaction with the postwar Asia-Pacific. Concomitant with their critiques of Western and Japanese imperial practices across the Asia-Pacific, blacks contemplated the legacies – and the future – of America's colonial practices across the region. African Americans had been implicated in transforming the Pacific into an "American lake," and the Pacific War affirmed that they accepted many of the cultural and political assumptions underpinning that process. Yet alongside their condescension toward other nonwhite peoples, their wartime experiences had also highlighted the tension between America's stated mission as a liberating force, and the realities of American power. For African Americans, the underlying tension between nationality and race further clouded the

---

[55] Rowe, "G.I. Bigotry Threatens U.S. Plan in Japan." For a contemporary explanation of Japanese women's motives for resorting to prostitution, see Rebecca Stiles Taylor, "Activities of Women's National Organizations: Baroness Ishimoto Tells of Movement of Women in Japan," *Chicago Defender*, January 24, 1942.

indistinct line between "liberator" and "occupier." Indeed, their identity as "African Americans" – even before that phrase became part of common parlance – was fundamental to their understanding of the US postwar role as the dominant power across the Asia-Pacific. As Allied victory became more certain during 1944 and early 1945, African Americans' allegiance to the United States – an allegiance tested by the remorseless realities of American racism – continued to be counterpoised against their ambivalence toward the nonwhite peoples of the Asia-Pacific region.

A key figure in shaping African American attitudes toward the postwar Asia-Pacific was the prominent black journalist and activist, Walter White. Having asserted in 1942 that "White Invincibility" was "doomed," in 1945 he described the black struggle in the United States as "part and parcel" of the worldwide "struggle against imperialism and exploitation." The war, he wrote, had "given to the Negro a sense of kinship with other colored – and also oppressed – peoples of the world." Presuming that African Americans would be leaders of this transnational alliance, and invoking language and ideas reminiscent of Marcus Garvey and other proponents of "Black Internationalism," White argued "that as time proceeds" the "identification of interests will spread even among some brown and yellow peoples who today refuse to see the connection between their exploitation by white nations and discrimination against the Negro in the United States."[56]

White's optimism regarding the prospect of internationalist sentiment among nonwhite peoples was tempered, however, by his apprehensions regarding the immediate future of the postwar world. Using the imprimatur of his position as Executive Secretary of the National Association for the Advancement of Colored People (NAACP), he railed against colonialism and insisted that the European powers be prevented from reasserting their colonial authority at war's end. White's perspective was global – he spent considerable time denouncing the colonization of Africa, for instance – but he reserved some of his most vehement language and arguments for his vision of the postwar Asia-Pacific. In early 1945, White toured the Pacific Theater. At the end of his 36,000-mile tour, he registered his distress at many people's "calm acceptance" that the "colonial empires" would be reestablished in the wake of Japan's defeat. Condemning the natives' impoverished condition, their lack of education, and their "physical condition" as "terrible" indictments "of

---

[56] "'White Invincibility Doomed' – Walter White," *Pittsburgh Courier*, May 23, 1942; Walter White, *A Rising Wind* (Garden City, NY: Doubleday, Doran and Co., 1945), 144.

their British, Dutch and French exploiters," he explained that the victims of colonialism were "bewildered and dismayed that winning a war
for 'freedom'" would apparently not lead to a "change in their status."
Accepting that American power had been decisive in securing victory,
and endorsing the promise of American exceptionalism, White agreed
that the United States had particular global responsibilities. Both the US
Government and the American people, he demanded, "must wake up"
to what was happening across the Pacific "and make it clear to allies
and enemies alike" that the war was not being fought "to restore colonial systems."[57] White's argument was based not just on a determination
to prevent "continued misery" for African Americans, or on his sense
of transnational racial justice and his aversion to colonialism, however.
Insisting that the "white overlordship over brown, yellow and black people of the world" must end, he also appealed to white self-interest. If
the "global problem of color" was not ameliorated, and if the colonial
powers were permitted to reestablish their colonial power, White wrote,
it would "inevitably ... breed another war."[58]

Warning that America's racial policies, and the "attempts of some
Americans to spread race hatred in the Pacific," were creating confusion
and "anti-American feeling," White contended that the "perilous effects"
of racial prejudice extended "beyond American Negroes to the natives
whose aid we need now in winning the war and whose friendship we will
need after the war if we are to have peace."[59] White's analysis was unambiguous: American racism – at home and abroad – was jeopardizing the
nation's attempts to shape the postwar Asia-Pacific. The friendship of the
native peoples of the Asia-Pacific region would remain important even
after the defeat of Japan. White was not alone in not alone in grasping
the significance of maintaining friendly relations with America's wartime
allies. By continuing to praise the martial qualities of the native peoples
of the Asia-Pacific, black reporters insinuated that African Americans preferred to be allies rather than adversaries of those peoples, even after the
war ended.[60] As Fletcher P. Martin had explained in mid-1944, the Fijians'

[57] "Empire Colonial Policy in Pacific is Seen in Danger," *Pittsburgh Courier*, April 21, 1945.
[58] Walter White to Editors (of "Negro Newspapers"), January 7, 1944, Reel 24, *Papers of the NAACP, Part 17: National Staff Files, 1940–1955*, Microfilm, eds. John H. Bracey, Jr., and August Meier (Bethesda, MD: University Publications of America, 1994); "Empire Colonial Policy in Pacific is Seen in Danger."
[59] "Empire Colonial Policy in Pacific is Seen in Danger." Walter White, cited in "White Warns Prejudice May Void UNCIO," *Atlanta Daily World*, July 8, 1945.
[60] "Dutch Natives Kill Many Japs on Island," *Atlanta Daily World*, August 18, 1945.

wartime exploits had created a "deeper impression." In common with the "millions" of other "so-called natives in the Pacific," he stated, the Fijians had shown that given "the opportunity, they can be useful in winning the peace as well as waging the war."[61]

Black activists such as Walter White reserved some of their most strident criticism for America's allies, particularly those determined to preserve white hegemony throughout the Asia-Pacific. As Gerald Horne has demonstrated, African Americans took a keen interest in Indians' struggle for independence.[62] "An independent India," declared Edgar T. Rozeau in April 1942, would help African Americans secure their rights. Conceding that "Negroes" had "little in common with Moslems and Hindus," Rozeau explained that the negotiations then taking place on the subject of Indian independence "may well decide the future of the Black American."[63] In Rozeau's analysis, not only were cultural distinctions between African Americans and other nonwhite peoples less significant than the political advantages that would accrue from a recognition of their shared political oppression, but – unusually – in this instance African Americans were not being depicted as the leaders of the international struggle against racism and colonialism. Three years later, in 1945, a visit to the United States by Vijaya Lakshmi Pandit, President of the All-India Women's Conference, and a sister of Jawaharlal Nehru, the leader of the Indian independence movement, attracted wide and positive attention from the black press. In contrast to many black servicemen, who regarded India and Indians principally as objects of pity, the *Afro-American*'s report on Pandit's visit to the United States highlighted India's early and significant contribution to the war against Japan. Reiterating a theme that had been evident in African American musings on the Pacific War since Pearl Harbor, the *Afro-American* was again linking nonwhites' battlefield contributions with the political structures that would prevail across the postwar Asia-Pacific.[64]

British, French, and Dutch attempts to reestablish their colonial authority attracted widespread opprobrium from African Americans. But black

[61] Fletcher P. Martin, "Fijians Gain Respect of Enemy and Allies," *Philadelphia Tribune*, May 27, 1944.

[62] See Gerald Horne, *The End of Empires: African Americans and India* (Philadelphia, PA: Temple University Press, 2008).

[63] Edgar T. Rozeau, "'An Independent India Would Help Black America Get Rights' – Rozeau," *Pittsburgh Courier*, April 4, 1942.

[64] S. A. Haynes, "India Stands for Equality, Leader Tells Baltimoreans," *Afro-American*, April 14, 1945.

activists recognized that the European powers were not the only guilty white nations: at the end of the war Australia continued to loom large in the black consciousness. Alongside his criticism of Australia's ongoing refusal to relax its laws prohibiting the immigration of Asians and Pacific Islanders, Walter White condemned the Australian government's determination to maintain its colonial hold on New Guinea. Australia's colonial policies, he stated, were part of the wider European imperial venture, and Australia's refusal to abandon those colonial practices could play a part in provoking another global conflict. "Apparently," he wrote, "if the articulate element" in Australia had its way, "imperialism" would survive. "And thus," he despaired, "will be sown the seeds of World War III."[65]

In referring to Australia's role in the postwar Asia-Pacific, White had raised an issue of deep concern to those Australians who hoped the war would not permanently disrupt the racial hierarchies that had prevailed across the Asia-Pacific. Key to the restoration of colonial authority was ensuring that the formerly colonized subjects did not develop expectations of equality. Given their surprise at white Americans' determination to subjugate African Americans stationed in wartime Australia, it was, at the very least, paradoxical that Australians hoped to thwart aspirations of equality among Pacific Islanders. But racism rarely demands consistency, and just as the hopes of black servicemen stationed in Australia could not be contained, nor could Pacific Islanders' yearning for freedom be stifled. Further confounding matters, Australians recognized that their attempts to restore their authority in the Pacific region were being complicated by the attitudes and interventions of their wartime allies, notably African Americans. Worried about American servicemen's easy familiarity with the natives, Private Eddie Allan Stanton, an Australian serving in New Guinea, was troubled particularly by the sight of "American Negroes teaching" the natives "how to box."[66] No doubt with knowledge of Joe Louis's feats and reputation in mind, for Stanton the spectacle of African Americans teaching the skills of pugilism to oppressed natives portended more than symbolic trouble from the formerly colonial subjects of New Guinea, and elsewhere. Emboldened by their wartime

---

[65] Walter White to "Dear Folks," March 23, 1945, Reel 24, *Papers of the NAACP, Part 17*; See also Kenneth Robert Janken, *White: The Biography of Walter White, Mr. NAACP* (New York, NY: Free Press, 2003), 296.

[66] See Stanton's diary entry, January 8, 1944, in *The War Diaries of Eddie Allan Stanton: Papua 1942–45, New Guinea 1945–46* (Sydney: Allen and Unwin, 1996), 206–7. See also Lachlan Grant, *Australian Soldiers in Asia-Pacific in World War II* (Sydney: NewSouth Publishing, 2014), 124.

experiences, including their contacts with African Americans, colonized peoples would no longer respect the hierarchies of race and power upon which the colonial enterprise had rested.

For their part, African Americans could be surprised by the ways in which Australians treated Pacific Islanders. Lieutenant Jimmy Hicks, an African American serving with the 92nd Quartermaster Company, referred to the "Aussies" who "pay the natives one shilling for a week's work," but who "bellyache because a bloody yank will come along and give the poor devil a half pound note just to see him climb a coconut tree." Betraying a condescension toward "natives" that sat easily alongside the racial attitudes of white Americans and their Australian allies, Hicks was not seeking consciously to overturn the established order in New Guinea. Nonetheless, his remarks hinted at African Americans' interest and role in the transformations wrought by the Pacific War.[67]

Those transformations threatened the economic as well as political bases of the colonial enterprise. Recognizing the significance of transforming economic relations across the Asia-Pacific, Walter White lamented that the "rights of native peoples to share in the benefits of raw materials and their own labor" were "completely unthought of, except by the natives themselves."[68] Yet while African Americans demanded the abolition of colonial economic systems, some linked their exceptionalist assumptions to the redemptive power of American capitalism. Seeking to join US economic power to their own anticolonial and antiracist ideals, African Americans and their progressively minded white allies confronted a dilemma during the postwar years, as the emerging anticolonial nationalist forces were increasingly associated with left-wing – and often communist – philosophies that were anathema to American capital and American policymakers.

White's plans for a transnational nonwhite alliance confronted other obstacles, too. Although many African American leaders endorsed the idea of such an alliance, a partnership of that type would not be comprised of equals. Reflecting the exceptionalist assumptions that had long characterized African American thought, black leaders continued to assume they would lead an international antiracial and anticolonial coalition. The experiences of the Pacific War had not undermined African

---

[67] Jimmy Hicks, "This Is My Island," *Cleveland Call and Post*, November 27, 1943.
[68] White Warns, "Wake Up to Pacific Happenings," *Atlanta Daily World*, April 15, 1945. See also *Interracial News Service* (May, 1945), 6, Published by the Department of Race Relations, Federal Council of Churches, New York, Reel 13, *Papers of the NAACP Papers, Part 14*.

Americans' sense of difference from other nonwhite peoples. Moreover, not only was White's vision of an African American-led racial alliance predicated upon assumptions regarding the superiority of Western – in practice, that meant "American" – values, but it also overlooked distinctions between other non-European peoples. As the Pacific War demonstrated, national and ethnic loyalties problematized a one-dimensional analysis of "white" versus "nonwhite." There were occasions when wartime black discourse complicated African American visions of the postwar world, and countered US plans to transform international relations across the Asia-Pacific region. Commending those "natives" who had "allied themselves with the U.S." and who were "helping to win the war against the followers of Tojo," an August 1943 article in the *Pittsburgh Courier* suggested that the indigenous inhabitants of "many sections of the South Pacific" had "formed a lasting dislike for the Asiatics."[69] The *Courier's* reference to "Asiatic" was made with Japan in mind. And as evidenced by the contrast they drew between peace-loving Chinese peasants and warlike Japanese, African Americans' perceptions of so-called "Asiatic" racial groups reflected the importance they attached to distinctions of nationality. Nonetheless, sometimes-casual references to "Asiatics" and "natives" were antithetical to the notion of a transnational alliance of nonwhite peoples.

Perhaps aware of those limitations to African American internationalism, some observers challenged blacks' professed interest in the fate of other nonwhite peoples. Writing for the *Chicago Defender*, the Canadian-Japanese academic and activist S. I. Hayakawa suggested in June 1945 that African Americans' "curiosity about the fate of other colored peoples" did "not rise spontaneously from generosity or imagination or breadth of vision." "On the contrary," he submitted, it arose because white American racism "forced the Negro to identify himself with all other people of color." Suggesting that African Americans were essentially ignorant about nonwhites outside the borders of the United States, Hayakawa contended blacks would be better off working with friends closer to home – namely, the "millions of white Americans who bear no ill will towards Negroes."[70] There was some validity to Hayakawa's suggestion that African Americans' professed identification with other nonwhite peoples was ill-informed and self-interested. And he was not

[69] "They Prefer to Fight for Uncle Sam," *Pittsburgh Courier*, August 7, 1943.
[70] S. I. Hayakawa, "Second Thoughts: Interest in Colored Peoples," *Chicago Defender*, June 16, 1945.

the first to propose an alliance between blacks and sympathetic whites. Yet the fact that African Americans' interest in the transnational challenge to white supremacy was born principally of a reaction *against* a specific form of oppression – white American racism – was not unusual. Ideologies and movements, whatever their hue and whatever their form, rarely arise with the spontaneity which Hayakawa implied. The imagined community of black internationalism was a powerful ideological reference point, but like any exercise in activism it was characterized by conflicting loyalties and realpolitik.

Notwithstanding the limits of black internationalism, the end of the Pacific War reaffirmed the need for global opposition to white supremacy. This was a cultural as well as political project. Recognizing the transnational implications of American cultural power, African Americans condemned the "ignorant and untrue fables" that were "poisoning" the minds of Pacific Islanders. As long as "anti-Negro films" and "Uncle Tom plays" continued to present African Americans in a negative light, and so long as African American actors were willing to accept roles that demeaned nonwhite characters, "the Negro race will never be respected" anywhere in "the world."[71] As they witnessed the peoples of the Asia-Pacific imitating racial idioms presented by Hollywood, and as they once again presented African Americans as leaders of nonwhite people everywhere, black servicemen at the frontlines of America's postwar Pacific mission understood that what would subsequently be described as "soft power" was explicitly racialized.

Just as Walter White and others had prophesied, the power of American example could not be underestimated. Identifying an emerging pattern of "Jim Crow" across the postwar "South Seas," black commentators expressed frustration that Pacific Islanders were adopting the "ways" of white Americans.[72] As the *Pittsburgh Courier* reported in mid-1946, the "intolerance and prejudice" of many American officers serving across the Pacific was poisoning relations with the region's indigenous inhabitants.

---

[71] "Marines Say Films Poisoning Native Islanders toward Race," *Atlanta Daily World*, June 6, 1945; "Letters to [the] Editor," *Atlanta Daily World*, August 24, 1945. See also "Uncle Tom Films Poisoning Islanders' Minds – Marines," *Afro-American*, June 9, 1945. In mid-1943 Vincent Tubbs had reported that black servicemen stationed in Australia considered some of Hollywood's depictions of "colored characters" – the 1942 film *The Vanishing Virginian* was singled out for its disparaging images of African Americans – as "particularly embarrassing." See Tubbs, "Tubbs Visits Camp in Australia; Finds it Equal to Best in U.S.A.," *Afro-American*, June 12, 1943.

[72] Fleming R. Waller, "Jim Crow in the South Seas: Natives Adopt the Ways of U.S. White Folk," *Afro-American*, February 9, 1946.

Utilizing a term destined to become even more notorious in subsequent wars, white American officers were reportedly contemptuous of the "gooks."[73]

One group of so-called "gooks" in whom African Americans took a particular interest were the Filipinos. As a former colony of the United States, the Philippines' strategic significance was complemented by emotional – albeit paternalistic – bonds between Americans and Filipinos, symbolized by Douglas MacArthur's 1942 promise to return and liberate the islands from Japanese occupation. African Americans were conscious of their nation's colonial role, and President Franklin D. Roosevelt's wartime undertaking to grant full independence to the Philippines "the moment" that Japanese power was "destroyed" was reported widely in the black press.[74] It was characteristic of the racial complexities of the Pacific War, however, that even as the Allies were liberating the Philippines from Japanese occupation, African Americans recognized the long-term implications of Japan's earlier success in overthrowing US authority. The Filipinos, wondered *Afro-American* journalist Irene West in late 1944, might "prefer Jap bosses to snooty Americans." While it was too soon to "calculate how the sudden change from a white boss to a yellow boss may have affected" the Filipinos' "psychology," West hypothesized that Americans might encounter "trouble" from "revengeful citizens" determined to assert their independence. "When the Americans come to" reclaim the towns and cities of the Philippines, she asserted, they might well "learn for the first time how immensely they were hated" – just as "the British learned the bitter truth in Singapore and the Malay States."[75] White Americans imagined that US rule over the Philippines was a benign alternative to the cruelties of the European colonial enterprise; African Americans knew otherwise.

Racial and strategic issues were hence as inseparable in the Philippines as they were in those parts of the Asia-Pacific formerly under the tyranny of European colonial authority. As African Americans contended, the ability of the United States to implement its plans for the postwar world would be affected by past behavior. Although Roosevelt had promised to grant independence to the Philippines when the war was over, the editors of the *Afro-American* emphasized that Filipinos are "colored," and that

[73] "Say Natives Neglected," *Pittsburgh Courier*, July 6, 1946.
[74] "Full Independence for Filipino People Promised by Roosevelt," *Atlanta Daily World*, August 13, 1943.
[75] Irene West, "Filipinos May Prefer Jap Bosses to Snooty Americans," *Afro-American*, November 11, 1944.

"for forty-five years they have known what United States imperialism and race prejudice mean."[76] In early 1945, the paper editorialized about the meaning of "liberation." Reflecting on the impact of liberation on the Filipinos – the "98 per cent of the islands' 17,000,000 population" – the *Afro-American* suggested one could not help but be skeptical about "the term 'liberation' as applied to the Philippines." If the "past performances of America in her colonial relations is any criterion of what the future holds," the editors contended, "'liberation' would not mean the same to many of the Filipinos" as it did to Europeans "freed from Axis domination." "Because white Americans are generally inclined to transplant their color prejudices to all parts of the world," and because they "find it difficult to solve a simple bi-racial problem here at home," the *Afro-American* despaired of whites' capacity to "reconcile properly all of the complexities of the Far East." It was no surprise, the paper noted, that "some Filipinos considered the whole war between America and Japan" as "simply a choice of two evils." "Let us hope that MacArthur and his men are carrying some real democracy in their knapsacks, jeeps, tanks, and planes," concluded the *Afro-American*, "so that the term 'liberation' will have some real meaning for the masses of the Philippine peoples," rather than merely just a "change of one master for another."[77]

The final months of the Pacific War brought these questions of race, colonial authority, and postwar power to the fore. As the ascendant military force across the region, the United States was in a position of power; but that power was not absolute, and was the subject of negotiation between the liberators, the liberated, and those seeking to restore colonial authority. When American forces liberated particular areas, their first priority was to ensure military security. In some instances, the most straightforward means of doing so was by cooperating with former colonial officials.

These circumstances were vexing for all concerned. But they were particularly complicated for African Americans, given the black leadership's determination to extend freedom to the formerly colonized peoples of the Asia-Pacific and provide a counter to white American imperialism. As early as mid-1943 it was hypothesized that African American soldiers might play a "key role" in "policing" the postwar South Seas. If the anticipated role of African Americans was ambiguous – the phrase "policing" implied that blacks would be in positions of authority – the foundation

[76] "Race and Color Are Now a Chief Issue in the War," *Afro-American*, March 21, 1942.
[77] "Philippine 'Liberation?'" *Afro-American*, February 17, 1945.

of that role was clear: the wartime friendships "established between dark-skinned South Seas Islanders and American Negro soldiers" meant that "if the United Nations must police these isles when peace comes, the Negro soldier will be the logical man for the job."[78] By early 1945, when Allied forces had liberated much of the Asia-Pacific, those assumptions appeared perspicacious. Black reporter Charles H. Loeb noted that African American troops had been "welcomed by the Filipinos with joyful shouts and open arms."[79] Claiming a special bond between African Americans and the Filipinos – the "Filipino has been more jovial and social with the Negro than any other group he has met in the Southwest Pacific" – Fletcher P. Martin intimated that black troops were particularly equipped to perform occupation duties.[80]

Confident that they were destined to play a role in the postwar Asia-Pacific, African Americans expressed skepticism regarding the process by which Allied – specifically, United States – military forces were reestablishing control across the region. Following the liberation of the Philippines, African Americans worried that the exercise of US military power, on the local level, entailed political consequences extending well beyond the immediate objective of defeating Japan. John Robert Badger reported that although Filipino guerrilla forces had valiantly resisted the Japanese occupiers, they were promptly disarmed by the returning US forces. This display of American power was doubly galling. Having worn "down the Japanese," and after marching "through the countryside" to meet the liberating Americans, "many guerrillas" had "established local government" and "maintained law and order." In other words, they had demonstrated their capacity for self-government, under the most adverse circumstance. To be "ousted from their posts 'in the name of law and order,'" wrote Badger, was not just an affront to the guerrillas, and by extension, all Filipinos, but also an inauspicious portent of the form of "independence" that would be granted to the Philippines. The analogy with domestic racial politics in the United States was unmistakable: "the 'independence' and 'democracy' to be 'granted' to the Filipinos," wrote Badger, would be "very similar to that in Dixie – democracy in form only." The United States, he opined, would be imposing "the worst

[78] "Negro Soldiers May Prove Key to South Seas Policing Following War," *Atlanta Daily World*, June 9, 1943.
[79] Charles H. Loeb, "Filipinos Welcome Tan-Hued Yanks; Glad Freed of Japs," *Cleveland Call and Post*, February 24, 1945.
[80] Fletcher P. Martin, "Philippine Children Go Back to School," *Cleveland Call and Post*, December 9, 1944.

kind of oppression and tyranny" on the Philippines. Consequently, regardless of Badger's professed optimism regarding decolonization – "I do not believe," he declared, that "the imperialists" would "be successful in suppressing the peoples of Asia" – many African Americans had concluded already that the lofty rhetoric emanating from the San Francisco Conference was essentially a ruse, which would not translate anytime soon into meaningful freedom. Endorsing W. E. B. Du Bois's apprehensions regarding "American imperialism," Badger concluded that the means by which MacArthur was reestablishing US authority in the Philippines was confirmation of American intentions.[81]

Ostensibly, then, African Americans expressed unambiguous hostility to colonialism. On the former frontlines, however, black servicemen could find themselves complicit in the return of colonial authority. This tension was evident in the former Dutch East Indies. While African Americans acknowledged the Javanese determination to overthrow the "harsh domination of the Dutch masters who had ruled" the region "since 1596," an almost incidental remark from the intelligence officer assigned to the 93rd Infantry Division – "Dutch officials," he reported, had been "very cooperative" by "helping select" local "guides familiar with areas in question" – suggested a degree of local cooperation between US forces and Dutch colonial authorities intent on reestablishing control.[82] Whether the African American troops of the 93rd Division endorsed that cooperation is difficult to ascertain, but as black seaman L. J. Taggart's 1945 reference to "our unique race" suggested, black servicemen remained certain that they were different from the Pacific Islanders and Asians they had encountered during the war.[83] This sense of African American ethnocentrism, reflecting a cultural relativism informed by notions of American exceptionalism, was continuing to shape black attitudes toward the non-white peoples of the Asia-Pacific. Betraying a form of African American orientalism, when African Americans contemplated their role in the postwar Asia-Pacific, they did so with a clear understanding of their sense of difference from – and, less euphemistically, their sense of superiority

[81] John Robert Badger, "World View: Ill Winds in the Pacific," *Chicago Defender*, July 7, 1945.
[82] James H. Hill, "The Brown Winds Rise," *Afro-American*, November 17, 1945; S2, 369th Infantry Regiment, "Use of Natives," in G2 Weekly Summary, No. 29, May 26, 1945, RG 407, Box 11331, 291.2 Race, Records of the Adjutant General's Office, National Archives and Records Administration, College Park, Maryland (NARA).
[83] L. J. Taggart, "What the People Say: Natives of S. W. Pacific Area Appreciate American Negro," *Chicago Defender*, June 30, 1945.

to – the nonwhite majorities who were in the process of asserting their
independence. And, acknowledging the horrors of the Pacific War, African
Americans suggested the conflict had ushered in positive changes. As
Fletcher P. Martin noted in April 1944, in the wake of the allied libera-
tion of New Guinea from the Japanese, the island had been "changed."
"Civilization," wrote Martin, had "crept in."[84]

African American correspondents such as Martin were certain that
the former colonies of the Asia-Pacific region required leadership, or
stewardship, from more developed nations. These assumptions could be
expressed in apparently innocuous ways. In praising the wartime cooperation between blacks and Filipinos – such as the celebrated exploits of
a "Filipino guerrilla band" led by an African American, Captain Frank
Merith – Martin also implied differences, including physical differences,
between the two groups. These physical differences could symbolize a
racial hierarchy. Claiming that the African American guerrilla leader
was known to "three out of five Filipinos on Leyte," Martin's evocative
description of Merith as a "giant Negro" suggested that his physical
stature distinguished him from the majority of the Filipinos.[85] More significantly, implicit within the black press's celebrations of both Merith's
deeds and the cooperation between Merith and the Filipinos were familiar assumptions regarding African Americans' capacity for leadership
over other nonwhite peoples.

African American condescension was evident elsewhere, too. Even
while they condemned the "brutal treatment" to which black troops were
routinely subjected across the Philippines, and lamented that there was
"much friction between" white and black Americans, African Americans
were themselves treating Filipinos as less-than-equals.[86] Expressing his
frustration at white officers' ongoing mistreatment of the black troops of
the 93rd Infantry Division, Lloyd F. Graves exposed an implicit hierarchy
between black servicemen and the Filipinos. Angry that white officers

---

[84] Fletcher P. Martin, "Martin Finds New Guinea Changed by 'Civilization,'" *Atlanta Daily World*, April 20, 1944.

[85] Fletcher P. Martin, "Negro Leads Filipino Snipers against Japs," *Atlanta Daily World*, December 6, 1944. See also Fletcher P. Martin, "American on Leyte Famed as Guerrilla Band Leader," *Afro-American*, December 9, 1944; Fletcher P. Martin, "Seeks Giant Leader of Guerrilla Band," *Pittsburgh Courier*, December 9, 1944.

[86] Chester S. Perry et al., to the NAACP, October 6, 1945, "Camp Investigations-Overseas Pacific, 1945–1948," Group II, Box G2, NAACP-LoC. On African American Marines' ongoing discontent at their mistreatment at the hands of white commanders, see Rolonal (sic) L. Ingram to William T. Andrews, November 7, 1945, "Camp Investigations-Overseas Pacific, 1945–1948," Group II, Box G2, NAACP-LoC.

were preventing local Filipinos from performing "odd jobs" such as washing the black servicemen's clothes, Graves explained that the Filipinos were effectively segregated from African American troops.[87] It is possible that the black soldiers' frustration stemmed in part from their failure to avoid tasks commonly assigned to women: combat troops such as the black infantrymen of the 93rd were particularly attuned to any affront to their masculinity. Yet if Graves was concerned by this example of emasculation of black servicemen, his letter avoided the subject. Rather, his principal concern was that the men of his unit were being denied access to a ready supply of cheap Filipino labor. Graves left no sign that he was embarrassed by – or even aware of – the contradiction underpinning his critique of the segregation of African American troops from the local Filipinos. The men of the 93rd well understood the discrimination to which they were subjected, but like other black servicemen they did not always recognize their complicity in the subjugation of others.

That tension between a transnational racial identity and an abiding sense of difference from other nonwhite peoples was evident in African Americans' responses to their wartime encounters with poverty and deprivation across Asia and the Pacific. Confronting living conditions far worse than those witnessed by their counterparts serving in the European Theater, and implicitly associating cleanliness with progress and even modernity, African Americans who served in the Asia-Pacific Theatre expressed revulsion at the conditions under which many Asians and Pacific Islanders lived. India, in particular, was singled out as the antithesis of Western cleanliness. Soon after referring disparagingly to "filthy disease-ridden Calcutta," *Chicago Defender* correspondent Deton J. Brooks described the "stinking mass of humanity of the poorest classes" who traveled in the "pig-stye-like" third-class train carriages.[88] African American revulsion at such conditions could be manifested as a pride in – or feelings of superiority about – the United States. Interviewed long after the war, black Navy veteran Bobby Wallace recalled vividly his disgust at the conditions in Karachi, Pakistan: "the odor that we smelled, open toilets, no drainage, no sewage, no nothing ... and I said thank God for America." Flush with faith in the possibility of the American

[87] Lloyd F. Graves to "Miss [Mary White] Ovington," November [?], 1945, "Soldier Complaints," Part II, Box G1, NAACP-LoC.
[88] Deton J. Brooks, "Negro GI's Jim Crowed in India; Red Cross Worker Quits in Protest," Chicago Defender, July 14, 1945; Brooks, "Gandhi Still India's 'No. 1,'" *Chicago Defender*, July 28, 1945. See also Frank Bolden, "Discrimination Cause of Low Morale among Tan Yanks in India and Burma," *Afro-American*, October 13, 1945.

dream, Wallace's wartime travels convinced him of the limitless possibilities offered by the United States. "In America," he stated, "you can go from rags to riches, regardless of race, color, or creed. You can't do that in no other country on this earth." Echoing Wallace's confidence in the American dream, his fellow Pacific War veteran William Henry Harvey stated that seeing "what goes on in these other countries" made him want to keep the United States "free."[89] In this way, black veterans such as Wallace and Harvey affirmed their faith in the precepts of American exceptionalism.

As well as situating notions of "race" within hierarchies shaped by history, nationality, and culture, African Americans' continuing sense of exceptionalism was also articulated in biological terms. Although they decried the notion of biological distinction between the races – African Americans criticized the segregation of "black" and "white" blood supplies, for example – there were occasions when they themselves deployed the language of biologically determined racial difference.[90] This issue arose in the context of one of the war's most tangible, if understated legacies: the offspring born of liaisons between American troops and local women in the areas fought over during World War Two.[91] Irene West, reporting for the *Afro-American*, reflected on this question soon after the Japanese surrender. Urging Americans to embrace the children born of wartime dalliances between American servicemen and Pacific Islanders and Asians, West anticipated that by the time such children reached the United States, the nation's "anti-color psychology will have altered." "Any half-caste, illegitimate child that I ever meet," she asserted, "with American soldier, sailor or marine blood in his veins will be very dear to my heart." The scenario painted by West – whereby children born to American fathers would be welcomed by their relatives in the United States – was both optimistic and naïve. Equally significantly, her references to "blood" betrayed deep-seated assumptions regarding race and racial difference, and suggested an essentialist view of what constituted

[89] Bobby Wallace, AFC/2001/001/4736, VHP-LoC; William Henry Harvey, AFC/2001/001/27509, VHP-LoC.

[90] For a critique of the wartime separation of "black" and "white" blood, see Charles H. Loeb, "Methuselah's Prayer," *Cleveland Call and Post*, January 10, 1942. See also Gilbert Ware, *William Hastie: Grace under Pressure* (New York, NY: Oxford University Press, 1984), 107–9; Phillip McGuire, *He, Too, Spoke for Democracy: Judge Hastie, World War II, and the Black Soldier* (New York, NY: Greenwood, 1988), 73–7.

[91] See Judith A. Bennett and Angela Wanhalla, eds., *Mothers' Darlings of the South Pacific: The Children of Indigenous Women and U.S Servicemen, World War II* (Dunedin: Otago University Press, 2016).

an "American." When "foreign dark-skinned Americans" reached the United States, she argued, they should be welcomed warmly, since flowing through their veins "was good American blood that offered up its life that we may live free."[92] The sacrifices of black servicemen were thereby joined to both the future of the regions they had liberated and the promise of a more racially enlightened United States.

Irene West's optimistic assessment of Americans' capacity to accept racial change, along with her faith that African Americans' wartime sacrifices were not in vain, should be viewed alongside blacks' ongoing apprehensions regarding race relations. Reporting from Tokyo soon after Japan's surrender, Charles Loeb noted that African American servicemen were "doubtful of the future of race relations after the war."[93] For many blacks, those doubts turned quickly to despair, as wartime hope gave way to segregation, lynching, and the unfinished struggle for civil and political equality. While African Americans condemned American racism, however, their visions of the postwar, postcolonial world continued to reflect American values. Not for the first time, African Americans were endorsing and seeking to transplant American ideals, if not American racial practices. There was a symbiosis between blacks' lasting belief in American exceptionalism, and their enduring hope in the possibility of change at home, and of an American-led regeneration abroad. At the same time, therefore, as they were repudiating colonialism and denouncing white American racism, African Americans were symbols and agents of American power across the Asia-Pacific. Amid an international system that prized stability above equality, the tension between racial and national identity that long characterized African American political and cultural life endured. As ensuing decades would reveal, when African Americans projected US power abroad they remained sharply critical of the disjunction between the lofty, idealistic rhetoric of American international power and the realities of American globalism.

---

[92] West, "Japs Will Bear Strange Fruit."
[93] Loeb, "Troops 'Take' Tokyo".

Conclusion

We fought the good fight. We contributed more than our share to defend a democracy that thus far excluded us ... This could be a new beginning. The greatest catastrophe in human history was at an end. Caught up in the euphoria of victory and peace, there was reason to believe a new world was in birth and America, too, would change.[1]

African American veterans of the Pacific War perceived and portrayed themselves as part of a great crusade that had defeated fascist tyranny. Yet the issues of liberation and equality raised by World War Two transcended the immediate goals of defeating the Axis Powers. From their own often-bitter experiences, African Americans understood the limits of American freedom. Their determination to defeat fascism was hence inseparable from their determination to overcome American racism. This dual struggle – the Double V campaign – prompted profound questions regarding race and identity. For African Americans fighting against Japan, negotiating the vexed relationship between race and nationality proved a complex and sometimes-contradictory process.

African Americans' prewar attitudes toward Japan exemplified those complexities. During the 1920s and 1930s Japanese authorities had sought to win the hearts and minds of black America. To the enduring consternation of white American authorities, African Americans – or, more specifically, elements of the black leadership – had been impressed by Japan's self-declared status as leader of the family of nonwhite peoples. In the aftermath of Pearl Harbor, however, African Americans made

---

[1] Nelson Peery, *Black Radical: The Education of an American Revolutionary* (New York, NY: New Press, 2007), epigraph.

clear their determination to remain part of the American family, notwithstanding that family's racialized dysfunctionality. Reaffirming their patriotism and recognizing that "Pearl Harbor" was a transnational moment that did much more than bring a reluctant United States into a global war, African Americans intuited that the Pacific War was challenging the racial hierarchies that had scarred the prewar Asia-Pacific.

When African Americans offered their services to their nation, the nation questioned their right to fight. White America's determination to deny or restrict black military service was tantamount to denying African Americans the rights of citizenship. And when blacks did enter military service they confronted forms of institutionalized discrimination and segregation that were little different from those encountered most recently by their forbears in World War One, but which stretched back painfully to the Revolutionary era. The United States was no exemplar of democracy. The black mission, then, became one of transformation as well as preservation, as they vowed that the United States that would emerge victorious from World War Two would live up to its democratic ideals. It was only when the United States fulfilled those ideals, African Americans insisted, that the nation could rightly assume the mantle of international leadership.

Black leaders recognized the global implications of American racism. Writing in 1945, Walter White connected the racist practices of the US military to America's self-proclaimed role as a leader and beacon of liberty for the free world. The "soldiers of Canada, New Zealand, and strangely enough – in light of her laws forbidding admission to that island of any but whites – Australia," he warned, would "take home with them" from the war's "battle fronts greatly augmented suspicion and mistrust against the United States because of her treatment of Negro soldiers." "America's generosity, idealism, and heroism," wrote White, "are being immeasurably diminished by these resentments."[2] The relegation of African Americans to the margins of American democracy was compromising both the US war effort and its self-proclaimed role as a force for global democracy and freedom.

Conscious of these domestic and international racial imperatives, African Americans hoped their contributions to the war effort would earn them the right to play their part in shaping the postwar world. From the beginning of US involvement in the Pacific War, African Americans' dual mission of preservation and transformation was unambiguously

---

[2] Walter White, *A Rising Wind* (New York, NY: Doubleday, Doran and Co., 1945), 146–7.

transnational, as they sought to carry with them American values of democracy and equality. As they confronted American racism, and demanded the rights of citizenship on the basis of their military service, African Americans challenged the racism that was both cause and effect of the colonial order across the Asia-Pacific region. Celebrating their role in winning the war, African Americans perceived themselves as liberators in the vanguard of the struggle against the associated evils of colonial and racial oppression.

African American participation in the Pacific War was underpinned by the notion – sometimes explicit, sometimes implicit – of an international alliance of nonwhite peoples, which would subvert racism and colonialism. Yet while African Americans serving in the Pacific Theater understood and experienced the indignities of white racism, they rarely recognized their own complicity in the subjugation of other nonwhite peoples. Accordingly, while they unanimously endorsed the principles of universal freedom, the imagined transnational community of nonwhite peoples articulated by some African Americans was itself characterized by hierarchies. Influenced by the longstanding Western myths of the Pacific region that exercised a powerful hold over the African American imagination, blacks' wartime experiences confirmed their continuing sense of difference – cultural, social, and political – from Pacific Islanders and Asians. That sense of difference – a form of African American orientalism – rested on many of the same Western assumptions and values upon which colonialism was predicated – and which African Americans had renounced.

This paradox, or contradiction, exposed the limits of African American internationalism. It also implied that the principles underpinning the notion of American exceptionalism transcended the racial divide within the United States. Even as they repudiated white American racism, African Americans revealed the influence of the United States in shaping their world view. In the face of often-overwhelming white racism, the enduring appeal of "America" was the promise of what it might be, internationally, as well as at home. African Americans sought to carry that promise with them as they served in the Asia-Pacific. The United States was undeniably racist, yet it still represented – in possibility, albeit not in practice – "civilization" and "democracy."

The Pacific War, then, concurrently challenged and affirmed African Americans' sense of difference from other nonwhite peoples. Reflecting and appropriating the rhetoric and principles of American exceptionalism, African Americans continued to regard themselves as more advanced than the colonized and otherwise oppressed peoples they encountered during the course of the Pacific War. Notions of American exceptionalism therefore complicated the tension between race and nationality. American democracy had not delivered racial equality, but African Americans remained confident in the ideal of democracy. It was their duty, and their mission, to carry those principles abroad, even as they continued the fight for civil rights at home. Challenging the racialized and racist military power projected by the United States during World War Two, African Americans were carrying not just their rifles across the Asia-Pacific – they were confident they were also bringing democratic ideas and ideals.

One of the most powerful expressions of the racism that characterized American military power was white America's reluctance to allow African Americans to serve in combat. The politics of African Americans' frontline military service across the Pacific Theater reveal much about the wider politics of race during the mid-twentieth century. Combat was a test of African American manhood, and an opportunity for blacks to prove their valor. But it was also much more. Refuting long-standing racial assumptions that they were temperamentally and physiologically ill-equipped for combat, African Americans on the frontlines were also claiming their democratic rights within the United States, and forcefully asserting their right to play a part in shaping the postwar Asia-Pacific. Like white America's wartime reluctance to allow blacks to serve in combat, the ongoing refusal to acknowledge African American demonstrations of battlefield valor is a potent example of the significance attached to black combat duty. Even many decades after the war's end, the struggle continues to award appropriate service medals to African American veterans of the Pacific War. Writing in late 1943, the black correspondent Edgar T. Rozeau had anticipated that African Americans' contribution to winning World War Two would be put to one side in popular memory. Lamenting that "historians only glorify the deeds of the fighting men and not those of the supply and services," Rozeau wondered "how much value future generations of Americans" would "place on the contributions of Negro soldiers during this war, if the disparity between white and Negro combat troops should continue as it is present."[3] African American combat service thus transcended the immediate goal of vanquishing the enemy on the battlefield.

[3] Edgar T. Rozeau, "'Insist on Combat Duty' – Rozeau: Unable to Find Negroes Manning Gun on Frontline," *Pittsburgh Courier*, January 1, 1944.

There were other ways, too, in which African American combat service, and the consequent challenge to white notions of black passivity, challenged white masculine hegemony. White Americans' attempts to regulate blacks' interactions with foreign women – particularly, but not exclusively foreign white women – further exposed their own masculine anxieties. The specter of African American men proving themselves in combat, or interacting "inappropriately" with women, compromised the distinctions between black and white men – and made it more difficult to deny social and civil equality to African Americans. These concerns reflected underlying white fears regarding the intersections of race and gender. Singularly, each raised concerns; in tandem, they provoked anxieties that struck deep at white Americans' self-identity and authority. As the Pacific War revealed, the regulation and control of black manhood, in both the private and public sphere, was essential for the preservation of segregation and other forms of American racism.

Wartime attempts to circumscribe and control African American manhood were symptomatic of the broader white American concerns prompted by the presence of African Americans in the Pacific. White Australians shared many of these same racial and sexual anxieties. Their longstanding legislative and judicial responses to those anxieties – the exclusion of nonwhite immigrants, and the regulation and separation of indigenous Australians – were immediately familiar to many Americans. However, by denying Australia's post-Pearl Harbor request to not deploy African Americans Down Under, US authorities not only placed military expediency above Australia's racial anxieties: unwittingly, they had let the genie out of the bottle. The consequences of the African American presence in wartime Australia were both unintended and significant. As with so many aspects of African Americans' analysis of the Pacific War, their understanding of Australia's racial policies, and of the importance of Australians' perceptions of American racism, was explicitly transnational. Troubled deeply by the prospect of defending a nation whose democracy was founded on principles of racial exclusion, African Americans resolved to transform Australians' racial sensibilities. Contrary to African Americans' fears, however, from early 1942 Australians frequently displayed warmth, gratitude, and sometimes even affection to African Americans. Perceiving black Americans as a component of American military power – Australians realized the United States was the only Allied power capable of staunching the Japanese advances of late 1941 and early 1942 – and assured that African Americans were wartime visitors rather than potential permanent immigrants, many Australians welcomed black service personnel.

The disjunction between the White Australia Policy on the one hand, and Australians' wartime attitudes toward and treatment of African Americans on the other, provided a powerful example of the possible fate of Southern segregation. Americans – black and white alike – recognized the significance of the tension between legislative expressions of white racism, and the cultural bases upon which such policies were predicated: if the latter was not immutable, there was hope that the former might also be overcome. The implications for the African American struggle against Southern segregation were clear: race relations in the United States need not be locked in the eternal segregationist time warp envisaged by many white Southerners. And while it would be going too far to suggest that Australians had performed a wartime volte-face on questions of race – it was not until 1973 that the last legislative vestiges of the White Australia Policy were abolished – the African American presence in wartime Australia was one aspect of the wider challenge to the racist principles and habits associated with that policy. As the African American presence in Australia tested the tenets of white supremacy in both Australia and the United States, Australians' reactions to the presence of black Americans in wartime Australia became a transnational symbol of the possibility of racial reform.

African Americans' wartime experiences confirmed their skepticism toward Japan's claim to be the most formidable opponent of international white supremacy. While elements of the African American community, including the black military community, recognized the ongoing importance of Japan's challenge to white racism and colonialism, Japanese behavior during the Pacific War persuaded many blacks to accept the prevailing wartime Allied narrative regarding the Japanese "character." Japan's often-vicious mistreatment of Allied soldiers and prisoners-of-war – of all races – coupled with their contempt for the very peoples they claimed to be liberating, convinced African Americans that Japan had forfeited any right to be considered an honorable enemy or a symbol of nonwhite racial power. That conviction shaped black attitudes toward the Japanese nation, and the Japanese people. Debates continue regarding the American decision to use nuclear weapons on Japan. But for African Americans who had experienced firsthand the excesses of the Pacific War, the bombing of Hiroshima and Nagasaki was a necessary nadir of a merciless conflict that exposed the worst of humanity. Furthermore, the cruelty that African Americans witnessed across the Pacific Theater – participants from all sides were capable of normally unimaginable acts of callous inhumanity – led them to reflect on the links between the brutalities they witnessed in war and the violence they endured at home. International and national manifestations of racism were indivisible.

In October 1945, just a few weeks after Japan's surrender, the Reverend William H. Jernigen, Director of the Washington Bureau of the Fraternal Council of Negro Churches, urged the black soldiers of the 93rd Infantry Division to "keep up the good work and return to civilian life." It was incumbent upon "every serviceman," he insisted, to "improve race relations in his own sphere."[4] Of course, many African American servicemen sought nothing other than a prompt and peaceful return to civilian life. Yet the challenges confronting black America remained stark. The immediate postwar period brought little joy for African Americans, and black veterans frequently encountered white racism no less virulent than that which they had endured during the prewar years. Evidently, the status quo ante must not be allowed to prevail. In affirming that the scourge of white supremacy was not bound by national borders, military service in the Pacific War had raised the consciousness of African Americans. But the impact of black military service on white America was less certain. Consequently, while President Harry Truman's 1948 Executive Order integrating the armed forces was a potent symbol of racial progress, when the United States next went to war in the Asia-Pacific – in 1950, in the so-called "police action" to thwart the advance of communism in Korea – black military service again threw into sharp relief the dispiriting contrast between the rhetoric of American democracy and the realities of American racism.

---

[4] Address by Reverend William Jernigan, October 30, 1945, Papers of Gen. Leonard Russell Boyd, Box 2, Hoover Institution Archives, Stanford University, Stanford, California.

Bibliography

PRIMARY SOURCES

Manuscript Materials

Australian War Memorial, Canberra.
- Department of Defence, Minute Paper, December 28, 1942, 54, 506/1/1
- Private Papers of David Tratten, PR0021
- Papers of Sergeant Charles Walmsby, PR00742

Hoover Institution Archives, Stanford University, Stanford, California.
- Papers of General Leonard Russell Boyd

Library of Congress, Washington, DC.
- Records of the National Association for the Advancement of Colored People
- *Papers of the NAACP* (Microfilm) Ed. John H. Bracey, Jr., and August Meier (Bethesda, MD: University Publications of America, 1993–1994)
  - Part 14: Race Relations in the International Arena, 1940–1955
  - Part 17: National Staff Files, 1940–1955
- Interviews with African American veterans of the Pacific War, included in the Veterans History Project (American Folklife Center)

Lyndon B. Johnson Presidential Library, Austin, Texas.
- Robert Sherrod, undated report, with processing note, "[Public activities-Biographical Information-Navy] Australia Material," Lyndon Baines Johnson Archives Collection

National Archives and Records Administration, College Park, Maryland.
- RG 107: Records of the Office of the Secretary of War
- RG 160: Records of U.S. Army Services Forces (World War II)
- RG 165: Records of the War Department General and Special Staffs
- RG 247: Records of the Office of the Chief of Chaplains
- RG 313: Records of the Naval Operating Forces
- RG 337: Records of Headquarters Army Ground Forces

- RG 338: Records of U.S. Army Operational, Tactical, and Support Organizations (World War II and Thereafter)
- RG 407: Records of the Adjutant General's Office
- RG 495: Records of Headquarters, United States Army Forces, Western Pacific (World War II)
- RG 496: Records of the General Headquarters, Southwest Pacific Area and United States Army Forces, Pacific (World War II)

United States Army Military History Institute, United States Army Heritage and Education Center, Carlisle, Pennsylvania.

- Daniel J. Brown Papers
- Cork M. Goff Papers
- Maurice C. Pincoffs Papers
- World War II Veterans Survey. 93rd Infantry Division

Norris L. Brookens Library, Archives/Special Collections, University of Illinois at Springfield.

- Dr. Edwin A. Lee Memoir

Schomburg Center for Research in Black Culture, New York Public Library, New York City.

- World War II Letters from African American Soldiers

Newspapers and Magazines

Atlanta Daily World, 1940–1945
Baltimore *Afro-American*, 1924, 1930, 1940–1946
Chicago Defender, 1922, 1926, 1936–1937, 1940–1946
Chicago Tribune, 1944
Cleveland Call and Post, 1930, 1939–1946
New York Amsterdam Star-News (variously titled as *New York Amsterdam News*), 1940–1946
Norfolk Journal and Guide (variously titled as *New Journal and Guide*), 1941–1945
Philadelphia Tribune, 1928–1929, 1940–1945
Pittsburgh Courier, 1926–1928, 1939–1945
MidPacifican, 1942–1945
Perth *Daily News*, 1928
Spartanburg (SC) *Herald*, November 1, 1943
The Crisis, 1941–1945
Time, 1941–1945
Yank Down Under, 1943–1944

Interviews

"Interview with Leon Canick," October 11, 1994, Kurt Piehler and Patrick Gordon, Rutgers Oral History Archives, http://oralhistory.rutgers.edu/interviewees/851-canick-m-leon

Published Sources

Campbell, Alfred S. *Guadalcanal Round-Trip: The Story of an American Red Cross Field Director in the Present War*. Lambertville, NJ: Printed privately, 1945.

Cozzens, James Gould. *Guard of Honor*. New York, NY: Harcourt, Brace, 1948.

Davis, Benjamin O., Jr. *Benjamin O. Davis, Jr.: American: An Autobiography*. New York, NY: Plume, 1992.

Department of the Navy. *The Negro Sailor*. Directed by Henry Levin. United States Navy Motion Film Productions, 1945.

Downey, Bill. *Uncle Sam Must Be Losing the War: Black Marines of the 51st*. San Francisco, CA: Strawberry Hill Press, 1982.

Du Bois, W. E. B. *The Souls of Black Folk* (1903). Edited by Henry Louis Gates, Jr. and Terri Hume Oliver. New York, NY: W. W. Norton, 1999.

"A Chronicle of Race Relations." *Phylon* 3, no. 2 (1942): 206–20.

Franklin, John Hope. *Mirror to America: The Autobiography of John Hope Franklin*. New York, NY: Farrar, Straus, and Giroux, 2005.

Hall, Gwendolyn Midlo, ed. *Love, War, and the 96th Engineers: The World War II New Guinea Diaries of Captain Hyman Samuelson*. Urbana, IL: University of Illinois Press, 1995.

Hastie, William H. "The Negro in the Army Today." *The Annals of the American Academy of Political and Social Science* 223, no. 1 (September 1942): 55–9.

Historical Section, 93rd Infantry Division. *93rd Infantry Division. Summary of Operations in World War II*. March, 1946.

Honey, Maureen, ed. *Bitter Fruit: African American Women in World War II*. Columbia, MO: University of Missouri Press, 1999.

International Labor Defense. *For Equality of Military Justice: 1,100 Leaders and Organizations Join in Endorsing Appeal for Clemency for Privates Frank Fisher, Jr. and Edward R. Loury, Victims of "the Army Scottsboro Case."* New York, NY: International Labor Defense, 1944.

Isom, George Hemingway. *What Is That Boy Going to Do Next?: A Memoir*. Lincoln, NE: iUniverse, 2005.

Killens, John O. *And Then We Heard the Thunder*. New York, NY: Knopf, 1963.

Knapp, George Edward. *Buffalo Soldiers at Fort Leavenworth in the 1930s and Early 1940s*. Fort Leavenworth, KS: Combat Studies Institute, U.S. Army Command and General Staff College, 1991.

Logan, Rayford W. ed. *What the Negro Wants*. Chapel Hill, NC: University of North Carolina Press, 1944.

MacDonald, Nancy and Dwight MacDonald. *The War's Greatest Scandal!: The Story of Jim Crow in Uniform*. New York, NY: The March on Washington Movement, 1943.

McGuire, Phillip, ed. *Taps for a Jim Crow Army: Letters from Black Soldiers in World War II*. Lexington, KY: University Press of Kentucky, 1983.

Moss, Carlton. *The Negro Soldier*. Directed by Frank Capra. War Activities Committee of the Motion Picture Industry, 1944.

Motley, Mary Penick, ed. *The Invisible Soldier: The Experience of the Black Soldier, World War II*. Detroit, MI: Wayne State University Press, 1975.

Nalty, Bernard C., and Morris J. MacGregor, eds. *Blacks in the Military: Essential Documents*. Wilmington, DE: Scholarly Resources, 1981.

Nelson, Hank, ed. *The War Diaries of Eddie Allan Stanton: Papua 1942–45, New Guinea 1945–46*. Sydney: Allen and Unwin, 1996.

Newtown, Adolph. *Better than Good: A Black Sailor's War, 1943–1945*. Annapolis, MD: Naval Institute Press, 1999.

O'Donnell, Patrick K., ed. *Into the Rising Sun: World War II's Pacific Veterans Reveal the Heart of Combat*. New York, NY: Free Press, 2002.

Ottley, Roi. *"New World A-Coming": Inside Black America*. Boston, MA: Houghton Mifflin, 1943.

Peery, Nelson. *Black Fire: The Making of an American Revolutionary*. New York, NY: The New Press, 1994.

Black Radical: The Education of an American Revolutionary. New York, NY: New Press, 2007.

Rampersad, Arnold, ed. *The Collected Works of Langston Hughes: Volume 2, The Poems, 1941–1950*. Columbia, MO: University of Missouri Press, 2001.

Randolph, A. Philip. "Pro-Japanese Activities among Negroes." *The Black Worker*, September, 1942, 4.

Reddick, Lawrence. "Of Motion Pictures" (1944). In *Black Films and Filmmakers: A Comprehensive Analogy from Stereotype to Superhero*, edited by Lindsay Patterson, 3–24. New York, NY: Dodd Mead, 1975.

Rickerl, Stephen. "Mosley Accepts Overdue Honor," *The Southern Illinoisan*, November 13, 2011.

Sebring, Lewis. "Negroes Make Good Soldiers." *SALT: Authorized Education Journal of Australian Army and Air Force* 3, no. 7 (May 18, 1942): 16–19.

Shenk, Robert, ed. *Authors at Sea: Modern American Writers Remember Their Naval Service*. Annapolis, MD: Naval Institute Press, 1997.

Sherrod, Robert. "Australia Wants the GIs Back." *Life*, September 22, 1947, 9–16.

Special Services Division, Army Service Forces, United States Army. *A Pocket Guide to Australia*. Washington, DC: War and Navy Departments, 1942.

Special Services Division, Services of Supply, United States Army. *Instructions for American Servicemen in Australia*. 1942

Terkel, Studs. *"The Good War": An Oral History of World War II*. 1984; reprinted, New York, NY: Ballantyne Books, 1985.

The Best from Yank, The Army Weekly: Selected by the Editors of Yank. New York, NY: E. P. Dutton, 1945.

This is Our War: Selected Stories of Six War Correspondents Who Were Sent Overseas by the Afro-American Newspapers. Baltimore, MD: Afro-American Company, 1945.

Tweed, George R. *Robinson Crusoe, USN: The Adventures of George R. Tweed, RM1C, on Jap-held Guam*, as told to Blake Clark. New York, NY: Whittlesey House, 1945.

United States War Department. *Command of Negro Troops*. Washington, DC: U.S. Government Printing Office, 1944.

Waters, Enoch P. *American Diary: A Personal History of the Black Press*. Chicago, IL: Path Press, 1987.
White, Walter. *A Rising Wind*. Garden City, NY: Doubleday, Doran and Co., 1945.
A Man Called White: The Autobiography of William White. London: Gollancz, 1949.
"Willo and Brillo" [William Haymes]. *The Aussies and the Yanks: Front Line Fact, Fun and Fiction*. Sydney: F. Johnson, 1943.
Wilson, Ruth Danenhower. *Jim Crow Joins Up*. Rev. Ed. New York, NY: William J. Clark, 1944.
Wilson, Sloan. *Voyage to Somewhere*. New York, NY: A. A. Wyn, 1946.
"Women and War Work." (Sydney) *Truth*, January 16, 1944.
World War II Scrapbook, Fort Huachuca Images, Fort Huachuca Museum, Arizona, http://huachuca.army.mil/files/History_WWIIScrapbook.pdf (Accessed February 2, 2015).
X. Malcolm, and Alex Haley. *The Autobiography of Malcolm X. With the Assistance of Alex Hailey*. 1965; reprinted, New York, NY: Grove Press, 1966.

SECONDARY SOURCES

Allen, Ernest, Jr. "When Japan Was the 'Champion of the Darker Races': Satokata Takahashi and the Flowering of Black Messianic Nationalism." *Black Scholar* 24 (Winter, 1994): 23–46.
Alkebulan, Paul. *The African American Press in World War II: Toward Victory at Home and Abroad*. Lanham, MD: Lexington Books, 2014.
Alpers, Benjamin L. "This is the Army: Imagining a Democratic Military in World War II." *Journal of American History* 85, no. 1 (1998): 129–63.
Altman, Alex. "Were African-Americans at Iwo Jima?" *Time*, June 9, 2008, http://content.time.com/time/nation/article/0,8599,1812972,00.html (Accessed October 9, 2016)
Anderson, Carol. "From Hope to Disillusion: African Americans, the United Nations, and the Struggle for Human Rights, 1944–1947." *Diplomatic History* 20, no. 4 (1996): 531–63.
Eyes off the Prize: The United Nations and the African American Struggle for Human Rights, 1944–1955. Cambridge: Cambridge University Press, 2003.
Andrews, Robert Hardy. *Bataan*. Directed by Tay Garnett. Metro-Goldwyn-Mayer, 1943.
Arrowsmith, Robyn. *All the Way to the USA: Australian WWII War Brides*. Mittagong: Robyn Arrowsmith, 2013.
Associated Press, *Pearl Harbor: Day of Infamy*. np: AP Publishers, 2015.
Astor, Gerald. *The Right to Fight: A History of African Americans in the Military*. Novato, CA: Presidio, 1998.
Bailey, Beth, and David Farber. "The 'Double-V' Campaign in World War II Hawaii: African Americans, Racial Ideology, and Federal Power." *Journal of Social History* 26, no. 4 (1993): 817–43.
The First Strange Place: The Alchemy of Race and Sex in World War II Hawaii. New York, NY: Free Press, 1992.

Baker, Anni P. *American Soldiers Overseas: The Global Military Presence.* Westport, CT: Praeger, 2004.

Barbeau, Arthur E. *The Unknown Soldiers: Black American Troops in World War I.* Philadelphia, PA: Temple University Press, 1974.

Barker. Anthony J., and Lisa Jackson. *Fleeting Attraction: A Social History of American Servicemen in Western Australia during the Second World War.* Nedlands: University of Western Australia Press, 1996.

Bell, Philip, and Roger Bell. *Implicated: The United States in Australia.* Melbourne: Oxford University Press, 1993.

Bell, Roger. *Unequal Allies: Australian-American Relations and the Pacific War.* Carlton: Melbourne University Press, 1977.

Bellafaire, Judith L. *The Army Nurse Corps: A Commemoration of World War II Service.* Washington, DC: U.S. Army Center of Military History, 1993.

Bennett, Judith A. *Natives and Exotics: World War II and Environment in the Southern Pacific.* Honolulu, HI: University of Hawai'i Press, 2009.

Bennett, Judith A., and Angela Wanhalla, eds. *Mothers' Darlings of the South Pacific: The Children of Indigenous Women and U.S. Servicemen, World War II.* Dunedin: Otago University Press, 2016.

Bergerud, Eric. *Touched with Fire: The Land War in the South Pacific.* New York, NY: Penguin Books, 1997.

Bérubé, Allan. *Coming Out under Fire: The History of Gay Men and Women in World War Two.* New York, NY: Free Press, 1990.

Bielakowski, Alexander. *African American Troops in World War II.* Oxford: Osprey, 2007.

Blauner, Robert. "Internal Colonialism and Ghetto Revolt." *Social Problems* 16, no. 4 (1969): 393–408.

Bodnar, John. *"The Good War" in American Memory.* Baltimore, MD: Johns Hopkins University Press, 2010.

Borstelmann, Thomas. *The Cold War and the Color Line: American Race Relations in the Global Arena.* Cambridge, MA: Harvard University Press, 2001.

Bowers, William T., William M. Hammond, and George L. MacGarrigle. *Black Soldier, White Army: The 24th Infantry Regiment in Korea.* Washington, DC: Center of Military History, United States Army, 1996.

Brandt, Nat. *Harlem at War: The Black Experience in World War II.* Syracuse, NY: Syracuse University Press, 1996.

Brawley, Sean. *The White Peril: Foreign Relations and Asian Immigration to Australasia and North America, 1919–1978.* Sydney: University of New South Wales Press, 1995.

Brawley, Sean, and Chris Dixon. "Jim Crow Downunder: African American Encounters with White Australia, 1942–1945." *Pacific Historical Review* 71, no. 4 (2002): 607–32.

"Colonel Zimmer's Sea Shell Collection: Souvenirs, Experience Validation, and American Service Personnel in the Wartime South Pacific." In *Coast to Coast and the Islands in Between: Case Studies in Modern Pacific Crossings,* edited by Prue Ahrens and Chris Dixon, 77–87. Newcastle-upon-Tyne: Cambridge Scholars Publishing, 2010.

Hollywood's South Seas and the Pacific War: Searching for Dorothy Lamour. New York, NY: Palgrave Macmillan, 2012.

The South Seas: A Reception History from Daniel Defoe to Dorothy Lamour. Lanham, MD: Lexington Books, 2015.

Brokaw, Tom. *The Greatest Generation.* New York, NY: Random House, 1998.

Broussard, Jinx Coleman, and John Maxwell Hamilton. "Covering a Two Front War: Three African American Correspondents during World War II." *American Journalism* 22, no. 3 (2005): 33–54.

Broussard, Jinx Coleman. *African American Foreign Correspondents: A History.* Baton Rouge, LA: Louisiana State University Press, 2013.

Buchanan, A. Russell. *Black Americans in World War II.* Santa Barbara, CA: Clio Books, 1977.

Buckley, Gail. *American Patriots: The Story of Blacks in the Military from the Revolution to Desert Storm.* New York, NY: Random House, 2001.

Byers, Jean. *A Study of the Negro in Military Service.* Washington, DC: Department of Defense, 1950.

"Caesar Stephens Bassette, Jr." www.bassettbranches.org/tng//getperson.php?personID=I40&tree=276B (Accessed May 26, 2015)

Campbell, Rosemary. *Heroes and Lovers: A Question of National Identity.* Sydney: Allen and Unwin, 1989.

Center of Military History. "African American Medal of Honor Recipients," https://history.army.mil/moh/mohb.html (Accessed October 20, 2017)

Chapman, Ivan. *Private Eddie Leonski.* Sydney: Hale and Iremonger, 1982.

Chester, Robert K. "'Negroes' Number One Hero': Doris Miller, Pearl Harbor, and Retroactive Multiculturalism in World War II Remembrance." *American Quarterly* 65, no. 1 (2013): 31–61.

Clayton, James D. *The Years of MacArthur, Vol. 2, 1941–1945.* Boston, MA: Houghton Mifflin, 1975.

Coates, Ken, and W. R. Morrison. "The American Rampant: Reflections on the Impact of United States Troops in Allied Countries during World War II." *Journal of World History* 2, no. 2 (1991): 201–21.

Converse, III, Elliot V., et al. *The Exclusion of Black Soldiers from the Medal of Honor in World War II. The Study Commissioned by the United States Army to Investigate Racial Bias in the Awarding of the Nation's Highest Military Decoration.* Jefferson, NC: McFarland and Co, 1997.

Courtney, Susan. *Hollywood Fantasies of Miscegenation: Spectacular Narratives of Gender and Race, 1903–1967.* Princeton, NJ: Princeton University Press, 2005.

Cripps, Thomas. *Slow Fade to Black: The Negro in American Film, 1900–1942.* New York, NY: Oxford University Press, 1977.

Making Movies Black: The Hollywood Message Movie from World War II to the Civil Rights Era. New York, NY: Oxford University Press, 1993.

Culp, Robert K. *The First Black United States Marines: The Men of Montford Point.* Jefferson, NC: McFarland & Co., 2007.

D'Emilio, John. *Sexual Politics, Sexual Communities: The Making of a Homosexual Minority in the United States, 1940–1970.* Chicago, IL: University of Chicago Press, 1983.

Dalfiume, Richard M. "The 'Forgotten Years' of the Negro Revolution." *Journal of American History* 55, no. 1 (1968): 90–106.

Desegregation of the U.S. Armed Forces: Fighting on Two Fronts, 1939–1953. Columbia, MO: University of Missouri Press, 1969.

Daniels, Roger. *Prisoners without Trial: Japanese Americans and World War II.* New York, NY: Hill and Wang, 1993.

Darian-Smith, Kate. *On the Home Front: Melbourne in Wartime, 1939–1945.* Oxford: Oxford University Press, 1990.

Dixon, Chris, and Sean Brawley. "'Tan Yanks' Amid a 'Semblance of Civilization': African American Encounters with the South Pacific, 1941–1945." In *Through Depression and War: Australia and the United States*, edited by Peter Bastian and Roger Bell, 92–109. Sydney: Australian-American Fulbright Commission, 2002.

Dower, John. *War without Mercy: Race and Power in the Pacific War.* New York, NY: Pantheon, 1986.

Drea, Edward J. "'Great Patience Is Needed': America Encounters Australia, 1942." *War & Society* 11, no. 1 (1993): 21–51.

Dudziak, Mary L. *Cold War Civil Rights: Race and the Image of American Democracy.* Princeton, NJ: Princeton University Press, 2000.

Dyja, Thomas. *Walter White: The Dilemma of Black Identity in America.* Chicago, IL: Ivan R. Dee, 2008.

Edgerton, Robert B. *Hidden Heroism: Black Soldiers in America's Wars.* Boulder, CO: Westview Press, 2001.

Estes, Steve. *I am a Man! Race, Manhood, and the Civil Rights Movement.* Chapel Hill, NC: University of North Carolina Press, 2005.

Fidcock, Jane. "The Effect of the American 'Invasion' of Australia 1942–45." *Flinders Journal of History and Politics* 11 (1985): 91–101.

Finkle, Lee. *Forum for Protest: The Black Press during World War II.* Cranbury, NJ: Fairleigh Dickinson University Press, 1975.

Fischer, Perry E., and Brooks E. Gray. *Blacks and Whites Together through Hell: U.S. Marines in World War II.* Turlock, CA: Millsmont Publishing, 1994.

Flynn, George Q. "Selective Service and American Blacks during World War II." *Journal of Negro History* 69, no. 1 (1984): 14–25.

Foner, Jack D. *Blacks and the Military in American History: A New Perspective.* New York, NY: Praeger, 1974.

Franklin, John Hope. "Their War and Mine." *Journal of American History* 77, no. 2 (1990): 576–9.

Franklin, John Hope and Alfred A. Moss, Jr. *From Slavery to Freedom: A History of African Americans.* 8th edn. New York, NY: Alfred A. Knopf, 2000.

Fujitani, Takashi. *Race for Empire: Koreans as Japanese and Japanese as Americans.* Berkeley, CA: University of California Press, 2011.

Fujitani, Takashi, Geoffrey M. White, and Lisa Yoneyama. *Perilous Memories: The Asia-Pacific War(s).* Durham, NC: Duke University Press, 2001.

Furstenberg, Francois. "Beyond Freedom and Slavery: Autonomy, Virtue, and Resistance in Early American Political Discourse." *Journal of American History* 89, no. 4 (2003): 1295–330.

Gailey, Harry A. *Bougainville, 1943–1945: The Forgotten Campaign.* Lexington, KY: University Press of Kentucky, 1991.

Gallicchio, Marc. *The African American Encounter with Japan and China: Black Internationalism in Asia, 1895–1945.* Chapel Hill, NC: University of North Carolina Press, 2000.

Geiger, Jeffrey. *Facing the Pacific: Polynesia and the American Imperial Imagination.* Honolulu, HI: University of Hawaii Press, 2007.

Gillespie, Michael Boyce. *Film Blackness: American Cinema and the Idea of Black Film.* Durham, NC: Duke University Press, 2016.

Gilyard, Keith. *John Oliver Killens: A Life of Literary Black Activism.* Athens, GA: University of Georgia Press, 2010.

Graham, Herman, III. *The Brothers' Vietnam War: Black Power, Manhood, and the Military Experience.* Gainesville, FL: University Press of Florida, 2003.

Grant, Lachlan. *Australian Soldiers in Asia-Pacific in World War II.* Sydney: NewSouth Publishing, 2014.

"Grave Information for Hampson H. Fields." https://billiongraves.com/grave/Hampson-H-Fields/10188316#/ (Accessed October 12, 2016).

Green, Michael Cullen. *Black Yanks in the Pacific: Race in the Making of the American Military Empire after World War II.* Ithaca, NY: Cornell University Press, 2010.

Hachey, Thomas E. "Jim Crow with a British Accent: Attitudes of London Government Officials toward American Negro Soldiers in England during World War II." *Journal of Negro History* 59, no. 1 (1974): 66–77.

Hall, Robert A. *Black Diggers: Aborigines and Torres Strait Islanders in the Second World War.* Canberra: Aboriginal Studies Press, 1997.

Hall, Stuart. "What Is This 'Black' in Black Popular Culture?" *Social Justice* 20, nos. 1–2 (1993): 104–14.

Hardy, Travis J. "Race as an Aspect of the U.S.-Australian Alliance in World War II." *Diplomatic History* 38, no. 3 (2014): 549–68.

"Strangers in a Strange Land." Paper presented to the 2017 Australian and New Zealand Studies Association of North America Conference, Washington, DC, February, 2017.

Hastings, Max. *All Hell Let Loose: The World at War 1939–1945.* London: HarperPress, 2011.

Henningham, Stephen. "The French Administration, the Local Population, and the American Presence in New Caledonia 1943–1944." *Journal de la Société des Océanistes* 98, no. 1 (1994): 21–41.

Hervieux, Linda. *Forgotten: The Untold Story of D-Day's Black Heroes, at Home and at War.* New York, NY: Harper, 2015.

Hoberman, Robert. "A Fighting Press: The African-American Press and the Early Cold War, 1945–1955." *Honors thesis*, Rutgers University, 2008.

Horne, Gerald. *Race War!: White Supremacy and the Japanese Attack on the British Empire.* New York, NY: New York University Press, 2004.

The End of Empires: African Americans and India. Philadelphia, PA: Temple University Press, 2008.

Houston, Ivan J. *Black Warriors: The Buffalo Soldiers of World War II.* New York, NY: iUniverse, 2009.

Huebner, Andrew J. *Warrior Image: Soldiers in American Culture from the Second World War to the Vietnam Era.* Chapel Hill, NC: University of North Carolina Press, 2008.

Hutchinson, Earl Ofari. "Flags of Our Fathers Whitewashes War History," *The Huffington Post*, May 26, 2011, http://www.huffingtonpost.com.au/entry/flags-of-our-fathers-whit_b_32402 (Accessed October 9, 2016).

James, Jennifer Corrine. "'Sable Hands' and National Arms: African-American Literature of War, the Civil War-WWII." PhD dissertation, University of Maryland, 2001.

James, Jennifer C. *A Freedom Bought with Blood: African American War Literature from the Civil War to World War II*. Chapel Hill, NC: University of North Carolina Press, 2007.

Janken, Kenneth Robert. *White: The Biography of Walter White, Mr. NAACP*. New York, NY: Free Press, 2003.

 Walter White: Mr. NAACP. Chapel Hill, NC: University of North Carolina Press, 2006.

Jannings, Christopher Michael. "Lest We Forget: The Library of Congress's Veterans History Project and 'Radical Trust.'" PhD dissertation, Western Michigan University, 2010.

"Japanese Offered 5,000 Peso Reward for Coleman's Head." *Ebony* 15, no. 5 (1960): 78–82.

Jarvis, Christina Sharon. "The Male Body at War: American Masculinity and Embodiment during World War II." PhD dissertation, Pennsylvania State University, 2000.

Jefferson, Robert F. *Fighting for Hope: African American Troops of the 93rd Infantry Division in World War II and Postwar America*. Baltimore, MD: Johns Hopkins University Press, 2008.

Jolly, Margaret. "From Venus Point to Bali Ha'i: Eroticism and Exoticism in Representations of the Pacific." In *Sites of Desire, Economies of Pleasure: Sexualities in Asia and the Pacific*, edited by Lenore Manderson and Margaret Jolly, 99–122. Chicago, IL: University of Chicago Press, 1997.

Jun, Helen H. "Black Orientalism: Nineteenth-Century Narratives of Race and U.S. Citizenship." *American Quarterly* 58, no. 4 (2006): 1047–66.

Kachun, Mitch. *First Martyr of Liberty: Crispus Attucks in American Memory*. New York, NY: Oxford University Press, 2017.

Kaplan, Amy, and Donald E. Pease, eds. *Cultures of United States Imperialism*. Durham, NC: Duke University Press, 1993.

Kearney, Reginald. "Afro-American Views of Japanese, 1900–1945." PhD dissertation, Kent State University, 1991.

 African American Views of the Japanese: Solidarity or Sedition? Albany, NY: State University of New York Press, 1998.

Knauer, Christine. *Let Us Fight as Free Men: Black Soldiers and Civil Rights*. Philadelphia, PA: University of Pennsylvania Press, 2014.

Knoblock, Glenn A. *Black Submariners in the United States Navy, 1940–1975*. Jefferson, NC: McFarland & Co., 2005.

Koppes, Clayton R., and Gregory D. Black. "Blacks, Loyalty, and Motion-Picture Propaganda in World War II." *Journal of American History* 73, no. 2 (1986): 383–406.

Krenn, Michael L., ed. *The African American Voice in U.S. Foreign Policy since World War II*. New York, NY: Garland, 1998.

The Color of Empire: Race and American Foreign Relations. Lincoln, NE: University of Nebraska Press, 2003.

Kruse, Kevin M., and Stephen Tuck, eds. *Fog of War: The Second World War and the Civil Rights Movement.* New York, NY: Oxford University Press, 2012.

Kryder, Daniel. *Divided Arsenal: Race and the American State during World War II.* Cambridge: Cambridge University Press, 2001.

Lake, Marilyn. "Female Desires: The Meaning of World War II." In *The World War Two Reader*, edited by Gordon Martel, 359–76. New York, NY: Routledge, 2004.

Lanning, Michael Lee. *The African-American Soldier: From Crispus Attucks to Colin Powell.* Secaucus, NJ: Birch Lane Press, 1997.

Latourette, Debra J., et al. *African Americans in World War 2: Struggle against Segregation and Discrimination.* Directed by Jonathan J. Nash. Miami, FL: Department of Defense 50th Anniversary of World War II Commemorative Committee, 1997.

Lee, Ulysses. *The Employment of Negro Troops.* Washington, DC: Office of the Chief of Military History, United States Army, 1966.

Lentz-Smith, Adriene. *Freedom Struggles: African Americans and World War I.* Cambridge, MA: Harvard University Press, 2009.

Linderman, Gerald. *The World within War: America's Combat Experience in World War II.* New York, NY: Free Press, 1997.

Lindstrom, Lamont, and Geoffrey M. White. *Island Encounters: Black and White Memories of the Pacific War.* Washington, DC: Smithsonian Institution Press, 1990.

Lipsitz, George. "'Frantic to Join … the Japanese Army': The Asia Pacific War in the Lives of African American Soldiers and Civilians." In *The Politics of Culture in the Shadow of Capital*, edited by Lisa Lowe and David Lloyd, 324–53. Durham, NC: Duke University Press, 1997.

Longley, David J. "Vincent Tubbs and the Baltimore Afro-American: The Black Press, Race, and Culture in the World War II Pacific Theater." *Australasian Journal of American Studies* 35, no. 2 (2016): 61–80.

"Victory at Home and Abroad: Overseas Correspondents, the African American Press, and the Long Civil Rights Movement, 1939–1946." PhD dissertation, Monash University, 2018.

Longmate, Norman. *The G.I.'s: The Americans in Britain, 1942–1945.* London: Hutchinson, 1975.

Luszki, Walter A. *A Rape of Justice: MacArthur and the New Guinea Hangings.* Lanham, MD: Madison Books, 1991.

Lyons, Paul. *American Pacificism: Oceania in the U.S. Imagination.* New York, NY: Routledge, 2006.

MacGregor, Morris J., Jr. *Integration of the Armed Forces, 1940–1965.* Washington, DC: Center of Military History, United States Army, 1981.

Manchester, William. *American Caesar: Douglas MacArthur, 1880–1964.* Boston, MA: Little, Brown, & Co., 1978.

Marable, Manning, and Vanessa Agard-Jones. *Transnational Blackness: Navigating the Global Color Line.* New York, NY: Palgrave MacMillan, 2008.

Martin, Waldo E., Jr. *No Coward Soldiers: Black Cultural Politics and Postwar America.* Cambridge, MA: Harvard University Press, 2005.

Masaharu, Satu, and Barak Kushner. "'Negro Propaganda Operations': Japan's Short-Wave Radio Broadcasts for World War II Black Americans." *Historical Journal of Film, Radio and Television* 19, no. 1 (1999): 5–26.

Melson, Charles D. *Condition Red: Marine Defense Battalions in World War II.* Washington, DC: History and Museums Division, Headquarters, U.S. Marine Corps, 1996.

Mershon, Sherie, and Steven Schlossman. *Foxholes and Color Lines: Desegregating the U.S. Armed Forces.* Baltimore, MD: Johns Hopkins University Press, 1998.

McCuaig, Nicole, and Veronica Fury. *Black Soldier Blues.* Directed by Nicole McCuaig. Sydney: Australian Broadcasting Corporation/Big Island Pictures, 2005.

McEuen, Melissa A. *Making War, Making Women: Femininity and Duty on the American Home Front, 1941–1945.* Athens, GA. University of Georgia Press, 2010.

McFerson, Hazel M. "'Part-Black Americans' in the South Pacific." *Phylon* 43, no. 2 (1982): 177–80.

McGuire, Phillip. *He, Too, Spoke for Democracy: Judge Hastie, World War II, and the Black Soldier.* New York, NY: Greenwood, 1988.

McIntyre, Darryl. "Paragons of Glamour: A Study of U.S. Military Forces in Australia." PhD thesis, University of Queensland, 1989.

McKernan, Michael. *All In!: Australia during the Second World War.* Melbourne: Thomas Nelson, 1983.

McKerrow, John. *The American Occupation of Australia, 1941–1945: A Marriage of Necessity.* Newcastle-upon-Tyne: Cambridge Scholars Publishing, 2013.

McLaurin, Melton A. *The Marines of Montford Point: America's First Black Marines.* Chapel Hill, NC: University of North Carolina Press, 2007.

Mead, Margaret. *New Lives for Old: Cultural Transformations – Manus, 1928–1953.* 1956; New York, NY: William Morrow and Co., 1966.

Meriwether, James H. *Proudly We Can Be Africans: Black Americans and Africa, 1935–1961.* Chapel Hill, NC: University of North Carolina Press, 2002.

Meyer, Leisa D. "Creating G. I. Jane: The Regulation of Sexuality and Sexual Behavior in the Women's Army Corps during World War II." *Feminist Studies* 18, no. 3 (1992): 581–601.

Michaeli, Ethan. *The Defender: How the Legendary Black Newspaper Changed America.* Boston, MD: Houghton Mifflin Harcourt, 2016.

Moore, Christopher Paul. *Fighting for America: Black Soldiers – The Unsung Heroes of World War II.* New York, NY: One World/Ballantine, 2005.

Moore, John Hammond. *Over-sexed, Over-paid, and Over Here: Americans in Australia, 1941–1945.* St. Lucia: University of Queensland Press, 1981.

Morehouse, Maggi M. *Fighting in the Jim Crow Army: Black Men and Women Remember World War II.* Lanham, MD: Rowman and Littlefield, 2000.

Moye, J. Todd. *Freedom Flyers: The Tuskegee Airmen of World War II.* New York, NY: Oxford University Press, 2010.

Mullen, Bill V. *Afro-Orientalism.* Minneapolis, MN: University of Minnesota Press, 2004.

Muller, William G. *The Twenty-Fourth Infantry: Past and Present.* 1923; reprinted, Fort Collins, CO: Old Army Press, 1972.

Munholland, Kim. *Rock of Contention: Free French and Americans at War in New Caledonia, 1940–1945*. New York, NY: Berghahn, 2005.

Myrdal, Gunnar. *An American Dilemma: The Negro Problem and Modern Democracy*. New York, NY: Harper and Row, 1944.

Nalty, Bernard C. *The Right to Fight: African-American Marines in World War II*. Washington, DC: History and Museums Division, Headquarters, U.S. Marine Corps, 1995.

Strength for the Fight: A History of Black Americans in the Military. New York, NY: Free Press, 1986.

Nelson, Dennis D. *The Integration of the Negro into the U.S. Navy*. New York, NY: Farrar, Strauss, and Young, 1951.

O'Brien, Kenneth Paul, and Lynn Hudson Parsons, eds. *The Home Front War: World War II and American Society*. Westport, CT: Greenwood, 1995.

Okada, Yasuhiro. "Negotiating Race and Womanhood across the Pacific: African American Women in Japan under U.S. Military Occupation, 1945–1952." *Black Women, Gender, and Families* 6, no. 1 (2102): 71–96.

Onishi, Yuichiro. *Transpacific Antiracism: Afro-Asian Solidarity in 20th-Century Black America, Japan, and Okinawa*. New York, NY: New York University Press, 2013.

"The New Negro of the Pacific: How African Americans Forged Racial Cross-Solidarity with Japan, 1917–1922." *Journal of African American History* 92, no. 2 (2007): 191–213.

Osur, Alan M. *Blacks in the Army Air Force during World War II: The Problems of Race Relations*. Washington, DC: Office of Air Force History, 1977.

Parker, Juliete. *A Man Named Doris*. Longwood, FL: Xulon Press, 2003.

Patton, Gerald W. *War and Race: The Black Officer in the American Military, 1915–1941*. Westport, CT: Greenwood Press, 1981.

Perry, Earnest L., Jr. "A Common Purpose: The Negro Newspapers Publishers Association's Fight for Equality during World War II." *American Journalism* 19, no. 2 (2002): 31–43.

Phillips, Kimberley L. *War! What Is It Good For? Black Freedom Struggles and the U.S. Military, from World War II to Iraq*. Chapel Hill, NC: University of North Carolina Press, 2012.

Pietila, Antero, and Stacy Spaulding. "The Afro-American's World War II Correspondents: Feuilletonism as Social Action." *Literary Journalism Studies* 5, no. 2 (2013): 37–58.

Plummer, Brenda Gayle. *Rising Wind: Black Americans and U.S. Foreign Affairs, 1935–1960*. Chapel Hill, NC: University of North Carolina Press, 1966.

"'Pop' Coleman, Pride of the Philippines." *Ebony* 15, no. 5 (1960): 78–9.

Potts, Annette and Lucinda Strauss. *For the Love of a Soldier: Australian War-Brides and Their GIs*. Sydney: ABC Enterprises, 1987.

Potts, E. Daniel, and Annette Potts. "The Negro and the Australian Gold Rushes, 1852–1857." *Pacific Historical Review* 37, no. 4 (1968): 381–99.

Yanks Down Under: The American Impact on Australia. Melbourne: Oxford University Press, 1985.

"The Deployment of Black Servicemen Abroad during World War Two." *Australian Journal of Politics and History* 35, no. 1 (1989): 92–6.

Putney, Martha. *When the Nation Was in Need: Blacks in the Women's Army Corps during World War II*. Metuchen, NJ: Scarecrow Press, 1992.

Quarles, Benjamin. *The Negro in the American Revolution*. 1961; reprinted, Chapel Hill, NC: University of North Carolina Press, 1996.

Ralph, Barry. *They Passed This Way: The United States of America, The States of Australia and World War II*. East Roseville, NSW: Kangaroo Press, 2000.

Reddick, L. D. "The Negro Policy of the United States Army, 1775–1945." *Journal of Negro History* 34, no. 1 (1949): 9–29.

Reynolds, David. "The Churchill Government and the Black American Troops in Britain during World War II." *Transactions of the Royal Historical Society* 35 (1985): 113–33.

Rich Relations: The American Occupation of Britain, 1942–1945. London: Harper-Collins, 1995.

Ripley, Herbert S., and Stewart Wolf. "Mental Illness among Negro Troops Overseas." *American Journal of Psychiatry* 103, no. 4 (1947): 499–512.

Riseman, Noah. *Defending Whose Country: Indigenous Soldiers in the Pacific War*. Lincoln, NE: University of Nebraska Press, 2012.

Roark, James L. "American Black Leaders: The Response to Colonialism and the Cold War, 1943–1953." *African Historical Studies* 4, no. 2 (1971): 253–70.

Robinson, Neville K. *Villagers at War: Some Papua New Guinea Experiences in World War II*. Canberra: Australian National University, 1979.

Rose, Kenneth D. *Myth and the Greatest Generation: A Social History of Americans in World War II*. New York, NY: Routledge, 2008.

Rosenberg, Emily S. *A Date Which Will Live: Pearl Harbor in American Memory*. Durham, NC: Duke University Press, 2003.

Rosenberg, Jonathan. *How Far the Promised Land? World Affairs and the American Civil Rights Movement from the First World War to Vietnam*. Princeton, NJ: Princeton University Press, 2006.

Sales, Peter M. "White Australia, Black Americans: A Melbourne Incident, 1928." *Australian Quarterly* 46, no. 4 (1974): 74–81.

Saunders, Kay. "Racial Conflict in Brisbane in World War II: The Imposition of Patterns of Segregation upon Black American Servicemen." *Brisbane at War. Brisbane History Group Papers*, 4 (1986): 29–34.

"Conflict between the American and Australian Governments over the Introduction of Black American Servicemen into Australia during World War Two." *Australian Journal of Politics and History* 33, no. 2 (1987): 39–46.

"Reassessing the Significance of the Battle of Brisbane." *Journal of the Royal Historical Society of Queensland* 15, no. 1 (1993): 70–3.

"The Dark Shadow of White Australia: Racial Anxieties in Australia in World War II." *Ethnic and Racial Studies* 77, no. 2 (1994): 325–41.

"In a Cloud of Lust: Black GIs and Sex in World War II." In *Gender and War: Australians at War in the Twentieth Century*, edited by Joy Damousi and Marilyn Lake, 178–90. Cambridge: Cambridge University Press, 1995.

Saunders, Kay, and Helen Taylor. "The Reception of Black American Servicemen in Australia during World War II: The Resilience of 'White Australia.'" *Journal of Black Studies* 25, no. 3 (1995): 331–48.

Schrijvers, Peter. *Bloody Pacific: American Soldiers at War with Japan*. New York, NY: Palgrave Macmillan, 2010.

Scipio, L. Albert. *Last of the Black Regulars: A History of the 24th Infantry Regiment (1869–1951)*. Silver Springs, MD: Roman Publications, 1983.

Scott, Lawrence P., and William M. Womack, Sr. *Double V: The Civil Rights Struggle of the Tuskegee Airmen*. East Lansing, MI: Michigan State University Press, 1992.

Shaw, Henry I. and Ralph W. Donnelly. *Blacks in the Marine Corps*. Washington, DC: History and Museums Division, Headquarters, U.S. Marine Corps, 1975.

Silvera, John D., comp. *The Negro in World War II*. New York, NY: Arno Press and the New York Times, 1969.

Sims-Wood, Janet Louise. "'We Served America Too!': Personal Recollections of African American Women in the Women's Army Corps during World War II." PhD dissertation, Union Institute, 1994.

Sitkoff, Harvard. "Racial Militancy and Interracial Violence in the Second World War." *Journal of American History* 58, no. 3 (1971): 661–81.

Skinner, Byron Richard. "The Double 'V': The Impact of World War II on Black America." PhD dissertation, University of California, Berkeley, 1978.

Sklaroff, Lauren Rebecca. "Constructing G.I. Joe Louis: Cultural Solutions to the 'Negro Problem' during World War II." *Journal of American History* 89, no. 3 (2002): 958–83.

Smith, Graham. *When Jim Crow Met John Bull: Black American Soldiers in World War II Britain*. London: Tauris, 1987.

Smaal, Yorick. *Sex, Soldiers and the South Pacific, 1939–45: Queer Identities in Australia in the Second World War*. Basingstoke: Palgrave Macmillan, 2015.

Stein, Judith. *The World of Marcus Garvey: Race and Class in Modern Society*. Baton Rouge, LA: Louisiana State University Press, 1986.

Stouffer, Samuel, et al. *The American Soldier. Vol. 1: Adjustment during Army Life*. Princeton, NJ: Princeton University Press, 1949.

Stevens, John D. *From the Back of the Foxhole: Black Correspondents in World War II*. Journalism Monographs, 27, Lexington, KY: Association for Education in Journalism, February, 1973.

Sturma, Michael. "Loving the Alien: The Underside of Relations between American Servicemen and Australian Women in Queensland, 1942–1945." *Journal of Australian Studies* 13, no. 24 (1989): 3–17.

Sutherland, Jonathan. *African Americans at War: An Encyclopedia*. Santa Barbara, CA: ABC-Clio, 2004.

Sweeney, Michael S., and Patrick S. Washburn. "'Aint Justice Wonderful': The *Chicago Tribune*'s Battle of Midway Story and the Government's Attempt at an Espionage Act Indictment in 1942." *Journalism & Communication Monographs* 16, no. 1 (2014): 7–97.

Takaki, Ronald. *Double Victory: A Multicultural History of America in World War II*. Boston, MA: Little, Brown and Co., 2000.

Taketani, Etsuko. *The Black Pacific Narrative: Geographic Imaginings of Race and Empire between the World Wars*. Hanover, NH: Dartmouth College Press, 2014.

Thompson, Peter, and Robert Macklin. *The Battle of Brisbane: Australians and Yanks at War*. Sydney: ABC Books, 2000.

Thorne, Christopher. *Allies of a Kind: The United States, Britain, and the War against Japan, 1941–1945*. New York, NY: Oxford University Press, 1978.

Tomblin, Barbara Brooks. *G.I. Nightingales: The Army Nurse Corps in World War II*. Lexington, KY: University Press of Kentucky, 1996.

Treadwell, Mattie E. *The Women's Army Corps*. Washington, DC: Office of the Chief of Military History, Department of the Army, 1954.

van Rijn, Guido. *Roosevelt's Blues: African-American Blues and Gospel Songs on President FDR*. Jackson, MS: University Press of Mississippi, 1997.

Vogel, Todd, ed. *The Black Press: New Literary and Historical Essays*. New Brunswick, NJ: Rutgers University Press, 2001.

Von Eschen, Penny M. *Race against Empire: Black Americans and Anticolonialism, 1937–1957*. Ithaca, NY: Cornell University Press, 1997.

Wald, Elijah. *Josh White: Society Blues*. Amherst, MA: University of Massachusetts Press, 2000.

Ware, Gilbert. *William Hastie: Grace under Pressure*. New York, NY: Oxford University Press, 1984.

Washburn, Patrick S. *A Question of Sedition: The Federal Government's Investigation of the Black Press during World War II*. New York, NY: Oxford University Press, 1986.

"The *Pittsburgh Courier's* Double V Campaign in 1942." *American Journalism* 3, no. 2 (1986): 73–86.

"The Black Press: Homefront Clout Hits a Peak in World War II." *American Journalism* 12, no. 3 (Summer 1995): 359–66.

Waterhouse, Richard. *From Minstrel Show to Vaudeville: The Australian Popular Stage, 1788–1914*. Sydney: NSW University Press, 1990.

"Empire and Nation: Australian Popular Ideology and the Outbreak of the Pacific War." *History Australia* 12, no. 3 (2015): 30–54.

Weeks, Charles, J., Jr. "The American Occupation of Tonga, 1942–1945: The Social and Economic Impact." *Pacific Historical Review* 56, no. 3 (1987): 399–426.

Westheider, James. *Fighting on Two Fronts: African Americans and the Vietnam War*. New York, NY: New York University Press, 1997.

The African American Experience in Vietnam: Brothers in Arms. Lanham, MD: Rowman and Littlefield, 2008.

Williams, Chad L. *Torchbearers of Democracy: African American Soldiers in the World War I Era*. Chapel Hill, NC: University of North Carolina Press, 2010.

Woodruff, Nan Elizabeth. "The Image of the Negro during World War II as Revealed in the White Popular Press." MA dissertation, University of Arkansas, 1973.

Wynn, Neil A. "The Impact of the Second World War on the American Negro." *Journal of Contemporary History* 6, no. 2 (1971): 42–53.

"Black Attitudes toward Participation in the American War Effort, 1941–1945." *Afro-American Studies* 3, no. 1 (June, 1972): 13–19.

The Afro-American and the Second World War. London: Paul Elek, 1976.

The African American Experience during World War II. Lanham, MD: Rowman and Littlefield, 2010.

Yardley, Jonathan. "The Thunder of Protest without the Lightning of Art." *Washington Post*, July 24, 2003.

Index

Taggart, L. J., 249
Taketani, Etsuko, 5
Taylor, Cowie, 66
Taylor, Leon W., 47, 48
This Our Life (1942), 10
Thompson, James G., 34
Thompson, Jannett, 103
Time magazine, 39
Time–Life, 153
Tinsley, Franklin Howard, Sr., 75
Tokyo Rose, 212. *See also* propaganda
Toles, Marke, 214
Tonga, 83, 209
tourist, serviceman as, 77
training facilities in the American South,
    60–62
transnational racial liberation
    in African American discourse, 33, 240,
        243, 244, 255
    African American internationalism,
        27, 239
    African American servicemen as agents
        in, 7, 18, 59, 66, 93, 94, 149,
        221, 255
    challenges to forging nonwhite alliance,
        57, 88, 94, 244, 245, 252. *See also*
        exceptionalism; racial stereotyping;
        black orientalism
    and domestic racism in United States,
        7, 41, 49
    and Japanese expansionism, 47, 218
    racial solidarity and alliance of nonwhite
        peoples, 42, 47, 76, 87, 94, 196, 222,
        229, 231, 243, 244, 256. *See also*
        imagined community
    and white anxieties, 41, 170
    and white Australia, 18, 138, 148, 149,
        170, 171, 194, 258, 259
Tratten, David (Chaplain), 159
Triple V campaign, 136. *See also* Double V
    campaign
Trout, James (Private), 197
Truman, Harry S., 225, 260
Truth (Sydney), 151, 160, 168
Tubbs, Vincent
    as activist, 15
    on Australia, 112, 146
    on domestic racism in the United States,
        231
    on encounters between US personnel and
        Pacific Islanders, 112
    on Japanese American internees, 45

on racial significance of the Pacific
    War, 4
views on the Japanese, 215, 231, 233
views on the South Pacific, 81, 86
Tuskegee Airmen, 38
Tweed, George R., 89
typhus, 81

Uncle Tom's Cabin, 72. *See also* Stowe,
    Harriet Beecher
"Uncle Tom plays", 245
white officers likened to Simon
    Legree, 72
United Kingdom. *See* Great Britain
United Nations, 40, 220, 222, 248
United Services Organization (USO), 113
    African American performers,
        103, 112, 133
    segregation and exclusion, 70, 83
    women performers, 103
United States Army
    discriminatory practices, 39, 40, 60, 64,
        65, 69, 75, 115, 120, 130, 184, 185,
        187, 193, 203
United States foreign policy
    as benevolent, 6, 27, 250
    domestic racial politics and, 3, 13, 28.
        See also transnational racial
        liberation
United States Marine Corps
    African American marines in,
        66, 69, 72
    discriminatory practices, 69, 107, 188,
        189, 191, 203, 204, 212
    and masculinity, 189
United States Navy
    discriminatory practices, 39, 50, 51, 55,
        68, 69, 84, 99, 130, 131
United States Navy Department, 10, 37
United States War Department, 10, 15, 50,
    60, 123, 187
Universal Negro Improvement Association
    (UNIA), 43
USS *Devilfish* (submarine), 204
USS *Harrison* (ship), 196
USS *Liscome Bay* (ship), 56
USS *San Francisco* (ship), 91
USS *West Virginia* (ship), 54

Vandegrift, Alexander (General), 202
venereal disease, 105–6, 107–8, 165, 236
Vissuk, Chief of Vanuatu, 90

Walker, Oliver R., 35
Wallace, Bobby, 251, 252
Ward, Harold E., 91
Waters, Enoch P., 113, 162, 165, 166, 169,
171, 194, 196, 230, 233
Watson, George, 198
West, Irene, 236, 238, 246, 252, 253
White Australia Policy
African American understandings of, 18,
137, 145, 146, 148, 171
and African American personnel, 140,
141, 157, 159, 163, 174, 176, 258
and African American press, 144, 146,
160, 170, 171, 174, 175
challenges to, 138, 143, 157, 167, 176
discursive links with Southern
segregation, 147, 259
and nonwhite labor, 159
and treatment of Aboriginal Australians,
170
and US–Australia alliance, 140
white masculine hegemony, 18, 95, 116,
138, 258
white officers
African American attitudes toward, 72,
75, 184, 197, 198, 203
attitudes toward African American
troops, 71, 84, 106, 107, 155, 164,
167, 188, 189, 198
attitudes toward nonwhite peoples, 246
treatment of African American
servicemen, 71, 72, 73, 74, 84, 184,
189, 191, 203, 250
White Savage (1943), 97
white servicemen
attitudes toward African American
troops, 73, 84, 129, 184, 191, 206
military efforts to mediate relations with
African American servicemen, 14, 73,
80, 189
relations with African American
servicemen, 67, 68, 71, 73, 129, 154,
203, 204, 205, 206, 250

white servicewomen and nurses, 116–18,
125, 134
white supremacy, 4, 18, 24, 39, 136, 231,
245
subversion of in Australia, 138, 259
White, Josh, 53
White, Lloyd L. (Private), 126. *See also*
Milne Bay case
White, Walter. *See also* National
Association for the Advancement of
Colored People (NAACP)
Australia, 165, 175, 242
combat, African Americans in,
177, 194, 201
discrimination in United States armed
forces, 51, 69, 194, 255
disillusionment of African American
personnel, 220
Pacific War as transformative experience,
39, 187, 222, 243
tensions between black and white
servicemen, 127
transnational racial liberation,
239, 243
Wilkins, Roy, 39, 44, 131. *See also*
National Association for the
Advancement of Colored People
(NAACP); *Crisis, The*
Williams, Ellis D. (Warrant Officer),
marriage to Eugenia Diloy, 113
Williams, Francis H. (Captain), 153.
See also race riots, "Townsville
Mutiny"
Women's Army Corps (WAC), 116, 118,
130, 131

Yamamoto, Isoroku (Admiral), 56–57
Yellow Peril, Australian fears of Asian
invasion, 148. *See also* White Australia
Policy
Yi, Chien Lung (Doctor), 92
Yon, E. M. (Colonel), 201
Young, Bernard P., 15